Behold
The King

Behold
The King

A Study of
Matthew

Stanley D. Toussaint

MULTNOMAH PRESS
PORTLAND, OREGON 97266

First Edition

Second Printing, 1981

BEHOLD THE KING
© 1980 by Multnomah Press
Portland, Oregon 97266

Library of Congress Cataloging in Publication Data

Toussaint, Stanley D.   1928-
   Behold the King.

      Bibliography: p. 337
      Includes indexes
      1. Bible. N.T. Matthew—Commentaries.
I. Bible. N.T. Matthew. English. New American Standard Bible. 1980.
II. Title.
               BS2575.3.T67   226'.2077   80-13410
   ISBN 0-930014-39-1

Printed in the United States of America

To my faithful and loving wife,
Maxine

Preface

The Gospel of Matthew was the focal point of my doctoral studies at Dallas Theological Seminary some twenty years ago. Since then it has been my privilege to teach this Gospel in part or in whole a number of times from both the Greek and English texts. The basic conclusions arrived at when my dissertation was written have been confirmed by years of further study. I trust that it will prove to be a blessing in use to those who name and love our Savior, the Lord Jesus Christ.

While the approach of this volume is clearly dispensational and premillennial, there are some distinctions from historical dispensationalism in this study. This will be seen especially in such areas as the approach to the Sermon on the Mount, the parables of Matthew 13, and the definitions of the Kingdom of God and the Kingdom of Heaven.

By no means is this commentary strictly a word by word analysis of the verses in the book of Matthew. Rather, its goal is to set forth the flow of thought of Matthew's Gospel as it relates to his purpose.

I am much indebted to Dr. S. Lewis Johnson, Jr., who as my Greek exegesis professor gave direction for my studies both in content and method; to my wife who so faithfully proofread and typed the manuscript; to Multnomah Press for their support and help in making this book a reality; and to my friends who encouraged me to put this work into print.

Matthew's Gospel is undoubtedly one of the key books of the Bible; it certainly was not a mere circumstance that it heads the New Testament. Careful study of this Gospel will not only reveal who Jesus is but also will show the discerning reader God's program for the church and Israel. It is with this hope and desire that the author humbly submits the work to the reader.

Stanley D. Toussaint

Table of Contents

Introduction
to the Gospel of Matthew

Introduction

I. The Study of the Gospel of Matthew

The Gospels have always been held as precious documents of the Christian faith. As such they have been carefully studied by saints since the time they were penned. Although they are now nearly two thousand years old, they are still the object of careful scrutiny and study on the part of both layman and scholar.

Generally speaking there have been two methods of studying the Gospels. One method approaches them in the light of their doctrinal content. Those who study the Gospels in this way often compare the doctrines of the Gospels with the doctrines of the epistles, or they may look for the doctrinal emphasis of each of the gospel writers. In this approach the Gospels become source books for theology.

The other system of study looks at the Gospels as simply containing a narrative of the life of Christ. Those who use this approach often attempt to harmonize the Gospels with one another in reconstructing the life of Jesus. In this method the Gospels become source books for a history of Jesus Christ.

Both of these methods have made a vital and blessed contribution to the church. They have shown that there is no contradiction between the doctrines of Jesus and the apostles. Gospel harmonies provide insights into and details concerning the life of Christ on earth. However, these two approaches have failed to grasp the significance of *each* Gospel as it relates to the life of Christ. These books were not written merely to convey theological concepts or to relate a story. These are important, but the primary purpose of the gospel writers was to prove a point. In other words, they wrote their Gospels with the intention of setting forth an argument. In order to attain this objective the evangelists were very selective in their choice of materials. Those elements were placed in the fore which would assist them in accomplishing their purpose. Therefore one writer may at times emphasize doctrine; at other times he may underscore a series of events. Both doctrine and narration may be used, but their use is all for the sake of setting forth an argument.

The writer of the Gospel of Matthew is no exception. His account is not a simple biography or a theological treatise. Both elements are included but only because Matthew is arguing for a point. Therefore one errs greatly when he approaches Matthew's Gospel as though it were merely a doctrinal treatise or a record of the life of Jesus. An analysis of different writers' styles demonstrates the correct approach of finding the author's purpose for writing a book.

> There is a difference between biography and monograph. The biography is an attempt at the appraisal of a life from birth to death. A monograph, when written of a life, presents merely one phase of that life. Books have been written concerning certain great men which omit entire phases of their lives, simply because the writers were limiting themselves to one particular aspect of their theme. One volume may portray a leader as a statesman; another may present him as a military strategist; still another may write of his home-life or the steps in his rise to political power.[1]

It was no great innovation for Matthew to use this method of argument. The recounting of a narrative as a method of proving something was well established by the time Matthew wrote his Gospel.

> It must be remembered that it was in accordance with the literary method of the first Christian century and of the adjacent periods to employ historical material into the form of an argument, or even stating anywhere in the course of the narrative what the facts were intended to prove. It was assumed that the reader or hearer would be shrewd enough to discover this for himself, and this assumption was apparently amply justified.[2]

There are several illustrations of this method in the New Testament itself. One of the clearest is that of John's Gospel. "Many other signs therefore Jesus also performed in the presence of the disciples, which are not written in this book; but these have been written that you may believe that Jesus is the Christ, the Son of God; and that believing you may have life in His name." (John 20:30-31). In Luke 4:16-27 the Lord uses a simple narrative to establish a point. Stephen's sermon in Acts

---

1. Donald Grey Barnhouse, *His Own Received Him Not, But . . .*, pp. 12-13.
2. Ernest DeWitt Burton, *A Short Introduction to the Gospels*, p. 13.

seven is another illustration. There are many others. Because of these facts one can hardly be accused of being presumptuous in asserting that Matthew as well as the other gospel writers set down their Gospels in written form with a definite argument in view.

Now if Matthew wrote his Gospel with an argument in mind, what is his purpose and how does he pursue it? Herein lies the problem. The answer can only be found by observing the main emphases of Matthew's Gospel and noting the logical development of those emphases. The solution to the problem of Matthew's argument is all-important since it is the backbone of the book. Neither the significance of the life of Christ narrated by Matthew or the doctrines contained in his Gospel are intelligible without an understanding of his argument. This discernment of the argument provides the key to the comprehension of the Gospel according to Matthew.

Note: See the appendix for comments regarding the date and authorship of the Gospel of Matthew.

II. The Jewish Character of the Book

The Style of Writing

One can sum up the character of the book in a word by saying it is Jewish.[3] This is shown in several ways. It is seen first of all in the author's style. The Greek grammarian, A. T. Robertson, comments on this by saying, "He has the instinct for Hebrew parallelism and the Hebrew elaboration, and his thought and general style are Hebraistic .... "[4] Matthew's use of "then, at that time" τότε reflects the Jewish character of the book. "The Greek τότε ('then') occurs 90 times (six times in Mark, fourteen times in Luke, ten times in John)." Matthew may use this connective because he thought in Aramaic.[5]

The Vocabulary

Matthew's vocabulary as well as his style of writing is Hebraistic.

3. See Frederick C. Grant, ed., *Nelson's Bible Commentary*, 6:25; William Hendriksen, *New Testament Commentary, Exposition of the Gospel According to Matthew*, pp. 86-87; David Hill, *New Century Bible, The Gospel of Matthew*, pp. 39-41.
4. Archibald Thomas Robertson, *A Grammar of the Greek New Testament in the Light of Historical Research*, p. 119.
5. Henry Clarence Thiessen, *Introduction to the New Testament*, p. 139.

Matthew is the Jewish Gospel, dealing with the King and the Kingdom. In Greek, the term "kingdom of heaven" occurs thirty-three times, and the term "kingdom of God," four times. Jesus is called "Son of David" nine times (three times in Mark, three times in Luke, and never in John).[6]

The term *kingdom of heaven* is especially significant since it occurs in no other Gospel. This phrase is distinctly Jewish.[7] Jerusalem is called the "holy city" (4:5; 27:53) and the "city of the great King" (5:35). The Jewish people are called "the lost sheep of the house of Israel" (10:6; 15:24). The term *Son of Man* is Jewish and looks back to the prophecy of Daniel 7:13. "The words 'righteous' and 'righteousness' occur more often in Matthew than in all the other three Gospels combined."[8] The vocabulary is Jewish and clearly indicates its Hebraistic character.

The Subject Matter

The subject matter is also Jewish. Such subjects as the law, ceremonial defilement, the Sabbath, the kingdom, Jerusalem, the temple, David, the Messiah, the fulfillment of Old Testament prophecies, and Moses are all discussed from the Jewish viewpoint for Jewish readers.

The Old Testament Quotations

Still another indication of the Jewishness of the book is seen in the Old Testament quotations which appear so frequently in Matthew. "There are 129 Old Testament references: 53 of them are citations, and 76 are allusions."[9]

> The number of argumentative quotations from the Old Testament introduced by the writer, and the almost total absence of such quotations from Mark and Luke—John has more than Mark and Luke, but fewer than Matthew—suggest also Jewish readers.[10]

Usually the quotations are made to prove a point to Jewish readers. This is especially true with reference to Christ.

6. Ibid., p. 138.

7. Willoughby C. Allen, *A Critical and Exegetical Commentary on the Gospel According to S. Matthew*, p. lxxvi.

8. Thiessen, *Introduction*, p. 139.

9. W. Graham Scroggie, *A Guide to the Gospels*, p. 270.

10. Ernest DeWitt Burton, "The Purpose and Plan of the Gospel of Matthew," *The Biblical World* 11 (January 1898):44.

> No less than thirteen times Matthew says that Jesus performed
> some act "that it might be fulfilled which was spoken by the
> prophet." . . . the cumulative effect of these passages makes the
> person of Christ the focus of God's purpose and of the prophets'
> predictive utterances during all preceding centuries.[11]

The Genealogy

Another mark of the Jewish character of Matthew's Gospel is found
in the genealogy of chapter one. Matthew traces the record of ancestors
of Jesus back through David to Abraham, the father of the Jewish race.

The Emphasis on Peter

The emphasis on Peter in this Gospel points to a Jewish readership.
Peter was the apostle to the Jews and would attract Jewish readers.
Allen notices this and reaches much the same conclusion.[12]

The Unexplained Customs

Still another token of the Jewish nature of the Gospel is its unexplained customs. The fact that Matthew refers to so many Jewish customs and leaves them unexplained points in this direction.

> Compare, for example, Matthew's references to the Jewish rulers
> (2:1, 22; 14:1) with Luke's (2:1, 2; 3:1, 2), or his unexplained
> mention of the Jewish custom of ceremonial cleansing (15:2) with
> Mark's detailed explanation (7:3, 4). The seeming exception in
> 27:15 is not properly such. The custom of releasing a prisoner at
> the passover season, not otherwise known to us, was probably not
> of Jewish but of Roman origin . . . .[13]

The Testimony of Tradition

A final proof of the Jewishness of Matthew's Gospel is the testimony
of tradition.

> Irenaeus says: "Matthew issued a written Gospel among the He-
> brews," and "The Gospel of St. Matthew was written for the

---

11. Merrill C. Tenney, *The Genius of the Gospels,* p. 53.
12. Allen, *Commentary on Matthew,* p. lxxxi.
13. Burton, "Purpose of Matthew," p. 43.

Jews." Origen says, "St. Matthew wrote for the Hebrew."
Eusebius says: "Matthew ... delivered his gospel to his country-
men." The complexion and content of the Gospel abundantly confirm this view.[14]

One must conclude that Matthew's Gospel is directed toward Jewish
readers since it is so Jewish in character. This conclusion is evidenced
by the author's style, by the vocabulary of the Gospel, by its subject
matter, by the use it makes of Old Testament quotations, by the genealogy of chapter one, by its emphasis on Peter, by the unexplained customs related in the book, and by the testimony of tradition.

III. The Purpose of the Book

Matthew has a twofold purpose in writing his Gospel. Primarily he
penned this Gospel to prove Jesus is the Messiah, but he also wrote it to
explain God's kingdom program to his readers. One goal directly involves the other. Nevertheless, they are distinct.

The Purpose is to Prove Jesus is the Messiah

Matthew portrays Jesus in the way he does to prove that He is the
fulfillment of the Old Testament prophecies concerning the promised
Messiah. The term *Messiah* is a Hebrew word equivalent to the Greek
word for Christ ($X\rho\iota\sigma\tau\acute{o}\varsigma$). Both terms are equivalent to the English
expression *Anointed One*. The ritual of anointing was characteristic of
the official introduction into three offices—prophet, priest, and king.
Since the prophecies of the Old Testament indicated that Israel's hopes
were founded in Him who would be a prophet, priest, and king, He was
referred to as the Anointed One, the Christ, or the Messiah (1 Samuel
2:10; Psalms 2:2; 18:50; 132:17; Daniel 9:26).

> In Jewish literature the term came to be a title for the king who
> would bring salvation in the final age, and probably it derives from
> such passages as Ps. 2:2; 18:50; 1 Sam. 2:10; etc. In the Psalms of
> Solomon and other pre-Christian writings the form is usually "the
> anointed of the Lord" (Ps. Sol. 17:36; cf. Luke 2:26); later it is
> simply "the Messiah," as in II Esdras 7:28-29, II Baruch 29:3, and
> rabbinical literature. The rabbis often refer to the future age as the
> "days of the Messiah."[15]

14. Scroggie, *Guide to Gospels,* p. 248.
15. Sherman E. Johnson and George A. Buttrick, "The Gospel According to St.
Matthew," *The Interpreter's Bible,* 7:251.

The term thus embraces all of the prophecies concerning the Coming Deliverer. Matthew shows that Jesus is this Messiah.

> The genealogy (chap. i) shows His royal descent; the Magi were looking for a King (ii. 1,2). The discourses, so prominent in this Gospel, embody His prophetic ministry; and His atoning death reveals Him to be both the Priest and the Sacrifice.[16]

Thus Matthew writes to prove that Jesus is the predicted Messiah of the Old Testament.

The Purpose Is to Present the Kingdom Program of God

A nonbelieving Jew would scoff at any assertion of the Lord Jesus being the Messiah, let alone King. "If Jesus is the Messiah of Israel, where is His kingdom? Where is the fulfillment of the Old Testament promises to Israel?" he would ask. After all, the Hebrew Scriptures are replete with foreviews of a Utopian age headed by Israel and their Messiah. Therefore, the objector would contend Jesus could not be the Messiah because He did not fulfill Old Testament prophecies promising a kingdom for Israel.

Because of the validity of this objection, Matthew explains God's kingdom program as it relates to Jesus, to Israel, and to the church. He shows first of all that the Jews rejected an earthly kingdom when they rejected their King (21:28-22:10; 11:16-24). He then goes on to show that because Israel rejected its King, its Kingdom is postponed. It is very important to notice that the kingdom is *postponed* and the promises are yet to be fulfilled. The promises to Israel are *not cancelled* because it failed to accept its King at His first coming. Matthew shows this clearly (19:28; 20:20-23; 23:39; 24:29-31; 25:31-46).

In the meantime God has inaugurated an entirely new and previously unknown program. It involves the church of the present age which Christ predicted in Matthew 16:18. Because of the universal character of the church, Matthew also has an emphasis on Gentiles. Only Matthew mentions the word *church*. He refers to the Magi from the East, the Gentile centurion's great faith, the Canaanitish woman, the promise of the universal proclamation of the kingdom (24:14), and the final great commission. Matthew has a definite universal emphasis to prove that the kingdom program of God also embraces Gentiles.

Didn't God know before?

16. Scroggie, *Guide to Gospels*, p. 255.

Therefore, to say that Matthew has only one purpose, to prove Jesus is the Messiah, is erroneous.

> The author's aim is by no means attained when he has advanced evidence that Jesus is the Messiah. He reaches his goal only when, with this as the first step of his argument, he has shown that Jesus the Messiah founded a kingdom of universal scope, abolishing all Jewish limitations.[17]

Thus Matthew also shows how the Gentiles are related to the Jewish kingdom program. When Matthew's Gospel was written, the gospel message was already being proclaimed to Gentiles; Judaism was a separate and distinct entity.[18] The Jews would need an explanation and Matthew accomplishes this in his Gospel.

Matthew then presents the kingdom program in three aspects. First, the earthly literal kingdom was offered to Israel in the person of Jesus, the Messiah, at His first coming. Second, the kingdom was postponed because Israel rejected its Messiah. This postponed kingdom will be established at Christ's second coming. Third, Christ Jesus is now engaged in building His church, composed of those who in this age are the heirs of the kingdom. Matthew thus agrees with Paul who writes, "For I say that Christ has become a servant to the circumcision on behalf of the truth of God to confirm the promises given to the fathers, and for the Gentiles to glorify God for His mercy" (Romans 15:8-9).

IV. The Theme of the Book

Of the three offices of the Messiah—prophet, priest, and king— Matthew clearly places a special stress on the royal aspect of the Lord's person and ministry. And there are many factors which indicate Jesus the Messiah is especially a king.

In the opening verse of the book He is called "The son of David" who in turn is described as "David the King" in verse six. Joseph, the Lord's legal father, is addressed by an angel as "Joseph, son of David" in 1:20. The magi searched for Him as one who is born "King of the Jews" (2:2). The prophecy of Micah 5:2 predicting the great ruler of Israel would be born in Bethlehem is applied to the Lord Jesus (2:6). A number of times Christ Jesus is addressed or obliquely referred to as the *Son of David* (9:27, 12:23; 15:22; 20:30-31; 21:9, 15; 22:45). The many

---

17. Burton, *A Short Introduction to the Gospels*, p. 17.
18. Hill, *Matthew,* pp. 39-44.

references to Christ and His kingdom support the idea that Matthew emphasizes the royal facet of the Savior's character and work—"the kingdom of heaven is at hand" (3:2, 4:17; 10:7); "the kingdom of God has come upon you" (12:28); "the Son of Man coming in His kingdom" (16:28); " .. your kingdom" (20:21); " .. in My Father's kingdom" (26:29). The book concludes with Jesus holding all authority in heaven and earth (28:18).

Perhaps the most pointed of all the royal references is Matthew 21:5 containing a quotation of Zechariah 9:9 and introduced by a clause from Isaiah 62:11, "Say to the daughter of Zion, 'Behold your King is coming to you, gentle, and mounted upon a donkey, even upon a colt, the foal of a beast of burden.'" Clearly then Jesus is portrayed not only as the Christ, but as the *royal* Messiah.

> The royal aspect of Jesus' career is stressed in Matthew. Not only was He descended from royal stock, but in infancy He was also the recipient of gifts such as would be given to a king—gold, frankincense, and myrrh (2:11). His famous Sermon on the Mount was really the inaugural address of a king, embodying the essential principles of a new policy. His conflict with evil was the clash of two antagonistic kingdoms (12:26, 27). The parables of chapter 13 are the "parables of the kingdom." The transfiguration was a sample of the Son of Man coming in His kingdom (16:28, 17:1, 2), and from the transfiguration to the Passion in Jerusalem Jesus proclaimed insistently that He would come again "in his kingdom" (20:20-23, 25:31-46).[19]

The reason Matthew emphasized this aspect of the Messiah's ministry is comparatively simple. The Jews stressed this phase of the work of Messiah in their own thinking. Even the Old Testament Scriptures accented the kingly aspect of Messiah.[20] Since Matthew wrote for Jewish readers, he would naturally point to the Lord's royalty in order to convince them. He meets them on their own ground.

V. The Plan of the Book—A Didactic Structure

The Grouping of Material

Commentators have noticed that Matthew makes a practice of grouping his materials so that three, five, six, or seven incidents, miracles,

19. Tenney, *The Genius of the Gospels,* p. 53.
20. Thomas R. English, "The Purpose and Plan of Matthew's Gospel," *The Bible Student,* 1 (April 1900):221.

sayings, or parables appear together. A concise list of many of these is given by Allen.[21] This clustering of materials was not done for any mystical reason but for a very practical purpose; that goal was a pedagogical one. "Jewish-Christian catechists would use them in their catechumen classes, and in this way much narrative and teaching could be held in the mind."[22] Plummer notes that every indication of grouping does not prove a didactic purpose, but he does concede, "... some of his numerical groups may have had this aim."[23]

A fact to be noted in this connection relates to the order of the Gospel. Since so much material is grouped, it is impossible for Matthew to be in perfect chronological order. Rather Matthew uses groups where it suits his purpose and places these groups in a chronological framework. Thiessen says, "The first four chapters of Matthew are chronological; chs. 5-13 are topical; and chs. 14-28 are again chronological ...."[24] This is very plausible and fits the Gospel of Matthew well.

The Emphasis on Discourses

While the didactic character of the book is displayed primarily by its groupings of material, it is also shown by its emphasis on the discourses.[25]

> Matthew's Gospel is didactic in emphasis. It contains the largest single block of discourse material found in the Gospels (chaps. 5, 6, and 7), and there are other long passages (chaps. 10, 13, 18, 23, 24, 25) which reproduce Jesus' teaching.[26]

The value of this Gospel in teaching doctrine can readily be seen. No other gospel contains as much of the teachings of Jesus.

The Use of Prophecy

A third evidence of the didactic character of the Gospel of Matthew is shown by Matthew's use of prophecy, those Old Testament Scriptures which were so very familiar to the Jewish people. These prophecies

21. Allen, *Commentary on Matthew,* p. lxv.; cf. Alfred Plummer, *An Exegetical Commentary on the Gospel According to S. Matthew,* pp. xix-xxiii.
22. Scroggie, *Guide to Gospels,* p. 311.
23. Plummer, *Exegetical Commentary,* p. xxiii.
24. Thiessen, *Introduction,* p. 138.
25. *See pp. 24-25, below.
26. Merrill C. Tenney, *New Testament Survey,* p. 150.

therefore proved invaluable in instructing the Jews concerning Jesus. Matthew was very adept at doing this as his Gospel proves.

> By continuity is meant the fundamental pedagogical principle of proceeding from the known to the unknown. Every preacher and every teacher follows this principle when he tries to convey a new thought to an audience. Matthew made the Old Testament his apperceptive basis. Evidently those for whom he intended his Gospel were either quite familiar with the law and the prophets, or else they acknowledged their authority.[27]

Quite obviously the use of the Hebrew Scriptures was also helpful in defending Christianity. Many times Matthew states that something occurred or was done " ... that the Scriptures might be fulfilled." Some such formula introduces quotation after quotation to show God was unfolding His sovereignly ordered program in the ministry of the Lord Jesus.

The Grammar

A fourth indication of the pedagogical emphasis of Matthew is found in his grammar. It is that of an historian. Scroggie writes, "The aorist tense is very prominent in Matthew, and denotes simply and graphically what has taken place."[28] "The common use of the genitive absolute indicates the same thing."[29] This emphasis on the historical record makes it valuable to use to instruct as well as to convince. Evidently it was used for both purposes.

The Use of the Verb *"to disciple"*

A fifth and last evidence of the didactic character of Matthew's Gospel is his use of the verb "to disciple." This verb, $\mu\alpha\theta\eta\tau\epsilon\dot{\upsilon}\omega$, means either "to be a disciple" or "to make a disciple," but in either case learning is involved. It occurs three times in Matthew (13:52; 27:57; 28:19) and only once elsewhere (Acts 14:21).[30] The fact that Matthew is the only one of the gospel writers to use this word indicates his thinking. *Luke wrote Acts!* He evidently thought highly of making disciples by teaching and had this in mind when he wrote his Gospel.

didn't site $\mu\alpha\theta\eta\tau\eta\varsigma$ - throughout gospels!

27. Tenney, *The Genius of the Gospels*, p. 75.
28. Scroggie, *Guide to Gospels*, p. 110.
29. Robertson, *Grammar*, p. 513.
30. Scroggie, *Guide to Gospels*, p. 277.

The Outline of the Book

There have been various theories proposed concerning the structure of Matthew. One of the more novel propounds the idea that the sections of Matthew's Gospel correspond to the Jewish liturgical year.[31] Another suggestion dating back to Papias (ca. 60-130 A.D.) relates the structure of Matthew's Gospel to the first five books of the Old Testament, the Pentateuch. In Matthew's Gospel there are five discourses, all concluded with the same formula (7:28; 11:1; 13:53; 19:1; 26:1). It is propounded Matthew is introducing a New Pentateuch or New Order with Jesus as the New Moses.[32] However, there is really no correlation between the five sections of Matthew and the Pentateuch.

Frederick Grant has noted the parallel with the five books of Moses and also other five-fold divisions in the Old Testament—the five books of Psalms (Psalms 1-41, 42-72, 73-89, 90-106, 107-150), and the five "Megilloth" (The Song of Songs, Ruth, Lamentations, Ecclesiastes, and Esther).[33] He feels the arrangement is simply Judaistic and catechetical. The order certainly seems to have more significance than simply a five-fold sectional arrangement. Fenton suggests a chiasmus—a, b, c, c, b, a—with the central breaking point being the middle of the parabolic discourse of chapter 13.[34] This however is too artificial. Generally students see three blocks of thought in each gospel—the presentation of Jesus to the people, a period of consideration, and the rejection of Jesus by the people.

The outline here presented follows Matthew's argument as it is based on the recurrence of "and it came about that when Jesus had finished," (καὶ ἐγένετο ὅτε ἐτέλεσεν ὁ Ἰησοῦς), which Matthew evidently used to mark the divisions of his Gospel. This identical clause occurs in Matthew 7:28; 11:1; 13:53; 19:1 and 26:1, and always at the end of an address. The fact the addresses are rather extended and they occur at the end of each section implies they are climactic. It appears Matthew uses the narrative sections of his Gospel as an introduction to and a setting for the discourses of Jesus. Because of this the events generally recede into the background and the discourses assume the important role. Interestingly, the narratives of Matthew's Gospel are almost always briefer

31. P. P. Levertoff and H. L. Goudge, "The Gospel According to St. Matthew," *A New Commentary on Holy Scriptures Including the Apocrypha*, pp. 128-29.
32. A. W. Argyle, *The Gospel According to Matthew*, p. 2; cf. W. D. Davies, *The Sermon on the Mount*, pp. 6-10.
33. Grant, *Nelson's Bible Commentary*, 6:24.
34. J. C. Fenton, *Saint Matthew*, pp. 15-16.

than the corresponding ones in the Gospel of Mark, this in spite of the fact Mark is much shorter than Matthew. Some 606 of Mark's verses are pressed into 500 of Matthew's.[35] Of course this is not to say the events are unimportant; they are crucial, since the discourses would be meaningless and contradictory without them. Except for the prologue and the epilogue of Matthew, each of the movements ends with a discourse; the outline is therefore arranged accordingly.

I. The Incarnation and the Preparation of the King (1:1-4:11)

    A. The Incarnation of the King (1:1-2:23)

        1. The genealogy of the King (1:1-1:17)
        2. The birth of the King (1:18-1:25)
          a. The betrothal (1:18-1:19)
          b. The annunciation (1:20-1:21)
          c. The fulfillment of prophecy and His birth (1:22-1:25)
        3. The childhood of the King (2:1-2:23)
          a. In Bethlehem (2:1-2:12)
          b. In Egypt (2:13-2:18)
          c. In Nazareth (2:19-2:23)

    B. The Preparation of the King (3:1-4:11)

        1. The forerunner of the King (3:1-3:12)
        2. The baptism of the King (3:13-3:17)
        3. The temptation of the King (4:1-4:11)

II. The Declaration of the Principles of the King (4:12-7:29)

    A. The Introduction to the Ministry of the King (4:12-4:25)

        1. The occasion (4:12-4:16)
        2. The message of the King (4:17)
        3. The call of four disciples (4:18-4:22)
        4. A summary of the ministry of the King (4:23-4:25)

    B. The Principles of the King (5:1-7:29)

        1. The setting (5:1-5:2)
        2. The subjects of the kingdom (5:3-5:16)
          a. Their character and their portion in the kingdom (5:3-5:12)
          b. Their calling and their position in the world (5:13-5:16)

---

35. Hendriksen, *Matthew*, p. 25; cf. Eduard Schweizer, *The Good News According to Matthew*, p. 210.

3. The explanation of genuine righteousness (5:17-7:12)
   a. The principle of righteousness and the law (5:17-5:48)
      1) The confirmation of the law (5:17-5:20)
      2) The interpretation of the law (5:21-5:48)
         a) The law regarding murder (5:21-5:26)
         b) The law regarding adultery (5:27-5:30)
         c) The law regarding divorce (5:31-5:32)
         d) The law regarding the taking of an oath (5:33-5:37)
         e) The law regarding retaliation (5:38-5:42)
         f) The law regarding love (5:43-5:48)
   b. The practice of righteousness (6:1-6:18)
      1) The maxim (6:1)
      2) The motives for good deeds (6:2-6:18)
         a) The rewards for giving (6:2-6:4)
         b) The rewards for praying (6:5-6:15)
         c) The rewards for fasting (6:16-6:18)
   c. The perspectives of righteousness (6:19-7:12)
      1) With respect to wealth (6:19-6:34)
      2) With respect to brethren (7:1-7:5)
      3) With respect to the spiritually hostile (7:6)
      4) With respect to God (7:7-7:12)
4. The warnings of the King (7:13-7:27)
   a. Regarding the narrow gate (7:13-7:14)
   b. Regarding false prophets (7:15-7:20)
   c. Regarding false profession (7:21-7:27)
5. The response of the people (7:28-7:29)

III. The Manifestation of the King (8:1-11:1)

  A. The Demonstration of the Power of the King (8:1-9:34)

    1. Miracles of healing (8:1-8:17)
      a. Leprosy (8:1-8:4)
      b. Paralysis (8:5-8:13)
      c. Sickness and demons (8:14-8:17)
    2. The demands of disciples (8:18-8:22)
      a. Regarding possessions (8:18-8:20)
      b. Regarding paternal relations (8:21-8:22)
    3. Miracles of power (8:23-9:8)
      a. In the realm of nature (8:23-8:27)
      b. In the realm of the supernatural (8:28-8:34)
      c. In the realm of the spiritual (9:1-9:8)

B. The Illustrations of the Opposition to the King (12:1-12:50)

    1. The contention concerning the Sabbath (12:1-12:21)

        a. The relationship of the Sabbath to man (12:1-12:8)

        b. The relationship of the Sabbath to good deeds (12:9-12:21)

    2. The contention concerning the power of the King (12:22-12:37)

    3. The contention concerning the signs of the King (12:38-12:45)

    4. The question concerning the kin of the King (12:46-12:50)

C. The Adaptation of the King to His Opposition (13:1-13:53)

    1. The parables spoken to the multitudes (13:1-13:35)

        a. The setting (13:1-13:2)

        b. The introduction (13:3-13:23)

            1) The parable of the sower (13:3-13:9)

            2) The purpose of the parables (13:10-13:17)

            3) The parable of the sower explained (13:18-13:23)

        c. Three parables of the Kingdom (13:24-13:33)

            1) The parable of the wheat and the darnel (13:24-13:30)

            2) The parable of the mustard seed (13:31-13:32)

            3) The parable of the leaven and the meal (13:33)

        d. The fulfillment of the prophecy (13:34-13:35)

    2. The parables spoken to the disciples (13:36-13:53)

        a. The explanation of the parable of the wheat and the darnel (13:36-13:43)

        b. Three parables of the Kingdom (13:44-13:50)

            1) The parable of the hidden treasure (13:44)

            2) The parable of the pearl of great price (13:45-13:46)

            3) The parable of the dragnet (13:47-13:50)

        c. Conclusion: the parable of the householder (13:51-13:53)

V. The Reaction of the King (13:54-19:2)

A. The Withdrawal of the King (13:54-16:12)

    1. The unbelief of the people of Nazareth (13:54-13:58)

    2. The opposition of Herod (14:1-14:36)

        a. The beheading of John (14:1-14:12)

VI. The Formal Presentation and Rejection of the King (19:3-25:46)

A. The Continued Instruction of the Disciples (19:3-20:34)

1. Concerning marriage (19:3-19:12)
   a. The problem of divorce (19:3-19:9)
   b. Marriage and the kingdom (19:10-19:12)
2. Concerning childlikeness (19:13-19:15)
3. Concerning the snare of wealth (19:16-19:26)
4. Concerning rewards (19:27-20:16)
   a. Peter's question (19:27-19:30)
   b. The parabolic illustration (20:1-20:16)
5. Concerning the passion (20:17-20:19)
6. Concerning position (20:20-20:28)
7. The healing of the blind men (20:29-20:34)

B. The Formal Presentation of the King (21:1-21:17)

1. The preparation (21:1-21:7)
2. The entrance into Jerusalem (21:8-21:11)
   a. The homage (21:8-21:9)
   b. The response (21:10-21:11)
3. The entrance into the temple (21:12-21:17)
   a. The cleansing of the temple (21:12-21:13)
   b. The healing ministry in the temple (21:14-21:17)

C. The Rejection of the King by the Nation (21:18-22:46)

1. The fig tree (21:18-21:22)
2. The conflict with the chief priests and the elders (21:23-22:14)
   a. The question of authority (21:23-21:27)
   b. The parable of the two sons (21:28-21:32)
   c. The parable of the wicked husbandmen (21:33-21:46)
   d. The parable of the royal feast (22:1-22:14)
3. The conflict with the Pharisees and the Herodians (22:15-22:22)
4. The conflict with the Sadducees (22:23-22:33)
5. The conflict with the Pharisees (22:34-22:46)

D. The Rejection of the Nation by the King (23:1-23:39)

1. The admonition of the multitudes and the disciples (23:1-23:12)
2. The indictment of the scribes and Pharisees (23:13-23:36)
3. The lamentation over Jerusalem (23:37-23:39)

E. The Predictions of the Rejected King (24:1-25:46)

1. The setting (24:1-24:2)
2. The questions of the disciples (24:3)
3. The warning concerning deception (24:4-24:6)
4. The general description of the end time (24:7-24:14)
5. The abomination of desolation (24:15-24:22)
6. The coming of the Son of Man (24:23-24:31)
7. The parabolic admonition (24:32-25:30)
   a. The parable of the fig tree (24:32-24:42)
   b. The parable of the watchful householder (24:43-24:44)
   c. The parable of the two servants (24:45-24:51)
   d. The parable of the ten virgins (25:1-25:13)
   e. The parable of the talents (25:14-25:30)
8. The judgment of the nations (25:31-25:46)

VII. The Crucifixion and the Resurrection of the King (26:1-28:20)

A. The Crucifixion of the King (26:1-27:66)

1. The preparation (26:1-26:46)
   a. The setting (26:1-26:5)
   b. The anointing at Bethany (26:6-26:13)
   c. The agreement to the betrayal (26:14-26:16)
   d. The Passover supper (26:17-26:29)
   e. The prediction of the denials (26:30-26:35)
   f. The agonizing in Gethsemane (26:36-26:46)
2. The arrest (26:47-26:56)
3. The trials (26:57-27:26)
   a. Before Caiaphas (26:57-26:68)
   b. The denials of Peter (26:69-26:75)
   c. The remorse of Judas (27:3-27:10)
   d. Before Pilate (27:1-27:2, 27:11-27:26)
4. The cross (27:27-27:56)
   a. The mocking (27:27-27:31)
   b. The passing of the King (27:32-27:50)
   c. The supernatural occurrences (27:51-27:56)
5. The burial (27:57-27:66)
   a. The burial by Joseph of Arimathea (27:57-27:61)
   b. The sealing of the tomb (27:62-27:66)

B. The Resurrection of the King (28:1-28:20)

    1. The empty tomb (28:1-28:10)

    2. The false report (28:11-28:15)

    3. The final instructions of the King (28:16-28:20)

Commentary
on the Gospel of Matthew

I. The Incarnation and the Preparation of the King (1:1-4:11)

A. The Incarnation of the King (1:1-2:23)

1. The genealogy of the King (1:1-1:17)
2. The birth of the King (1:18-1:25)
   a. The betrothal (1:18-1:19)
   b. The annunciation (1:20-1:21)
   c. The fulfillment of prophecy and His birth (1:22-1:25)
3. The childhood of the King (2:1-2:23)
   a. In Bethlehem (2:1-2:12)
   b. In Egypt (2:13-2:18)
   c. In Nazareth (2:19-2:23)

B. The Preparation of the King (3:1-4:11)

1. The forerunner of the King (3:1-3:12)
2. The baptism of the King (3:13-3:17)
3. The temptation of the King (4:1-4:11)

I. The Incarnation and the Preparation of the King

Two main subjects are discussed by Matthew in the early chapters of his Gospel—the birth of the King and the preparation of the King for His ministry and manifestation to Israel. Because these two subjects are so closely related in Matthew's argument, they are considered under one section heading.

A. The Incarnation of the King
1:1-2:23

1. The Genealogy of the King, 1:1-1:17

One of the primary questions a Jew would ask concerning a claimant to the title of Messiah would be, "Is he a son of Abraham and of the house of David?" This interrogation would be completely valid since God had given marvelous promises to Abraham (Genesis 12:1-3; 13:14-18; 15:1-21; 17:1-19; 22:15-18) and to David (2 Samuel 7:12-16) to be fulfilled by the one who was to be the Messiah. Because this question concerning the King of Israel is so important, and because it forms a logical starting point for a document which sets about to prove the Messiahship of Christ, Matthew presents first the genealogy of Jesus (1:1-1:17).

The Superscription, **1:1.** ***The book of the genealogy of Jesus Christ, the son of David, the son of Abraham.*** The first words of Matthew, "the book of the genealogy of" (βίβλος γενέσεως), refer to the Lord's family tree. There is little doubt that this superscription was formed with the Septuagint version of Genesis in mind. The identical phrase occurs in the Septuagint in Genesis 2:4 and 5:1. Genealogical lists are found throughout Genesis (6:9, 10:1; 11:10, 27; 25:12, 19; 36:1, 9 and 37:2) and are often used by Bible students as a basis for outlining the book. It is interesting to note that in Genesis each genealogical table is followed by a brief narrative. It may be that Matthew is following Moses' example in this respect by presenting the genealogy of Jesus and then a brief narrative of His birth (1:18-25). However, it is more probable that Matthew is referring here to the genealogical table only since γένεσις occurs again in Matthew 1:18 in a different sense.[1] There it means "birth." It seems best therefore to conclude that Matthew 1:1 refers to the genealogical table and 1:18 introduces the narrative of the birth of the King.

The phrase in 1:1 must not be passed over as merely a superscription to a genealogical table. It is that, but it is also much more. Schweizer asserts, " ... it is implied that the story of Jesus, to be told in what follows, is not merely the genetic but the logical outcome of God's history as recounted in this opening section."[2] A thought connection with the usage in Genesis can also be found. Relative to its occurrences in Genesis, Tenney says, "Each use of the formula introduces a new stage in the development of God's purpose in the propogation of the Seed through which He planned to effect redemption."[3] Generally speaking this observation is true. The last time the term occurs in the Old Testament in connection with the Messianic line is Ruth 4:18 where the genealogy terminates with David. Matthew picks up the genealogy at this juncture and links it to Jesus.[4] The term is used by him to mark the continuation and consummation of God's program in the person and work of Jesus Christ, the Son of David and the Son of Abraham. The plan which God inaugurated in the creation of *man* is to be completed by *the Man,* Christ Jesus.

It is of importance to note that the order of the superscription is *Son of David* and then *Son of Abraham.* Matthew has a definite purpose in inverting the chronological order of the names. The promises given to David were restricted; that is, they were Jewish, national, and royal in character. To David was promised an eternal throne, an eternal king, and an eternal kingdom (2 Samuel 7:12-17; Psalm 89). On the other hand, the promises given to Abraham were more comprehensive, being personal, national, *and universal* (Genesis 12:1-3; 13:14-17; 15:13-21; 17:1-8; 22:16-19). Abraham was given the promise among others that in him

1. Alan Hugh M'Neile, *The Gospel According to St. Matthew, p. 1.*
2. Eduard Schweizer, *The Good News According to Matthew,* p. 24.
3. Merrill C. Tenney, *The Genius of the Gospels,* p. 52.
4. Merrill C. Tenney, *New Testament Survey,* p. 143.

should all the nations of the earth be blessed. The pattern of Matthew's Gospel emphasizes the Davidic aspect first and then the Abrahamic. Matthew shows that the Lord Jesus, restricting His early ministry to Israel (Matthew 10:5-7), comes as the King of Israel offering Himself to them as their Messiah. After Israel has rejected their King the emphasis falls on the universal character of the ministry of the Messiah (Matthew 28:16-20). This is the second aspect of Matthew's presentation.

> Christ came with all the reality of the kingdom promised to David's Son. But if He were refused as the Son of David, still, as the Son of Abraham, there was blessing not merely for the Jew, but for the Gentile. He is indeed the Messiah; but if Israel will not have Him, God will during their unbelief bring the nations to taste of His mercy.[5]

Paul establishes this interpretation in his Epistle to the Romans (Romans 15:8-9).

By this brief superscription Matthew discloses the theme of his book. Jesus is the One who shall consummate God's program. In His first coming He was presented as the Son of David first and then as the Son of Abraham. The emphasis falls on His royalty and then on His universality. "First He is Sovereign, then Savior."[6] This is the order Matthew follows in the development of his argument.

Abraham, 1:2. To Abraham was born Isaac; and to Isaac, Jacob; and to Jacob, Judah and his brothers. There are some observations pertinent to the argument of Matthew which must be made regarding the genealogy itself. It is interesting to note that the genealogy commences with Abraham and not Adam. This indicates the Jewish character of this list. For legal reasons a Jew need not go beyond Abraham, the father of the Jewish race, but the Messiah must of necessity be a Jew. It is also interesting to note that Matthew uses Abraham, the covenant name, and not Abram. Abraham as a name denotes the covenant privileges of the Jewish race.

Judah. Another factor in the genealogy which contributes to the argument is found in verse two. There Matthew writes, "and to Jacob [was born] Judah and his brothers." Judah is singled out from his brothers since the Messianic promise of sovereignty was given to him

---

5. William Kelly, *Lectures on the Gospel of Matthew,* p. 14.
6. S. Lewis Johnson, Jr., "The Argument Of Matthew," *Bibliotheca Sacra* 112 (April 1955): 143.

(Genesis 49:10). Because of this fact it becomes necessary for Matthew to show that Jesus is a descendant of Judah. The phrase *and his brothers* also occurs in verse eleven in connection with Jeconiah. However, the expression is used there in a very different sense.

> There is pathos in this second allusion to brotherhood. "Judah and his brethren," partakers in the promise (also in the sojourn in Egypt); "Jeconiah and his brethren," the generation of the promise eclipsed.[7]

The second occurrence thus emphasizes the significance of the first.

Perez, **1:3-1:5.** *and to Judah were born Perez and Zerah by Tamar; and to Perez was born Hezron; and to Hezron, Ram; and to Ram was born Amminadab; and to Amminadab, Nahshon; and to Nahshon, Salmon; and to Salmon was born Boaz by Rahab; and to Boaz was born Obed by Ruth; and to Obed, Jesse;* Verse three makes mention of Judah's twin sons, Perez and Zerah. However, the genealogy is traced through Perez only. This is not done without a reason. M'Neile says, "Jewish tradition traced the royal line to Perez (Ruth iv. 12, 18 ff.), and 'son of Perez' is a Rabb. expression for the Messiah."[8] In showing that Jesus follows the Messianic line of David as it proceeded from Perez, Matthew follows the genealogy given in Ruth 4 and in 1 Chronicles.

David the King, **1:6-1:15.** *and to Jesse was born David the king.*
And to David was born Solomon by her who had been the wife of Uriah; and to Solomon was born Rehoboam; and to Rehoboam, Abijah; and to Abijah, Asa; and to Asa was born Jehoshaphat; and to Jehoshaphat, Joram; and to Joram, Uzziah; and to Uzziah was born Jotham; and to Jotham, Ahaz; and to Ahaz, Hezekiah; and to Hezekiah was born Manasseh; and to Manasseh, Amon; and to Amon, Josiah; and to Josiah were born Jeconiah and his brothers, at the time of the deportation to Babylon.
And after the deportation to Babylon, to Jeconiah was born Shealtiel; and to Shealtiel, Zerubbabel; and to Zerubbabel was born Abiud; and to Abiud, Eliakim; and to Eliakim, Azor; and to Azor was born Zadok; and to Zadok, Achim; and to Achim, Eliud;

7. Alexander Balmain Bruce, "The Synoptic Gospels," *The Expositor's Greek Testament,* 1:64.
8. M'Neile, *St. Matthew,* p. 1.

and to Eliud was born Eleazar; and to Eleazar, Matthan; and to Matthan, Jacob; There is also a subtle suggestion within the genealogy in that only David is called *king*.[9] Even the grammatical construction emphasizes the regal character of David's person. M'Neile recognizes this and comments, "The art. before Δαυίδ is strictly incorrect when τὸν βασιλέα is added; the addition emphasizes the fact that the genealogy is royal."[10] Fenton adds, "The addition of the title, *the king*, marks the end of this period of waiting, and points forward to Jesus, *the Son of David, the Christ, the King of the Jews.*"[11]

Solomon, too, was a king, but he is not called such since he was not the one who fulfilled the promises made to his father. This indicates two things. First, it shows that the line of Jesus was a royal one. He could claim David the king as His forefather. Second, it intimates that no one was the fulfillment of the promised king of 2 Samuel 7 until the birth of Jesus the Messiah.

Joseph the Husband of Mary, **1:16.** *and to Jacob was born Joseph the husband of Mary, by whom was born Jesus, who is called Christ.* In Matthew 1:16 an important peculiarity is found. Previous to this verse γεννάω ("was born" NASB, "begat" KJV) is always used in the active voice with the husband as the subject ("Abraham *begat* Isaac"—"Jacob *begat* Joseph," KJV). But in verse sixteen it is used in the passive voice and is not connected with Joseph. Rather Joseph is called "the husband of Mary, of *whom* was born Jesus, who is called Christ" (KJV). The pronoun "whom" (ἧς) is feminine and refers to Mary. Therefore Matthew is hinting at that which he later openly declares, the virgin birth of Jesus (1:23).

The clause "who is called" (ὁ λεγόμενος) in 1:16 is not used to imply doubt as to the Messiahship of Jesus; it is simply used to identify the Jesus whose genealogy is being presented. In referring to Matthew's use of this phrase Scroggie writes that it " . . . is a favourite expression of this Evangelist in announcing the names of persons, or places, or surnames . . ."[12] It occurs twelve times in the Gospel of Matthew (1:16; 2:23; 4:18; 10:2; 13:55; 26:3, 14, 36; 27:16, 17, 22, 33). From these occurrences it can be seen that the expression is used throughout the Gospel for identification. That is exactly how Matthew employs it here.

9. A. C. Gaebelein, *The Gospel Of Matthew,* 1:24.
10. M'Neile, *St. Matthew,* p. 2.
11. J. C. Fenton, *Saint Matthew,* p. 38.
12. W. Graham Scroggie, *A Guide To the Gospels,* p. 277.

Matthew 1:16 shows that Jesus can be called the son of Joseph although
He was virgin born of Mary.

The Four Women. It is of great importance to mark the mention of the
four women in the genealogy. The enumeration of women in a Jewish
genealogy was very uncommon. The remarkableness of their mention is
accentuated by their character. The names of the women are Tamar,
Rahab, Ruth, and the wife of Uriah. Matthew's method of referring to
Bathsheba as the wife of Uriah emphasizes the heinousness of David's
sin. "Of the four mentioned two—Rahab and Ruth—are foreigners, and
three—Tamar, Rahab and Bathsheba—were stained with sin."[13]
Matthew has a twofold purpose in doing this. He shows the discerning
reader that the Lord Jesus came to seek and to save the lost and to
minister to them. He was to be the embodiment of God's grace. Those
of the lowest state are raised to the highest royal line. Matthew also
indicates by their mention the universal character of the Messiah's
ministry. The reference to these alien women is " ... meant to prefigure
God's activity—to culminate in Jesus (28:19)—that will embrace not
only the Jews but all Gentiles as well."[14] It was to result in the extension
of mercy to the Gentiles as well as to the Jews.

The Deletions. It will be noted that there are a number of names which
are not included in the genealogy which are actually in the line of
descent. This can be explained by several factors. First, it was not at all
uncommon to leave names out of a genealogy. The purpose of such a list
was to establish proof of one's ancestry, and therefore every name is not
a necessity. Second, Matthew intended, for mnemonic purposes, to
include only fourteen names in each division; therefore it was necessary
to leave out some names. Finally, the infamous character of some of the
persons may explain their deletion. Ahaziah, Joash, and Amaziah may
have been omitted for this reason. Certainly Matthew had accurate
genealogical tables at hand. It can be inferred, therefore, that the deletion of certain names from his genealogical record was made for a
purpose. That purpose is found in one or more of the above explanations.

The Divisions, **1:17.** ***Therefore all the generations from Abraham
to David are fourteen generations; and from David to the deportation to Babylon fourteen generations; and from the deportation to***

13. A. Carr, *The Gospel According To St. Matthew,* p. 81.
14. Schweizer, *Good News,* p. 25.

Babylon to the time of Christ fourteen generations. One last observation needs to be made concerning the genealogy. The divisions of the genealogy are very significant. The names are placed in three groups, each of which is characterized by the person or event with which it culminates. "In David the family rose to royal power ... At the captivity it lost it again. In Christ it regained it."[15] Another has noted a major covenant was given in each of the three periods.[16] In the first the Abrahamic covenant was established, in the second the Davidic covenant, and in the third the new covenant. All were to be fulfilled in the person and work of Jesus the Messiah.

As a mnemonic device Matthew summarizes the three groups by stating that there are fourteen names in each group (v. 17). To do this he counts David twice and omits several names. It is recognized that this was a common rabbinic device. Matthew may have derived the number fourteen from the Hebrew spelling of David's name. In the Hebrew language the letters of the alphabet have numerical value. The Hebrew spelling of David is דָּוִד . These three letters have the numerical value of four, six, four, respectively, their total being fourteen. This is a possible and very plausible explanation of why Matthew chose fourteen as a basic number for his divisions. If this be true Matthew would again be emphasizing the royal character of the genealogy of Jesus. He is not saying there were only fourteen people in each section of the actual genealogy. This was simply a typical Rabbinic aid to memory. The names of the women are not included in Matthew's counting.

Conclusion. Matthew uses the genealogy in two ways to prove the royal lineage of Jesus the Messiah. First of all, for the cursory reader he employs it in the *general way* to prove the direct lineage of Jesus through Joseph to David and Abraham. This is the impression one would get immediately when looking at the genealogy as a whole. Second, he writes the genealogy in a *detailed way* so that a person making a careful study of the names and more minute features cannot help but find Messianic implications. Some of these details have been pointed out, such as his use of the name Abraham, the way he singles out Judah from his brethren, the reference to David as king, and the grammatical changes in 1:16. This is the more particular method he employs to convey the same general message: Jesus is the Messiah.

15. Willoughby C. Allen, *A Critical and Exegetical Commentary on the Gospel According to S. Matthew,* p. 2.
16. S. Lewis Johnson, Jr., "The Gospel Of Matthew," unpublished class lecture notes.

2. The Birth of the King, 1:18-1:25

This subject is discussed by Matthew in his Gospel from 1:18-2:23. The annunciation to Joseph and the birth of the King are considered in 1:18-25, while Matthew 2:1-23 contains an account of the King's infancy.

a. The Betrothal, **1:18-1:19.** *Now the birth of Jesus Christ was as follows. When His mother Mary had been betrothed to Joseph, before they came together she was found to be with child by the Holy Spirit. And Joseph her husband, being a righteous man, and not wanting to disgrace her, desired to put her away secretly.* The "now" (δέ) of 1:18 marks the transition from the genealogy to the narrative. As the superscription of the genealogy (1:1) acts as a title to Matthew 1:1-17, so the first sentence of 1:18 presents the subject of the next section (1:18-25).

Matthew is very careful to inform the reader of his Gospel as to the way in which the Messiah came into this world. The words "as follows" (οὕτως) indicate the manner of the birth (1:18). The Evangelist desires the reader to grasp immediately the supernatural character of Jesus Christ and points to His miraculous birth with this οὕτως.

The actual narrative of the birth commences with the time of the discovery of the pregnancy of Mary.[17] The fact became known *after* her betrothal but *before* her marriage. The Jewish laws of marriage looked at a betrothed couple in such a way that they could not break their engagement without divorce proceedings. Yet an engaged couple had no conjugal rights.

> ... a betrothed girl was a widow if her *fiance* died (Kethub. i.2),
> and this whether the man had "taken" her into his house or not.
> After betrothal, therefore, but before marriage, the man was
> legally "husband" ....[18]

This becomes significant to Matthew's argument. Joseph, being a "just man" (δίκαιος), would hardly be engaged to a woman of loose morals. His piety is further affirmed by the note Matthew makes of his consternation and the struggle which ensued between his conscience and his love for Mary. Being betrothed, they would not be involved in connubial relationships. If they had been married, the child born of Mary would doubtless have been attributed to Joseph. But Matthew guards

17. The Greek text uses a genitive absolute here, a characteristic of Matthew's style.
18. M'Neile, *St. Matthew*, pp. 6-7.

against this by saying Mary was found to be pregnant *before* they came together.[19] Every circumstance indicates that Mary could not have become pregnant by a human man. This is exactly what Matthew is attempting to prove. The conception of Jesus was supernatural, being by (causal ἐκ) the Holy Spirit. To assert that it was otherwise would be to completely discount Matthew's veracity and reliability.

Joseph's consternation is explained more clearly when the chronology of Luke's Gospel is placed alongside Matthew's. Luke 1:26-38 states the annunciation to Mary was made in the sixth month of Elizabeth's pregnancy. Mary promptly went to visit her cousin, Elizabeth, and was with her for three months; then she returned to Nazareth. It was only then much to his chagrin Joseph discovered Mary was in her third month; to all appearances she had been unfaithful to him!

The breaking of the engagement contract by divorce seemed to be the only alternative. Probably because of his love for Mary and possibly also to spare his own reputation he decided to pursue the course of divorce privately. In this case the certificate of divorce would be " . . . handed to her privately, only in the presence of two witnesses."[20]

b. The Annunciation, 1:20-1:21. But when he had considered this, behold, an angel of the Lord appeared to him in a dream, saying, "Joseph, son of David, do not be afraid to take Mary as your wife; for that which has been conceived in her is of the Holy Spirit. And she will bear a Son; and you shall call His name Jesus, for it is He who will save His people from their sins." While Joseph was turning the whole matter over in his mind, an angel appeared by a dream and explained the cause of Mary's pregnancy to him (1:20-1:21).[21]

The name and work of this one who is to be born of a virgin is not without significance. The angel first tells Joseph that His name shall be

19. συνελθεῖν denotes the accomplishment of marriage. *Ibid*, p. 7.

20. Alfred Edersheim, *The Life and Times of Jesus the Messiah*, 1:154.

21. Matthew appeals to the Jewish reader in a number of ways in this section. He first makes reference to an angel of the Lord. In the Old Testament the term *Angel of the Lord* denoted an appearance of the Son of God Himself. (Charles Hodge, *Systematic Theology*, 1:485). This is impossible here, however, and so it refers to *an* angel from the Lord. To a Jew a message brought by angels was unquestionably authoritative (Galatians 3:19; Hebrews 2:2).

Another indication that the book is written for Jewish readers is seen in the use of the interjection "Behold" (ἰδού). It is definitely Hebraic and occurs throughout the Gospel of Matthew (M'Neile, *St. Matthew*, p. 8).

A very important clause as far as the Israelites are concerned is found in verse twenty. This phrase is "Joseph, son of David" (Ἰωσὴφ υἱός Δαυιδ). This form of address is a supernatural acknowledgment of exactly what the genealogy just preceeding was attempting to prove. The affirmation of the angel confirms the declaration of the genealogy.

Jesus. This appellation, which means *Jehovah is Savior,* was not unique with the Messiah. Joshua is the Hebrew equivalent and so the name was well known to Israel; nevertheless, this designation had special significance in this case. The connective "for" (γάρ) indicates why. "He will save His people from their sins." The pronoun "He" (αὐτός) is very emphatic, so the sentence is rendered, "It is He Who shall save ... " This is important, for the Jews looked for a Messiah who not only would be a political power but also a redeemer from sin.[22] The Jewish character of the Gospel is again seen in that the work of salvation is related to His people, the Jews. The word "people" (λαός) refers to the Jews as distinct from "Gentiles" (ἔθνη).[23] God's angel declares that this Jesus is the promised Messiah who shall save.

The circumstances of Mary's pregnancy have verified the miraculous birth of Jesus. Now the message of the angel confirms it with the additional information that He shall perform the work of a redeemer.

c. The Fulfillment of Prophecy and His Birth, **1:22-1:25.** *Now all this took place that what was spoken by the Lord through the prophet might be fulfilled, saying,*

> *"Behold, the virgin shall be with child, and shall bear a Son, and they shall call His name Immanuel;" which translated means, "God with us."*

And Joseph arose from his sleep, and did as the angel of the Lord commanded him, and took her as his wife, and kept her a virgin until she gave birth to a Son; and he called His name Jesus. Matthew now relates these events to the famous prophecy of Isaiah. The formula, "what was spoken ... fulfilled" (πληρωθῇ τὸ ῥηθὲν) recurs often throughout the Gospel (2:15, 17, 23; 4:14; 8:17; 12:17; 13:35; 21:4; 27:9; cf 26:56). It points to the fulfillment of the Old Testament Scriptures. Divine sovereignty was working out the details on behalf of the Messiah for the purpose of fulfilling Old Testament prophecy.[24] The first instance of many fulfilled prophecies occurs here in Matthew 1:22. No doubt this would strike the Jew who read this Gospel very forcibly.

This quotation (Isaiah 7:14), taken from the Septuagint, has occasioned much discussion and is famous for its difficulties. The first problem involves the meaning of "virgin" (παρθένος). Generally

---

22. Gustaf Dalman, *The Words of Jesus,* p. 297.

23. M'Neile, *St. Matthew,* p. 8.

24. The "that" (ἵνα) indicates purpose. Archibald Thomas Robertson, *Word Pictures in the New Testament,* 1:11.

speaking this Greek noun refers to a virgin.[25] Several factors make it patently clear Matthew uses the term with this meaning. This is seen first from the context. Twice, in verses eighteen and twenty, the birth is affirmed to be a supernatural one. In verse twenty-five Joseph is said not to have known Mary until she gave birth to Jesus.[26] A clearer declaration of the virgin birth could hardly be made. A second indication of the sense in which the noun ($\pi\alpha\rho\theta\acute{e}\nu\omicron\varsigma$) is used here is the usual meaning of the word. Delling, in discussing the history of the noun, writes, "The word then went through an obvious process of narrowing down ... and $\pi\alpha\rho\theta\acute{e}\nu\omicron\varsigma$ came to be used for 'virgin.'"[27] This is its consistent New Testament meaning.

Another problem in this question of Isaiah is the meaning of the equivalent for "virgin" in the Hebrew text of Isaiah 7:14. It is commonly argued the word עַלְמָה means "young woman of marriageable age." While this is true, it must be conceded its every occurrence in the Old Testament either refers to a virgin or allows this meaning.[28] Because the New Testament interprets it to mean virgin in its prophetic fulfillment, this must also be its sense in Isaiah 7:14.

There is still another question revolving about the problem of the contemporary significance of Isaiah 7:14. All conservative students of Scripture agree Isaiah 7:14 has its ultimate fulfillment in Christ's birth as recorded in Matthew one. But what did the prophecy mean in Isaiah's day? The sign given to Ahaz had to have some contemporary importance. Isaiah seven says the child to be born in his day will be a sign to Ahaz. Before the boy reaches the age of accountability the two kings Ahaz feared would come to nothing.

The virgin of Isaiah 7:14 was first then a virgin of Isaiah's time who would marry, conceive, and bear a child. Who the virgin was is an open question. Smith wrote, " ... and those who embark upon curious inquiries, as to who exactly the mother might be, are busying themselves with what the prophet had no interest in, while neglecting that in which

---

25. M'Neile, *St. Matthew*, p. 9. This is so despite the fact it is used in Genesis 34:3 in the Septuagint to describe Dinah after her virginity had been violated forcibly by Shechem.

26. The imperfect tense "kept," lit., "was not knowing" ($\dot{\epsilon}\gamma\acute{\iota}\nu\omega\sigma\kappa\epsilon\nu$) asserts beyond the shadow of a doubt that Joseph had no conjugal relationship with Mary until after Jesus was born.

27. Gerhard Delling, "$\pi\alpha\rho\theta\acute{e}\nu\omicron\varsigma$" *Theological Dictionary of the New Testament*, 5:827.

28. Willis J. Beecher, *The Prophets and the Promise*, footnote, p. 334; cf. Genesis 24:43; Exodus 2:8; Psalm 68:25 (26); Proverbs 30:19; Song of Songs 1:3; 6:8; Isaiah 7:14. These are all of its Old Testament occurrences.

really lay the significance of the sign he offered."[29] When the predicted events came to pass in a few years the sign was proven true. However, the ultimate fulfillment of the Immanuel prophecy is seen in the Messiah. In other words, the Isaiah 7:14 prophecy has a double fulfillment—a near and far accomplishment of the prediction with the ultimate being the final fulfillment in the care of the virgin Mary and the virgin birth of Jesus Christ.

The prophecy goes on to state that His name shall be called Immanuel, which means *God with us*. At first sight this seems to conflict with Matthew 1:21, but as Gaebelein writes, "He is Emmanuel, and as such Jehovah the Saviour, so that in reality both names have the same meaning."[30] Matthew, by quoting this prophecy, proves conclusively that Jesus is the Messiah promised by God through the prophet Isaiah.

The Legal Emphasis. In looking back over the first chapter of Matthew one cannot help but see the emphasis on the legal aspect of this section. This is seen in the important role of Joseph, even though the Messiah was virgin born. The genealogy is that of Joseph. In contrast to the account of Luke, the angel appears to Joseph to make the annunciation, and Joseph is the one who names the infant. This, too, is in distinction to Luke's account.

The Person Of the King. Matthew places a special emphasis on the person of the King in this chapter. He first stresses the humanity of the Lord in the genealogy. The second emphasis rests on the divine character of Messiah's person as seen in His miraculous conception by the Holy Spirit in the virgin Mary. Both natures of the theanthropic person are vitally important to Matthew's argument. Gaebelein writes:

> If Matthew i:1-17 were all that could be said of His birth, He might then *have had* a legal right to the throne, but He could never have been He who was to redeem and save from sin. But the second half before us shows Him to be truly the long promised One, the One of whom Moses and the prophets spake, to whom all the past manifestations of God in the earth and the types, pointed.[31]

The first chapter of Matthew explicitly sets forth the person of the Messiah. He is both the Son of David and Son of Abraham, and also the Son of God, Immanuel, God with us. The credentials which Matthew

29. George Adam Smith, *The Book of Isaiah,* 1:134.
30. Gaebelein, *The Gospel Of Matthew,* 1:37.
31. Ibid, 1:27.

presents are three—the genealogy, the virgin birth, and the fulfillment of prophecy.

3. The Childhood of the King, 2:1-2:23

   Matthew, in chapter two, traces the childhood of the King from Bethlehem (2:1-2:12) to Egypt (2:13-2:18) to Nazareth (2:19-2:23). The primary purpose of this chapter is not to portray the King in His infancy and childhood; there is nothing in the chapter which describes Jesus Himself. The leading aim is to indicate the reception given to the Messiah by the world. The Jews are antipathetic and Gentiles worship Him. Skillfully Matthew employs this series of events to anticipate the reception which shall be given by Jew and Gentile to the Messiah. This chapter sets the stage for the remainder of the book.

   Chapter two is an ideal illustration of Matthew's style of writing which plays such an important part in the development of his argument. When Matthew mentions a subject for the first time he seldom makes an outright declaration concerning that subject. Rather, he makes an implication and then goes on to build on it, showing how this original implication is brought to its conclusion. In chapter two Matthew indicates the existence of apathy on the part of Israel. Later he shows how Jewish opposition to the Messiah increases in its intensity, culminating finally in the death of the King.

   A secondary purpose of the chapter is to show the fulfillment of Old Testament Scriptures in the Lord Jesus. This is evidenced by the number of allusions to the Old Testament prophets and prophecies (2:5-6, 15, 17-18, 23).

   a. In Bethlehem, **2:1-2:12.** *Now after Jesus was born in Bethlehem of Judea in the days of Herod the king, behold, magi from the East arrived in Jerusalem, saying, "Where is He Who has been born King of the Jews? For we saw His star in the East, and have come to worship Him." And when Herod the king heard it, he was troubled, and all Jerusalem with him. And gathering together all the chief priests and scribes of the people, he began to inquire of them where the Christ was to be born. And they said to him, "In Bethlehem of Judea; for so it has been written by the prophet,*

   > *'And you, Bethlehem, land of Judah; are by no means least among the leaders of Judah; for out of you shall come forth a Ruler, who will shepherd My people Israel.'"*

Then Herod secretly called the magi, and ascertained from them the time the star appeared. And he sent them to Bethlehem, and said, "Go and make careful search for the Child; and when you have found Him, report to me, that I too may come and worship Him." And having heard the king, they went their way; and lo, the star, which they had seen in the East, went on before them, until it came and stood over where the Child was. And when they saw the star, they rejoiced exceedingly, with great joy. And they came into the house and saw the Child with Mary His mother; and they fell down and worshiped Him; and opening their treasures they presented to Him gifts of gold and frankincense and myrrh. And having been warned by God in a dream not to return to Herod, they departed for their own country by another way.

It is evident that the events of chapter two transpire a considerable time after the birth of Jesus. The words of verse one are translated, "Now after Jesus was born in Bethlehem ... " This is a good rendering.[32] However, the text does not state how long it was after Jesus was born that the wise men came. The length of time is indicated by several factors. The word used to describe the infant is "child" ($\pi\alpha\iota\delta\iota o\nu$, v. 11) and not "infant" ($\beta\rho\epsilon\phi o\varsigma$, Luke 2:12, 16). The child is now residing in a house and not in the manger described by Luke. The fact that Herod commanded all children in the area of Bethlehem who were two years old and under to be slaughtered would indicate a time interval between the birth of Jesus and the visit of the Magi. In addition, the poor people's sacrifice described in Luke 2:24 (cf. Leviticus 12:6-8) hardly would have been appropriate after the gifts of gold, frankincense, and myrrh presented by the Magi. Joseph and Mary certainly would not have restricted themselves in the sacrifices to a pair of turtledoves or two young pigeons if they would have had the money to supply the regularly commanded sacrifice of Leviticus 12. The gifts must have been brought by the Magi after the days of purification were over. Finally, the intention of Joseph and Mary to return to Judea from Egypt (v. 22) indicates that they had taken up residence there. Jesus must have been about a year old when the Magi worshiped Him.

The Response Of the Magi, 2:1-2, 7-12. The outstanding event marking the stay at Bethlehem is the visit of the Magi. The "now" ($\delta\epsilon$) in 2:1

---

32. The aorist participle ("was born"), which occurs in the genitive absolute of verse one, usually indicates action antecedent to the main verb ("arrived").

marks a change of subject.[33] The Magi are simply described to the Jewish reader. The "behold" (ἰδού) is Hebraic and points out the wise men. The only description of the Magi is the phrase "from the East" (ἀπὸ ἀνατολῶν). However, much can be gleaned from these words. These wise men could be either fraudulent sorcerers or a more honorable class of astrologers.[34] Here they are the latter. "*From the east* not only specifies their origin but also confirms this view of their calling."[35] In the East they were looked upon as professionals.

It may be that these men became acquainted with the Jewish Scriptures by means of the deportations of Israel to Babylon and to Medo-Persia.[36] The prophecy concerning the star contained in Numbers 24:17 would associate the astrological occurrence with the birth of the Messiah. In addition, the prophecy of Daniel's seventy weeks in Daniel 9 would cause great anticipation for the coming of the King at this time. It is not without significance David was well known as a "wise man" in the royal courts of Babylon. Since the Magi were astrologers, the sign of the star was highly significant. This with their evident knowledge of some of the Old Testament prophecies brought them to Jerusalem.

Matthew affirms the supernatural birth of the King by noting the reference the Magi make to the star. Morgan writes, "It was an extraordinary and special movement in the stellar spaces, designed to lead these men to Christ."[37] Such a significant display in the heavens would cause no little stir among those who were looking for the coming of a king. That there was at this time a universal expectation of a world deliverer is both asserted[38] and denied.[39] In either case the Magi were evidently acquainted with the Old Testament prophecies, and because of the stellar manifestations which they saw, had come to Jerusalem to seek out the Messiah of Israel.

It is highly significant that the Magi came to "worship" (προσ-κυνέω) Him. This verb is a favorite with Matthew and occurs thirteen

33. "The δέ in ver. 1, as in 1:18, is adversative only to the extent of taking the attention off one topic and fixing it on another connected and kindred." Bruce, "The Synoptic Gospels," *The Expositor's Greek Testament*, p. 69.
34. William Hendriksen, *New Testament Commentary, Exposition of the Gospel According to Matthew*, p. 152; Robertson, *Word Pictures*, 1:15.
35. William H. McClellan, "Homiletical Notes on the Magi: Gospel for the Feast of Epiphany," *The Catholic Biblical Quarterly 1* (January 1939): 72.
36. Hendriksen, *Matthew*, pp. 150-151.
37. G. Campbell Morgan, *The Crises of the Christ*, p. 98.
38. Alfred Plummer, *An Exegetical Commentary on the Gospel According to S. Matthew*, p. 12.
39. Edersheim, *The Life and Times of Jesus the Messiah*, 1:203.

times in his Gospel. It may refer to the homage one pays to men or to God.[40] However, it is affirmed by Moulton and Milligan that it is " . . . used generally of a god."[41] That it is employed in this sense is seen in the fact that the Magi seem to be completely cognizant of the Messianic implications of the One Who was born King of the Jews. If they were ignorant of this, why would they bother to come to a tiny nation under the recognition of supernatural occurrences? A final proof that the Magi worshipped Jesus in the true sense of the word is seen in the New Testament usage. Προσκυνέω usually refers to the worship of a deity in the New Testament. A good illustration of the religious significance of the word is found in Acts 10:25-26.

When the Magi leave Herod in Jerusalem and proceed on their way to Bethlehem, the star reappears to guide them to the house where Jesus was. The prophecy of Micah 5:2 guided them to Bethlehem; the star directed them to the house in Bethlehem. The star was also a verification of all that the Magi were doing. They would have much cause to be discouraged. The one who was born King was not to be found in the capital city, Jerusalem. He Who ruled was a usurper interested only in his own power. Even the people of Israel were disinterested. The religious leaders knew the answer to the question of the Magi, but they were too apathetic to prove their own answer. The Magi were finally sent to the poor village of Bethlehem. The supernatural manifestation of the same star which had first prompted the journey now vindicated them in their search. That it is the same star which caused them such great joy is indicated by the article of previous reference in verse ten (*the* star). This unusual stellar manifestation attests the supernatural character of the person the Magi were seeking. It is included in Matthew's argument for this apologetic reason.

When the Magi find the child King, they respond with worship; this is their purpose in coming (v. 2). It is well to note the primacy of Jesus in this passage. All centers about Him. Mary is seen only as she is associated with Him as His mother. Many see in the bringing of gold and incense a fulfillment of Isaiah 60:6. However, this is rather unlikely since the Isaiah passage is clearly dealing with the Millennial Kingdom that is to be established after the second coming of Christ. Matthew's

40. Walter Bauer, *A Greek-English Lexicon of the New Testament and Other Early Christian Literature,* pp. 716-717.
41. James Hope Moulton and George Milligan, *The Vocabulary of the Greek Testament,* p. 549.

narrative may be a preview of what is portrayed in Isaiah 60, but it is unlikely that Matthew 2:11 is a fulfillment of that prophecy.

Having worshipped the King, the magi are warned not to return to Herod but to withdraw to their own country by another way. The word "depart" (ἀναχωρέω) is significant in Matthew and he uses the term more often than any other gospel writer. It carries with it the implication of danger.[42] Moulton and Milligan write, " ... 'retire' is too weak for ἀναχωρέω. The connotation of 'taking refuge' from some peril will suit most of the NT passages remarkably well."[43] Matthew often in his narrative uses the word to show the withdrawal of the King in the face of opposition. Even the Magi who worship Him are forced to take refuge from the wrath of Herod.

The first to worship the King in Matthew's Gospel are Gentiles, an implication of the last command of the Messiah. The supernatural stellar manifestations attest the divine character of the person of Jesus. Matthew also notes the fact that the Magi who worship the Messiah of Israel are forced to take refuge from Bethlehem. This, too, is a hint of the future antagonism of Israel to their King.

The Response Of Israel, 2:4-8. When the Magi came to Jerusalem asking, "Where is He who has been born King of the Jews?" the response of Israel was pitifully apathetic. They were concerned about Herod's disposition, but they cared little about the matter of their Messiah. However, there was just cause for their fear of Herod. He was a ruthless murderer who killed the members of his own family out of fear of their plotting against him. "Augustus is said to have remarked that he would rather be Herod's pig (ὗς) than his son (υἱός)."[44] The inhabitants of Jerusalem knew only too well what the rage of Herod would do and they feared it.

The leaders of Israel in their spiritual blindness fail to grasp the significance of the question of the Magi. This is the first mention of the scribes and chief priests in the Gospel. By implication Matthew begins here in denouncing the religious leaders of Israel. In response to the question they reply without reservation, "In Bethlehem of Judea." This little phrase is very significant. " ... the name Bethlehem signified the sovereignty of Christ; for Bethlehem, rich in tradition, was the well-

42. G. Abbott-Smith, *A Manual Greek Lexicon of the New Testament,* p. 35.
43. Moulton and Milligan, *The Vocabulary of the Greek Testament,* p. 40.
44. Sherman E. Johnson and George A. Buttrick, "The Gospel According to St. Matthew," *The Interpreter's Bible,* 7:260.

spring of a royal stream . . . . "[45] It was at Bethlehem that David was born and anointed king. The town was called Bethlehem *of Judea* not to distinguish it from the Bethlehem in Galilee, but to show that the King was to be born of the tribe of Judah.[46]

To substantiate their answer the scribes and priests very loosely quote Micah 5:2 (v. 6). The last clause, which describes the type of governor who shall rule, is taken from 2 Samuel 5:2 and is important. The word "who" (ὅστις) is a qualitative pronoun and can be translated *such a one as, of such a nature*. This pronoun is described by the verb "shepherd" (ποιμαίνω), which refers to the work of a shepherd who feeds and guides his sheep. Thus the character and work of the Messiah is described by the Jewish leaders as they refer to the Old Testament. The marked contrast to that which characterized the rule of Herod must have been clear to the most unobserving.

Even though Israel is cognizant of the prophecies, they are blind to spiritual realities. The King of Israel is worshiped by Gentiles, while His own people do not bother to own Him as their King. The condition of Israel is clearly implied in the early verses of Matthew's Gospel. They are cold and indifferent.

The Response Of Herod. Complete antagonism characterizes the response of the cunning Herod. The coming of the Magi caused Herod no little consternation. The question which they were asking was worded in such a way that Herod was made to look like an inferior. The significance of "who has been born king" (ὁ τεχθεὶς βασιλεύς) in verse two is seen in that Herod, who ruled as king, was not a born king. "It was long since there had been a *born king* among the Jews."[47] Herod, of the Idumaean dynasty, was a usurper.

Herod had another reason to fear. Lange traces his consternation to a statement in 1 Maccabees 14:41.[48] The context of this portion of the Apocrypha records the conferral of royal power to the Maccabees. The passage in view shows that this was done with the reservation that their power would cease with the coming of the Messiah. Later the Herodian dynasty displaced the Hasmonean. It may be that Herod was acquainted with this stipulation and was concerned over the Jewish reaction to news of one who was born king.

---

45. Ibid, 7:256.
46. Plummer, *Exegetical Commentary*, p. 12.
47. James Morison, *A Practical Commentary on the Gospel According to St. Matthew*, p. 14.
48. John Peter Lange, "Matthew," *Commentary on the Holy Scriptures*, p. 56.

Herod, too cunning to display anger, inquires of the religious leaders where the Jewish Messiah is to be born. In his typical craftiness he places before them a theological proposition and not a fact of history.[49] The word "then" (τότε) in verse seven introduces Herod's action in response to the answer given to him by the Jewish leaders. This particle is characteristic of Matthew's style, occurring some ninety times in his Gospel. He often uses it to bring the reader from one event in the narrative to the next.[50] The wily Herod craftily sends the wise men on their way with the command to report back to him with their findings.

The next time Herod steps on the stage of events he is all rage. Evaded by the Magi he commands all of the children two years of age and under in Bethlehem and its surrounding environs to be slaughtered. This is done in desperate fear of the Messiah of Israel.

The Gentile wise men worship the King of the Jews; the Jews are apathetic; and Herod is concerned only for his throne. Herod's interest in his own political well-being marks the attitude of the governmental authorities throughout the remainder of the Gospel.

b. In Egypt, **2:13-2:18.** *Now when they had departed, behold, an angel of the Lord appeared to Joseph in a dream, saying, "Arise and take the Child and His mother, and flee to Egypt, and remain there until I tell you; for Herod is going to search for the Child to destroy Him." And he arose and took the Child and His mother by night, and departed for Egypt; and was there until the death of Herod; that what was spoken by the Lord through the prophet might be fulfilled, saying, "Out of Egypt did I call My Son."*

Then when Herod saw that he had been tricked by the magi, he became very enraged, and sent and slew all the male children who were in Bethlehem and in all its environs, from two years old and under, according to the time which he had ascertained from the magi. Then that which was spoken through Jeremiah the prophet was fulfilled, saying,

"A voice was heard in Ramah, weeping and great mourning, Rachel weeping for her children; and she refused to be comforted, because they were no more."

The Fulfillment Of Prophecy. One of the characteristics of Matthew's style of writing is his use of Old Testament prophecy for apologetic purposes. In chapter two of his Gospel Matthew uses prophecy for this

49. Edersheim, *Life and Times,* 1:205.
50. M'Neile, *St. Matthew,* pp. 16-17.

purpose very effectively. For instance, in verses six and seven he shows how the religious leaders were completely cognizant of the birthplace of the Messiah from their study of prophecy. That Matthew uses this passage to further his argument is noted by Robinson, who writes, "Even the classes who later were to be the bitterest opponents of Jesus testify to the fact that his birth at Bethlehem is a direct fulfillment of this well known passage in Micah v. 2."[51] The case is so well proven that Matthew does not even say Jesus was born in Bethlehem "in order that" Micah 5:2 should be fulfilled. This fact is so evident that the most casual reader would grasp its significance relative to the birth of Jesus Christ.

Matthew makes a second reference to prophecy in the second chapter of his Gospel (Matthew 2:15). While Joseph, Mary, and the child Jesus are still in Bethlehem, Joseph is supernaturally warned in a dream to flee into Egypt to escape Herod's wrath. In obedience Joseph withdraws ($\dot{\alpha}\nu\alpha\chi\omega\rho\dot{\epsilon}\omega$) into Egypt and remains there until Herod dies. Matthew sees in this a fulfillment of Hosea 11:1. But since Hosea 11:1 is simply a declaration of God's past workings with Israel, a problem is raised concerning Matthew's use of the Old Testament Scriptures. In particular, in what sense is Hosea 11:1 fulfilled by Jesus?

It will be noted that Matthew never in chapter two says a *prophecy* is being fulfilled. In guarded language he writes that the events occurred that *the word spoken* through the prophets might be fulfilled. The prophet's main task was to give God's word to men. Speaking from Jehovah's vantage point they may dip into the past or look ahead into the future. Therefore it is not necessary to make every statement of the prophet Hosea a prophecy of some future event. This is especially true of Hosea 11:1. Hosea simply makes reference to the deliverance of the nation Israel from its bondage in Egypt as seen from God's viewpoint. It was simply a matter of God calling His son, Israel, out of Egypt.

It will also be noted that Matthew uses three phrases to point to the fulfillment of a statement made by an Old Testament prophet—$\tilde{\iota}\nu\alpha$ $\pi\lambda\eta\rho\omega\theta\tilde{\eta}$ (1:22), $\ddot{o}\pi\omega\varsigma$ $\pi\lambda\eta\rho\omega\theta\tilde{\eta}$ (2:23), and $\tau\dot{o}\tau\epsilon$ $\dot{\epsilon}\pi\lambda\eta\rho\dot{\omega}\theta\eta$ (2:17). Each of these formulas occurs in the first two chapters. Some see great significance in the difference between them.

> I would also remark here that the Old Testament prophecies are quoted in three ways, which must not be confounded:—"that it might be fulfilled"; "so that it was fulfilled"; and, "then was fulfilled." In the first case it is the object of the prophecy; Matthew

51. Theodore H. Robinson, *The Gospel of Matthew*, p. 8.

1:22, 23 is an instance. In the second it is an accomplishment
contained in the scope of the prophecy, but not the sole and complete thought of the Holy Ghost; Matthew 2:23 may serve as an
example. In the third it is simply a fact which corresponds with the
quotation, which in its spirit applies to it, without being its positive
object—chapter 2:17, for instance.[52]

While this explanation has much to commend it, it has some rather
serious faults. It fails to translate ὅπως πληρωθῇ correctly. The aorist
subjunctive with ὅπως should be translated "in order that it might be
fulfilled." In addition, it is generally acknowledged that in Matthew ἵνα
and ὅπως may be thought of as practically synonymous, although ἵνα is
generally recognized as having a broader usage. Both may be translated
"in order that." Finally, Darby's explanation fails to meet the problem.
In what way is Hosea 11:1 fulfilled by Christ? This theory cannot answer
the problem.

The meaning of the word "fulfill" (πληρόω) is the key. When used
in reference to prophecies it means "completely to establish."[53] If a
prophet looks into the future, as Micah did in Micah 5:2, the prophecy is
completely established by the event coming to pass, as it was in the birth
of Jesus at Bethlehem. When a prophet looks at a past event, the record
of that event is often looked upon as being confirmed or fulfilled by
another event which is much like it coming to pass at a later time. A
good illustration of this use of πληρόω is found in James 2:23. It is in
this sense that Matthew uses Hosea 11:1. Israel is called God's son in
Exodus 4:22; using the same term Hosea refers to Israel in his writings.
Since Jesus is *the* Son of God (Matthew 2:15; 3:17; 4:3,6; 8:29; 11:27;
14:33; 16:16; 17:5; 26:63; 27:40, 43, 54), the history of Israel is " ... a
typical anticipation of the life of the Messiah."[54] Thus that which God
accomplished in delivering Israel is confirmed in His workings with His
Son. All this was not left to haphazard circumstances. The flight into
Egypt (v. 14) is looked at as a purposeful fulfillment of Hosea 11:1, the
word "that" (ἵνα) in verse fifteen indicating purpose and not result.[55]

A third reference to prophecy is made by Matthew (2:17-18). While
the family of Joseph is in Egypt, Herod discerns that he was deluded by
the Magi, and he becomes infuriated. In his rage he commands all of the
male children two years of age and under in Bethlehem and the sur-

52. J. N. Darby, *Synopsis Of the Books Of the Bible*, 3:21.
53. Hermann Cremer, *Biblico-Theological Lexicon of New Testament Greek*, p. 500.
54. Plummer, *Exegetical Commentary*, p. 19.
55. M'Neile, *St. Matthew*, p. 9.

rounding regions to be slaughtered. In this Matthew sees a fulfillment of
Jeremiah 31:15. Jeremiah in poetic imagery describes the entombed
Rachel weeping for the Israelites who are being deported to Babylon.
Matthew uses these words of Jeremiah in the same manner in which he
used Hosea's. Rachel, whose tomb was near Bethlehem (Genesis
35:19), was " . . . to the Hebrew family a mother for Israel in all time,
sympathetic in all her children's misfortunes."[56] The fulfillment is again
seen in the typology of the statement. Matthew alters the expression
slightly because he did not want to attribute the slaughter to God's
purpose.[57]

   c. In Nazareth, **2:19-2:23.** *But when Herod was dead, behold, an*
angel of the Lord appeared in a dream to Joseph in Egypt, saying,
"Arise and take the Child and His mother, and go into the land of
Israel; for those who sought the Child's life are dead." And he arose
and took the Child and His mother, and came into the land of Israel.
But when he heard that Archelaus was reigning over Judea in place
of his father Herod, he was afraid to go there; and being warned by
God in a dream, he departed for the regions of Galilee, and came
and resided in a city called Nazareth; that what was spoken through
the prophets might be fulfilled, "He shall be called a Nazarene." A
fourth fulfillment of Old Testament prophecy is found in the supernatural recall of Joseph and his family to the land of Israel. It is significant that the land is called Israel and not the land of Canaan or Judea or
Galilee. This is the only occurrence of *land of Israel* in the New Testament, and it is used here since it designates the promises and blessings
bestowed by God on Jacob and his descendants. The word "warn"
($\chi\rho\eta\mu\alpha\tau\iota\zeta\omega$) occurs twice in this chapter of Matthew (vs. 12, 22) and
indicates the significance of Jesus in God's program. With the warning
that an enemy still reigned in Judea, the family withdraws or "departs"
($\dot{\alpha}\nu\alpha\chi\omega\rho\dot{\epsilon}\omega$) to Galilee and dwells in a city called Nazareth.

   Matthew sees the fulfillment of the prophecy in Jesus' dwelling in
Nazareth, and again the Evangelist's use of the Old Testament causes a
problem for the New Testament student. The fact of the matter is there is
no Old Testament prophet who said, "He shall be called a Nazarene."
There have been various explanations to the problem. All recognize that
no one prophet or prophecy is in mind since Matthew refers to "the
prophets" ($\tau\tilde{\omega}\nu \ \pi\rho o\phi\eta\tau\tilde{\omega}\nu$).

---

56. Bruce, "The Synoptic Gospels," 1:76.
57. M'Neile, *St. Matthew*, p. 19.

The first explanation is that which associates Nazarene with Nazareth (Judges 13:5). However, this can be discounted because the Lord was not a Nazarite (Matthew 11:19).[58] In addition, the etymology of the word is wrong for this interpretation.[59] A second explanation states that the word is to be explained by the Hebrew נֵצֶר which occurs in Isaiah 11:1, a Messianic passage.[60] This Hebrew word means *shoot* and sounds much like the Greek word for Nazareth. A similar word, צֶמַח meaning *branch* occurs with reference to the Messiah in Isaiah 4:2; Jeremiah 23:5; 33:15; Zechariah 3:8, and 6:12. However, this explanation has a difficulty. What does this Hebrew title have to do with the town of Nazareth apart from similarity of pronunciation? Certainly Matthew has more in mind. In addition, this term occurs in only one prophecy of one prophet, while Matthew refers to more than one prophet.

A third view is more plausible. It looks at the Old Testament prophecies of reproach such as Psalm 22:6-9 and Isaiah 53 as being summed up in the title *Nazarene*. *"To be called a Nazarene was to be spoken of as despicable."*[61] Matthew is pointing to those prophecies in the Old Testament which portray the Messiah as rejected and despised and claiming their fulfillment in the fact that Jesus is reared at Nazareth. Israel's feeling of contempt for their King is indicated by this verse and is proven by the chapter which Matthew has just written.

Generally speaking, Matthew has made three points in chapter two. The first relates to the Gentiles. The Magi come from the East and worship the King of the Jews. A glimmering foreview of all the nations of the earth being blessed in Abraham is seen in this act. "Jesus is essentially the Messiah of the Jews, but his kingdom is to be worldwide, and already the 'first fruits of the Gentiles' come to offer their homage."[62] The second point Matthew makes concerns the Jews. They are shown to be unconcerned and indifferent to any report concerning Him. Finally, Matthew, by his use of the Old Testament, proves that Jesus is the promised Messiah. He is the fulfillment of all that is anticipated in their Scriptures. These three things form the basis of Matthew's Gospel. Jesus is presented as the Messiah prophesied and promised in the Old Testament. The Jews reject Him. Because of this rejection the King

58. Plummer, *Exegetical Commentary*, p. 18.
59. R. C. H. Lenski, *The Interpretation of St. Matthew's Gospel*, p. 88.
60. Carr, *St. Matthew*, p. 95.
61. Morison, *A Practical Commentary*, p. 25.
62. Robinson, *The Gospel of Matthew*, p. 7.

turns to the Gentiles and the kingdom program for the Jews is post-poned.

Chapter one declares the theanthropic character of the person of the Messiah. The reception which is to be given the claims of the Messiah is set forth in chapter two. Matthew three begins the narrative of the historical account of the presentation of Israel's Messiah to that nation.

B. The Preparation of the King
3:1-4:11

The King born in Judea is forced to flee to Egypt. After Herod, His antagonist, dies He returns to his own land, but not to reign on a throne. As yet He must be manifested to Israel for their acceptance—or rejection. Matthew quickly and silently passes over the childhood of the King to present the account of the preparation of the King for His presentation to Israel.

1. The Forerunner of the King, 3:1-3:12

In all propriety the King has a forerunner. Matthew, more interested in presenting a closely knit argument than a precise historical narrative, introduces this phase of the King's presentation with the very general, temporal phrase "in those days" ($\dot{\epsilon}\nu$ $\tau\alpha\hat{\iota}\varsigma$ $\dot{\eta}\mu\dot{\epsilon}\rho\alpha\iota\varsigma$ $\dot{\epsilon}\kappa\epsilon\hat{\iota}\nu\alpha\iota\varsigma$). In commenting on the pronoun, "those" ($\dot{\epsilon}\kappa\epsilon\hat{\iota}\nu\sigma\varsigma$), and its use with general time designations, Robertson says, "It usually occurs at a transition in the narrative . . . .)[63] With this phrase Matthew introduces John the Baptist as the forerunner of the King. John, indeed, is the forerunner of Jesus. He precedes Him in His birth, in His appearance, and in His death.

a. His Work, **3:1-3:2.** *Now in those days John the Baptist came, preaching in the wilderness of Judea saying, "Repent, for the kingdom of heaven is at hand."* The Baptist comes preaching in the wilderness of Judea. Actually *preach* is not a precise English equivalent of $\kappa\eta\rho\dot{\upsilon}\sigma\sigma\omega$. It really means *to act as a herald, to publish.*[64] The verb has also a more specific connotation. A. M. Hunter writes, "In the New Testament the verb does not mean 'to give an informative or hortatory or edifying discourse expressed in beautifully arranged words with a

---

63. A. T. Robertson, *A Grammar of the Greek New Testament in the Light of Historical Research,* p. 708.
64. Joseph Henry Thayer, *A Greek-English Lexicon of the New Testament,* p. 346.

melodious voice; it means to proclaim an event' . . . [65] John came, then, heralding an event, and that event was the drawing near of the kingdom. In proclaiming this event, John was acting as a forerunner for the King, preparing the way ahead of Him. (See Proclamation of the Forerunner, pp. 60-61, for further discussion about John's message).

b. His Fulfillment of Prophecy, **3:3. For this is the one referred to by Isaiah the prophet, saying,**

> **"The voice of one crying in the wilderness, 'Make ready the way of the Lord, make His paths straight!' "**

Matthew links John's ministry to the prophecy of Isaiah 40:3 with the conjunction "for" (γάρ). "He preached repentance, *for* that was necessary in one who was to fulfill the prophet's words."[66] The words "one referred to" (ὁ ῥηθείς) refer to the pronoun "this" (οὗτος). In this way Matthew definitely identifies John with the one spoken of by Isaiah. In Isaiah the voice cries out exhorting the people to prepare for the coming of God as He brings Israel back from their dispersion. The prophet then goes on to describe the blessings of the kingdom that follow their return. Thus Matthew, by identifying John the Baptist with the voice of Isaiah 40, verifies the message of John. The kingdom is indeed near at hand.

c. His Uniqueness, **3:4-3:6. Now John himself had a garment of camel's hair, and a leather belt about his waist; and his food was locusts and wild honey. Then Jerusalem was going out to him, and all Judea, and all the district around the Jordan; and they were being baptized by him in the Jordan River, as they confessed their sins.** The uniqueness of John is especially seen in his rite of baptism. Some attach it to the ceremonial washings of the Old Testament such as those prescribed in Exodus 19, Leviticus 15, and Numbers 19.[67] Others associate it with the washing which was required of proselytes to Judaism.[68] In both cases purification is signified. Therefore, the meaning of John's baptism is the same if it is derived from either one. While this is the significance of John's baptism, his rite is different. In ceremonial cleansing and in proselyte baptism the individual washed or

---

65. Archibald M. Hunter, *The Message of the New Testament,* p. 24.
66. M'Neile, *St. Matthew,* p. 25.
67. Geerhardus Vos, "The Ministry of John the Baptist," *The Bible Student* 1 (January 1900):28.
68. Robertson, *Word Pictures,* 1:23.

baptized himself.[69] John is the first to baptize *others*, and this may account for his name, John *the Baptist*.[70]

His baptism is also new in that it was marked by confession of the one who was baptized. Both collective confession and individual confession were known in Israel, but a " ... great, spontaneous, self-unburdening of penitent souls ... " was before unknown.[71] This unique baptism marked out his singular eschatological message.[72]

John was not only unique with regard to his rite of baptism and his message, but the same was true of his dress, his diet, and his being in the wilderness. All these things in a special way marked John out as the forerunner of the Messiah. It is possible that his ascetic appearance and his preaching in the wilderness could illustrate Israel's spiritual poverty and their future rejection of their Messiah.[73] However, several other factors appear to be more important and explain his uniqueness more clearly. His uniqueness with regard to his appearance, his location, and his baptism lend support to the singular importance of his message.

A second reason for his being in the wilderness is pointed out by Matthew; it is simply the fulfillment of Isaiah's prophecy, for the messenger was to cry in the wilderness. Another explanation for his location is that the people who were looking for the coming of the Messiah would be especially marked out. Finally, those who were baptized identified themselves in a very definite way with John's peculiar message.

d. The Proclamation of the Forerunner.

Repentance. John's message was an imperative, "Repent!" Contrary to popular thinking, repent does not mean *to be sorry*. The Greek word μετανοέω means " ... *to change one's mind* or *purpose* ... "[74] In the New Testament, it " ... indicates a complete change of attitude, spiritual and moral, towards God."[75] The primary meaning involves a turning to God which may indeed make a person sorry for his sins, but that sorrow is a by-product and not the repentance itself. In this exhortation to repentance John has been likened to the Old Testament prophets by many.[76] "They frequently called upon Israel to turn to God from their

69. Morison, *A Practical Commentary*, p. 32.
70. Ethelbert Stauffer, *New Testament Theology*, p. 22.
71. Bruce, "The Synoptic Gospels," *The Expositor's Greek Testament*, 1:81.
72. F. W. Green, *The Gospel According To Saint Matthew*, p. 115.
73. Gaebelein, *The Gospel Of Matthew*, 1:59-60.
74. Abbott-Smith, *A Manual Lexicon*, p. 287.
75. Moulton and Milligan, *The Vocabulary of the Greek Testament*, p. 403.
76. Plummer, *Exegetical Commentary*, p. 22.

backslidden condition, using the Hebrew verb *shuv* (cf. Joel 2:12; Isa. 55:7; Ezek. 33:11, 15)."[77] In a word, John's command to the people of Israel was for them to turn from their sins to God in anticipation of their Messiah.

The Kingdom of the Heavens. Matthew states that John's message was, "Repent, for the kingdom of the heavens has drawn near." At this point one may ask several questions, the first being, "What does John mean by 'the kingdom of the heavens'?" Several answers have been propounded, and McClain succinctly summarizes the positions.

> But the question has been raised: Was this Kingdom identical with the Kingdom of Old Testament prophecy? Or was it something different? To these questions the various current answers can be summarized under five heads:
>
> First, the *Liberal-Social* view: that Christ took over from the Old Testament prophets their ethical and social ideals of the kingdom, excluding almost wholly the eschatological element, and made these ideals the program of a present kingdom which it is the responsibility of His followers to establish in human society on earth here and now . . . .
>
> Second, the *Critical-Eschatological* view: that Jesus at first embraced fully the eschatological ideas of the Old Testament prophets regarding the Kingdom, and to some extent the current Jewish ideas; but later in the face of opposition He changed His message; or, at least, there are conflicting elements in the gospel records. As to the precise nature and extent of this change, or the alleged conflicts, the critics are not agreed . . . .
>
> Third, the *Spiritualizing-Anti-millennial* view: that our Lord appropriated certain spiritual elements from the Old Testament prophetical picture, either omitted or spiritualized the physical elements (excepting the physical details involved in the Messiah's first coming!), and then added some original ideas of His own . . . .
>
> Fourth, the *Dual-Kingdom* view: that Christ at His first coming offered to Israel and established on earth a purely spiritual kingdom; and that at His second coming He will establish on earth a literal Millennial Kingdom . . . .
>
> Fifth, the *One-Kingdom Millennial* view: that the Kingdom announced by our Lord and offered to the nation of Israel at His first coming was identical with the Mediatorial Kingdom of Old Testament prophecy, and will be established on earth at the second coming of the King. This might well be called the *Biblical* view because it is supported by the material in both Testaments taken at its normal or face value.[78]

77. S. Lewis Johnson, Jr., "The Message of John the Baptist," *Bibliotheca Sacra,* 113 (January 1956):32.

78. Alva J. McClain, *The Greatness of the Kingdom,* pp. 274-276.

John has in mind the eschatological, earthly kingdom as anticipated by the Old Testament prophets. This is evident for several reasons. First, the simple fact that John and Christ made no explanation of the kingdom is a clear indication of this fact.[79] If the concept had been a different one, John and the Lord would have pointed it out. But neither John, Jesus, nor the twelve disciples make any such explanation when they preach the nearness of the kingdom. A second cogent reason is seen in the restriction of the message to the Jewish nation (Matthew 10:5-6). If this message involved a spiritual kingdom only, why limit it to Israel? This message was preached to the Jews exclusively because the coming of the kingdom prophesied in the Old Testament was contingent upon the reception of it by the nation of Israel.

A third reason for believing John refers to the Millennial Kingdom is found in the disciples' anticipation of a literal kingdom (Matthew 20:20-21; Acts 1:6). The request of Matthew 20 could be explained as a mistaken notion if it were made early in the disciples' career. However, this request is made after they had heard the doctrine of the kingdom as taught by the Lord for many months. In fact, they were the very disciples whom the Lord had pronounced blessed because of their insight into the mysteries of the kingdom of the heavens (Matthew 13:11-17). A fourth reason is based on simple logic. The kingdom in view cannot refer to the church since the church was not yet revealed. It cannot be God's universal kingdom because it is an eternal kingdom always present. Some contend that the kingdom in view is a spiritual one in which God rules in men's hearts. McClain presents a very forcible argument in opposition to this view.

> We may also add that if the Kingdom, announced as "at hand" by the Lord, had been exclusively a "spiritual kingdom," or as some have defined it, "the rule of God in the heart," such an announcement would have had no special significance whatever to Israel, for such a rule of God had *always* been recognized among the people of God. Compare the psalmist's affirmation concerning the righteous, *The law of his God is in his heart (37:31).* Any denial of this would certainly be a new kind of dispensationalism.[80]

The only conclusion at which one can arrive is that the proclamation of John refers to a literal, earthly kingdom in fulfillment of the Old Testament promises and prophecies.

79. George N. H. Peters, *The Theocratic Kingdom of Our Lord Jesus, the Christ, as Covenanted in the Old Testament and Presented in the New Testament,* 1:195.
80. McClain, *The Greatness of the Kingdom,* p. 303.

It was the Jewish eschatological kingdom which had drawn near. The verb here is ἐγγίζω which means *to draw near* and not *to be here*. A good illustration is found in Matthew 21:1 ("And when they *drew nigh* unto Jerusalem, ... " KJV). The perfect tense points to the fact that the kingdom had drawn near and was then in a condition of nearness. This very position of nearness connotes the idea of a kingdom offer. All that is needed to bring it here is the acceptance of it by the Jewish nation. Their acceptance would be indicated by their reception of the Messiah.

The kingdom of the heavens was near in a very real sense in that the King was here and it was the Messiah's work to bring the kingdom. McNeile, certainly not a dispensationalist, concurs with this by writing, "But with the King is bound up the Kingdom."[81] Thus for John the kingdom was near in that the King was near. When Jesus and His disciples heralded the drawing near of the kingdom, the King was there, but the kingdom was still only near. If Israel had accepted its Messiah, the earthly kingdom would have been inaugurated by the King.

The Divine Program. Some object to the doctrine of a kingdom offer on the basis that it nullifies the work on the cross by Christ. They contend the cross has no part in any scheme which considers the kingdom of John, Jesus, and His disciples an earthly kingdom offered to the Jews. A champion of the view which voices this objection is Oswald T. Allis, who explains his view of the kingdom offer. "As preached at the first advent it did not include or involve the Cross; as preached at the second advent it will not include or presuppose the Cross."[82] Such an interpretation of the dispensational viewpoint is entirely erroneous and even presumptuous.

The premillennialist believes that Christ came to offer the kingdom by means of the cross.[83] This is clearly declared by the Old Testament Scriptures. Jesus could not have been the Messiah without suffering on the cross. Such passages as Psalm 22, Isaiah 53, Daniel 9, and Zechariah 13 clearly indicate the Messiah must suffer and enter into glory. It is significant to note that in Psalm 22 and Isaiah 53 the glory chronologically follows the suffering of the Messiah. Zechariah 12:10 and 13:6 are very explicit in showing that the glory follows the suffering.

81. A. H. McNeile, *An Introduction to the Study of the New Testament*, p. 10.
82. Oswald T. Allis, *Prophecy And the Church*, p. 234.
83. Erich Sauer, *The Triumph of the Crucified*, p. 25.

This is in exact accord with the New Testament interpretation of the sufferings of Christ as they relate to His glory and the promised kingdom of the Jews (Luke 24:25-26; Acts 3:17-21; 26:23). A case in point is 1 Peter 1:10-11.

> As to this salvation, the prophets who prophesied of the grace that would come to you made careful search and inquiry, seeking to know what person or time the Spirit of Christ within them was indicating as He predicted the sufferings of Christ and the glories to follow.

Here the sufferings are clearly said to precede the glory.

Some may object by saying the glory is that which Christ enjoys in the present age and throughout eternity. A careful study of the Scriptures will indicate that in some cases it refers to the glory of Christ in the present age, but in others the manifestation of His glory in the future millennial age is anticipated. Examples of the former are Hebrews 2:7; 1 Peter 1:21; 5:10; 2 Peter 3:18, and Jude 24. That it also refers to the glory which shall be His at the establishment of the kingdom is shown by many passages of God's Word (Numbers 14:21; Isaiah 60:1-3; 66:18; Habakkuk 2:14; Matthew 16:27; 19:28; 24:30; 25:31; Romans 8:18; Colossians 3:4; 2 Thessalonians 1:7-10; 1 Peter 4:13).

One can only conclude that Christ came to offer the kingdom by way of the cross. This presents no difficulty when one realizes that the Old Testament eschatological program did not have the church age in view. The program of the Lord in case of His acceptance by Israel would be in this order: (1) the acceptance of Jesus as the Messiah, (2) the cross, (3) the seven years of Jacob's trouble, and (4) the return of the Messiah to establish the kingdom. If Jesus were accepted *or* rejected as the Messiah, His death was a divine necessity.

> This was, from one point of view, a necessary stage in the development of the divine purpose. If the Son of Man was to appear on the clouds of heaven in His kingdom, He must first return to the Father in heaven to be invested with the divine glory. Thus the Son of Man "must" suffer (16:21). This was a part of the divine scheme (16:23). It had been foretold in prophecy (26:24, 54).[84]

Many have speculated as to how the crucifixion of the Messiah would have been brought about had the Jews accepted Jesus as their Saviour. However, it is almost ludicrous for humans to theorize on what would have happened in God's program had some event occurred which did

84. Allen, *Commentary on Matthew*, p. lxvii.

not transpire. Still, it may be said that had the Jews accepted the kingdom offer, God would have providentially arranged for the crucifixion of Christ since His sufferings were prophesied in the Old Testament.

Some may object that the offer of the kingdom was not a valid one. Had not the eternal purposes of God already determined that Israel would reject her Messiah? This objection is open to refutation.

> Those who cavil at the idea of an offer which is certain to be rejected betray an ignorance, not only of Biblical history (cf. Isa. 6:8-10 and Ezek. 2:3-7), but also of the important place of the legal proffer in the realm of jurisprudence.[85]

That the coming of the kingdom was contingent upon the acceptance of Jesus as the Messiah by the Jews is indicated by Matthew 11:14.[86] One may conclude then that the offer of the kingdom in no way nullifies the program of Christ's death on the cross.

The Kingdom of the Heavens and the Kingdom of God. A considerable amount of literature exists discussing the meaning of the term *the kingdom of the heavens* in its relationship to *the kingdom of God*. Many premillenarians believe the terms have distinctive meanings, while others say they are used interchangeably. Needless to say, for one to state they are used interchangeably in nowise makes him an amillennialist, although the amillennialist does hold this view. Nevertheless, it is important for premillennialists to clarify the terminology which has become the focal point of much discussion among themselves and considerable debate with amillenarians.

In this discussion the problem will be considered from the premillennial viewpoint since this doctrine has already been asserted in stating that the proclamation of the nearness of the kingdom by John, Jesus, and the disciples referred to the earthly kingdom promised to the Jews. Since Israel rejected her Messiah, this kingdom was postponed and was to be established in the future at the second coming of Jesus Christ. The tenets of those who hold to a distinction between the terms will be presented, and then the arguments of those who believe the terms are used interchangeably will follow.

Held in abeyance

Those who draw a distinction between the terms usually assert the primary difference is seen in that the kingdom of God refers to the sphere of reality, and the kingdom of heaven, while including reality,

85. McClain, *The Greatness of the Kingdom,* p. 344.
86. Ibid., p. 218.

also has profession in it.[87] John 3:3 is cited as proof of the fact that the kingdom of God contains only those who are born again. The fact that there are "professors" as well as genuine believers in the kingdom of the heavens is indicated by the parable of the wheat and the darnel.[88] Further proof of the difference in character between the two kingdoms is seen in the use Luke makes of the parables. Luke, who speaks only of the kingdom of God, omits the parable of the wheat and darnel and of the dragnet, while Matthew applies both to the kingdom of the heavens.[89] The inference is the kingdom of God contains only believers while the kingdom of the heavens includes professors as well.

A second difference between the two kingdoms is seen by Scofield. He states that Matthew uses the kingdom of the heavens with reference to the earthly Messianic kingdom, and the kingdom of God with reference to the inward and spiritual.[90] A third difference is claimed. Miller believes there is also a topographical distinction.

> *The Kingdom of Heaven* is concerned only with the re-establishment of the will of God upon *earth* as it is established in heaven. *The Kingdom of God,* on the other hand, is a much broader term, for it reaches out far beyond the earth into the three heavens and to the utmost bounds of the universe. Topographically the Kingdom of Heaven is within the bounds of the Kingdom of God, but a great deal of what is considered in the Kingdom of Heaven is not generically in the Kingdom of God.[91]

Finally, those who hold to a distinction between the terms argue that if all else is disproved, one must account for the reason Matthew uses both phrases.

For a number of reasons it seems best to hold to the view that the terms are used interchangeably. First, none of the differences which are said to exist between the two terms can actually be proven. The assertion that there is profession in the kingdom of the heavens cannot be substantiated. On the contrary, Jesus lays down strict specifications for entrance into the kingdom of the heavens.

> *"For I say to you, that unless your righteousness surpasses that of the scribes and Pharisees, you shall not enter the kingdom of heaven"* (Matthew 5:20). *"Not every one who says to Me, 'Lord,*

87. Charles L. Feinberg, *Premillennialism or Amillennialism?*, p. 298-99.
88. Earl Miller, *The Kingdom of God and the Kingdom of Heaven*, pp. 63-64.
89. C. I. Scofield, ed., *The Scofield Reference Bible*, p. 1003.
90. Ibid.
91. Miller, *The Kingdom Of God*, pp. 60-61.

66

*Lord,' will enter the kingdom of heaven; but he who does the will
of My Father who is in heaven"* (Matthew 7:21). *"Truly I say to
you, unless you are converted and become like children, you shall
not enter the kingdom of heaven"* (Matthew 18:3).

It is hardly valid to argue that hypocritical profession is a part of the
kingdom of the heavens on the basis of the parables. Actually the darnel
and the bad fish are never said to be in the kingdom of the heavens.
There is no profession without reality in either the kingdom of God or
the kingdom of the heavens (cf. Luke 13:20-21).

It is also erroneous to say the kingdom of God is primarily inward and
spiritual while the kingdom of the heavens is earthly. The kingdom of
God used in its eschatological sense is no less earthly than the kingdom
of the heavens. Christ announced the nearness of the kingdom of God in
Mark 1:14-15 and Matthew 12:28. Luke records the account of the
Lord's sending out His disciples with the same message (Luke 10:9).
Therefore, the kingdom of God must be limited, earthly, and Messianic
in its significance.

To assert that a topographical difference exists because the kingdom
of God is broader than the kingdom of the heavens is without basis.
Both are pronounced near at hand. On what grounds, therefore, can the
kingdom of the heavens be said to be within the kingdom of God?

The reason Matthew uses two terms in his Gospel can be explained. It
must be remembered that Matthew's Gospel is peculiarly Jewish, and
the use of Matthew's terms must be viewed in this light. It is very
significant that the term, *the kingdom of the heavens,* is based on the
Aramaic portion of Daniel (2:44; 4:26; 7:27). Since the Palestinian Jew
of Christ's day could not read Hebrew, and because Aramaic was the
vernacular of that time, the expression would be especially well known.

> Our Lord, Who spoke in Aramaic, would always use this phrase,
> and when writing in Greek, Matthew, in keeping with the special
> scope and character of his Gospel retained it, whereas, in the other
> Gospels the figure was translated as being what it also, although
> not exclusively, meant, the Kingdom of God.[92]

Matthew retained the phrase because the Jews, instead of employing *the
kingdom of God,* simply used *the kingdom of the heavens.* This was
done because of their reverence for the name of Jehovah.[93] Dalman
gives conclusive evidence that this was common enough.[94] However, it

92. Scroggie, *Guide to Gospels,* p. 300.
93. Sauer, *The Triumph of the Crucified,* p. 23.
94. Dalman, *The Words of Jesus,* pp. 91-93.

seems that Matthew, though generally using the kingdom of the heavens, had a special reason for employing the kingdom of God. Whenever Matthew uses the latter term it seems that he desires to stress the divine character of the kingdom. The kingdom of the heavens denotes the fulfillment of the Old Testament prophecies, while the kingdom of God stresses the character of that kingdom. For instance, in Matthew 12:28 the character of God's kingdom is contrasted to that of Satan's. There the kingdom of God is a more fitting term than the kingdom of the heavens. Thus the same kingdom is always in view but Matthew uses the two terms to suit his purpose.

What then do the two terms mean? Throughout the entire Gospel of Matthew both terms always refer to the literal, earthly kingdom promised and prophesied in the Old Testament. When the church is mentioned in connection with the kingdom, the church and the kingdom are not to be confused. The church will be in the kingdom as its spiritual nucleus, but the church is not the kingdom or *vice versa*. It is clear that Matthew maintains this distinction throughout his Gospel as he unfolds the kingdom program presented by the King.

e. The Preaching of the Forerunner. After Matthew has presented the "proclamation" (κήρυγμα) of John, his position, his appearance, and the response to his proclamation, he goes on to give a sample of his preaching. The Evangelist presents three aspects—his rebuke of the Pharisees and the Sadducees, the warning of the coming judgment, and the greatness of the Messiah.

The Rebuke of the Pharisees and Sadducees, 3:7-3:9. But when he saw many of the Pharisees and Sadducees coming for baptism, he said to them, "You brood of vipers, who warned you to flee from the wrath to come? Therefore bring forth fruit in keeping with your repentance; and do not suppose that you can say to yourselves, 'We have Abraham for our father'; for I say to you, that God is able from these stones to raise up children to Abraham." In verse seven of Matthew 3 the Evangelist presents the first *marked* instance of animosity towards the Pharisees and Sadducees.[95] It is significant that this first mention of the Pharisees and Sadducees in the Gospel marks them out as being hypocritical. They were coming "for" (ἐπί, with the accusative) baptism without genuine repentance. This hypocrisy characterizes them throughout the rest of the book. John points out this trait by

95. Plummer, *Exegetical Commentary,* p. 28.

telling them to bring forth fruit worthy of repentance and to stop ascribing merit to their Abrahamic lineage. Most of the Israelites of John's day were taught that every Jew would automatically enter the kingdom at its institution.[96] By including the record of this rebuke, Matthew gives a hint of a later movement in the book as to why the Jews did not receive the kingdom with the coming of the Messiah. They refused to turn to God and trusted instead in their self-ascribed merits.

The Warning of Judgment, **3:10-3:12.** *"And the axe is already laid at the root of the trees; every tree therefore that does not bear good fruit is cut down, and thrown into the fire. As for me, I baptize you in water for repentance; but He who is coming after me is mightier than I, and I am not even fit to remove His sandals; He Himself will baptize you with the Holy Spirit and fire. And His winnowing fork is in His hand, and He will thoroughly clean His threshing floor; and He will gather His wheat into the barn, but He will burn up the chaff with unquenchable fire."* The reason Israel was to repent is introduced by the conjunction "for" (γάρ) in verse two. Since judgment was to precede the manifestation of the kingdom according to the Old Testament prophets (Isaiah 1:27; 4:4; 5:16; 13:6-19; 42:1; Jeremiah 33:14-16; Daniel 7:26-27), this call to repentance is completely in order.[97] In fact, to the Jew, the concept of repentance was constantly and closely connected with the Messianic age.[98] In verses ten to twelve Matthew shows that John recognized this judgment as being immediately at hand. "And the axe is already laid at the root of the trees; every tree therefore that does not bear good fruit is cut down *(futuristic present)* and thrown *(futuristic present)* into the fire." The judgment is further emphasized by the mention of wrath (3:7), the fire (3:12), and the winnowing fork (3:12).

John's preaching was to have a twofold effect. It was to cause individuals to repent for personal salvation and to bring national salvation to Israel if it repented.

> John preached *both* a personal salvation, involving the remission
> of sins (Mark 1:4), *and* a national salvation, involving the estab-
> lishment of the millennial kingdom with Israel delivered out of the
> hand of their enemies (Matt. 3:2; Luke 1:71-75).[99]

96. Edersheim, *Life and Times,* 1:271.
97. See also McClain, *The Greatness of the Kingdom,* pp. 179-80, 201-202, 286.
98. C. G. Montefiore, "Rabbinic Conceptions of Repentance," *The Jewish Quarterly Review,* 16 (January 1904):211.
99. S. Lewis Johnson, Jr., "The Message Of John the Baptist," p. 36.

Thus John warned both the individuals of Israel and Israel as a nation to repent because of the judgment which was at hand with the kingdom.

The Greatness of the Messiah.   Since the primary purpose of the Baptist was to prepare the way for the coming of the Messiah, John emphatically extolled the greatness of the Coming One. In doing so John portrayed Christ both as a Savior and as a Judge. In describing the superior work of the Messiah John used the phrase "with the Holy Spirit and fire" (ἐν πνεύματι ἁγίῳ καὶ πυρί, Matthew 3:11). This phrase has caused some difficulty.

The question is this: Does "fire" (πυρί) speak of purification or of judgment? It is possible that two distinct baptisms are spoken of—one a baptism of the Holy Spirit and the other a judgment of fire. This view has much to commend it. The contexts immediately preceding and following verse eleven speak of judgment. There is good fruit and bad fruit; there is wheat and chaff. It is possible that John follows the parallelism by referring to a baptism of the Spirit and a judgment of fire. In addition the apostles make reference to the baptism of the Spirit with no mention of fire. Even in Acts 1:5 and 11:16 where John's baptism is compared with Spirit baptism, as it is in Matthew 3, nothing is said about fire.

Despite the commendable features of this view, there is a better interpretation. The better approach takes "fire" (πυρί) to be one aspect of Spirit baptism, that of purification. Since the two nouns are joined by the conjunction "and" (καί) and one preposition is used with both, only a baptism of the Holy Spirit is in view. While it is true that in Greek one preposition used with two nouns does not always place them in the same category, this usually is the case.[100] The cases where the preposition is to be supplied before the second noun are very few. It is best, therefore, to follow the usual grammatical significance of the construction and say the "fire" (πυρί) is an aspect of Spirit baptism. Furthermore, fire is mentioned in connection with Spirit baptism in Acts 2:3. Edersheim,[101] Morison,[102] and M'Neile[103] hold this view.

The introduction of Spirit baptism by Jesus introduces another thought which verifies the greatness of the person of Jesus as the Messiah. Throughout the Old Testament prophecies the Holy Spirit is asso-

---

100. Robertson, *Grammar,* p. 566.
101. Edersheim, *Life And Times,* 1:272.
102. Morison, *A Practical Commentary,* p. 36.
103. M'Neile, *St. Matthew,* p. 29.

ciated with the coming of the Messiah. It is one of the marks which identifies Him (Isaiah 32:15; Ezekiel 11:19; 36:26-27; 37:14; Joel 2:28-29). Not only was the Messiah to bring judgment but also a baptism of the Holy Spirit.

Still another problem presents itself. What is the significance of Spirit baptism to John the Baptist? It is correctly affirmed by dispensationalists that Spirit baptism is the means whereby the body of Christ, the church, is constituted today (1 Corinthians 12:13; Colossians 1:24; Ephesians 1:22-23). Since the church was unknown to John before Christ revealed it, how could the term have any significance in the days of John's ministry? It can only be said that to John, the baptism of the Holy Spirit was God's means of identifying His people. Paul and Luke used the concept with far greater significance to refer to the manner in which the church is marked out as God's people in this age.

2. The Baptism of the King, 3:13-3:17

Matthew 3:13-3:17 contains the record of the baptism of Jesus. It is introduced by the "then" ($\tau \acute{o} \tau \epsilon$). M'Neile says the particle " ... means little more than 'the next event to be related is—' . . . ."[104] Thus Christ's baptism is very loosely connected with the preceding passage.

The Reason for the Baptism, **3:13-3:15.** *Then Jesus arrived from Galilee at the Jordan coming to John, to be baptized by him. But John tried to prevent Him, saying, "I have need to be baptized by You, and do You come to me?" But Jesus answering said to him, "Permit it at this time; for in this way it is fitting for us to fulfill all righteousness." Then he permitted Him.* This passage is difficult because the reason for Christ's baptism poses a problem. In a sense Jesus answered it when He said it was necessary for John to baptize Him "to fulfill all righteousness" (3:15). But what did Jesus mean by this statement?

Several solutions have been proposed. Many believe Jesus was baptized to identify Himself with the godly remnant of Israel. Some who hold this view are Bruce,[105] Robinson,[106] Darby,[107] Gaebelein,[108]

---

104. Ibid., p. 30.
105. Bruce, "The Synoptic Gospels," *The Expositor's Greek Testament,* 1:86.
106. Robinson, *The Gospel of Matthew,* p. 18.
107. Darby, *Synopsis,* 3:28.
108. Gaebelein, *The Gospel of Matthew,* 1:74.

Kelly,[109], Morgan,[110] Plummer,[111] and Feinberg.[112] A battery of great men do indeed support this position. However, this interpretation does not clearly fit the meaning of "to fulfill all righteousness." Being identified with God's people may be a *result* of fulfilling all righteousness, but it can hardly be said to be *the purpose* of Christ's baptism.

Others believe Jesus was baptized as a Messianic anointing. Green[113] and Vos[114] hold this view. However, an anointing would not fulfill all righteousness either.

Chafer holds a position which states that Christ's baptism was His consecration to the priesthood.[115] Again, this does not explain clearly the fulfillment of all righteousness, nor is the baptism necessarily associated with His priesthood.

Some commentators hold that the baptism of Christ fulfilled all righteousness in that it indicated His submission to the law of Moses. Shepard,[116] Montefiore,[117] and Carr[118] see this in the baptism of Christ by John. This has the serious difficulty of uniting John's baptism with the law. Since John's baptism was new, it would be chronologically impossible for his baptism to be a fulfillment of the requirements of the law. There is no direct connection between John's baptism and the law.

English claims the baptism pictured the work of Christ which He would accomplish on earth by His death and resurrection.[119] Still another view is presented by Robertson.[120] He believes the baptism linked the two ministries of John and Christ together. These things indeed are true, but again, they fail to give meaning to the phrase "to fulfill all righteousness" in verse fifteen.

The meaning of the phrase need not be so specific. Rather it evidently is a general rule of Christ's earthly life which refers to His voluntary subjection to the ordinances which belonged to men, whether they were religious or secular. It would be the reason for Christ's obedience to the

109. Kelly, *Lectures on Matthew*, p. 64.
110. Morgan, *The Crises of the Christ*, pp. 120-121.
111. Plummer, *Exegetical Commentary*, p. 30.
112. Feinberg, *Premillennialism*, p. 30.
113. Green, *Saint Matthew*, pp. 116-117.
114. Vos, "The Ministry of John the Baptist," p. 29.
115. Lewis Sperry Chafer, *Systematic Theology*, 5:61-62.
116. J. W. Shepard, *The Christ of the Gospels*, p. 71.
117. Montefiore, *The Synoptic Gospels*, 2:16-17.
118. Carr, *St. Matthew*, p. 102.
119. E. Schuyler English, *Studies in the Gospel According to Matthew*, p. 34.
120. Robertson, *Word Pictures*, 1:28-29.

Old Testament laws and His subservience to the laws of civil government. Since they were instituted by God, it became Him to obey them in order "to fulfill all righteousness." Because God had led John to baptize, it was proper for Christ to receive the ordinance at the hands of the Baptist. It is interesting to note that the word "fitting" ($\pi\rho\acute{\epsilon}\pi\epsilon\iota$) refers to that which is becoming, proper, and fitting. This certainly fits the interpretation. The plural pronoun "us" ($\dot{\eta}\mu\hat{\iota}\nu$) supports this view also in that it implicates John in the act very definitely. Finally, the words "at this time" ($\ddot{\alpha}\rho\tau\iota$) show that this condition of being in subjection to all of the ordinances belonging to men is to be contrasted with some other time: in this case a later time when Jesus would be glorified.

The Results of the Baptism. Generally the confusion arises over a failure to differentiate between the *purpose of* Christ's baptism and its *results*. The purpose was to fulfill all righteousness; the results were manifold.

One very definite result was the identification of Jesus with the believing remnant. This was important. Those who were baptized indicated by their act of subjection to the ordinance their need for repentance as well as their anticipation of the coming kingdom. Now they were prepared for the Messiah. The King, because of His baptism, is now bound up with His subjects. A second result is the authentication of John's message by Jesus. John had been preaching the nearness of the kingdom. Jesus in His baptism verified this concept of the eschatological kingdom. Some may accuse John of having an erroneous concept of the kingdom. If he did, Jesus did also since he affirmed John's concept by being baptized.

A third result of the baptism is the manifestation of the Messiah to Israel. Matthew does not indicate this fact, but John very clearly does (John 1:29-34). A fourth result was the anointing of Jesus with the Holy Spirit (Acts 10:37-38). This is not to say that Jesus did not have the Spirit before. He who was conceived by the Holy Spirit was surely always filled with the Spirit. This anointing was a divine mark of God's appointment of Jesus to His Messianic work.

The Divine Authentication of the King, **3:16-3:17.** *And after being baptized, Jesus went up immediately from the water; and behold, the heavens were opened, and he saw the Spirit of God descending as a dove, and coming upon Him; and behold, a voice out of the heavens, saying, "This is My beloved Son, in whom I am well-pleased."* A final result of Christ's baptism was the divine authentication of the sonship of Jesus. To Matthew this event is highly significant for the voice from heaven affirmed the righteous person of Jesus. "This is My beloved Son" seems to be a reference to Psalm 2:7 where the Messiah points to the affirmation of His sonship by Jehovah. Psalm 2 goes on to describe how this Anointed One shall receive the nations in a most glorious way as His inheritance. "In whom I am well-pleased" seems to be a reference to Isaiah 42:1. Again the passage is Messianic, associating the judgment of the nations with the servant in whom Jehovah delights. Here "the Beloved One" is a Messianic title.[121]

In chapter three Matthew makes another significant contribution to his argument. Chapter one declared the glories of the Messiah's person. Chapter two gives a preview of the reception which was to be given to the Messiah. Now in chapter three Matthew presents the forerunner of the King as to his work of preparation for the coming kingdom. The Messiah in being baptized is divinely authenticated as to His person.

3. The Temptation of the King, 4:1-4:11

The genealogy and the virgin birth show that the King is legally qualified to reign. At the baptism Jesus received divine approval. Now the King is proven as to His moral character (Matthew 4:1-11).

The Divine Character of the Temptation, **4:1. Then Jesus was led up by the Spirit into the wilderness to be tempted by the devil.** Since the temptation follows the baptism in every one of the Synoptics, it can be inferred that they are definitely linked together. Mark joins them with the adverb "immediately" (εὐθύς), Luke uses the conjunction "and" (δέ), and Matthew employs his characteristic adverb "then" (τότε). In other words, Satan now tests the veracity of God's declaration at the baptism of Jesus. The character of the Messiah must be blameless, and the Adversary now proves that character.

The significance of the temptation is pointed out well by the Greek text. First of all, the phrase "was led up by the Spirit" (ἀνήχθη ὑπὸ τοῦ πνεύματος) indicates divine *providence*. It was not by reason of mere circumstances that Jesus was in the wilderness and was confronted with temptations by Satan. The passive verb with ὑπό indicates Jesus was led *by the Spirit* into the wilderness. The passive infinitive "to be tempted" (πειρασθῆναι) indicates a divine *purpose*. Πειράζω means " ... *to make proof of* ... *to test, try, prove* ...."[122] It can also be used

---

121. Allen, *Commentary on Matthew,* p. 29.
122. Abbott-Smith, *A Manual Lexicon,* p. 351.

of solicitation to evil, but James 1:13 negates that though here. Jesus was tested with the idea of proving His righteous character in order that He might be approved.

Commentators have approached the three tests from various vantage points. However, most of these fail to relate the temptations to Matthew's argument. The most accurate and pertinent approach is that which sees the attacks of Satan as being personal, national, and universal in their implications.[123]

The Personal Temptation, **4:2.** ***And after He had fasted forty days and forty nights, He then became hungry.*** The first temptation is recorded in Matthew 4:2-4. It commences with the Lord's fasting for forty days and forty nights. Moses, the great lawgiver, and Elijah, a prominent Old Testament prophet, had both fasted for the same length of time (Deuteronomy 9:9; 1 Kings 19:8). The number was significant to Israel. Throughout the Old Testament forty is often associated with sin (Genesis 7:4, 12; Numbers 14:33; 32:13; Deuteronomy 9:25; 25:3; Psalm 95:10; Jonah 3:4).[124] The Lord is thus associated with Moses and Elijah, and the reader is prepared for the entrance of Satan on the scene.

4:3 ***And the tempter came and said to Him, "If You are the Son of God, command that these stones become bread."*** The "tempter" (ὁ πειράζων) begins his temptation with a first class conditional clause, the condition of assumed reality—"If You are the Son of God" (εἰ υἱὸς εἶ τοῦ θεοῦ). "The temptation, to have force, must be assumed as true. The devil knew it to be true. He accepts that fact as a working hypothesis in the temptation."[125] The temptation did not exist in an attempt to make Jesus doubt His sonship; both Satan and Christ were completely cognizant of the fact. Ever since the baptism there was no doubt of it for them. The substantive "son" (υἱός) links the clause with the declaration of 3:17. If the temptation were aimed at the fact of sonship, the Lord's reply would have little bearing on the temptation.

The test consisted of an attempt to make Jesus act independently of God. Christ has fasted and now hungers. The devil commands Him to turn stones to loaves, the basis of this imperative being the recognized sonship of Jesus. Thus Satan urged Jesus to use His divine prerogative independently of God to satisfy His desire for food.

123. Johnson, "Argument Of Matthew," p. 146.
124. Richard Chenevix Trench, *Studies in the Gospels,* pp. 14-16.
125. Robertson, *Grammar,* p. 1009.

4:4. *But He answered and said, "It is written, 'Man shall not live on bread alone, but on every word that proceeds out of the mouth of God.'"* In reply Jesus quotes Deuteronomy 8:3. The first important word here is "alone" (μόνῳ). Man shall not live by bread *only*. Jesus is saying that man shall not live apart from the will of God; he is to walk in dependence upon God. The second significant word is "man" (ἄνθρωπος). By it Jesus as Messiah identifies Himself with the human race. Tempted to act as God, He responds as the theanthropic person— both God and man. He answers as the Messiah, Immanuel, and not as God only. Matthew here shows that Jesus is not God only, but an unique theanthropic person, *personally* qualified to be King of Israel.

The National Temptation, **4:5-4:6.** *Then the devil took Him into the holy city; and he stood Him on the pinnacle of the temple, and said to Him, "If You are the Son of God throw Yourself down; for it is written,*

> *'He will give His angels charge concerning You; and on their hands they will bear You up, lest You strike Your foot against a stone.'"*

The second temptation, presented in Matthew 4:5-4:7, has national connotations. These are seen by the references to the holy city and the temple (4:5). Satan had a very evident purpose in placing the Lord at this scene for this temptation. According to a rabbinic tradition, the coming of the Messiah to mark the deliverance of Israel would be indicated by His appearance on the temple roof. Edersheim quotes a rabbi as saying, "Our Rabbis give this tradition: In the hour when King Messiah cometh, He standeth upon the roof of the Sanctuary."[126]

For Jesus to leap unhurt from the place the Messiah was to appear would certainly identify Him as the King of Israel. John 6:30 shows the Jews anticipated the Messiah would manifest Himself with such a sign as this. Therefore, the temptation takes on national significance, though Satan on the surface does not intimate such a thing. Bruce argues against this view since there is no mention in the gospels of a crowd to witness this event.[127] However, no crowd was needed; only a few witnesses, of which there certainly were some, would attest to the truthfulness of the feat (cf. Matthew 16:1).

The temptation is significant. Jesus is to prove to Israel in a visible way that He is God's Son. The first temptation was with regard to the

---

126. Edersheim, *Life and Times,* 1:293. Cf. Malachi 3:1.
127. Bruce, "The Synoptic Gospels," *The Expositor's Greek Testament,* 1:90.

faith of Jesus in God. The second is made with regard to God's faithfulness to His Son. Satan tempts Jesus to prove and to display that faithfulness by hurling Himself from a high point of the temple.

4:7. Jesus said to him, "On the other hand, it is written, 'You shall not tempt the Lord your God.'" Jesus replies with a quotation from Deuteronomy 6:16, introducing it with words "on the other hand" (πάλιν). The Greek word has the sense of " . . . on the other hand, not contradicting but qualifying." [128] Deuteronomy 6:16 is most fitting since this passage guards against presumptuous acts whereby the faithfulness of God is tested. Ἐκπειράζω means " . . . *to prove* or *test thoroughly, to find by testing.*" [129] Shepard says, "He declared by this reference to Israel at Massah that testing is not trusting." [130] Once again Jesus takes His place as a man and responds as the Messiah. Matthew declares that Jesus is a faithful Messiah morally qualified to rule the *nation*.

The Universal Temptation, **4:8-4:9.** *Again, the devil took Him to a very high mountain, and showed Him all the kingdoms of the world, and their glory; and he said to Him, "All these things will I give You, if You fall down and worship me."* Matthew 4:8-11 concludes the record of Christ's temptation with this last test relating to the kingdoms of the world. Satan displays all the kingdoms with their glory to Christ. He approaches Jesus this time as a man and not as God. Jesus, knowing that with the declaration of sonship comes the promise of universal dominion (Psalm 2), was tempted to obtain that power by worshipping His arch enemy.

4:10-4:11. *Then Jesus said to him, "Begone, Satan! For it is written, 'You shall worship the Lord your God, and serve Him only.'" Then the devil left Him; and behold, angels came and began to minister to Him.* But Jesus, answering as the Messiah, speaks with all of the authority of the Christ and orders Satan to depart. Worship and service belong only to God and are not to be given to Satan. With Satan's departure angels come and begin to worship Christ. Jesus the Christ is morally qualified to rule on a *universal* scale.

It is important to note that each of the temptations relates to Jesus' Messiahship. The first temptation relates to Him as a person, the second to the Jews as the Son of David, and the third to the world as the Son of Abraham. This is exactly parallel with the superscription of the geneal-

---

128. Ibid.
129. Cremer, *Biblico-Theological Lexicon,* p. 497.
130. Shepard, *The Christ of the Gospels,* p. 78.

ogy given in Matthew 1:1.[131] In conjunction with this it is interesting to
see that Jesus always responded as the Messiah. This shows not only
His moral qualifications but also His ultimate defeat of Satan. As Messiah He overcame Satan, and therefore He shall ultimately wrest the
kingdoms of the world from him (Revelation 11:15).

One further observation needs to be made. The temptations prove that
an earthly, literal kingdom is in view in Matthew.[132] Some state that the
third temptation consisted of an enticement to gain a temporal instead of
a spiritual dominion.[133] That is, it would have been sinful for Christ to
accept an earthly kingdom. However, this interpretation is not legitimate. It must be remembered that each temptation is dependent upon the
possibility of Jesus doing or having the thing spoken of. Jesus did not
deny the reality of the earthly kingdom which should ultimately be His;
He did object to the method of obtaining it.

> In the first temptation Jesus does *not deny* that He is hungry and
> able to make bread; in the second, He does *not deny* that He is the
> Son of God, and under special protection; and in the third, He does
> *not deny* the Kingdom or dominion which is to be given to Him,
> but only rejects *the mode* by which it is to be obtained. As ob-
> served, if such a Kingdom is not covenanted, predicted, and in-
> tended, the temptation would not have any force.[134]

Matthew has carefully presented the legal genealogy of the King, His
supernatural birth in fulfillment of prophecy, His confirmation of
prophecy by His childhood, His forerunner, His baptism, and His temptation. In every detail the King is qualified—legally, scripturally, and
morally. All is now in readiness for the presentation of the Messiah to
Israel.

131. Johnson, "Argument of Matthew," p. 146.
132. Peters, *Theocratic Kingdom,* 1:698.
133. M'Neile, *St. Matthew,* p. 41.
134. Peters, *Theocratic Kingdom,* 1:700.

II. The Declaration of the Principles of the King (4:12-7:29)

   A. The Introduction to the Ministry of the King (4:12-4:25)
      1. The occasion (4:12-4:16)
      2. The message of the King (4:17)
      3. The call of four disciples (4:18-4:22)
      4. A summary of the ministry of the King (4:23-4:25)

   B. The Principles of the King (5:1-7:29)
   Introduction to Various Interpretations of the Sermon on the Mount
      1. The setting (5:1-5:2)
      2. The subjects of the kingdom (5:3-5:16)
         a. Their character and their portion in the kingdom (5:3-5:12)
         b. Their calling and their position in the world (5:13-5:16)
      3. The explanation of genuine righteousness (5:17-7:12)
         a. The principle of righteousness and the law (5:17-5:48)
            1) The confirmation of the law (5:17-5:20)
            2) The interpretation of the law (5:21-5:48)
               a) The law regarding murder (5:21-5:26)
               b) The law regarding adultery (5:27-5:30)
               c) The law regarding divorce (5:31-5:32)
               d) The law regarding the taking of an oath (5:33-5:37)
               e) The law regarding retaliation (5:38-5:42)
               f) The law regarding love (5:43-5:48)
         b. The practice of righteousness (6:1-6:18)
            1) The maxim (6:1)
            2) The motives for good deeds (6:2-6:18)
               a) The rewards for giving (6:2-6:4)
               b) The rewards for praying (6:5-6:15)
               c) The rewards for fasting (6:16-6:18)
         c. The perspectives of righteousness (6:19-7:12)
            1) With respect to wealth (6:19-6:34)
            2) With respect to brethren (7:1-7:5)
            3) With respect to the spiritually hostile (7:6)
            4) With respect to God (7:7-7:12)
      4. The warnings of the King (7:13-7:27)
         a. Regarding the narrow gate (7:13-7:14)
         b. Regarding false prophets (7:15-7:20)
         c. Regarding false profession (7:21-7:27)
      5. The response of the people (7:28-7:29)

II. The Declaration of the Principles of the King

A. The Introduction to the Ministry of the King
4:12-4:25.

With the introduction of the King's forerunner the scene is set for the coming of the King. The King Himself is prepared for His ministry and presentation to Israel in two ways—He fulfills all righteousness by being baptized, and He indicates His moral preparedness by being tested by Satan. In anticipation of the famous sermon of the Messiah, Matthew briefly introduces the reader to the ministry of the King. This concise introduction, composed of a brief resume of His work, is contained in Matthew 4:12-25.

1. The Occasion, 4:12-4:16.

4:12. *Now when He heard that John had been taken into custody, He withdrew into Galilee* ... The occasion for the commencement of the ministry of the Messiah is the imprisonment of His forerunner, John the Baptist. The close time relationship is indicated by the word "now" (δέ) plus the aorist participle "when He heard" in 4:12. The phrase "from then" (ἀπὸ τότε) of verse seventeen further affirms this. Matthew is careful to record his narrative so that it leaves his reader with the impression that John's imprisonment is the occasion for the commencement of the King's ministry. In royal protocol the King does not make His appearance in public until the forerunner has finished his work. Matthew, emphasizing the official and regal character of Jesus, follows this procedure exactly.[1] It was because Jesus heard of John's

---

1. S. Lewis Johnson, Jr., "The Argument of Matthew," *Bibliotheca Sacra* 112 (April 1955):146.

imprisonment that he "withdrew" (ἀναχωρέω) into Galilee to begin His ministry there.[2] Thus Matthew quietly passes over one whole year of the Lord's Judean ministry which is recorded in John's Gospel.

It is interesting to note that even though Jesus moved to Galilee, He remained under the governmental authority of the Herod who had imprisoned John, for Herod Antipas also ruled over Galilee. However, the Lord felt His safety would be greater in Galilee in that there would be less chance for violence at the hands of the religious leaders at Jerusalem (John 4:1-3; 5:1-16). These rulers were not in sympathy with the movement John had started. If they had approved of John and had accepted his proclamation, Herod would not have dared to imprison the Baptist because of the explosive political situation which was ever present in Palestine. The passive verb "to be taken into custody" (παρεδόθη) may even suggest that the leaders had a hand in John's imprisonment. It is the same word which is used throughout Matthew for the betrayal of Jesus at the hands of Judas (Matthew 26:15, 16, 21, 23, 25; 27:3, 4). It may be inferred, therefore, that Jesus withdrew to Galilee in order to escape the religious leaders whose headquarters were in Jerusalem.

4:13. *and leaving Nazareth, He came and settled in Capernaum, which is by the sea, in the region of Zebulun and Naphtali.* Omitting the ugly incident recorded in Luke 4:16-31, Matthew traces the steps of Jesus from Nazareth to Capernaum. Matthew says Jesus "left" or forsook (καταλείπω) Nazareth and took up a permanent dwelling (κατοικέω) in Capernaum. This is further verified by Matthew 9:1 which calls Capernaum "His own city."

4:14-16. *This was to fulfill what was spoken through Isaiah the prophet, saying,*

> *The land of Zebulun and the land of Naphtali, by the way of the sea, beyond the Jordan, Galilee of the Gentiles. The people who were sitting in darkness saw a great light, and to those who were sitting in the land and shadow of death, upon them a light dawned.*

In this incident Matthew sees the fulfillment of another Old Testament prophecy (Isaiah 9:1-2). Isaiah pictures the darkness of oppression that existed under the hands of the Assyrians. According to the prophecy, the Messiah was to marvelously emancipate the people by the power of God. Though Galilee at the time of Christ was no longer under the rule

2. Alan Hugh M'Neile, *The Gospel According to St. Matthew*, p. 42.

of Assyria, it was still under a foreign yoke, that of Rome. Therefore, the reference to the darkness and shadow of death is very appropriate in its *historical* application.

The references to Zebulun and Naphtali correspond with the land of Galilee so that the prophecy is also fitting in its *geographical* application. Because the population of Galilee is of a mixed Gentile and Jewish character, the prophecy is also proper in its *ethnological* application.[3] Finally, the *contextual* application of Isaiah 9 is appropriate since it is definitely Messianic and eschatological in character. Of course, there is no doubt Matthew is also referring to their *spiritual* darkness and deadness, but that is only implicated by his quoting the prophecy here.

2. The Message of the King, 4:17.

4:17. *From that time Jesus began to preach and say, "Repent, for the kingdom of heaven is at hand."* The message of the King is introduced by the words "from that time Jesus began" (ἀπὸ τότε ἤρξατο ὁ Ἰησοῦς), a clause which occurs in the Gospel of Matthew only here in 4:7 and in 16:21. Here it indicates the beginning of the public preaching of Jesus. It has a very different purpose in 16:21 since the King there stands as rejected. In 4:17 He proclaims the nearness of the Kingdom; in 16:21 He announces the approach of His passion and resurrection. The first occurrence introduces the account of His presentation to Israel; the second commences the account of the culmination of Israel's rejection. One commentator has observed that whenever Matthew uses the verb "to begin" (ἤρξατο), it marks the inception of the continuous action, or it describes a new phase in the narrative.[4]

It is very important to note that the message of the King is the same as that proclaimed by His forerunner. Since Jesus makes no explanation of His concept of the kingdom, it must have been the same eschatological, earthly kingdom which was preached by John.[5] While many commentators agree John's concept was eschatological, they affirm Christ's was soteriological.[6] However, John's message was both soteriological and eschatological. These concepts were not exclusive of one another.[7] The

3. Alexander Balmain Bruce, *The Galilean Gospel*, p. 7.
4. M'Neile, *St. Matthew*, p. 45.
5. George N. H. Peters, *The Theocratic Kingdom of Our Lord Jesus, the Christ, as Covenanted in the Old Testament, and Presented in the New Testament*, 1:266.
6. J. W. Shepard, *The Christ of the Gospels*, pp. 62, 123.
7. See above, p. 69.

King Himself now announces the nearness of the *earthly* kingdom. The subjects are to prepare themselves *spiritually,* since the kingdom is founded by Messiah, the Righteous One.

3. The Call of Four Disciples, 4:18-4:22.

4:18-4:22. *And walking by the sea of Galilee, He saw two brothers, Simon who was called Peter, and Andrew his brother, casting a net into the sea; for they were fishermen. And He said to them, "Follow Me, and I will make you fishers of men." And they immediately left the nets, and followed Him. And going on from there He saw two other brothers, James the son of Zebedee, and John his brother, in the boat with Zebedee their father, mending their nets; and He called them. And they immediately left the boat and their father, and followed Him.* To impress his reader with the authority of the King, Matthew records the call of four disciples (4:18-22). There is certainly no doubt that these incidents do illustrate the power of Christ over men. Plummer comments, "But it is with regal authority that He calls His first disciples."[8] The adverb "immediately" ($\epsilon\dot{\upsilon}\theta\acute{\epsilon}\omega\varsigma$) is significant in verses twenty and twenty-two in that it marks a fitting response to the call of a king. He but speaks and there is immediate, implicit obedience.

4. A Summary of the Ministry of the King, 4:23-4:25

4:23. *And Jesus was going about in all Galilee, teaching in their synagogues, and proclaiming the gospel of the kingdom, and healing every kind of disease and every kind of sickness among the people.* A brief resume of the ministry of the King is presented in Matthew 4:23-25. This ministry is described by three words—teaching, preaching, and healing. Although His work is located in Galilee of the Gentiles, the ministry of the King is limited to the Jewish people. This is clearly indicated by three facts. First, the King practices His teaching ministry in their synagogues, a Jewish institution. Second, He preaches a Jewish message, the gospel of the kingdom. Third, the people among whom He performs His healing ministry are designated by the Greek word $\lambda\alpha\acute{o}\varsigma$. To a Jewish reader this meant Israel.[9]

8. Alfred Plummer, *An Exegetical Commentary on the Gospel According to S. Matthew,* p. 48.

9. M'Neile, *St. Matthew,* p. 47.

4:24-4:25. *And the news about Him went out into all Syria; and they brought to Him all who were ill, taken with various diseases and pains, demoniacs, epileptics, paralytics; and He healed them. And great multitudes followed Him from Galilee and Decapolis and Jerusalem and Judea and from beyond the Jordan.* As a result of the ministry of the King, His fame is noised to the Gentiles of Syria. The phrase "into all Syria" (εἰς ὅλην τὴν Συρίαν) in verse twenty-four stands in sharp contrast to "in all Galilee" (ἐν ὅλῃ τῇ Γαλιλαίᾳ) in verse twenty-three. The former is a designation of that which is predominantly Gentile, the latter that which is Jewish.[10] These Gentiles bring their sick, diseased, demon-possessed, epileptics, and paralytics. He heals them all. In addition, crowds from Galilee, Decapolis, Jerusalem, Judea, and beyond the Jordan follow Him. Evidently many of the disciples of John mentioned in Matthew 3:5 would also be included in these crowds.

While Jesus begins His ministry with the Jews only, His fame becomes so widespread that both Jews and Gentiles respond. This is clearly a foreview of the kingdom. The King is present with both Jews and Gentiles being blessed, the Gentiles coming to the Jewish Messiah for blessing (Zechariah 2:10-12; 8:18-23; Isaiah 2:1-4).

Verses twelve to twenty-five of this chapter form a fitting introduction to the discourse which follows. The King has called forth disciples. Large crowds follow in great anticipation as a result of His message and His work. In the light of this anticipation the King presents an extended discourse. This discourse is commonly known as the Sermon on the Mount.

B. THE PRINCIPLES OF THE KING
5:1-7:29.

Perhaps no other sermon, oration, or address has attracted as much attention as the famed Sermon on the Mount found in chapters five through seven of Matthew's Gospel. Christian and non-Christian alike have studied it and have considered its teachings. Yet, after nineteen hundred years of careful investigation, fundamental problems still exist with regard to it. Of these, the primary problem concerns its basic interpretation.

---

10. *Ibid.*

Introduction to Various Interpretations
of the Sermon on the Mount.

Numerous interpretations have been posited as the solution to the understanding of this sermon, many of which are widely divergent from one another. Of the great number of interpretations, a few of the more important and representative are presented here.

The Soteriological Approach. This interpretation, once widely held by liberals, has now been generally abandoned. Simply stated, it posits that men may attain their salvation through governing their lives by the principles set forth in the Sermon on the Mount.

> The Kingdom of God, like the Kingdom of Science, makes no other preliminary demand from those who would enter it than that it should be treated experimentally and practically as a working hypothesis. "This do and thou shalt live."[11]

This approach involves a number of duties.

> The Faith of the Fellowship of the Kingdom would be expressed in its Creed-Prayer, the Lord's Prayer. No other affirmation of faith would be required. To pray that Creed-Prayer daily from the heart would be the prime expression of loyal membership. The duties of membership would be the daily striving to obey the Two Great Commandments and to realize in character and conduct the ideals of the Seven Beatitudes: the seeking of each member to be in his environment "the salt of the earth" and "the light of the world:" and the endeavour to promote by every means in his power the coming of the Kingdom of God among mankind. Membership of the Fellowship would be open to all men and women—whether Christians, Jews, Mohammedans, or members of any religion or of no religion at all—who desired to be loyal to the Kingdom of God and discharge its duties.[12]

The very fact that this view has been generally abandoned bears testimony to its weakness. To interpret the Sermon on the Mount as a guide to good works which will bring salvation is erroneous simply because it is out of accord with the rest of Scripture. It is the universal testimony of the Bible that one can obtain eternal life only by grace through faith. A second error of the soteriological interpretation is found when one studies the sermon itself. The high standards set forth in the discourse absolutely prevent any human from attaining them. If salvation depended on these standards, none could be saved. The soteriologi-

11. H. D. A. Major, *Basic Christianity,* p. 48.
12. *Ibid.,* pp. 67-68.

cal interpretation of the Sermon on the Mount is indeed found to be woefully lacking.

The Sociological Approach. An approach which is closely allied to the soteriological interpretation is the sociological approach. Those who come to the discourse with this view see in it a guide to the salvation of society.

> What would happen in the world if the element of fair play as enunciated in the Golden Rule— "Do unto others as you would that men should do unto you"—were put into practice in the various relationships of life? ... What a difference all this would make, and how far we would be on the road to a new and better day in private, in public, in business, and in international relationships!"[13]

It must be admitted that if the precepts which are presented in this sermon were followed by Christ's disciples, society would be improved, but it would not be cured. Since men are fallen creatures, and because there is no one to administer justice as it should be administered under its precepts, it can be no cure for today's society. Tolstoy's famous experiment bears vivid testimony to this fact. In addition, it is clear that the improvement of society for society's sake was not the intention of Jesus in giving the sermon. This view fails for the simple reason that it has no relevance to the context. To interpret the sermon from the sociological viewpoint robs it of all meaning.

The Penitential Approach. Those who hold to the penitential interpretation approach the sermon as a body of law which makes one conscious of his sin and thereby drives him to God. The man who popularized this view in theological circles was the famous German, Gerhard Kittel. Others adopted his position.

> Thus what we have here in the Sermon on the Mount, is the climax of law, the completeness of the letter, the letter which killeth; and because it is so much more searching and thorough than the Ten Commandments, therefore does it kill all the more effectually .... The hard demand of the letter is here in the closest possible connexion with the promise of the Spirit.[14]

This view is weak in that it fails to note the people to whom the sermon is addressed. Jesus is speaking to His disciples, not the crowds.

13. Frederick Keller Stamm, *Seeing the Multitudes,* pp. 68-69.
14. Charles Gore, *The Sermon on the Mount,* pp. 4-5.

He tells them they *are* the salt of the earth and the light of the world. They are to pray to God and to address Him as "Our Father." Service and not salvation is spoken of in 6:24-34. God is referred to as their heavenly Father in 6:26. It is clear from these indications that Jesus is in these portions of the sermon speaking to His disciples. The penitential interpretation falls short simply because it fails to consider those who are addressed.

The Ecclesiastical Approach. By far the most common approach is the ecclesiastical interpretation. It has its proponents in virtually every theological position—liberals, fundamentalists, amillennialists, and premillennialists. Simply stated, those who posit this view believe the Sermon on the Mount by interpretation is addressed to the church. Thus, it becomes the rule of life for believers in this age. Hogg and Watson state, "We conclude, therefore, that the Sermon on the Mount is intended for the guidance of regenerate persons in an unregenerate world (Matt. 19.28, Tit. 3.5)."[15] Hunter calls it a "Design for Life" for the believers of today.[16] "It is a religious system of living which portrays how transformed Christians *ought* to live in the world," says Kepler.[17] These citations could be multiplied many times over, taken from representatives of as many doctrinal viewpoints.

Again this view is found to be lacking. First of all, the context militates against it. It has been established that both John and Jesus had been preaching the nearness of the earthly kingdom promised in the Old Testament. Why should the Lord suddenly interject teaching which belongs to the church age? The word *church* is not even mentioned until chapter sixteen, although the age is predicted in parabolic form as early as chapter thirteen.

Hogg and Watson contend that the discourse must be applied to the church because there are so many parallels between it and the doctrine contained in the epistles.[18] However, this is not a valid point, since God's standards are unchanging. It would be ridiculous to assert that a believer today is under the law since nine of the ten commandments are addressed to believers in the epistles. Although parallels may often indicate identity, they do not prove it. In addition, the fact that the sermon was delivered in the age of the law bears much weight against

15. C. F. Hogg and J. B. Watson, *On the Sermon on the Mount*, p. 19.
16. Archibald M. Hunter, *A Pattern for Life: An Exposition of the Sermon on the Mount*, p. 122.
17. Thomas S. Kepler, *Jesus' Design for Living*, p. 12.
18. Hogg and Watson, *On the Sermon on the Mount*, pp. 15-16, 136-160.

this interpretation. Contrary to popular knowledge, the age of grace did not begin with the birth of Christ. The Bible is clear that the Lord ministered under the law of the Old Testament (Galatians 4:4; Romans 15:8). This sermon, being delivered within the context of the law, can hardly be applied in a primary sense to those living within the age of grace.

It must be concluded that because the context and setting of the discourse strongly oppose an ecclesiological interpretation of the Sermon on the Mount, some other approach must be found.

The Millennial or Kingdom Approach. The common view held by premillenarians is that which applies the Sermon on the Mount to the future earthly kingdom which the Lord announced as being at hand.

> In our exegesis of the three chapters, (which of necessity we have to condense considerably) we shall always in every part look upon the sermon on the mount as the proclamation of the King concerning the Kingdom. The Kingdom is not the church, nor is the state of the earth in righteousness, governed and possessed by the meek, brought about by the agency of the church. It is the millennial earth and the Kingdom to come, in which Jerusalem will be the city of a great King .... While we have in the Old Testament the outward manifestations of the Kingdom of the heavens as it will be set up in the earth in a future day, we have here the inner manifestation, the principles of it.[19]

Similar statements are made by Kelly,[20] Pettingill,[21] Chafer,[22] and most of the premillenarians. They support their conclusion mainly by pointing to the context of the sermon in which Christ is offering the kingdom to the Jews. The fact that the listeners were Jewish is also used as an indication that the sermon by interpretation belongs to the kingdom age.

> While it is true that *some* of the *people* heard "The Sermon on the Mount" (Matt. 7:28), we know that it was spoken directly to the disciples of our Lord (Matt. 5:1, 2). Now the disciples were believers on the Lord Jesus Christ, believers in Him as King and as the promised Messiah. But we must remember that the disciples

19. A. C. Gaebelein, *The Gospel of Matthew,* 1:10.
20. William Kelly, *Lectures on the Gospel of Matthew,* pp. 103-6.
21. William L. Pettingill, *Simple Studies in Matthew,* p. 58.
22. Lewis Sperry Chafer, "The Teachings of Christ Incarnate," *Bibliotheca Sacra* 108 (October 1951):410.

were *Jewish* believers, that they were living under Law, not under Grace.[23]

Further evidence is seen in the fact that the kingdom was postponed. Involved in this postponement is a delay in the application of the kingdom's constitution and rule of life, the Sermon on the Mount.[24]

But this view has some very serious difficulties. The greatest is seen in the many references throughout the discourse to conditions which are incongruous to the millennial kingdom. For instance, the disciples are to be reviled and persecuted for Christ's sake (5:11-12); wickedness must be prevalent since the disciples are considered to be the salt of the earth and the light of the world (5:13-16); they are to pray for the coming of the kingdom (6:10); they are warned concerning false prophets (7:15). This is indeed a strange portrayal of that kingdom which was pictured by the Old Testament prophets!

Those who take the millennial interpretation are cognizant of this difficulty and attempt to defend themselves accordingly. They contend that those things contained in the Sermon on the Mount which are out of harmony with the kingdom age belong to the tribulation period preceding it.

> During the years of the reign of the Antichrist, God's own upon the earth will be pleading the causes of these great pictures of promise, and with the coming of the Lord Jesus Christ to the earth these principles shall come into effect as a constitution that shall never need an amendment.[25]

Campbell concurs in writing that "this discourse will be pertinent when during the Tribulation period the gospel of the kingdom, heralding the coming King, will again be preached."[26]

In arguing that this non-kingdom material belongs in the tribulation period the proponents of a millennial interpretation destroy their own position. This is due to the simple fact that there is so much subject matter which, according to their position, would belong in the tribulation period. If the Sermon on the Mount is the constitution of the kingdom age, it certainly contains a great amount of extraneous material about the tribulation. The millennial view simply leaves too much un-

23. E. Schuyler English, *Studies in the Gospel According to Matthew*, p. 51.
24. Donald Keith Campbell, "Interpretation and Exposition of the Sermon on the Mount," (Doctor's dissertation, The Dallas Theological Seminary, 1953), p. 57.
25. Donald Grey Barnhouse, *His Own Received Him Not, But . . .*, p. 47.
26. Campbell, "Interpretation of Sermon on the Mount," p. 66.

explained relative to the non-kingdom material and its relevance to the sermon.

A second criticism is especially damaging to the view held by the proponents of the kingdom application of the discourse. They assert that the Sermon on the Mount contains the constitution of the kingdom. Those who desire to inherit the kingdom must live up to the standards presented in the discourse.

> The conclusion growing out of this analysis of this discourse is that it is the direct and official pronouncement of the King Himself of that manner of life which will be the ground for admission into the kingdom of heaven and the manner of life to be lived in the kingdom.[27]

But according to this view, no one would be able to enter the kingdom. If the ten commandments present an unattainable standard of life, how much more the Sermon on the Mount? It must be admitted that this interpretation presents problems which are insuperable and leaves one with the desire for a better approach to the discourse.

The Interim Approach. Those who come to the Sermon on the Mount with the interim interpretation see in it an ethic for the time preliminary to the establishment of the kingdom. This idea of a special ethic, called an *Interimsethik,* was popularized by Albert Schweitzer.[28] Although this writer certainly does not advocate the theological position held by Schweitzer, there is a great deal of merit seen in his approach to the sermon. There are several factors which are considered in this interpretation.

First of all, this approach utilizes the grammatico-historical method of interpretation. No other approach places the address in its historical setting as well as the interim interpretation. It is clear that the kingdom is in the process of being offered to Israel. John had announced the coming of the King with the words, "Repent, for the kingdom of heaven is at hand!" The King of that kingdom then comes on the scene, and after His baptism and temptation makes the identical announcement. Miracles of healing authenticate this message, and the crowds, in great anticipation of the kingdom, flock to Jesus. It is in the historical context of this anticipation on the part of the crowds and the Lord's disciples that the address is delivered.

---

27. Lewis Sperry Chafer, *Systematic Theology,* 5:111.
28. Albert Schweitzer, *The Quest of the Historical Jesus,* p. 354.

A second factor is to be noted. Not only are the crowds and disciples looking forward to the establishment of the kingdom, but the message of the sermon is also anticipatory. This aspect is indicated by *the attitude* of anticipation which pervades the entire discourse. It looks forward to a time when people shall enter the kingdom (5:20; 7:21). It speaks of future rewards (5:12, 19, 46; 6:1, 2, 4, 5, 6, 18). The sample prayer includes a request for the coming of the kingdom (6:10). The King will carry out a judgment preceding its establishment (7:19-23). A second indication of this fact is *the prediction* concerning persecution and false prophets (5:11-12; 7:15-18). This indicates that there is to be a time lapse preceding the establishment of the kingdom, but the kingdom is still near at hand. A third indication of the attitude of anticipation is the abundant use of the *future tense* (5:4-9, 19-20; 6:4, 6, 14, 15, 18, 33; 7:2, 7, 11, 16, 20, 21, 22). Thus it is seen that the sermon itself gives an attitude of anticipation because of its contents.

There is a third factor which this approach considers, and that is the matter of the addressees. The discourse is addressed primarily to disciples. This is clearly evident from the statement of the setting given in Matthew 5:1-2. There are also many indications given throughout the sermon which evidence this fact. The listeners are called the salt of the earth and the light of the world (5:13-16). They are to address God in prayer by "Our Father" (5:9). They are admonished with regard to righteousness which should characterize their lives (5:19-7:12). God is called their Father (5:16, 45, 48; 6:1, 4, 6, 8, 9, 14, 15, 18, 26, 32; 7:11, 21). The discourse is concerned with service and "doing" (5:10-12, 13-16, 19-20, 21-48; 6:1-18, 19-34; 7:1-12, 15-23, 24-27). Jesus is not said to be preaching, but rather is said to be teaching and giving them a body of instructions (5:2, 19: 7:29). Rewards play a prominent part in the sermon (5:12, 19, 46; 6:1, 2, 5, 16). No doubt many of these disciples had been disciples of the forerunner and now had left John to follow the King (John 3:22-30; 4:1-2). It may also be inferred that these people were those who had repented or had at least been baptized as a testimony to their repentance (John 3:22, 4:1-2). It is certain that the term *disciples* is not a reference to the twelve only, but rather includes a much larger group (John 6:66).

It must be remembered that those who were called disciples were not necessarily true ones. John 6:66 records, "As a result of this many of His disciples withdrew, and were not walking with Him any more." Judas Iscariot is the striking example of a false disciple. When Jesus addresses the disciples here, He is speaking to a large group who were following

Him; some were true disciples, others were not. This accounts for the warnings given in Matthew 5:20 and 7:21-29, as well as the invitation of Matthew 7:13.

In this sermon Jesus is looking at the entire life of a disciple, from its inception to its culmination. It is a life begun by repentance and thereafter marked by good fruit. This is why the Lord emphasizes the works which are to characterize His followers. Even the warning of Matthew 5:20 follows an admonition concerning the doing and teaching of the commandments, clearly the work of a disciple. The invitation to enter the narrow gate is associated with the narrow life that is to follow (Matthew 7:13-14). Likewise the warnings of Matthew 7:21-29 are concerned with righteous works performed from a pure heart. True disciples are those who have repented and produce good fruit.

In addition, it must be noted that while the address was directed to the disciples, the multitudes also heard it, at least the last portion of it. Matthew 5:1-2 says that when Jesus saw the multitude He left them and went into the mountain. It seems as though He sought to avoid the crowds. When His disciples came to Him, He began to teach them. Since the sermon ends with the crowds praising the sermon, it may be inferred that they followed the disciples and reached the spot where Jesus was teaching somewhat later than the disciples. Therefore, they heard only a final portion of the whole sermon. This may be a reason for the invitation of Matthew 7:13, a warning of judgment in Matthew 7:21-23, and the parable of the two foundations given in Matthew 7:24-27. It will be noted that all of these are in the last portion of the sermon, that section which the multitudes would hear (cf. John 6:1-5).

A fourth factor which is considered in this approach is the subject matter of the sermon. John had said, "Bring forth fruit in keeping with your repentance . . . . Every tree therefore that does not bear good fruit is cut down and thrown into the fire" (Matthew 3:8, 10). The Sermon on the Mount, as was indicated in the discussion of the addressees of the discourse, is concerned with service and doing. In other words, the discourse presents a description of the good fruit, the fruit of repentance. It is concerned with the life the disciples were to live in the light of the coming kingdom. It is very significant that the only thing the Lord is recorded to have repeated of John's preaching is the sentence, "Every tree that does not bear good fruit is cut down and thrown into the fire" (Matthew 7:19). The Lord continues, "So then, you will know them by their fruits." The King is concerned about His subjects being true ones

who bring forth fruit worthy of repentance. That fruit is described by
Him in this address.

Many have noted the parallels between the Sermon on the Mount and
the Epistle of James, but the most striking similarity is seen in the use
each makes of good works. James speaks of good works as being the
natural evidence of a genuine faith (James 2:18). Jesus shows that good
fruit is the result of a true repentance (Matthew 5:17-20; 7:16-23). Being
and doing are inseparable. Just as the epistles set forth unattainable
standards of the Christian life (1 Peter 1:15; 1 John 2:1; Colossians 3:13;
Philippians 3:12), so Christ sets forth the life which is to be the mark of
His disciples. It is unattainable, but nevertheless is to be attempted by
His disciples in dependence upon God.

To say that the primary purpose of the sermon is to bring conviction of
sin is to misinterpret the sermon. The epistles addressed to believers
have the same high standards, and no one would say they are to be used
primarily to convict an unbeliever. The sermon is *primarily* addressed to
disciples exhorting them to a righteous life in view of the coming
kingdom. Those who were not genuine disciples were warned concerning the danger of their hypocrisy and unbelief. They are enjoined to
enter the narrow gate and to walk the narrow way. This is included in the
discourse, but it is only the *secondary* application of the sermon.

1. The Setting, 5:1-5:2.

5:1-5:2. *And when He saw the multitudes, He went up on the
mountain; and after He sat down, His disciples came to Him. And
opening His mouth He began to teach them, saying,* ... The setting
of the discourse has been discussed at considerable length in the examination of the various approaches to the Sermon on the Mount. The King
has commenced His ministry and multitudes follow Him in anticipation
of the establishment of their promised kingdom. The immediate setting
of the sermon is presented in Matthew 4:23-5:2. The King, seeing the
great multitudes, goes up into the mountain. His disciples follow Him,
and sitting in the manner of rabbinical teachers, He begins to instruct
them.

2. The Subjects of the Kingdom, 5:3-5:16.

a. Their Character and Their Portion in the Kingdom, 5:3-5:12. The
first portion of this lecture is commonly known as the beatitudes
(Matthew 5:3-12). In reality it is a consideration of the character of the

subjects of the kingdom and their part in that kingdom. These brief statements demonstrate that the kingdom in view is an earthly one. Wilson, a secular writer whose works are in a popular vein, notices the earthly emphasis although he fails to understand the significance of the sermon.

> In the language of the Sermon on the Mount, there is what seems a strange vacillation between promising, on the one hand, to "the poor in spirit" "the kingdom of *heaven*," and, on the other, to "the meek" that "they shall inherit the *earth*."[29]

5:3-5:10. *"Blessed are the poor in spirit, for theirs is the kingdom of heaven.*

"Blessed are those who mourn, for they shall be comforted.

"Blessed are the gentle, for they shall inherit the earth.

"Blessed are those who hunger and thirst for righteousness, for they shall be satisfied.

"Blessed are the merciful, for they shall receive mercy.

"Blessed are the pure in heart, for they shall see God.

"Blessed are the peacemakers, for they shall be called sons of God.

"Blessed are those who have been persecuted for the sake of righteousness, for theirs is the kingdom of heaven."

The character of the ones who are to inherit the kingdom is described from eight perspectives, each marked by the pronouncement of blessing. The meaning of μακάριος, used here in the beatitudes, needs to be differentiated from εὐλογητός, since both words are translated into English by the word *blessed*. Εὐλογητός has the implication of praise, the noun often referring to a bestowed benefit. The adjective μακάριος refers to a happy condition.[30] In the Septuagint it represents אֶשֶׁר ׳ which is interjectional and means "Oh, the happiness of _____!"[31] Moreover, the happiness spoken of is a particular type of joy, a religious happiness as the result of divine favor.[32] The conjunction "for" (ὅτι) in each case introduces the cause or reason for calling the person who possesses the spiritual quality blessed.[33] The ὅτι in each occurrence here is to be translated "because" in order to bring out the proper sense.

29. Edmund Wilson, *The Scrolls from the Dead Sea*, p. 96.
30. W. E. Vine, *An Expository Dictionary of New Testament Words*, 1:133.
31. M'Neile, *St. Matthew*, p. 50.
32. C. G. Montefiore, *The Synoptic Gospels*, 2:30.
33. Archibald Thomas Robertson, *Word Pictures in the New Testament*, 1:40.

Those who are to inherit the kingdom are called blessed *now* because all these things shall be theirs. All of the verbs are future in verses three through ten except two.

> The tense of ἐστίν ["is"] must not be pressed: it is timeless, and in Aram. the connecting verb would not be used. As a potential right, the kingdom is theirs now and always: as an actual possession it is still future, as is shown by the verbs in *vv.* 4-9, which describe various aspects of its bliss.[34]

Montefiore also makes an excellent comment on the tense of the copulative.

> The present tense of the copula "is" must not be pressed. There would have been no verb in the original. *The future tense* in the next verses makes it certain that the future is also meant here. The Kingdom is the eschatological Kingdom: the Kingdom which is to come.[35]

Two general statements concerning the beatitudes can be made which pertain to Matthew's argument. First, it will be noted that each of the beatitudes is pronounced on the one who possesses a certain spiritual quality. This indicates that entrance into the kingdom is based on one's spiritual condition.

Second, the basis of each blessing in every case is a reference to some phase of the Jewish kingdom prophesied in the Old Testament. In verses three and ten the reason for the pronouncement of blessing is the fact that the kingdom of the heavens is their inheritance. This term has already been shown to refer to the prophesied earthly reign of the Messiah.[36] A pronouncement of blessing is given in verse four because those who mourned should be comforted. *Comforter* was a name for the Messiah who was to come to reign (Luke 2:25; Isaiah 40:1; 66:13).

In verse five the cause of blessing is the inheritance of the earth, clearly a reference to the millennial kingdom (Psalm 2:8-9; 37:11). The mention of being filled with righteousness in verse six looks back to the kingdom prophecies of Isaiah 45:8; 61:10-11; 62:1-2; Jeremiah 23:6; 33:14-16; and Daniel 9:24. In verse seven the reference to mercy is based on such millennial prophecies as Isaiah 49:10, 13; 54:8, 10; 60:10; and Zechariah 10:6. One of the great blessings of the kingdom is the privilege of seeing God. This blessing, mentioned in Matthew 5:8,

34. M'Neile, *St. Matthew,* p. 50. cf. Eduard Thurneysen, *The Sermon on the Mount,* p. 32.
35. Montefiore, *The Synoptic Gospels,* 2:33.
36. See above, pp. 61-68.

looks back to the prophecies of Psalm 24:3-4; Isaiah 33:17; 35:2; and 40:5. Finally, verse nine refers to being called sons of God and looks to the kingdom blessing spoken of in Hosea 1:10. Verses eight and nine form the climax to the beatitudes. Verse eight sets the keynote for the entire sermon. The pure *in heart* shall see God. At the same time Matthew 5:8-10 is climactic in the blessings it presents. Seeing God, being manifested as the sons of God, and possessing the kingdom are accounted among the highest possible blessings.

The ordinary Jew of Christ's day looked only at the physical benefits of the kingdom which he thought would naturally be bestowed on every Israelite. The amillennialist of today, on the other hand, denies the physical existence of the promised Jewish kingdom by "spiritualizing" its material blessings. The beatitudes of the King indicate that it is not an either-or proposition, but the kingdom includes *both* physical *and* spiritual blessings. A careful study of the beatitudes displays the fact that the kingdom is a physical earthly kingdom with spiritual blessings founded on divine principles.

5:11-5:12. *Blessed are you when men revile you, and persecute you, and say all kinds of evil against you falsely, on account of Me. Rejoice, and be glad, for your reward in heaven is great, for so they persecuted the prophets who were before you.* In presenting the blessings that would accrue to those spiritually qualified to obtain the kingdom, the King does not forget to mention persecution. This, of course, is in accordance with the prophecy of Daniel's seventieth week of years (Daniel 9:24-27). The nearness of the kingdom is indicated by the Lord's statement regarding the disciples; they were to be those who would endure this persecution.

A threefold revelation of the greatness of the person of Jesus is also given here. First, the persecution is to be on account of Him. If someone would be persecuted for merely being a disciple of Jesus, then Jesus must lay claim to some sort of greatness in the eyes of men. Second, the fact that endurance of unjust persecution for the sake of Jesus will bring reward in heaven emphasizes His greatness in the eyes of God. The reward in heaven does not simply mean that they shall receive their reward when they get to heaven. Rather, it means the reward is now prepared in heaven for a future time of manifestation.[37] The mention of rewards affirms that the message is being delivered primarily to the disciples.

37. Gustaf Dalman, *The Words of Jesus,* pp. 206-208.

A third indication of the greatness of Jesus is found in the comparison between the disciples and the prophets in verse twelve. The prophets spoke for *God* and were persecuted; the disciples represented *Jesus* and they were to suffer. The analogy is clear. Jesus, by making this parallel identifies Himself with God. These statements of Jesus mark the first recorded instance in Matthew of the claims of the Lord to Messiahship. The conclusion is to be inferred, but it is clear and evident nevertheless.

b. Their Calling and Their Position in the World, 5:13-5:16. You are the salt of the earth; but if the salt has become tasteless, how will it be made salty again? It is good for nothing any more, except to be thrown out and trampled under foot by men. You are the light of the world. A city set on a hill cannot be hidden. Nor do men light a lamp, and put it under a peck-measure, but on a lampstand; and it gives light to all who are in the house. Let your light shine before men in such a way that they may see your good works, and glorify your Father who is in heaven. The calling of the subjects of the kingdom as it relates to their position in the world is given in this passage. Looking at His disciples the Lord says, "You are the salt of the earth . . . You are the light of the world." In each statement "you" ($\dot{v}\mu\epsilon\hat{\imath}\varsigma$) is emphatic. "Salt was precious in Palestine for preserving food, and it is probably its preservative power which Jesus has chiefly in mind," comments Hunter.[38] However, the figure more probably is explained in Luke 14:34-35. From that parable it is evident salt was used for making soil more productive. So the disciples were left here to cause the world to bring forth fruit to God. If they failed in this, they were useless as far as God's purposes are concerned. As light they were to give open testimony and witness to the presence of Jesus the King. The purpose for giving the testimony is introduced by the conjunction "that" ($\ddot{o}\pi\omega\varsigma$) in verse sixteen. Their method was to be the manifestation of good works in such a way that it would bring men to glorify the heavenly Father of the disciples.

The "good works" ($\tau\grave{\alpha}$ $\kappa\alpha\lambda\grave{\alpha}$ $\ddot{\epsilon}\rho\gamma\alpha$) mentioned in verse sixteen set the tone for the rest of the sermon. These good works which are to be performed out of a pure heart as the hallmark of the disciples' lives are set forth in Matthew 5:17-7:12.

---

38. Hunter, *A Pattern for Life*, p. 44.

3. The Explanation of Genuine Righteousness, 5:17-7:12.

a. The Principle of Righteousness and the Law, 5:17-5:48. The King passes from the subject of the testimony of the disciples by good works to the principle of righteousness as declared by the law.

(1) The Confirmation of the Law, 5:17-5:20. As a bridge between the two topics of works and righteousness from the law, Jesus declares His relationship to the law. **5:17.** *Do not think that I came to abolish the Law or the Prophets; I did not come to abolish, but to fulfill.* This statement was needful as a result of the ministry which He had already carried on. He says in verse seventeen, "Do not think that I came to abolish the Law or the Prophets."

> Such an expression implies that He knew that there was danger of their thinking so, and possibly that some had actually said this of Him. The Pharisees would be sure to say it. He disregarded the oral tradition, which they held to be equal in authority to the written Law; and He interpreted the written Law according to its spirit, and not, as they did, according to the rigid letter. He did not keep the weekly fasts, nor observe the elaborated distinctions between clean and unclean, and He consorted with outcasts and sinners. He neglected the traditional modes of teaching, and preached in a way of His own. Above all, He spoke as if He Himself were an authority, independent of the Law. Even some of His own followers may have been perplexed, and have thought that He proposed to supersede the Law.[39]

Even as He defends His relationship to the law He makes a striking implication as to His person by using the verb "come" ($\check{\eta}\lambda\theta o\nu$) twice in verse seventeen. The "Coming One" ($\dot{o}$ $\dot{\epsilon}\rho\chi\acute{o}\mu\epsilon\nu o\varsigma$) is a Messianic term. The verb "to fulfill" ($\pi\lambda\eta\rho\acute{o}\omega$) has the same meaning here as it did in Matthew 2:15 where it means to establish completely.[40] Rather than destroying the law or the prophets He establishes them. This He did by (1) perfectly conforming His life to its high standards, and (2) retrieving its true meaning from the niceties of its rabbinic interpretations.

5:18-5:19. *For truly I say to you, until heaven and earth pass away, not the smallest letter or stroke shall pass away from the Law, until all is accomplished. Whoever then annuls one of the least of these commandments, and so teaches others, shall be called least in the kingdom of heaven; but whoever keeps and teaches them, he*

---

39. Plummer, *Exegetical Commentary,* p. 75.
40. Hermann Cremer, *Biblico-Theological Lexicon of New Testament Greek,* p. 500.

shall be called great in the kingdom of heaven. The Jews had graded the commandments according to what they thought were the most important (Matthew 22:36).[41] The Lord tells His disciples to be careful to observe every precept of the law, even the least one, and to teach men accordingly. By so doing Jesus again affirms His high regard for the law.

The verb "to annul" (λύω, 5:19) was often used by the scribes and Pharisees to refer to that which according to their interpretation of the law was permitted. There is great significance in this word.

> The relaxing of the Law involves a familiar figure, which compares the Law to a chain. The ordinary rabbinic word for "forbidden" is one which literally means "bound," and that which is permitted is "free."[42]

5:20. *For I say to you, that unless your righteousness surpasses that of the scribes and Pharisees, you shall not enter the kingdom of heaven.* These statements of the Lord are a direct accusation of the scribes and Pharisees, who by their traditions and interpretations had emptied the law of all its meaning (Matthew 15:3-6). The disciples were not to say and do that which the scribes and Pharisees practiced. The reason they were not to follow the scribes and Pharisees is given in verse twenty. The type of outward righteousness which was theirs had no internal basis and would not avail for entrance into the kingdom of heaven. This is the first time the Lord uses the clause, "I say to you" (λέγω ὑμῖν). By it He shows His authority as King to determine who will enter the kingdom.

(2) The Interpretation of the Law, 5:21-5:48. In contrast to the voiding of the law, which was done by the scribes and Pharisees, Jesus interprets the law, giving it its true significance and meaning. He presents six illustrations of the true morality of the Old Testament to show the righteousness which should characterize His disciples.

Each time an Old Testament commandment or precept is given the Lord marks His interpretation with the authoritative words, "But I say ..." (ἐγὼ δὲ λέγω). Many, because of this clause, see a contrast between the morality of Jesus and that of the Old Testament. This is not a necessary inference. It is better to take the conjunction "but" (δέ) as connective rather than adversative so that the verses would be translated, "You have heard that the ancients were told .. . *and* I say to

41. M'Neile, *St. Matthew,* p. 59.
42. Theodore H. Robinson, *The Gospel of Matthew,* p. 36.

you ..." Matthew very often uses δέ as a connective. The morality never changed; Jesus is giving the original meaning of the law.[43] That a contrast is being presented cannot be denied, but it is a contrast between the righteousness which was to be the characteristic of the King's subjects and the hypocritical goodness displayed by the scribes and Pharisees. The pronoun "I" (ἐγώ) is used not to mark a sharp differentiation between Jesus Christ and Moses, but between Jesus and the scribes and Pharisees.

The disciples had heard in their synagogues the exposition of the law and the prophets according to the rabbinical interpretation. In the typical explanation, conformity to the law was only an external matter. Jesus shows that obedience to the law involves the whole man, motives and all. To expect an inner conformity to the law is the teaching of the Old Testament. The tenth commandment (Exodus 20:17; Romans 7:7) intimates the inner character of the whole law. Such passages as Leviticus 19:17; Deuteronomy 6:5; Psalm 19:14; 139:22-24; Isaiah 29:13; Ezekiel 33:31; and Amos 5:21-27 all bear testimony to the same fact. This is the aim of the Lord's instruction of His disciples, that is, the indoctrination of genuine holiness.

*(a) The Law Regarding Murder, **5:21-5:26.** You have heard that the ancients were told, 'You shall not commit murder;' and 'Whoever commits murder shall be liable to the court;' but I say to you that everyone who is angry with his brother shall be guilty before the court; and whoever shall say to his brother, 'Raca,' shall be guilty before the supreme court; and whoever shall say, 'You fool,' shall be guilty enough to go into the hell of fire. If therefore you are presenting your offering at the altar, and there remember that your brother has something against you, leave your offering there before the altar and go your way, first be reconciled to your brother, and then come and present your offering. Make friends quickly with your opponent at law while you are with him on the way; in order that your opponent may not deliver you to the judge, and the judge to the officer, and you be thrown into prison. Truly I say to you, you shall not come out of there until you have paid up the last cent."* The true interpretation of the law is first exemplified by a discussion of the sixth commandment. The law said no murder; Jesus interprets it to mean no anger, associating the commandment of Exodus 20 with Leviticus

43. Wm. M. McPheeters, "Christ As an Interpreter of Scripture," *The Bible Student*, 1 (April 1900):223-229.

101

19:17. God desires inner conformity to the law as well as external obedience. The difficulties of verse twenty-two are not insuperable.

> The Rabbis say that murder is liable to judgment, but I say that anger, its equivalent, is liable to (divine) judgment. And (the Rabbis say that) abusive language such as *raka* is punishable by the local court, but I say that abusive language such as *more,* its equivalent, is punishable by the fire of Gehenna.[44]

(b) The Law Regarding Adultery, **5:27-5:30.** *You have heard that it was said, 'You shall not commit adultery;' but I say to you, that every one who looks on a woman to lust for her has committed adultery with her already in his heart. And if your right eye makes you stumble, tear it out, and throw it from you; for it is better for you that one of the parts of your body perish, than for your whole body to be thrown into hell. And if your right hand makes you stumble, cut it off, and throw it from you; for it is better for you that one of the parts of your body perish, than for your whole body to go into hell.* The commandment regarding adultery is used as a second illustration of true righteousness as it is outlined by the law. The law said, "You shall not commit adultery." The Lord's interpretation is, "Every one who looks on a woman to lust for her has committed adultery with her already in his heart." There follows an admonition regarding temptation. It is not to be taken literally because the tearing out of an eyeball or the severing of a hand or foot would not remove the cause of the offense. The warning is to make no provision for temptation; every occasion which may lead to sin is to be cut off.

(c) The Law Regarding Divorce, **5:31-5:32.** *And it was said, 'Whoever divorces his wife, let him give her a certificate of dismissal;' but I say to you that every one who divorces his wife, except for the cause of unchastity, makes her commit adultery; and whoever marries a divorced woman commits adultery.* The third illustration of the righteousness which is to characterize the disciples of Jesus concerns the matter of divorce. A considerable controversy was being waged in the Lord's day concerning the practice of divorce. Some were very strict and others were exceedingly lax in their interpretation of the divorce law of Deuteronomy 24:1. There were two main Jewish schools of thought concerning the basis of divorce.

44. M'Neile, *St. Matthew,* p. 62.

Shammei and his disciples took it to mean some grave offense like adultery. Hillel and his followers held that a man could divorce his wife for no more serious misdemeanour than 'letting his food burn.'[45]

In His interpretation Jesus shows that the only cause for divorce is fornication, which is actually the breaking of the marriage bond in a physical way, and remarriage on the part of the guilty party is morally wrong.

(d) The Law Regarding the Taking of an Oath, **5:33-5:37.** *Again, you have heard that the ancients were told, 'You shall not make false vows, but shall fulfill your vows to the Lord.' But I say to you, make no oath at all; either by heaven for it is the throne of God; or by the earth, for it is the footstool of His feet; or by Jerusalem, for it is the city of the great King. Nor shall you make an oath by your head, for you cannot make one hair white or black. But let your statement be 'Yes, yes' or 'No, no;' and anything beyond these is of evil.* The subject of taking oaths is next considered in the Lord's discourse as He unfolds the righteousness inherently present in the law and the prophets. The adverb "again" ($\pi \acute{\alpha} \lambda \iota \nu$) marks a division in the subjects, this being the fourth of six which He discusses relative to genuine righteousness. The Jewish concept of taking oaths was based on a false interpretation of Leviticus 19:12, "You shall not swear falsely by My name." They thought that any oath, therefore, which did not include the name of God was not binding. Sometimes these oaths even came to be used as a means of deceit.[46] The King places His finger on the inconsistency of their reasoning by associating all of their oaths with the person and purpose of God. His disciples were to be characterized by simple, unadorned truth at all times. For them there was to be no external guarantee of truthfulness. The reason: the abundant use of oaths is necessary because of the evil one, and they were not to be identified with him or his work. The disciples by their truthfulness are to bear testimony of their relationship to the heavenly Father.

(e) The Law Regarding Retaliation, **5:38-5:42.** *You have heard that it was said, 'An eye for an eye, and a tooth for a tooth.' But I say to*

---

45. Hunter, *A Pattern for Life,* p. 56.
46. Hogg and Watson, *On the Sermon on the Mount,* p. 54.

you, do not resist him who is evil; but whoever slaps you on your right cheek, turn to him the other also. And if any one wants to sue you, and take your shirt, let him have your coat also. And whoever shall force you to go one mile, go with him two. Give to him who asks of you, and do not turn away from him who wants to borrow from you. The fifth interpretation of righteousness is given in connection with the Old Testament concept of retaliation. The Lord first alludes to the Old Testament phrases, "eye for an eye," and "tooth for a tooth" (Exodus 21:22-25; Leviticus 24:20; Deuteronomy 19:18-21). It cannot be doubted that the law made complete provision for absolute vengeance by its law of retaliation *(lex talionis)*. However, this provision was modified in two ways. First, the retaliation generally was not to be performed without the authority of a legal court (Exodus 21:22; Numbers 35:9-34). Second, while the letter of the law made provision for absolute retaliation, the spirit of the law and the Old Testament show a more excellent way. Such passages as Leviticus 19:17-18; Deuteronomy 32:35; Psalm 94:1; Proverbs 20:22; and Proverbs 24:29 show that a person was to leave the matter of vengeance to the Lord.

It is in the light of the *spirit* of the law that the Lord presents His interpretation; it is not a new meaning, but it is a higher meaning. There is evidence that the more discerning Jews had already seen this meaning in relationship to the law's provision for retaliation.[47] Jesus said that no retaliation was to be made. Rather, the injured party is to be gracious and beneficent to the one who has done the wrong. Four illustrations are given of this principle. It must be remembered that *personal* wrongs are in view and not social and governmental crimes.

> ... Jesus is here talking to his disciples, and speaking of personal relations: he is not laying down moral directives for states and nations, and such issues as the work of police or the question of a defensive war are simply not in his mind.[48]

(f) The Law Regarding Love, 5:43-5:48. The sixth illustration of the true interpretation of the law is given in Matthew 5:43-48 in relationship to the Old Testament concept of love to one's neighbor. **5:43-5:44.** *You have heard that it was said, 'You shall love your neighbor, and hate your enemy.' But I say to you, love your enemies, and pray for those who persecute you;* The command, recorded in Leviticus 19:18, is quoted by the Lord. However, the phrase *hate your enemies* is

---

47. Plummer, *Exegetical Commentary,* p. 85.
48. Hunter, *A Pattern for Life,* p. 57-58.

nowhere found in the Hebrew Scriptures. The clause is only an inference and an invention of the rabbis spoken as their exposition of the law in their synagogues.[49] By their interpretation the scribes and Pharisees had robbed the Old Testament concept of love of all of its meaning. Exodus 23:4-5 indicates that kindness is to be extended toward one's enemies. This, the true interpretation, is the one the Lord gives.

5:45. *in order that you may be sons of your Father who is in heaven; for He causes His sun to rise on the evil and the good, and sends rain on the righteous and the unrighteous.* Verse forty-five poses a problem. Is one to become a son of God by good works? Montefiore in dealing with this verse comments, "A nobler ὅπως [in order that] was never penned. Not to gain reward are the disciples to act thus, but that, through such action, they may become like unto God."[50] Plummer says, "They *show* their parentage by their moral resemblance to the God who is Love ..."[51] That this is the correct meaning is affirmed by the sentence in which it is found; God is *already* their heavenly Father. This use of the verb "to be" (γίνομαι) is not unique; it is used in the same sense in Matthew 10:16; 24:44; Luke 6:36; 12:40; and John 20:27.

5:46-5:48. *For if you love those who love you, what reward have you? Do not even the tax gatherers do the same? And if you greet your brothers only, what do you do more than others? Do not even the Gentiles do the same? Therefore you are to be perfect, as your heavenly Father is perfect.* The Lord continues with an admonition to His disciples to mold their lives after this true meaning of love. He concludes, "Therefore you are to be perfect, as your heavenly Father is perfect." No doubt this is an allusion to Leviticus 19:2 and Deuteronomy 18:13. While it is true that the adjective "perfect" (τέλειος) can mean maturity, it is certain that here it has the idea of complete goodness. The concept of completeness is inherent in the Hebrew word which is used in these two Old Testament passages. The aim of the disciples' lives is the molding of their lives after the person of their heavenly Father. This is the climax to and the standard of the Old Testament concept of righteousness.

To this point the King has pronounced those who were to inherit the kingdom of God blessed because of their spiritual character. He has also

---

49. James Morison, *A Practical Commentary on the Gospel According to St. Matthew,* p. 83.

50. Montefiore, *The Synoptic Gospels,* 2:81.

51. Plummer, *Exegetical Commentary,* p. 88.

established His relationship to the law and the prophets, (1) by refuting the righteousness practiced and advocated by the scribes and Pharisees, and (2) by showing the true morality which was taught by their Scriptures.

b. The Practice of Righteousness, 6:1-6:18. Chapter six of Matthew records a change of emphasis; the King now goes on to show how true righteousness is performed. He has dealt with the Old Testament precept of righteousness; now the King discusses its practice. Both need to be discussed. This is evident from Matthew 5:19 where the Lord says greatness in the kingdom is dependent on both rightly *doing* and correctly *teaching* the commandments. The Lord follows this order since doctrine always forms the foundation for practice.

The practice of righteousness is presented in two phases. In Matthew 6:1 the maxim or principle of performing righteous acts is given and the motives of worship are set forth in Matthew 6:2-18.

(1) The Maxim, **6:1.** *Beware of practicing your righteousness before men to be noticed by them; otherwise you have no reward with your Father who is in heaven.* The principle is simple. Righteous acts are not to be performed for the praise of men. The King is emphasizing the statement of Matthew 5:16 from a different view. The disciples are to live in such a way that men will glorify God on account of their good works. There are two types of rewards, depending on the motive for which a good work was performed. If a righteous act was done for men's glory, the one who did it has already received his reward in the form of praise from men. If it was performed in simple devotion to God, the act would be rewarded by God Himself. M'Neile succinctly writes, "... good deeds cannot merit more than one reward; to gain it from men is to lose it from God."[52] The fact that rewards are in view indicates that the discourse is still being addressed to disciples.

(2) The Motives for Good Deeds, 6:2-6:18. Each of the three illustrations of the improper and proper motives in worship is introduced, and thus marked off, by the temporal particle "when" (ὅταν) Matthew 6:2, 5, 16). Each illustration also contains the authoritative "Truly I say to you ..." (ἀμὴν λέγω ὑμῖν). Just as the King positively declares the principle of righteousness, so He authoritatively sets forth the motives of righteous living.

---

52. M'Neile, *St. Matthew,* p. 73; cf. I Corinthians 3:12-15.

The three illustrations—almsgiving, prayer, and fasting—are ideal examples of Jewish worship, for each was highly esteemed as an act of devotion. But even so, these, according to the King, could be performed incorrectly. The improper spring of action is that which motivates hypocrites (Matthew 6:2, 5, 16; 7:5). The hypocrites are not identified here, but Matthew 23 clearly indicates that they are the scribes and Pharisees (Matthew 23:13, 14, 15, 23, 25, 27, 29). A clearer illustration of a facet of Matthew's style can hardly be found. First he intimates a fact, then he builds on it, and finally he establishes it. Here the intimation concerns the hypocrisy of the scribes and Pharisees.

(a) The Rewards for Giving, **6:2-6:4.** **When therefore you give alms, do not sound a trumpet before you, as the hypocrites do in the synagogues and in the streets, that they may be honored by men. Truly I say to you, they have their reward in full. But when you give alms, do not let your left hand know what your right hand is doing; that your alms may be in secret; and your Father who sees in secret will repay you.** Almsgiving is the first illustration used by the Lord. The giving of alms is to be done in absolute secrecy where it will be seen by God and consequently rewarded.

(b) The Rewards for Praying, 6:5-6:15. The same principle applies to prayer, the second illustration. **6:5-6:15.** **And when you pray, you are not to be as the hypocrites; for they love to stand and pray in the synagogues and on the street corners, in order to be seen by men. Truly I say to you, they have their reward in full. But you, when you pray, go into your inner room, and when you have shut your door, pray to your Father who is in secret, and your Father who sees in secret will repay you. And when you are praying, do not use meaningless repetition, as the Gentiles do, for they suppose that they will be heard for their many words. Therefore do not be like them; for your Father knows what you need, before you ask Him.** The sample prayer is significant to Matthew's argument because of the peculiar character of its petitions. It may be that Matthew included this prayer because it is so replete with kingdom concepts.

The prayer consists of six requests, all of which have some connection with the promised kingdom. The first three are petitions for the coming of the kingdom, and the last three are appeals in the light of the coming of the kingdom. All are interim requests. In each petition urgency is denoted by the use of the aorist imperative. This is the prayer of a sincere disciple beseeching God to bring the kingdom.

6:9. Pray, then, in this way: 'Our Father who art in heaven, Hallowed be Thy name.' The first request is, "Hallowed be Thy name." "To 'hallow' is to treat as holy, to honour, to revere."[53] In the Bible "name" ($\check{o}\nu o\mu\alpha$) refers to the nature or person of an individual. The request, then, is for the revering of God's person by mankind, which will occur only with the coming of the kingdom. In the Old Testament Scriptures the Jewish kingdom and the sanctifying of God's name were closely associated (Isaiah 29:23; Ezekiel 36:23).

> In one respect His name is profaned when His people are ill-treated. The sin of the nation which brought about the captivity had caused a profanation of the Name, Is. 43:25; 48:11; Ezk. 36:20-23. By their restoration His name was to be sanctified. But this sanctification was only a foreshadowing of a still future consummation. Only when the 'kingdom' came would God's name be wholly sanctified in the final redemption of His people from reproach.[54]

Because of the theological context in which this sample prayer was given there can be no doubt that the first request looks to the time when all nations shall worship God in the millennial age.

6:10a. 'Thy kingdom come.' The second request, "[Let] Thy kingdom come," is clearly eschatological. Millar Burrows calls attention to the fact that the New Testament Scriptures and all of its concepts must be approached with all possible objectivity. Burrows, who by no means can be called a premillennialist, goes on to criticize those who with Platonic concepts subjectively spiritualize the future aspect of the kingdom of God in Christ's preaching. John Marsh, who wrote a book entitled *The Fulness of Time* (1952), is the special object of Burrow's attack.

> The conception of time determines the interpretation of eschatology. Marsh recognizes, for example, the doctrine of the coming age in the NT, but he repeatedly affirms that "the two ages were not consecutive" (pp. 32, 140); they were related not by succession but by fulfillment (p. 141). Now surely any conception of fulfillment which divorces it from temporal succession is far from being biblical. Aside from the fulfillment of prophecy, fulfillment in the Bible, OT and NT alike, means filling up an appointed measure of time. Biblical Hebrew does not speak of fulfilling time, but of fulfilling days or years. The Hebrew words for "time" indicate

53. Hunter, *A Pattern for Life*, p. 72.
54. Willoughby C. Allen, *A Critical and Exegetical Commentary on the Gospel According to S. Matthew*, p. 58.

ordinarily a point rather than an extended period of time. The Aramaic of Daniel, however, speaks of "seven times" (4:16, 25, 32) and of "a time, two times, and half a time" (7:25); this last expression, in fact, occurs in Dan. 12:7 in Hebrew. When Marsh contrasts succession and fulfillment, he introduces a decidedly unbiblical distinction.

My particular bone of contention with him, however, is that he carries back his non-temporal eschatology into the gospel as proclaimed by Jesus. 'Jesus had often made it plain, from the start of his ministry,' he said, 'that the kingdom of God, like the Son of man, had already come. Therefore it cannot now come for the first time, nor is it ever said that the kingdom will come again" (p. 131).

If that is so, I submit, it is passing strange that Jesus told his disciples to pray, 'Thy kingdom come.' Those who maintain that for Jesus himself the kingdom of God had already come in his own person and ministry inevitably treat this second petition of the Lord's prayer in a rather cavalier fashion. It must be interpreted, they say, in line with other sayings of Jesus. Why? And what other sayings? When all the evidence in the sayings of Jesus for 'realized eschatology' is thoroughly tested, it boils down to the ἔφθασεν ἐφ' ὑμᾶς ['has come upon you'] of Matt. 12:28 and Luke 11:20. Why should that determine the interpretation of Matt. 6:10 and Luke 11:2? Why should a difficult, obscure saying establish the meaning of one that is clear and unambiguous? Why not interpret the ἔφθασεν ['has come,' 12:28] by the ἐλθάτω ['come,' 6:10]; or rather, since neither can be eliminated on valid critical grounds, why not seek an interpretation that does equal justice to both?

John Marsh does not ignore this second petition of the Lord's Prayer, but he reads into it a meaning which excludes its plain, natural implication. He says that it 'was not a superfluity after the kingly rule had been wholly present in Christ's own life, for our prayer must always be that the same obedience that our Lord manifested might be found also in us and in every child of man' (p. 165). In effect this identifies the coming of the kingdom with the individual's taking upon himself the yoke of the kingdom of heaven; it is no longer God's act but man's. Marsh recognizes a future phase, so to speak, of the kingdom, but he insists that the kingdom of God is 'not the end-term of an historical series, nor yet the *absolutely other* realm that will supervene upon the destruction of the present order,' for 'since the kingdom of God was fulfilled in Christ, then none other than that same kingdom can come at the end of history' (pp. 165 f.). However sound that may or may not be as theology, or as an interpretation of NT theology in general, it cannot be derived from the recorded sayings of Jesus.[55]

55. Millar Burrows, "Thy Kingdom Come," *Journal of Biblical Literature* 74 (January 1955):4-5.

Burrows does have an interpretation of this passage.

> What does this mean? It can only mean one thing. Jesus' concep-
> tion of God's kingdom is not simply that of the universal
> sovereignty of God, which may or may not be accepted by men but
> is always there. That is the basis of his conception, but he com-
> bines with it the eschatological idea of the kingdom which is still to
> come. In other words, what Jesus means by the kingdom of God
> includes what the rabbinic literature calls the coming age.[56]

6:10b. *'Thy will be done, on earth as it is in heaven.'* The third
request is simply an amplification of the two former requests. This
clause, an appeal for God's sovereignty to be absolutely manifested on
earth, is the key to the interpretation of the sample prayer.

> Although the Kingdom of God was already ruling over all, there
> was nevertheless difference between the exercise of its rule 'in
> heaven' and 'on earth.' This difference arises out of the fact that
> rebellion and sin exist upon the earth, sin which is to be dealt with
> in a way not known in any other spot in the universe, not even
> among the angels which sinned. It is here that the great purpose of
> what I have named the Mediatorial Kingdom appears: On the basis
> of mediatorial redemption it must 'come' to put down at last all
> rebellion with its evil results, thus finally bringing the Kingdom
> and will of God *on* earth as it is in heaven.[57]

6:11. *'Give us this day our daily bread.'* The fourth request introduces the concern the King's disciples were to have for physical needs
in the time preceding the coming of the kingdom. "This day" ($\sigma\eta\mu\epsilon$-
$\rho o\nu$) indicates that the interim preceding the establishment of the kingdom is in view. It could hardly refer to the kingdom age, since there will
be no shortage of food at that time (Zechariah 8:12; Amos 9:13; Isaiah
65:21-22).[58]

**6:12. *'And forgive us our debts, as we also have forgiven our
debtors.'*** The fifth request concerns the spiritual desires of the disci-
ples. The word used for sin here is $\delta\phi\epsilon\iota\lambda\eta\mu\alpha$ which means debt and is
used here only in the sense of a spiritual debt. "The thought of sins ...
as debts was thoroughly Jewish ...."[59]

---

56. *Ibid.*, p. 8.

57. Alva J. McClain, *The Greatness of the Kingdom*, p. 35.

58. For a presentation of the view that the kingdom banquet is being requested here see T.
Herbert Bindley, "Eschatology in the Lord's Prayer," *The Expositor* 17 (October
1919):317-318.

59. M'Neile, *St. Matthew*, p. 80.

The Jewish concept of sin is indicative of the Jewish aspect of Matthew's Gospel and this prayer especially. God forgives their sins as they forgive others. This idea is explained further in verses fourteen and fifteen and is well illustrated in Matthew 18:21-35. Judicial forgiveness is not in view (Acts 10:43) but fellowship (1 John 1:5-9). It is impossible for one to be in fellowship with God as long as he harbors ill will in his heart. The disciples were to be always spiritually prepared for the coming of the kingdom.

6:13-6:15. *'And do not lead us into temptation, but deliver us from evil. (For Thine is the kingdom, and the power, and the glory, forever. Amen).' For if you forgive men for their transgressions, your heavenly Father will also forgive you. But if you do not forgive men, then your Father will not forgive your transgressions.* A sixth request is for protection in the light of the trial which is to precede the establishment of the kingdom. Robinson recognizes the possibility of this meaning and refers to the distress of Revelation 7:14.[60] M'Neile states that "temptation" ($\pi\epsilon\iota\rho\alpha\sigma\mu\acute{o}s$) " . . . is primarily the fiery trial which is about to usher in the End; cf. Apoc. iii.10, and 2Pet. ii.9 which is possibly an echo of this and the following clause."[61] The request for deliverance from "evil" ($\tau o\tilde{v}$ $\pi o\nu\eta\rho o\tilde{v}$) is also a reference to the time of tribulation preceding the establishment of the kingdom.

> Connected with this fiery trial of faith is a Spirit of apostasy and hostility to God, the $\pi o\nu\eta\rho\acute{o}s$, the Evil One, who is viewed under various aspects and guises, but whose business it is to test the faith of the elect. 'False Christs and false prophets shall arise, and shall shew great signs and wonders, so as to lead astray if possible even the elect' (Matt. xxiv.24). To St. Paul that spirit appeared as 'the man of lawlessness' (2 Thess. ii.3-12); to St. John as 'many antichrists, whereby ye know that it is the last hour' (1 John ii.18). The same idea occurred or was repeated in the *Sibylline Oracles* iii.64-71: 'Now shall Beliar return, and he shall move the high mountains, still the sea, make the great blazing sun and the bright moon stand still, shall raise the dead, and do many signs among men . . . . He leads many astray, and shall deceive many faithful and elect of the Hebrews, and lawless men besides who have never yet harkened to God's word.'
>
> May we not here again find in the Lord's Prayer a reference to this anticipation of times of trial? 'Bring us not unto the trial, but deliver us from the Evil one.'[62]

60. Robinson, *The Gospel of Matthew,* p. 52.
61. M'Neile, *St. Matthew,* p. 81.
62. Bindley, "Eschatology in the Lord's Prayer," pp. 319-320.

The sample prayer, it can be concluded, is given in the context of the coming kingdom. The first three requests are petitions for the coming of the kingdom. The last three are for the needs of the disciples in the interim preceding the establishment of the kingdom.

(c) The Rewards for Fasting, **6:16-6:18.** *And whenever you fast, do not put on a gloomy face as the hypocrites do; for they neglect their appearance in order to be seen fasting by men. Truly I say to you, they have their reward in full. But you, when you fast, anoint your head, and wash your face; so that you may not be seen fasting by men, but by your Father who is in secret; and your Father who sees in secret will repay you.* Matthew 6:16-18 contains the third illustration of the practice of false and true righteousness in worship. Fasting is to be carried on in secret as a matter between the disciple and God. Again there is a veiled stab at the hypocrisy of the scribes and the Pharisees.

c. The Perspectives of Righteousness, 6:19-7:12. Following the three illustrations of righteous acts of worship, the King discusses three prohibitions for the daily walk of the disciples (Matthew 6:19-7:6). These prohibitions are given in directing the disciples in their relationship to God and wealth (Matthew 6:19-34), to brethren (Matthew 7:1-5), and to unbelievers (Matthew 7:6).

(1) With Respect to Wealth, **6:19-6:34.** *Do not lay up for yourselves treasures upon earth, where moth and rust destroy, and where thieves break in and steal; but lay up for yourselves treasures in heaven, where neither moth nor rust destroys, and where thieves do not break in or steal; for where your treasure is, there will your heart be also. The lamp of the body is the eye; if therefore your eye is clear, your whole body will be full of light. But if your eye is bad, your whole body will be full of darkness. If therefore the light that is in you is darkness, how great is the darkness! No one can serve two masters; for either he will hate the one and love the other, or he will hold to one and despise the other. You cannot serve God and Mammon. For this reason I say to you, do not be anxious for your life, as to what you shall eat, or what you shall drink; nor for your body, as to what you shall put on. Is not life more than food, and the body than clothing? Look at the birds of the air, that they do not sow, neither do they reap, nor gather into barns; and yet your heavenly Father feeds them. Are you not worth much more than they? And which of you by being anxious can add a single cubit to his life's*

span? And why are you anxious about clothing? Observe how the lilies of the field grow; they do not toil nor do they spin, yet I say to you that even Solomon in all his glory did not clothe himself like one of these. But if God so arrays the grass of the field, which is alive today and tomorrow is thrown into the furnace, will He not much more do so for you, O men of little faith? Do not be anxious then, saying, 'What shall we eat?' or 'What shall we drink?' or, 'With what shall we clothe ourselves?' For all these things the Gentiles eagerly seek; for your heavenly Father knows that you need all these things. But seek first His kingdom, and His righteousness; and all these things shall be added to you. Therefore do not be anxious for tomorrow; for tomorrow will care for itself. Each day has enough trouble of its own. Their relationship to God is to be marked by singlehearted devotion which will be manifested even in their attitude toward treasures. They are to stop laying up (the negative particle μή, with the present imperative) treasures for themselves on earth. After giving two illustrations of the character of devotion—the single eye and the nature of slavery—the King makes the application. Their heavenly Father will take care of them. The primary work of the subjects of the kingdom in their relationship to God is to give implicit, complete, and wholehearted devotion to Him. This dedication will be marked by freedom from care, for God will sustain them.

(2) With Respect to Brethren, 7:1-7:5. Do not judge lest you be judged yourselves. For in the way you judge, you will be judged; and by your standard of measure, it shall be measured to you. And why do you look at the speck in your brother's eye, but do not notice the log that is in your own eye? Or how can you say to your brother, 'Let me take the speck out of your eye,' and behold, the log is in your own eye? You hypocrite, first take the log out of your own eye; and then you will see clearly enough to take the speck out of your brother's eye. The second relationship of the disciples of Jesus is their affiliation with one another. The prohibition is simple: stop judging (μή with the present imperative). The disciples of the King are to be critical of self but not of their brethren. The group is to be noted for their bond of unity, which is indicated by a lack of criticism. This is fitting, since the kingdom is characterized by peace. (Isaiah 9:7).

(3) With Respect to the Spiritually Hostile, 7:6. Do not give what is holy to dogs, and do not throw your pearls before swine, lest they trample them under their feet, and turn and tear you to pieces. In

their relationships with unbelievers the disciples are to use discretion in giving out the truth (Proverbs 9:7, 8; 23:9). "Economy must be exercised in communication of religious truth."[63] The term "dogs" (κύων) is used in the metaphorical sense of reproach in this passage. [64] It no doubt refers to those who did not believe in the coming of the kingdom in the person and work of Jesus. "Mire" (βόρβορος) is used in 2 Peter 2:22 to describe an unbeliever, as "swine" (χοῖρος) is employed here in Matthew 7:6. In giving this word of admonition and warning, Jesus gives the first intimation of His ultimate rejection. The disciples were to preach the gospel of the nearness of the kingdom, but the deeper truths of the kingdom were to be reserved only for receptive hearts (Matthew 11:25-26; 13:10-17; 16:20; 17:9).

The body of the message ends with these practical instructions. The King has shown His disciples the principle of the righteous life. Unlike the dead hypocritical righteousness which characterized the scribes and Pharisees, it is an inner life which is the result of one's relationship to God. This is the righteousness which is to be the mark of His disciples. Entrance into the kingdom is impossible without it.

(4) With Respect to God, 7:7-7:12.

7:7-7:11. *Ask, and it shall be given to you; seek, and you shall find; knock, and it shall be opened to you. For every one who asks receives; and he who seeks finds; and to him who knocks it shall be opened. Or what man is there among you, when his son shall ask him for a loaf, will give him a stone? Or if he shall ask for a fish, he will not give him a snake, will he? If you then, being evil, know how to give good gifts to your children, how much more shall your Father who is in heaven give what is good to those who ask Him!* One can easily visualize the growing audience as the King ministers the truth to His disciples. Having completed the instruction of His disciples, He then turns to the multitudes and speaks about the perspective of righteousness with respect to God. There can be no doubt, however, that the remainder of the sermon is also addressed to the disciples. He first invites them to pray (Matthew 7:7-11). The three verbs—"to ask, to seek, and to knock" (αἰτεῖτε, ζητεῖτε, and κρούετε)—are all in the present tense. The "good things" (ἀγαθά, 7:11), of the kingdom were near at hand. By consistent and persevering prayer from righteous hearts

---

63. W. Graham Scroggie, *A Guide to the Gospels*, p. 281.
64. James Hope Moulton and George Milligan, *The Vocabulary of the Greek Testament*, p. 366.

the good things of the kingdom would be theirs. The future tenses give assurance that what they desired from their heavenly Father would come to be.

It is interesting to note the Lord's use of *Father* in this Gospel. He says "my Father" (Matthew 7:21; 10:32, 33; 11:27, *et al.*) and "your Father" (Matthew 5:16, 45, 48; 6:1, 14, 15, 26, *et al.*, but never does the Lord associate Himself with others in praying or saying "our Father."[65] Thus the King is careful to maintain the dignity of His person.

7:12. *Therefore whatever you want others to do for you, do so for them; for this is the Law and the Prophets.* The well-known "golden rule" follows in verse twelve as the formal conclusion to the discourse. This concept was prevalent in seed form in the Old Testament (Leviticus 19:18; Exodus 23:4; Deuteronomy 15:7-8; Proverbs 24:17; 25:21). By giving heed to this command, the righteousness of the law and the prophets would be fulfilled. This is a fitting conclusion in that the fulfilling of the law and the prophets looks back to Matthew 5:17. There the King declares His ministry of fulfilling the Old Testament Scriptures.

4. The Warnings of the King, 7:13-7:27

a. Regarding the Narrow Gate, **7:13-7:14.** *Enter by the narrow gate; for the gate is wide, and the way is broad that leads to destruction, and many are those who enter by it. For the gate is small, and the way is narrow that leads to life, and few are those who find it.* After the King has asked the multitudes and the disciples to entreat God in prayer, He bids them to enter into the way which leads to life. It must be remembered that the Old Testament concept of eternal life was an endless life on earth. Even resurrected saints hoped for an earthly eternal life (Genesis 13:15; 49:29; 50:24-25; Deuteronomy 30:15, 19-20; Job 19:25; Proverbs 11:31; Isaiah 65:17; Daniel 11:45-12:3; Hebrews 11:9-16, 22, 39-40). When therefore the King spoke of the way which led to life, the audience would immediately think of the everlasting life which would be characteristic of the kingdom age.

It is interesting to note the method the King uses here. First He extends an invitation to enter the narrow gate. Then He shows His listeners that the gate one has entered is indicated by his present course of life. The two occurrences of the conjunction "for" (ὅτι) in verses thirteen and fourteen indicate that the gate and the way are closely

65. Plummer, *Exegetical Commentary*, p. 74.

associated. Just as a tree is known by its fruit, so the gate is known by the way.

The two ways would be compared to the two forms of righteousness which He has been contrasting throughout the discourse. Repentance is the narrow gate through which Christ invited His audience to enter. The narrow way represents the restrictions laid upon one who walks in the way of true righteousness which the King has just outlined. The broad way is the natural walk of all flesh, characterized oftentimes by Pharisaic hypocrisy and outward righteousness.

Even in this passage there is an emphasis on discipleship. This is seen in the emphasis on the way as well as the gate. *Gate* is mentioned for the benefit of those who were not true followers; *way* is mentioned as a definition of the life of the disciples of Jesus. This is why Matthew uses the word "gate" (πύλη) while Luke employs the word "door" (θύρα, Luke 13:24). Luke is concerned primarily with salvation. Here the King desires subjects for His kingdom, so He uses a word which implies a path is to be followed after entrance into life.

The complacency of the audience is displayed by Matthew's use of the word "find" (εὑρίσκω) in verse fourteen. Only a few were finding the way to kingdom life. They had only to seek to find (Matthew 7:7), but they would not bother. Thus Matthew gives a subtle hint as to the lethargic spiritual condition of Israel while the kingdom was near at hand.

b. Regarding False Prophets, 7:15-7:20. Beware of the false prophets, who come to you in sheep's clothing, but inwardly are ravenous wolves. You will know them by their fruits. Grapes are not gathered from thornbushes, nor figs from thistles, are they? Even so every good tree bears good fruit; but the rotten tree bears bad fruit. A good tree cannot produce bad fruit, nor can a rotten tree produce good fruit. Every tree that does not bear good fruit is cut down, and thrown into the fire. So then, you will know them by their fruits. Following the invitation of the Lord to entreat God for the good things of the kingdom and to enter into its life by spiritual preparation, He gives a warning concerning false prophets. In attempting to find the narrow gate the listeners were to be on their guard against false teachers. The instructions of the scribes and Pharisees were restrictive, but they failed to point out the road leading to life. A teacher is known by his fruit, for his doctrine and/or his practice bears testimony to his character. The King has indicated that true righteousness involves the

116

inner man; therefore He uses ἀγαθός in referring to the "good" fruit and σαπρός in referring to the "bad." The final inference is given in verse twenty, "You will know them by their fruits." The plural *fruits* seems to show that both doctrine and works are in view.

   c. Regarding False Profession, 7:21-7:27.

   7:21-7:23. *Not everyone who says to Me, 'Lord, Lord, will enter the Kingdom of Heaven; but he who does the will of My Father, who is in heaven. Many will say to Me on that day, 'Lord, Lord, did we not prophesy in Your name, and in Your name cast out demons, and in Your name perform many miracles? And then I will declare to them, 'I never knew you; depart from Me, you who practice lawlessness.'* The two verbs in the future tense in verses twenty-one and twenty-two indicate two aspects of the kingdom. The verb "will enter" (εἰσελεύσεται) shows that the kingdom of the heavens is not yet present. Entrance is still future. The verb "will say" (ἐροῦσιν) indicates that judgment shall precede the establishment of the kingdom. However, the outstanding feature of verse twenty-one is found in the claims of the Lord. He shows that entrance into the kingdom is contingent upon one's relationship to Him. "Not every one who says to Me, 'Lord, Lord,' will enter the kingdom of the heaven." The words "not every one" (οὐ πᾶς) infer that some who call Jesus "Lord" would not enter (Matthew 7:23).[66]

   Verse twenty-two indicates further that Jesus will be judge in the judgment preceding the kingdom. "Many will say *to me*." No one could miss the claim of this statement. The King presents Himself as Savior and Judge. This will all take place "in that day," which is almost a technical term for the Messianic age (Isaiah 2:11, 17; 4:2, 10:20; Jeremiah 49:22; Zechariah 14:6, 20, 21). Those who shall fail in the day of judgment are called workers of lawlessness. The word "lawlessness" (ἀνομία) fits well into the context of the sermon. The Messiah has shown the inner significance of the law; those who refuse to live accordingly are therefore called "workers of lawlessness."

   7:24-7:27. *Therefore every one who hears these words of Mine and acts upon them, may be compared to a wise man, who built his house upon the rock; and the rain descended, and the floods came, and the winds blew, and burst against that house; and yet it did not fall; for it had been founded upon the rock. And every one who*

---

66. A. T. Robertson, *A Grammar of the Greek New Testament in the Light of Historical Research*, p. 752.

hears these words of Mine, and does not act upon them, will be like a foolish man, who built his house upon the sand. And the rain descended, and the floods came, and the winds blew, and burst against that house; and it fell, and great was its fall. In verses twenty-four to twenty-seven the King warns further against false profession. The performing of the Lord's instructions is in view. The houses represent profession; the foundations represent the bases of their profession. Some build on hypocrisy; others build on the genuine obedience of faith. In this parable, as in the illustration of the two ways, a life is looked at in its entirety. Each house represents a life founded on a governing principle. This is again a reiteration of the sermon's theme: genuine righteousness involves the whole person. This conclusion has a twofold appeal. One is to the disciples, exhorting them to live a life characterized by righteousness. The other appeal is to the unrepentant, calling them to entrance into the narrow way leading to life.

5. The Response of the People, 7:28-7:29.

7:28-7:29. *The result was that when Jesus had finished these words, the multitudes were amazed at His teaching; for He was teaching them as one having authority, and not as their scribes.* Matthew concludes this section by introducing the response of the people with his transitional formula, "(the result was that) when Jesus had finished ..." (καὶ ἐγένετο ὅτε ἐτέλεσεν ὁ Ἰησοῦς).[67] The response of the people is sheer amazement. That this state, of awe, continued for some time is indicated by the imperfect tense "to amaze" (ἐξεπλήσσοντο). The reason for their amazement is given in verse twenty-nine. He taught with authority and not as their scribes. The possessive pronoun "their" (αὐτῶν) looks at the scribes as an antagonistic group separate from the disciples of Jesus.[68] Usually the scribes went to great lengths to quote others in order to give authority to their doctrine; however, Christ simply spoke as the authority. Andrews observes, "His language throughout is not that of a rabbi, or a prophet, but of a Law-giver and a King."[69] But there is still another respect in which He was authoritative, and that is in the content of His message.

> But it was not merely the manner of His teaching— although that, no doubt, was very grave and sweet—which conveyed this impres-

67. See above, p. 24.
68. M'Neile, *St. Matthew*, p. 99.
69. Samuel J. Andrews, *The Life of Our Lord Upon the Earth*, p. 274.

sion of authority to the listening multitude, but the truths He taught: it was more what He said than how He said it, as we may infer from the contrast which the people saw between His teaching and that of the Scribes . . . . If his style was new in its simplicity, its geniality, its freedom from scholastic terms and technicalities, much more was the substance of His teaching new . . . new in its freedom, in its power, in its recognition of a present and living Fountain of truth, in its appeal to the moral instincts and intuitions, in its preference of the inward over the outward, of the heart over the appearance, of a willing obedience to a reluctant conformity to commands.[70]

The King has proclaimed the nearness of the kingdom and has authenticated that message with great signs. With people flocking to Him He instructs His disciples concerning the character of those who shall inherit the kingdom. The kingdom, though earthly, is founded on righteousness. Thus the theme of His message is righteousness. The crowds who had come up the mountain while Christ was instructing His disciples (cf. John 6:1-5) are amazed at His doctrine and His manner of teaching, but they fail to respond with the obedience of repentance.

---

70. S. Carpus, "The Sermon on the Mount," *The Expositor* 1 (February 1875):130-32.

III. The Manifestation of the King (8:1-11:1)

   A. The Demonstration of the Power of the King (8:1-9:34)

     1. Miracles of healing (8:1-8:17)
       a. Leprosy (8:1-8:4)
       b. Paralysis (8:5-8:13)
       c. Sickness and demons (8:14-8:17)
     2. The demands of disciples (8:18-8:22)
       a. Regarding possessions (8:18-8:20)
       b. Regarding paternal relations (8:21-8:22)
     3. Miracles of power (8:23-9:8)
       a. In the realm of nature (8:23-8:27)
       b. In the realm of the supernatural (8:28-8:34)
       c. In the realm of the spiritual (9:1-9:8)
     4. The deportment of disciples (9:9-9:17)
       a. The call of Matthew (9:9-9:13)
       b. The question of fasting (9:14-9:17)
     5. Miracles of restoration (9:18-9:34)
       a. Life (9:18-9:26)
       b. Sight (9:27-9:31)
       c. Speech (9:32-9:34)

   B. The Declaration of the Presence of the King (9:35-11:1)

     1. The compassion of the King (9:35-9:38)
     2. The charge of the King (10:1-10:42)
       a. The delegation of authority (10:1-10:4)
         1) The authority (10:1)
         2) The apostles (10:2-10:4)
       b. The directions for their actions (10:5-10:42)
         1) The sphere and nature of their work (10:5-10:8)
         2) The provisions for their work (10:9-10:15)
         3) The perils of their work (10:16-10:25)
         4) The attitude of the workers (10:26-10:39)
           a) Toward God (10:26-10:33)
           b) Toward Jesus (10:34-10:39)
         5) The reward for hospitality (10:40-10:42)
     3. The work of the King resumed (11:1)

III. The Manifestation of the King

Matthew has laid the foundational structure for his argument in chapters one through seven. The genealogy and birth have attested to the legal qualifications of the Messiah as they are stated in the Old Testament. Not only so, but in His birth great and fundamental prophecies have been fulfilled. The King, according to protocol, has a forerunner preceding Him in His appearance on the scene of Israel's history. The moral qualities of Jesus have been authenticated by His baptism and temptation. The King Himself then commences His ministry of proclaiming the nearness of the kingdom and authenticates it with great miracles. To instruct His disciples as to the true character of righteousness which is to distinguish Him, He draws them apart on the mountain. After Matthew has recorded the Sermon on the Mount, he goes on to relate the King's presentation to Israel (Matthew 8:1-11:1).

A. The Demonstration of the Power of the King
8:1-9:34

Matthew 4 relates the ministry of the King as being threefold—teaching, preaching, and healing. In 4:17 the Lord is recorded as preaching; the teaching ministry is presented in 5:3-7:29; then Matthew goes on to show the third aspect of His ministry, His power over disease, demons, and nature (8:1-9:34). In order to properly understand this section as it relates to Matthew's argument one must approach it with Matthew 11:2-6 and 12:24-28 in mind. The character of the miracles bears witness to the Messiahship of Jesus and the nearness of the kingdom.

It is also well to note the arrangement of the miracles as they are here presented by Matthew. The order is not chronological; therefore Matthew must have had a purpose in choosing the events which he did and placing them in the section which deals with the King's presentation to Israel. It is evident that the miracles are placed here to show that the King authenticated His claims with great Messianic signs.

A third aspect of Matthew 8:1-9:34 is the gracious quality of the signs which the King performs; it shows the power of the King as it will be manifested in the kingdom age. This no doubt accounts for the fact that Matthew omits many details which are found in the other gospels. He is concerned only about giving examples of the Lord's power. Whereas Moses used plagues to prove his message, Jesus uses signs of blessings to authenticate His. The reason for this, of course, was to demonstrate His ability to bring the kingdom if Israel would accept it.

1. Miracles of Healing, 8:1-8:17.

The signs presented in this section are grouped; that is, there are nine signs separated into three groups by two brief discussions of discipleship. The first records miracles of healing (Matthew 8:1-17); the second cites miracles of power (Matthew 8:23-9:8); and the third includes miracles of restoration (Matthew 9:18-34).

a. Leprosy, **8:1-8:4.** *And when He had come down from the mountain, great multitudes followed Him. And behold, a leper came to Him, and bowed down to Him, saying, 'Lord, if You are willing, You can make me clean.' And stretching out His hand, He touched him, saying, 'I am willing; be cleansed.' And immediately his leprosy was cleansed. And Jesus said to him, 'See that you tell no one; but go, show yourself to the priest, and present the offering that Moses prescribed, for a testimony to them.'* The first sign recorded in Matthew 8:1-4 is the cleansing of the leper. Having touched the man and miraculously cleansed him, the King orders the cleansed leper to fulfill the law of Leviticus 14:2 by showing himself to the priest. By doing so the cleansed leper would bear testimony to two great facts to the priest. First, it would prove that Jesus had definitely healed the leper, and secondly, the subjection of the Messiah to the law of Moses would be established.

The Lord also commands the cleansed leper to tell no man about the miracle. Several reasons have been postulated as to why Christ gave this

injunction. No doubt the primary purpose was to prevent the Jews from
acting too hastily on their erroneous and preconceived ideas of the
Messiah. The Israelites conceived of the kingdom as being purely physical with little or no spiritual basis whatsoever. That God would found
an earthly kingdom on spiritual principles hardly occurred to the Jew of
Christ's day. A good illustration of this fact is John 6:15. This may
account for Matthew's emphasis on the discourses of Christ. Since they
contain such essential features of God's kingdom program, the discourses are imperative for a gospel written for Jewish readers.

Another reason for the injunction is the opposition which would be
raised against the Messiah because of the wave of public sentiment in
favor of Him. While the opposition was sure to come, it was not yet
time for the King to be crucified (Matthew 12:14-15). Finally, it may
have been a gracious act on the part of Christ to give this negative
command. Just as the parables prevented the truth from bringing greater
condemnation on those who refused to believe (Matthew 13:10-16), so
the silence of the cleansed leper would prevent further condemnation of
those who disbelieved.

?! So we ought to remain silent??

b. Paralysis, **8:5-8:13.** *And when He had entered Capernaum, a
centurion came to Him, entreating Him, and saying, 'Sir, my servant is lying paralyzed at home, suffering great pain.' And He said
to him, 'I will come and heal him.' But the centurion answered and
said, 'Lord, I am not qualified for You to come under my roof, but
just say the word, and my servant will be healed. For I too am a
man under authority, with soldiers under me; and I say to this one,
'Go!' and he goes, and to another, 'Come!' and he comes, and to my
slave, 'Do this!' and he does it.' Now when Jesus heard this, He
marveled, and said to those who were following, 'Truly I say to you,
I have not found such great faith with anyone in Israel. And I say to
you, that many shall come from east and west, and recline at table
with Abraham, and Isaac, and Jacob, in the kingdom of heaven;
but the sons of the kingdom shall be cast out into the outer darkness; in that place there shall be weeping and gnashing of teeth.'
And Jesus said to the centurion, 'Go your way; let it be done to you
as you have believed.' And the servant was healed that very hour.*
Matthew goes on to show the King's power by relating the incident of
the healing of the centurion's servant. The outstanding characteristic of
this event is the consequent remark of Jesus. It is because of the faith of
the Gentile centurion that the King makes His statement. For the Lord to

commend the faith of the Gentile above any which He had found in
Israel was a severe rebuke to the Jew. The typical Israelite was conscious only of his pre-eminent place in the kingdom. Plummer writes
concerning the Jewish concept of the kingdom, "The Jew expected that
the Gentile would be put to shame by the sight of the Jews in bliss."[1]
But here the unbelieving sons of the kingdom, who are the Jews and the
natural heirs, are prophesied as being cast out, while believing Gentiles
take part in it. The Lord indicates that as a result of their faith Gentiles
will have a definite part in the coming kingdom. Entrance into the
kingdom for Jew and Gentile is contingent upon the spiritual basis of
faith in Jesus the Messiah.

The verb "to recline" ($\dot{\alpha}\nu\alpha\kappa\lambda\dot{\iota}\nu\omega$) in verse eleven suggests a banquet, a term often used by the Jews to characterize the promised
blessings of the prophesied kingdom.

> The idea of the Messianic Banquet as at once the seal and the
> symbol of the new era was a common feature in apocalyptic writ-
> ings and an extremely popular subject of discussion, thought, and
> expectation.[2]

Many references in Jewish literature substantiate this observation
(Enoch 62:13-16; 2 Baruch 29:3-8; 2 Esdras 6:49-52). That the Jewish
kingdom is in view is well established by the naming of the three
patriarchs. Only a Jew could claim descent from all three. It is also
interesting to observe that the Gentile follows the Jew in the sequence of
healing events. This is in accord with Matthew's plan of presenting
Jesus first as Son of David and then as Son of Abraham.

   c. *Sickness and demons,* **8:14-8:17.** *And when Jesus had come to
Peter's home, He saw his mother-in-law lying sick in bed with a
fever. And He touched her hand, and the fever left her; and she
arose, and began to wait on Him. And when evening had come, they
brought to Him many who were demon-possessed; and He cast out
the spirits with a word, and healed all who were ill; in order that
what was spoken through Isaiah the prophet might be fulfilled,
saying, 'He Himself took our infirmities, and carried away our
diseases.'"* The Evangelist now turns again to the Jews. Peter's mother-
in-law is ill, and many other Jews are demon possessed and sick. The

1. Alfred Plummer, *An Exegetical Commentary on the Gospel According to S. Matthew,*
p. 127.
2. T. Herbert Bindley, "Eschatology in the Lord's Prayer," *The Expositor* 17 (October
1919):317. cf. William Barclay, *The Gospel of Matthew,* 1:309.

apologetic character of Matthew's Gospel is seen in the reference to the fulfillment of Isaiah 53:4. This Old Testament prophecy looks forward to Christ's work on the cross when He was to bear the sins of the world and thus make provision for removing the results of sin—sickness, death, and demon possession. The relationship of sin and sickness is graphically shown here and also in Matthew 9:5. Christ's work of taking away sin on the cross makes possible the removal of disease and deformity in the Kingdom and eternity. Thus the blessed conditions of the kindgom sovereignty were being displayed before the eyes of the Israelites as the healing ministry of the King previewed the results of the cross.

Some see great significance in Matthew's deliberate rearrangement of these miracles. Since Matthew did not follow the chronological order, it seems he intended to illustrate the plan of his Gospel. Accordingly, the first miracle shows Christ ministering to the Jews. His mighty works bore testimony to His person, but His testimony was rejected. Consequently, He turns to the Gentiles, who manifest great faith in Him. Later, He returns to the Jews, represented by the mother-in-law of the apostle to the Jews. He heals her and all who come to Him. This third picture is that of the millennium, when the King restores Israel and blesses all the nations.   *Far reaching emphasis ... could be. But stretching limits!*

2. The Demands of Disciples, 8:18-8:22.

a. Regarding Possessions, **8:18-8:20.** ***Now when Jesus saw a crowd around Him, He gave orders to depart to the other side. And a certain scribe came and said to Him, 'Teacher, I will follow You wherever You go.' And Jesus said to him, 'The foxes have holes, and the birds of the air have nests; but the Son of Man has nowhere to lay His head.'*** The first demand concerns the use of possessions. The impetuous outburst of an unthinking scribe causes the King to remark that discipleship does not necessarily bring fame and wealth but involves defamation and poverty.

In this discussion the King uses the term *Son of Man.* This phrase has attracted the attention of many scholars. Hunter succinctly writes, "Dead seas of critical ink have gone to the discussion of this enigmatic title; but scholars agree, on the whole, that it goes back *ultimately* to Dan. vii. 13."[3] There is no doubt that the term had Messianic connota-

3. Archibald M. Hunter, *The Message of the New Testament,* p. 58.

tions in the time of Jesus.[4] Peters agrees with this and shows that the
title is one which relates to the covenants of Israel.[5] This is seen in that
Jesus as the Son of Man sustains a physical relationship to David and
Abraham. Therefore, the term refers to the union of God and man in the
One who was to be the King of Israel.

The New Testament Scriptures substantiate this idea in numerous
places; some examples are Matthew 10:13-28; 24:27-30, 37-39; 26:63-
64; John 5:25-27; and John 12:34. It is interesting to note that the term,
except for Acts 7:56, is always used by Christ of Himself and never by
the gospel writers of Him. Consequently, it may be inferred that Christ
used the term to make a veiled revelation of Himself. Plummer concludes, "It is a Jewish, pre-Christian Messiah that is indicated by 'The
Son of Man'."[6]

The answer of the King to the statement of the scribes was designed
to show the scribe much the same truth as was given in the Sermon on
the Mount. The kingdom demands true righteousness and genuine faith
rather than hypocritical externalities. Matthew does not tell whether the
scribe followed Jesus or not; this is irrelevant to his argument. He is
concerned only with presenting the words of Jesus at this point.

b. Regarding Paternal Relations, **8:21-8:22.** *And another of the*
disciples said to Him, 'Lord, permit me first to go and bury my
father.' But Jesus said to him, 'Follow Me; and allow the dead to
bury their own dead.' A second person, a disciple, asks for permission
to bury his father. In reality this man wished to return to his home to
await the death of his father and then to bury him.[7] But the King
demands implicit obedience and allegiance.

These two incidents concerning possessions and paternal relations
portray two aspects of one truth. The King desires wholehearted disciples to learn of Him and to work in His harvest fields. Matthew includes
these two events to show how many misunderstood what it meant to be a
disciple of the King. One who desired to become a disciple was motivated by a desire for fame; another who was already a disciple took it as
something which could be dropped and picked up again. Both were
regarding discipleship as a small thing.

4. Willoughby C. Allen, *A Critical and Exegetical Commentary on the Gospel According*
to S. Matthew, p. lxxii.

5. George N. H. Peters, *The Theocratic Kingdom of Our Lord Jesus, the Christ, As*
Covenanted in the Old Testament, And Presented in the New Testament, 1:562.

6. Plummer, *Exegetical Commentary,* p. xxvi.

7. T. M. Donn, "'Let the Dead Bury Their Dead' (Mt. viii. 22, Lk ix. 60)," *The*
Expository Times 61 (September 1950):384.

3. Miracles of Power, 8:23-9:8.

The first group of miracles is used by Matthew to show that Jesus is capable of bringing those blessings of the kingdom which relate to the body. He then goes on to show that the Son of Man is powerful in every realm.

  a. In the Realm of Nature, **8:23-8:27.** *And when He got into the boat, His disciples followed Him. And behold, there arose a great storm in the sea, so that the boat was covered with the waves; but He Himself was asleep. And they came to Him, and awoke Him, saying, 'Save us, Lord; we are perishing!' And He said to them, 'Why are you timid, you men of little faith?' Then He arose, and rebuked the winds and the sea; and it became perfectly calm. And the men marveled, saying, 'What kind of a man is this, that even the winds and the sea obey Him?'* The first indication of the power of the King is His stilling of the storm. In verse twenty-seven Matthew refers to the disciples by calling them "men" (οἱ ἄνθρωποι). This he does to contrast them to their Lord who had just revealed Himself in such a supernatural way.[8] The question introduced by the pronoun ποταπός expresses the marvel with which the disciples beheld the event. It means "of what sort?"[9] Thus Matthew by his record implies the supernatural character and origin of Jesus. It may be that they had some acquaintance with Psalm 89:9 and Psalm 107:23-30, which attribute the stilling of seas to God.

A very significant aspect of the miracle is seen in the manner in which Christ accomplished it. He rebukes the winds and the sea as though they were animated by demons.

> This is important. The incident is related, not primarily for the sake of recording a miracle, but as an instance of the subduing of the power of evil, which was one of the signs of the nearness of the Kingdom; see xii. 28.[10]

  b. In the Realm of the Supernatural, **8:28-8:34.** *And when He had come to the other side into the country of the Gadarenes, two men who were demon-possessed met Him as they were coming out of the tombs; they were so exceedingly violent that no one could pass by that road. And behold, they cried out, saying, 'What do we have to*

8. Plummer, *Exegetical Commentary,* p. 131.
9. James Hope Moulton and George Milligan, *The Vocabulary of the Greek Testament,* p. 530.
10. Alan Hugh M'Neile, *The Gospel According to St. Matthew,* p. 111.

*do with You, Son of God? Have you come here to torment us before
the time?' Now there was at a distance from them a herd of many
swine feeding. And the demons began to entreat Him, saying, 'If
You are going to cast us out, send us into the herd of swine.' And He
said to them, 'Begone!' And they came out, and went into the swine,
and behold, the whole herd rushed down the steep bank into the
sea, and perished in the waters. And the herdsmen fled, and went
away to the city, and reported everything, including the incident of
the demoniacs. And behold, the whole city came out to meet Jesus;
and when they saw Him, they entreated Him to depart from their
region.* Matthew's account of the casting out of the demons from the
two demoniacs graphically displays the power of Christ in the supernatural realm. It is highly significant that the demons by addressing
Jesus as the Son of God recognize Him as the Messiah.[11] Such passages
as Luke 4:41 and Matthew 16:16 show that *the Son of God* is equivalent
to the term *Messiah*.

The phrase "before the time" ($\pi\rho\grave{o}\ \kappa\alpha\iota\rho o\tilde{v}$) in verse twenty-nine
indicates that the demons recognized that a time was coming when they
would be tormented as the result of Messiah's work. What caused them
such consternation was their fear that the time had come already.
M'Neile translates the clause, "Surely Thou hast come too early!"[12]

The demons recognize who Jesus is and His great power, but the
inhabitants of Gadara ask Him to leave. This is the first recorded instance in Matthew of opposition to the Messiah. It is significant that the
conflict is between the spiritual and the material. This is characteristic
of the opposition to the King. The Jews fail to see that the King could
give them physical blessings if they would only respond spiritually. But
Israel, jealous of its *status quo* and interested primarily in the material,
finally and ultimately refuses its King. Matthew builds up to that point
from this first instance of conflict which gives the character of the
opposition to the Messiah.

c. In the Realm of the Spiritual, **9:1-9:8.** *And getting into a boat, He
crossed over, and came to His own city. And behold, they were
bringing to Him a paralytic, lying on a bed; and Jesus seeing their
faith said to the paralytic, 'Take courage, My son, your sins are
forgiven.' And behold, some of the scribes said to themselves, 'This
fellow blasphemes.' And Jesus knowing their thoughts said, 'Why*

11. *Ibid.,* p. 112.
12. *Ibid.,* p. 113.

*are you thinking evil in your hearts? For which is easier, to say,
'Your sins are forgiven,' or to say, 'Rise, and walk?' But in order
that you may know that the Son of Man has authority on earth to
forgive sins' –then He said to the paralytic, 'Rise, take up your
bed, and go home.' And he rose, and went to his home. But when
the multitudes saw this, they were filled with awe, and glorified
God, who had given such authority to men.* Having crossed over the
Sea of Galilee, the King comes to His own city of Capernaum (Matthew
9:1). In the miracle of healing the paralytic the King simply states, "Be
of good cheer, child; your sins are forgiven." In this connection some of
the scribes say to themselves, "This one blasphemes!" This is the first
mention of the scribes in contact with Christ, and immediately a conflict
arises. Here they accuse the King of blasphemy when He asserts His
power.

In answer to the thoughts of the scribes Jesus shows the relationship ?
between sin and sickness. Had they studied the Old Testament they
would have seen that sin and sickness are associated (Psalm 103:3;
Isaiah 33:24). The forgiveness of sins is the basis for healing. For
believers of the church age the restoration of the body does not come
until the resurrection. Christ would not have had to restore the lad at this
time, but to prove His power to forgive He heals him. This is one of the
most significant signs Jesus performs relative to the kingdom program.
It shows that He is capable of forgiving sins *on earth.* The results of the
miracle are shown in the reaction of the crowd. They feared and
glorified God who gave such "authority" (ἐξουσία) to men. The crowd
saw the authority of God, but they failed to discern the Messiahship of
Jesus.

These three miracles give a wonderful foreview and glimpse into the
conditions of the kingdom. Thus the King displays His power to bring
these promised blessings to Israel. The stilling of the storm indicates the
ability of Christ to fulfill the prophecies of Isaiah 30:23-24; 35:1-7;
41:17-18; 51:3; 55:13; Joel 3:18; Ezekiel 36:29-38; and Zechariah 10:1.
Such kingdom passages as Zechariah 3:1-2; Daniel 7:25-27; 8:23-25;
and Daniel 11:36-12:3 are exemplified in Christ's casting out of the
demons. The miracle indicates He is capable of destroying Satan. That
Jesus is able to forgive sins and so bring about the conditions described
in Isaiah 33:24; 40:1-2; 44:21-22; and Isaiah 60:20-21 is well proven by
the incident of the healing of the paralytic. By this group of miracles
Matthew shows the King's power to bring the kingdom if Israel will
only respond by repentance.

4. The Deportment of Disciples, 9:9-9:17.

   a. The Call of Matthew, **9:9-9:13.** *And as Jesus passed on from there, He saw a man, called Matthew, sitting in the tax office; and He said to him, 'Follow Me!' And he rose, and followed Him.*
   And it happened that as He was reclining at table in the house, behold many tax-gatherers and sinners came and joined Jesus and His disciples at the table. And when the Pharisees saw this, they said to His disciples, 'Why does your Teacher eat with the tax-gatherers and sinners?' But when He heard this, He said, 'It is not those who are healthy who need a physician, but those who are ill. But go and learn what this means, 'I desire compassion, and not sacrifice;' for I did not come to call the righteous, but sinners.' The call of Matthew is included by Matthew primarily for the purpose of showing the increasing hostility of the religious hierarchy to Jesus. As Matthew recounts the event, he reflects the Jewish point of view by using the phrase "many tax-gatherers and sinners" (πολλοὶ τελῶναι καὶ ἁμαρτωλοί, 9:10). The antagonism of the hierarchy becomes more aggressive as they question the disciples of the King about His eating with tax-gatherers and sinners.
   Jesus refutes their criticism by referring to Hosea 6:6. If they had known the heart of the Lord, they would not have criticized Him for ministering to the lost since God desires mercy rather than formal religious externalities. It is interesting to note that the Evangelist in the brief span of five verses presents the twofold response to the King. Matthew, a tax-gatherer, follows the King in simple obedience; the Pharisees, on the other hand, stand aside and criticize.

   b. The Question of Fasting, 9:14-9:17. In this section the Gospel writer records an incident involving John's disciples and the question of fasting. **9:14-9:15.** *Then the disciples of John came to Him, saying, 'Why do we and the Pharisees fast, but Your disciples do not fast?' And Jesus said to them, 'The attendants of the bridegroom cannot mourn, as long as the bridegroom is with them, can they? But the days will come when the bridegroom is taken away from them, and then they will fast.'* Asked by John's disciples why His disciples did not fast, Jesus replies that it is not proper to fast in the presence of the Bridegroom. By calling Himself the Bridegroom Jesus associates Himself with certain definite Old Testament Messianic passages such as Psalm 45; Isaiah 62:5; Hosea 2:20; and the Song of Solomon. The "sons

130

of the bridechamber" of course are the disciples who are the groom's guests.[13]

The King gives the first intimation of His violent death in the verb which He uses. Ἀπαίρω does not simply mean *to depart* but *to take away*. This together with the fact that the verb is passive suggests that the Lord was to suffer violence at the hands of others. The aorist tense looks at it as a definite event. After Israel's Bridegroom has been taken away and all the consequent blessings of the kingdom postponed, the disciples and Israel shall fast again.

9:16-9:17. *'But no one puts a patch of unshrunk cloth on an old garment; for the patch pulls away from the garment, and a worse tear results. Nor do men put new wine into old wineskins; otherwise the wineskins burst, and the wine pours out, and the wineskins are ruined; but they put new wine into fresh wineskins, and both are preserved.'* Two parables are given by the King to illustrate the impropriety of His disciples' fasting at this time. The first illustration is the folly of sewing cloth that has not been "Sanforized" on an old garment. The second is the foolishness of putting new wine into old, dried-out wine skins. In both cases the old cannot contain the new. The word used to describe the old garment and wine skins is παλαιός which refers to that which is not only old but also worn out by use. Two words, "new" (νέος) and "fresh" (καινός), are used in verse seventeen to describe that which is new. Νέος denotes that which is recent in time, while καινός refers to newness of kind.

The kingdom which was at hand was new both in time and kind. The old dispensation had worn out and was not capable of containing the new doctrines of the kingdom or any other new age which would follow the coming of the Messiah. It is interesting to note that in the first parable the old garment is destroyed; in the second not only are the wine skins destroyed, but the wine is also poured out.[14] Thus the second illustration advances on the first and shows that it is impossible to preserve either the old or the new age if they are mixed.

These words of Jesus must have served as a mild remonstrance to the disciples of John. John belonged to the old age; Jesus was the One who was bringing a new dispensation. They should therefore leave the forerunner and join themselves to the King. Unless they did, they could

---

13. F. W. Green, ed., *The Gospel According to Saint Matthew*, p. 161.
14. Richard Chenevix Trench, *Studies in the Gospels*, p. 183.

not partake of any new dispensation which Jesus might bring, a fact well illustrated by Acts 19:1-7.

The dispensational aspect of these parables is important. The Jews of Matthew's day would wonder what their relationship should be to the Old Testament if their King had come and the kingdom had been postponed because of Jewish unbelief. Matthew, by including these parables, explains that the old age was worn out by use. In his characteristic style Matthew here hints that another new age will be brought in if the kingdom comes or not. This may be the first intimation of the church age in Matthew's Gospel.

5. Miracles of Restoration, 9:18-9:34.

a. Life, **9:18-9:26.** *While He was saying these things to them, behold, there came a synagogue official, and bowed down before Him, saying, 'My daughter has just died; but come and lay Your hand on her, and she will live.' And Jesus rose and began to follow him, and so did His disciples. And behold, a woman who had been suffering from a hemorrhage for twelve years, came up behind Him and touched the fringe of His cloak; for she was saying to herself, 'If I only touch His garment, I shall get well.' But Jesus turning and seeing her said, 'Daughter, take courage; your faith has made you well.' And at once the woman was made well. And when Jesus came into the official's house, and saw the flute-players, and the crowd in noisy disorder, He began to say, 'Depart; for the girl is not dead, but is asleep.' And they were laughing at Him. But when the crowd had been put out, He entered and took her by the hand; and the girl arose. And this news went out into all that land.* Thus far the miracles which the King has performed have been in the realms of healing and of power. The last triad are all miracles of restoration. The fact that they deal with restoration indicates that Jesus will yet restore all things as the Son of David despite the opposition to His first coming. In fact, all of the wonders bear testimony to this.

In the first miracle of the last triad the King restores the daughter of a Jewish leader to life. On the way to the ruler's house a woman with an issue of blood is healed by touching the hem of His garment. At the home of the ruler, Jesus, by taking the hand of the daughter, raises her back to life. Two things stand out in this miracle. Primarily, it reveals the restoring power of the King. It is also significant that some rulers were exercising faith in Jesus. As a result of this miracle the fame of the Lord went out into the whole land.

b. Sight, **9:27-9:31.** *And as Jesus passed on from there, two blind men followed Him, crying out, and saying, 'Have mercy on us, Son of David!' And after He had come into the house, the blind men came up to Him, and Jesus said to them, 'Do you believe that I am able to do this?' They said to Him, 'Yes, Lord.' Then He touched their eyes, saying, 'Be it done to you according to your faith.' And their eyes were opened. And Jesus sternly warned them, saying, 'See here, let no one know about this!' But they went out, and spread the news about Him in all that land.* When the King leaves the house two blind men follow Him beseeching Him for mercy and addressing Him as the Son of David. This is the first time Jesus is called by this title. Hereafter He is designated in this way six times (Matthew 12:23; 15:22, 20:30, 31; 21:9, 15). The term is decidedly Messianic.[15] As a result of their faith He touches the eyes of the blind men, and sight is restored to them. Then Jesus "sternly warned" (ἐμβριμάομαι) them to be silent about the miracle. Evidently he does this for the same reasons that He gave a like injunction to the cleansed leper.

Matthew includes this miracle to show the growing consciousness among the people of the Messianic character of Jesus. Plummer writes, "The appeal to Jesus as the 'Son of David' indicates that the idea that He may be the Messiah is increasing."[16] "This shows that His descent from that royal house was known and recognized," Andrews comments.[17] As a result of His mighty works the fame of Jesus as possibly being the Messiah was becoming more generally widespread.

c. Speech, 9:32-9:34. The last miracle of the third triplet deals with the restoration of speech to one who was demon possessed. **9:32-9:33.** *And as they were going out, behold, a dumb man demon-possessed was brought to Him. And after the demon was cast out, the dumb man spoke; and the multitudes marveled, saying, 'Nothing like this was ever seen in Israel.'* The importance of this miracle is seen in the response on the part of the crowds and the Pharisees. The people marvel at the uniqueness of the King's power. There is that which is commendable in their awe—they recognize the power of the Son of David.

---

15. Gustaf Dalman, *The Words of Jesus,* pp. 316-318.
16. Plummer, *Exegetical Commentary,* p. 143.
17. Samuel J. Andrews, *The Life of Our Lord Upon the Earth,* p. 307.

However, they fail to recognize Him as their Messiah and Savior; consequently, they do not worship Him.

9:34. *But the Pharisees were saying, 'He casts out the demons by the ruler of the demons.'* The Pharisees, on the other hand, explain His power by attributing it to Satan. By including this response of the opponents of Jesus Matthew cleverly shows that the miracles of Jesus were genuine. The Pharisees could not deny the reality of the works, so they relied on a false explanation.

Summary, 8:1-9:34. It is interesting to note the kingdom character of the signs which Matthew records in this portion of his Gospel. The first set of miracles, those emphasizing healing, confirms the promise of Isaiah 33:24 and 57:19. Examples of the conditions which will exist in the earthly kingdom are shown in the King's power over the storm (Isaiah 35:1-7), demons (Daniel 7:25-27), and sin (Isaiah 33:24). The blessings of the kingdom are also displayed in the raising of the ruler's daughter (Isaiah 65:17-20; Daniel 12:2), the restoration of sight (Isaiah 29:18; 35:5-6), and the healing of the dumb man (Isaiah 35:5-6). Therefore this person, Jesus, is capable of bringing the kingdom to Israel and must be the Messiah.

In this section (Matthew 8:1-9:34) Matthew has also marked out some important developments in his argument. One is the spreading of Jesus' fame. Matthew notes that His fame went into that whole country (9:26, 31, and 33). A second development is the increase of the idea that Jesus is the Messiah. This is indicated by the title by which the blind men call to Jesus. Still another result of the manifestation of the King's power is the belief of some of the religious leaders. The ruler came to Jesus and worshipped Him as he besought Jesus to raise his daughter. By noting the response of John's disciples to the life of Christ and His disciples, Matthew indicates still another development. Even John's disciples did not fully realize the significance of the presence of the King.

Finally, in this section the beginning of opposition to the presence of the King is seen. The people of the land of the Gadarenes ask the Deliverer to leave their country. The second instance of opposition is from the leaders who inwardly dispute His authority to forgive sins. The antagonism mounts until the Pharisees accuse Him of casting out demons by the ruler of demons.

While Matthew develops his argument by tracing the development of fame and opposition, his primary purpose has been to manifest the supernatural character of Jesus as one qualified to bring about the blessings of the kingdom. This no doubt accounts for the diversity in the kinds of miracles which Matthew records. But even though these miracles are tremendously important to the argument of the Evangelist, they also serve another purpose. Matthew also uses them to form an introduction to the second extended discourse of his Gospel, the charge of Jesus to His disciples.[18]

B. The Declaration of the Presence of the King
9:35-11:1

Matthew 9:35-10:42 contains an account of the King's concern over the condition of Israel in the light of the proximity of the kingdom, and, in addition, a record of His instructions to the twelve to proclaim the kingdom's nearness. To authenticate the proclamation the disciples were given power to perform signs. The charge contained in this portion is both similar to and unlike the discourse on the mount. It is similar in its general context; the kingdom is still near at hand (Matthew 10:7).

As the Sermon on the Mount is preceded by the authentication of the King as far as His legal rights and His morality are concerned, so this charge to the twelve is prefaced by a demonstration of the King's power. It is also similar in its immediate context. The general summary of the Lord's work given in Matthew 4:23 is almost identical to that of Matthew 9:35.

There are also dissimilar elements. The first is the difference in the response of the Lord at the sight of the crowds. In Matthew 5:1 He went up into a mountain to separate Himself from them, but here He is moved with compassion. In the former situation the King saw the need for instructing His *disciples* concerning the nature of true righteousness. This was the basic and primary lesson which the disciples had to learn. Now the King is exercised in heart about ministering to the *people of Israel* in words and works; therefore He delegates great authority to the disciples and sends them to the lost sheep of Israel.

This accounts for the difference in the content of the two discourses. One is basic to the understanding of the proclamation of the kingdom. The other contains a charge for the carrying out of the commission to announce the nearness of the kingdom. It is interesting to note that the two discussions of discipleship contained in Matthew 8:18-22 and 9:9-17 are so placed that they give hints as to the nature of the discourse which

18. Green, *Saint Matthew*, pp. 155-156.

is to follow. The narration of the various miracles is in accordance with Matthew's style of introducing a discourse with a series of events.

1. The Compassion of the King, 9:35-9:38.

At the sight of the crowds the King is moved to action by His great compassion, for the people have been mishandled and cast down as sheep without a shepherd. **9:35-9:36.** *And Jesus was going about all the cities and the villages, teaching in their synagogues, and proclaiming the gospel of the kingdom, and healing every kind of disease and every kind of sickness. And seeing the multitudes, He felt compassion for them, because they were distressed and downcast like sheep without a shepherd.* The verb "to feel compassion" (σπλαγχνίζομαι), except for its use in the parables, is used only of the Lord.[19] The pluperfect periphrastics describing the condition of the people (distressed, downcast) indicate that the results were still existing; consequently they were as sheep without a shepherd. Their lost condition is further described in Matthew 10:6 where they are called "the lost sheep" (τὰ πρόβατα τὰ ἀπολωλότα), sheep that have perished. The clause is no doubt an allusion to Jeremiah 50:6. This is a terrible indictment against the hypocritical righteousness of the scribes and the Pharisees. Because of them the people had been vexed and were lying helpless. The King who shall shepherd His people Israel is greatly exercised in heart because they are as sheep without a shepherd (Matthew 2:6).

9:37-9:38. *Then He said to His disciples, 'The harvest is plentiful, but the workers are few. Therefore beseech the Lord of the harvest to send out workers into His harvest.'* As a result of His compassion He issues a call for prayer to the Lord of the harvest that laborers will be sent into the great harvest field of Israel.

2. The Charge of the King, 10:1-10:42.

a. The Delegation of Authority, 10:1-10:4. The King, now concerned with gathering the lost sheep of Israel to Him, calls His twelve disciples.

(1) The Authority, **10:1.** *And having summoned His twelve disciples, He gave them authority over unclean spirits, to cast them out,*

---

19. Plummer, *Exegetical Commentary,* p. 144.

and to heal every kind of disease and every kind of sickness. Even as
He calls them He displays authority. In connection with the verb "to
summon" (προσκαλέω), M'Neile writes, "The Lord's personal authority, which expected obedience, made an ineffaceable impression
upon the disciples; cf. xv. 32, xx. 25 ..."[20] It is well to note that the call
is not now to discipleship, as it was in Matthew 4:18-22, but it is to the
position of apostles having delegated authority.

A second thing to note is the ability of the King to delegate such
authority and power to others (Matthew 10:1, 7-8). While Jesus displayed great power by His miracles, the delegating of miraculous power
to others was the clearest indication of the greatness of His person.

> Before giving the names of the Twelve he tells how the Messiah
> equipped them: He gave them authority to cast out unclean spirits,
> and to heal all manner of disease, as He Himself had been doing
> (iv. 23, 24, ix. 35). This was without a precedent in Jewish history.
> Not even Moses or Elijah had given miraculous powers to their
> disciples. Elijah had been allowed to transmit his powers to Elisha,
> but only when he himself was removed from the earth.[21]

(2) The Apostles, **10:2-10:4.** *Now the names of the twelve apostles
are these: The first, Simon, who is called Peter, and Andrew his
brother; and James the son of Zebedee, and John his brother;
Philip and Bartholomew; Thomas and Matthew the tax-gatherer;
James the son of Alphaeus, and Thaddaeus; Simon the Cananaean,
and Judas Iscariot, the one who betrayed Him.* A third factor which
is noteworthy is the mention of the twelve. This is the first mention of
them, and they are brought forth in Matthew's argument in connection
with their ministry to Israel. The number is significant in that it corresponds to the twelve tribes of Israel. It may be that the Lord chose
twelve disciples since the disciples were to minister first as apostles of
the Son of David. As apostles of the Son of Abraham the number would
be irrelevant. Hunter notes, "It is the number of the tribes of Israel. As
soon as he remarked that number, every Jew of any spiritual penetration
must have scented 'a Messianic programme.'"[22] This may also account
for Matthew's use of the word "apostle" (ἀπόστολος) here, the only
time it occurs in this Gospel. Writing for Jews, Matthew is interested in
the twelve as apostles only when they are sent to the lost sheep of Israel
exclusively.

20. M'Neile, *St. Matthew*, p. 130.
21. Plummer, *Exegetical Commentary*, p. 147.
22. Hunter, *The Message of the New Testament*, p. 62.

The use of the adjective "first" ($\pi\rho\hat{\omega}\tau\sigma s$) is another fact demanding consideration in connection with Matthew's argument. The word clearly shows the primacy of Simon.[23] Matthew, writing for Jewish readers, points to the supremacy of Peter, who was the apostle to the Jews in the early church. Again Matthew by one word gives a hint of what is to follow, the statement of Christ made in Matthew 16:17-19.

b. The Directions for Their Actions, 10:5-10:42. In the charge which the King gives to His twelve disciples several factors stand out in their relationship to Matthew's argument.

(1) The Sphere and Nature of Their Work, 10:5-10:8. First, He limits the sphere of their work to the lost sheep of the House of Israel. **10:5-10:6.** ***These twelve Jesus sent out after instructing them saying, 'Do not go in the way of the Gentiles, and do not enter any city of the Samaritans; but rather go to the lost sheep of the house of Israel.'*** Since the word "Gentiles" ($\dot{\epsilon}\theta\nu\hat{\omega}\nu$) is an objective genitive, they were not even to enter a road leading to the Gentiles, nor were they to enter a city of the Samaritans.[24] The exclusiveness of their ministry is further emphasized by the position of the phrases "in the way of the Gentiles" ($\epsilon\dot{\iota}s$ $\dot{\sigma}\delta\dot{\sigma}\nu$ $\dot{\epsilon}\theta\nu\sigma s$) and "(in the) city of the Samaritans" ($\epsilon\dot{\iota}s$ $\pi\dot{\sigma}\lambda\iota\nu$ $\Sigma\alpha\mu\alpha\rho\iota\tau\hat{\omega}\nu$). This restriction of the ministry of the twelve apostles to Israel has caused a great deal of trouble to many students of the Bible, specifically those who fail to hold to the dispensational viewpoint of Bible interpretation. The kingdom of the heavens which is still at hand is being offered to Israel. If it will accept its King, Israel will have its kingdom. Therefore, the King is concerned with manifesting His presence, but only as the Son of David.

10:7. ***And as you go, preach, saying, 'The kingdom of heaven is at hand.'*** A *second* important factor to note is the urgency of the situation. The phrase "and as you go, preach" ($\pi\sigma\rho\epsilon\nu\dot{\sigma}\mu\epsilon\nu\sigma\iota$ $\delta\dot{\epsilon}$ $\kappa\eta\rho\dot{\nu}\sigma\sigma\epsilon\tau\epsilon$) in verse seven shows that they were to preach on the move, as they were going from city to city and region to region.

> They are to be 'field preachers' moving on from place to place. No permanent organization is to be attempted. The sheep are all scattered, and the first thing is to awaken in them the desire for a

23. Plummer, *Exegetical Commentary*, p. 147.
24. Archibald Thomas Robertson, *Word Pictures in the New Testament*, 1:78.

shepherd and a fold. The Messiah and the Kingdom are ready
when they are ready.[25]

Plummer notes this despite the fact he is not a dispensationalist. The
kingdom has drawn near and will remain in the condition of nearness for
a comparatively short time. Therefore it is extremely urgent that as soon
as possible Israel be prepared and in a state of spiritual receptivity so
that it will come.

A *third* important thing to notice is the message which the disciples
were to proclaim (Matthew 10:7). It is the same message which John
had announced (Matthew 3:1) and the Lord was preaching (Matthew
4:17, 23; 9:35). The apostles were sent forth to proclaim that the anticipated kingdom of the Jews had drawn near and was only waiting for
their repentance. Though he is not a dispensationalist, M'Neile candidly
observes, "If the Jewish nation could be brought to repentance, the new
age would dawn; see Ac. iii. 19f., Jo. iv. 22."[26]

10:8. *'Heal the sick, raise the dead, cleanse the lepers, cast out
demons; freely you received, freely give.'* To authenticate their message concerning the nearness of the kingdom, the Lord gave them power
to perform signs. These miracles were not to be used merely to instill
awe, but to show that the kingdom was at hand (Matthew 12:28).

(2) The Provisions for Their Work, **10:9-10:15.** *'Do not acquire gold,
or silver, or copper for your money belts; or a bag for your journey,
or even two tunics, or sandals, or a staff; for the worker is worthy of
his support. And into whatever city or village you enter, inquire
who is worthy in it; and abide there until you go away. And as you
enter the house, give it your greeting. And if the house is worthy, let
your greeting of peace come upon it; but if it is not worthy, let your
greeting of peace return to you. And whoever does not receive you,
nor heed your words, as you go out of that house or that city, shake
off the dust of your feet. Truly I say to you, it will be more tolerable
for the land of Sodom and Gomorrah in the day of judgment, than
for that city.'* After discussing the content of their message, the King
speaks briefly about the provisions with which the disciples were to be
concerned as they went forth.

(3) The Perils of Their Work, 10:16-10:25. It is extremely important
for one to make a *fourth* observation in noting the program which the

---

25. Plummer, *Exegetical Commentary,* p. 149.
26. M'Neile, *St. Matthew,* p. 134.

King had in view. The King performed His ministry according to the
Old Testament Messianic calendar of events. According to the Hebrew
Scriptures the Messiah, after He appeared, was to suffer, die, and be
raised again (Daniel 9:26; Psalm 22; Isaiah 53:1-11; Psalm 16:10). Following the death and resurrection of the Christ there was to be a time of
trouble (Daniel 9:26-27; Jeremiah 30:4-6). The Messiah was then to
return to the earth to end this tribulation and to judge the world (Daniel
7:9-13, 16-26; 9:27; 12:1; Zechariah 14:1-5). Finally, the Messiah as
King would establish His kingdom with Israel as the head nation (Daniel
7:11-27; 12:1-2; Isaiah 53:11-12; Zechariah 14:6-11, 20-21). That this is
the program that is governing the King's earthly ministry to Israel is
indicated by a number of facts in this discourse.

The King anticipated His death and resurrection. While the immediate need was for the proclamation of the nearness of the kingdom
and the need for repentance on Israel's part, the next great event on the
program of the Messiah was His death and resurrection. This is shown
in Matthew 10:23 where Jesus says He is to come as the Son of Man.
Daniel 7:13, the Old Testament Scripture on which the Messianic concept of the Son of Man is founded, refers to the Son of Man as coming
"with the clouds of heaven." Therefore when Jesus says that the Son of
Man should come, He must have had in mind His death and resurrection
so that He could come in the manner described in Daniel 7:13. The
reference to the cross in verse thirty-eight may also be an indication of
the King's anticipation of His death.

10:16-10:25. *'Behold, I send you out as sheep in the midst of*
wolves; therefore be shrewd as serpents, and innocent as doves. But
beware of men; for they will deliver you up to the courts, and
scourge you in their synagogues; and you shall even be brought
before governors and kings for My sake, as a testimony to them and
to the Gentiles. But when they deliver you up, do not become anx-
ious about how or what you will speak; for it shall be given you in
that hour what you are to speak. For it is not you who speak, but it
is the Spirit of your Father who speaks in you. And brother will
deliver up brother to death, and a father his child; and children will
rise up against parents, and cause them to be put to death. And you
will be hated by all on account of My name, but it is the one who has
endured to the end who will be saved. But whenever they persecute
you in this city, flee to the next; for truly I say to you, you shall not
finish going through the cities of Israel, until the Son of Man comes.

'A disciple is not above his teacher, nor a slave above his master. It is enough for the disciple that he become as his teacher, and the slave as his master. If they have called the head of the house Beelzebul, how much more the members of his household!' The description of the disciples' persecution and the peril of their work is a clear reference to the seventieth week of Daniel, a time of tribulation following the cutting off of the Messiah. It is very evident that at the time the apostles were sent forth the Lord was enjoying great popularity. Therefore these predictions present a great problem to many commentators. For instance, M'Neile writes, "But there is no evidence that the apostles during their short tour were ever in peril; in Mt. ix. 36, x. 6 their hearers are πρόβατα [sheep]; they did not become wolves till the Lord's death."[27] The answer to the problem is simple. <u>The Messiah was simply looking past His death to the time of tribulation following. At that time the disciples would have the same message and possibly the same power.</u> The narrow road leading to the kingdom leads through the tribulation (Matthew 10:16), and this persecution is to be of a religious and political nature (Matthew 10:16-19).

The mention of the Spirit in verse twenty is an evident allusion to the coming of the Holy Spirit as prophesied in Joel 2:28. This is another indication that Jesus had Daniel's seventieth week in view. The context of Joel 2:28 is the tribulation preceding the establishment of the kingdom. Schweitzer observes, "It should be noticed that according to Joel iii. and iv. the outpouring of the Spirit, along with the miraculous signs, forms the prelude to the judgment. . . ."[28]

The tribulation character of the time which was before the disciples is also indicated by the fact that they were told to flee from city to city (Matthew 10:23). The Son of Man would come before they would have exhausted the cities of Israel.[29] This verse has caused commentators great difficulty.

> Some refer it to the Transfiguration, others to the Second Coming. Some hold that Matthew has put the saying in the wrong context. Others bluntly say that Jesus was mistaken, a very serious charge to make in his instructions to these preachers.[30]

The Lord made no error and clearly had "the coming" for judgment in mind. However, the coming is contingent upon Israel's acceptance

27. Ibid., p. 138.
28. Albert Schweitzer, *The Quest of the Historical Jesus,* p. 362.
29. M'Neile, *St. Matthew,* p. 142.
30. Robertson, *Word Pictures,* 1:82.

of its King. Because even after His resurrection, that nation refused Him, it became impossible to establish the kingdom (cf. Acts 3:18-26). In fact, the tribulation period did not come; if it had, the promise of the soon coming of the Son of Man would have been of great comfort to the apostles.

(4) The Attitude of the Workers, 10:26-10:39.

(a) Toward God, **10:26-10:33.** *'Therefore do not fear them, for there is nothing covered that will not be revealed, and hidden that will not be known. What I tell you in the darkness, speak in the light; and what you hear whispered in your ear, proclaim upon the housetops. And do not fear those who kill the body, but are unable to kill the soul; but rather fear Him who is able to destroy both soul and body in hell. Are not two sparrows sold for a cent? And yet not one of them will fall to the ground apart from your Father. But the very hairs of your head are all numbered. Therefore do not fear; you are of more value than many sparrows. Every one therefore who shall confess Me before men, I will also confess him before My Father who is in heaven. But whoever shall deny Me before men, I will also deny him before My Father who is in heaven.'* The emphasis on fear is a factor which shows that the time of Jacob's trouble prophesied in the Old Testament is considered as being about to be fulfilled. The verb "to fear" ($\phi o \beta \acute{\epsilon} \omega$) occurs in verses twenty-six, twenty-eight, and thirty-one. Fear of God and not of men is to govern their lives during the hectic days of persecution.

(b) Toward Jesus, **10:34-10:39.** *'Do not think that I came to bring peace on the earth; I did not come to bring peace, but a sword. For I came to set a man against his father, and a daughter against her mother, and a daughter-in-law against her mother-in-law; and a man's enemies will be the members of his household. He who loves father or mother more than Me is not worthy of Me; and he who loves son or daughter more than Me is not worthy of Me. And he who does not take his cross and follow after Me is not worthy of Me. He who has found his life shall lose it, and he who has lost his life for My sake shall find it.'* Although Christ brought the kingdom near, He also brought strife and division. These, of course, were to precede the establishment of the kingdom. The King says, "I did not come to bring peace, but a sword." This must have been a startling revelation to the disciples. Robertson comments, "A bold and dramatic climax. The aorist infinitive means a sudden hurling of the sword where peace was

expected."[31] The terrible dissensions in family relationships were a mark of the troublesome times preceding the kingdom. "Feud between members of a family is also mentioned in the Talmud as a sign of the coming of the Messianic age."[32] In referring to these critical dissensions the Lord quotes Micah 7:6, a description of the treacherous character of the people in the confused times of the tribulation.

The final indication of the perils which were awaiting the apostles is the mention of martyrdom (Matthew 10:21, 28, 39). They were to be faithful to Jesus Christ to death. A paraphrase of verse thirty-nine brings out the thought.

> He who uses his physical life to the fullest for himself will lose the purpose of life. On the other hand, he who loses his physical life for Christ's sake will find the reality and purpose of physical life.[33]

The program of the King not only includes the death of the Messiah and the arrival of the tribulation but also His second coming to the earth. This is what is in view in Matthew 10:23. His coming is to be as the Son of Man in the clouds of heaven (Daniel 7:13).

(5) The Reward for Hospitality, **10:40-10:42.** *'He who receives you receives Me, and he who receives Me receives Him who sent Me. He who receives a prophet in the name of a prophet shall receive a prophet's reward; and he who receives a righteous man in the name of a righteous man shall receive a righteous man's reward. And whoever in the name of a disciple gives to one of these little ones even a cup of cold water to drink, truly I say to you he shall not lose his reward.* The next event seen in the Lord's program is the judgment. This is clearly what is being discussed in verses fifteen, twenty-six, twenty-eight, thirty-two and thirty-three, and forty-one to forty-two. At the judgment, Christ will claim those who claim Him, and deny those who deny Him.[34]

The final event on the program is the establishment of the kingdom referred to in verse twenty-two. The Jewish Messianic concept of salva-

31. Ibid., 1:83.
32. C. G. Montefiore, *The Synoptic Gospels,* 2:152.
33. William Hendriksen, *Exposition of the Gospel According to Matthew,* p. 477.
34. M'Neile, *St. Matthew,* p. 146

tion was eschatological so that "salvation" (σωτηρία) is that which is to be given to the righteous who enter the kingdom.[35] (c.f. Hebrews 1:14-2:5)

Another observation that is pertinent to the argument of Matthew concerns the claims of Christ. In verse twenty-three He is seen as the Son of Man prophesied by Daniel. Persecutions will arise simply due to the fact that the apostles are associated with Him (verses twenty-four to twenty-five). In verse thirty-three He presents Himself as the One Who shall judge them. The King demands absolute allegiance to the point of death (verses thirty-seven to thirty-nine). Finally, in verse forty, He associates Himself with God. Matthew presents Jesus as the Messiah in all of His authority and majesty in this chapter.

This section of Matthew's Gospel presents the King in His power on the earth. He works all sorts of signs which prove the nearness of the kingdom. To further declare the nearness of the Messianic age He sends forth His disciples, delegating great authority to them. As He sends them forth He instructs them, keeping in mind the Old Testament eschatological calendar of events.

3. The Work of the King Resumed, 11:1.

And it came about that when Jesus had finished giving instructions to His twelve disciples, He departed from there to teach and preach in their cities. Having reached this point in his argument, Matthew closes this section with the King continuing His ministry to Israel. This conclusion is introduced with his characteristic transition "And it came about that when Jesus had finished ..." (καὶ ἐγένετο ὅτε ἐτέλεσεν ὁ Ἰησοῦς).

---

35. W. Adams Brown, "Salvation, Saviour," *A Dictionary of the Bible,* 4:359.

IV. The Opposition to the King (11:2-13:53)

A. The Evidence of the Rejection of the King (11:2-11:30)

   1. The antagonism to the forerunner and the King (11:2-11:19)
     a. The attestation of the person and program of the King (11:2-11:6)
     b. The commendation of the forerunner of the King (11:7-11:11)
     c. The identification of the forerunner of the King (11:12-11:15)
     d. The censoriousness of the generation of the King (11:16-11:19)
   2. The indifference to the message of the King (11:20-11:24)
   3. The invitation of the King (11:25-11:30)

B. The Illustrations of the Opposition to the King (12:1-12:50)

   1. The contention concerning the Sabbath (12:1-12:21)
     a. The relationship of the Sabbath to man (12:1-12:8)
     b. The relationship of the Sabbath to good deeds (12:9-12:21)
   2. The contention concerning the power of the King (12:22-12:37)
   3. The contention concerning the signs of the King (12:38-12:45)
   4. The question concerning the kin of the King (12:46-12:50)

C. The Adaptation of the King to His Opposition (13:1-13:53)

Including an Introduction to Parabolic Instruction

   1. The parables spoken to the multitudes (13:1-13:35)
     a. The setting (13:1-13:2)
     b. The introduction (13:3-13:23)
       1) The parable of the sower (13:3-13:9)
       2) The purpose of the parables (13:10-13:17)
       3) The parable of the sower explained (13:18-13:23)
     c. Three parables of the Kingdom (13:24-13:33)
       1) The parable of the wheat and the darnel (13:24-13:30)
       2) The parable of the mustard seed (13:31-13:32)
       3) The parable of the leaven and the meal (13:33)
     d. The fulfillment of prophecy (13:34-13:35)
   2. The parables spoken to the disciples (13:36-13:53)
     a. The explanation of the parable of the wheat and the darnel (13:36-13:43)
     b. Three parables of the Kingdom (13:44-13:50)
       1) The parable of the hidden treasure (13:44)
       2) The parable of the pearl of great price (13:45-13:46)
       3) The parable of the dragnet (13:47-13:50)
     c. Conclusion: the parable of the householder (13:51-13:53)

IV. The Opposition
to the King

Chapters eleven through thirteen are pivotal in Matthew's Gospel. The Evangelist has carefully presented the credentials of the King in relationship to His birth, His baptism, His temptation, His righteous doctrine, and His supernatural power. Israel has heard the message of the nearness of the kingdom from John the Baptist, the King Himself, and His disciples. Great miracles have authenticated the call to repentance. Now Israel must make a decision.

A. The Evidence of the Rejection of the King
11:2-11:30

Chapter eleven presents three evidences of the rejection of the King—the antagonism of Israel to John the Baptist and Jesus, the indifference to the message of the King, and the invitation of the King to individuals to come to Him. For Matthew to begin the history of the rejection of the King with these evidences is very characteristic of his method of arguing from an implication to a fact.

1. The Antagonism to the Forerunner and the King, 11:2-11:19.

a. The Attestation of the Person and Program of the King, **11:2-11:6.** *Now when John in prison heard of the works of Christ, he sent word by his disciples, and said to Him, "Are You the Coming One, or shall we look for someone else?" And Jesus answered and said to them, "Go and report to John the things which you hear and see: the blind receive sight and the lame walk, the lepers are cleansed and the deaf hear, and the dead are raised up, and the poor have the* *gospel preached to them. And blessed is he who keeps from stumbling over Me.*" John the Baptist, still in prison, with wavering faith sends a delegation of his disciples to inquire of Jesus concerning His Messianic office. Matthew includes the record of this interrogation for at least two reasons. First, the questioning of Jesus by John, a representative of the best in Israel, points up the misconception of Israel as to the program of the Messiah and His method. He had heard of the works of Jesus (Matthew 11:2), and they certainly appeared to be Messianic. However, Jesus did not suddenly assert His authority and judge the people as John probably had thought He would (Matthew 3:10-12). Because of this misconception he began to doubt. Perhaps his being in prison, a place which was certainly incongruous for the herald of the King, reinforced his doubts.

Several factors confirm that John's question concerned Messiahship. The mention of the works "of Christ" (τοῦ Χριστοῦ) and not "of Jesus" brings the subject to the reader's mind. In fact, this is the only place in Matthew where the name "Christ" (Χριστός) standing alone is used of Jesus.[1] In addition, the title "the Coming One" (ὁ ἐρχόμενος) is used of the Messiah (Mark 11:9; Luke 13:35; 19:38; Hebrews 10:37).[2] Finally the use of "someone else" (ἕτεροι) in contrast to "the Coming One" (λ ἐρχόμενος) points to the Messianic implications of the question. Either Jesus is the Messiah or He is a mere human being. If He is human, then John must look for a different kind of person. In answer to the question, Jesus simply points to His words and works.

The second purpose of these few verses (Matthew 11:2-6) is to reaffirm the concept that the works of Jesus prove His Messiahship. John's disciples are merely told to affirm that which John had heard. But the answer is phrased in such a way as to recall the prophetic oracles.[3] The works which are mentioned seem to be allusions to such Old Testament passages as Isaiah 29:18; 33:24; 35:5-6; and 61:1. The import and implications of this answer are great. Not only does it confirm the Messianic character of the person of Jesus, but it also shows the nature of the kingdom.

It is well to note that if John had an erroneous concept of the kingdom, this would have been the logical time for Christ to have corrected it. But He did no such thing.

1. Henry Alford, *The Greek Testament,* 1:114.
2. Alfred Plummer, *An Exegetical Commentary on the Gospel According to S. Matthew,* p. 159.
3. Alexander Balmain Bruce, "The Synoptic Gospels," *The Expositor's Greek Testament,* 1:170.

Such an answer was worth a thousand merely verbal affirmations. To John it was intended to show that he had not been mistaken about the identification of Jesus with the promised Mediatorial King of Old Testament prophecy, nor about the nature of His Kingdom. And to us Christ's words should prove what to John needed no proof; namely, that when the kingdom is established on earth, it will be a literal Kingdom, exhibiting all the varied aspects revealed by the Old Testament prophets.[4]

Even the signs which Jesus mentions emphasize the physical.

And it is worthy of note that, of the six items mentioned in Christ's answer to John, no less than five are concerned with human needs which are purely *physical*. Only one, i.e., the preaching of the Gospel, can be regarded as something *spiritual*, and even this has a *social* aspect—the "poor" are hearing it.[5]

The works of Christ attest both His own person and the character of the kingdom. They also proved that the Messianic age was very close.[6] For John this was all that was needed for a reaffirmation of his faith.

b. The Commendation of the Forerunner of the King, 11:7-11:11. Matthew goes on to record the commendation which Jesus makes of His herald, John the Baptist. Because the disciples of Jesus might be influenced by John's question, the Lord interjects these words concerning the Baptist. However, they do bear some weight on the argument.

11:7-11:10. *And as these were going away, Jesus began to say to the multitudes concerning John, "What did you go out into the wilderness to look at? A reed shaken by the wind? But what did you go out to see? A man dressed in soft clothing? Behold, those who wear soft clothing are in kings' palaces. But why did you go out? To see a prophet? Yes, I tell you, and one who is more than a prophet. This is the one about whom it was written,*

> *'Behold, I send My messenger before your face, Who will prepare your way before you.'"*

Matthew introduces the commendation with the verb "to begin" ($\check{\eta}\rho\xi\alpha\tau o$). M'Neile notes that in Matthew "... it either describes the beginning of a continuous action or marks a fresh start or phase in the narrative ..." [7] Here the King begins to show the superiority of John.

---

4. Alva J. McClain, *The Greatness of the Kingdom,* pp. 301-302.
5. Ibid., p. 302.
6. Alan Hugh M'Neile, *The Gospel According to St. Matthew,* p. 152.
7. Ibid., p. 45.

The people held John to be a prophet (Matthew 21:26); Jesus declares him to be more on the basis of two facts. He is greater since he was the one who proclaimed the nearness of the kingdom. His proximity to the kingdom and the King made him great. But his greatness rests on a second factor. He fulfills the prophecy of Malachi 3:1 as the forerunner of the Messiah. Both of these facts are significant to Matthew since it supports the fact that the kingdom was near at hand and being genuinely offered to Israel. These facts also show that Jesus was the Messiah promised in the Old Testament. The change of the pronoun "Me" ($\mu o\nu$) to "You" ($\sigma o\nu$) in Christ's quotation of Malachi 3:1 (verse 10) further affirms the greatness of His person.[8]

11:11. *"Truly, I say to you, among those born of women there has not arisen anyone greater than John the Baptist; yet he who is least in the kingdom of heaven is greater than he."* The conclusion of the commendation is significant in pointing up the greatness of the kingdom. Though John is as great as the greatest of the Old Testament saints, the least in the kingdom which is at hand is greater than John is now.[9] This statement further affirms that the kingdom was not then present, otherwise John would certainly have been in it. The kingdom was near and was being offered to Israel.

c. The Identification of the Forerunner of the King, 11:12-11:15. Some of the most significant words concerning John the Baptist and his position in God's program are recorded here. In this discussion Jesus speaks of the then present condition of the kingdom in verses twelve to thirteen. In verses fourteen to fifteen the potential coming of the kingdom is discussed.

11:12-11:13. *"And from the days of John the Baptist until now the kingdom of heaven suffers violence, and violent men take it by force. For all the prophets and the Law prophesied until John."* The first great problem which confronts the student of Matthew is the voice and meaning of the verb "to suffer violence" ($\beta\iota\acute{\alpha}\zeta\omega$) in Matthew 11:12. The verb form $\beta\iota\acute{\alpha}\zeta\epsilon\tau\alpha\iota$ can be deponent middle or passive. Those who believe it is middle argue from its use in Luke 16:16 and also lay claim to the context for support.[10] It then refers to the energy expended by the disciples to enter the kingdom. They must strive to the extent that

---

8. Alford, *The Greek Testament,* 1:116.

9. M'Neile, *St. Matthew,* p. 154.

10. Joseph Henry Thayer, *A Greek-English Lexicon of the New Testament,* p. 101.

entrance is violent.[11] However, it is better to take the verb as passive. The first evidence is the fact that the verb has no object.

> Taken as deponent, it would be utterly without sense, because βιάζεσθαι without an object or something equivalent thereto, such as πρόσω, εἴσω neither is nor can be used; it is not an independent, self-contained conception such as to exercise force, forcibly to step forward.[12]

Another indication is seen in the use of the verb "to take by force" (ἁρπάζω) which has the idea of snatching away violently. The feminine pronoun "it" (αὐτήν) shows that the kingdom is that which is being seized. Thus the kingdom suffers violence in that evil men snatch it. But when it is proven that the verb is passive, the meaning is still ambiguous.

The passive may yield several meanings. It may mean that men are snatching the kingdom from God's hands and thus forcing its coming.

> The saying has nothing to do with the entering of individuals into the Kingdom; it simply asserts, that since the coming of the Baptist a certain number of persons are engaged in forcing on and compelling the coming of the Kingdom. Jesus' expectation of the Kingdom is an expectation based upon a fact which exercises an active influence upon the Kingdom of God. It was not He, and not the Baptist who "were working at the coming of the Kingdom"; it is the host of penitents which is wringing it from God, so that it may now come at any moment.[13]

However, this view does not fit the context. Verse fourteen and verses twenty to twenty-six affirm the unwillingness of Israel to receive the kingdom. In addition it is noted by Cremer that the passive is never used in good sense; it is always used in a bad sense.[14]

There are still two meanings which the passive could give when all of the above factors are considered. The verb could be interpreted as referring to the political ambitions of some in attempting to instigate a revolution such as that of Barcochba in A.D. 135.[15] Or, it could mean the religious leaders of that day were offering resistance to the movement begun by John and Jesus. Although John 6:15 does make a reference to the former, there is no indication that such a revolutionary

---

11. J. N. Darby, *Synopsis of the Books of the Bible,* 3:59.

12. Hermann Cremer, *Biblico-Theological Lexicon of New Testament Greek,* p. 141.

13. Albert Schweitzer, *The Quest of the Historical Jesus,* p. 357.

14. Cremer, *Biblico-Theological Lexicon,* p. 142. cf. Gottlob Schrenk, *Theological Dictionary of the New Testament,* 1:609-614.

15. Theodore H. Robinson, *The Gospel of Matthew,* p. 102.

movement was under foot in the context of Matthew 11:12. Rather the opposite seems to be true.

It seems best therefore to refer βιάζεται to the movements of the religious leaders. Several factors favor this view. If it referred to a political revolution, why does Matthew refer to the time interval between John and "now" (ἄρτι) in verse twelve? There were certainly political revolutions preceding the appearance of John. What about the Maccabean revolt? The statement of Christ must have some reference to John the Baptist. In addition, Luke 16:16, when correctly interpreted, substantiates the view that the religious leaders of the people were snatching the kingdom from Israel. The preposition "into" (εἰς) in Luke 16:16 can easily mean against as it clearly does in Luke 12:10; 15:18; and Acts 6:11. On the basis of extra-biblical usage Cremer concludes that βιάζεται in Luke means to struggle against the coming of the kingdom.[16] This is correct. The occurrence of the verb in Matthew agrees exactly with this.

A third proof of the correctness of this view is seen in the accusation which Christ hurls at the scribes and Pharisees in Matthew 23:13. The leaders were attempting to wrest the reins of the kingdom from the Messiah and make the kingdom conform to their pleasures. Their hypocrisy and their hatred of Jesus and John caused the kingdom to suffer violence. By their opposition to it they snatched it from the people. The imprisonment of John was a cold and factual testimony to their rejection of his message, the same one proclaimed by the King and His evangelists. They were not willing to repent and to bring forth fruits worthy of repentance.

The present condition of the kingdom is for the first time seen in its place of rejection. However, it is still near at hand. That it began to be near with the appearance of John is seen in the use of the phrase "from the days of John" (ἀπὸ δὲ τῶν ἡμερῶν Ἰωάννου) in verse twelve and the phrase "until John" (ἕως Ἰωάννου) in verse thirteen. The period of time from John to the time Christ is speaking to the crowds is looked upon as a unique time anticipated by the law and the prophets. The prophets and the law prophesied until John because the time of fulfillment began with him. That the kingdom is still at hand when Christ is speaking is shown by the adverb "now" (ἄρτι) in verse twelve and the present tense of the verb "to care" (θέλω) in verse fourteen. The

16. Cremer, *Biblico-Theological Lexicon*, p. 143.

kingdom began to be near when John preached; it was still near at the time Christ spoke these words

11:14-11:15. *"And if you care to accept it, he himself is Elijah, who was to come. He who has ears to hear, let him hear."* The King has declared the present condition of the kingdom—it is suffering violence at the hands of the violent men who were the leaders of Israel. Now He goes on to show the potential of the coming of the kingdom. The kingdom would come *if* they would receive it. The conditional particle "if" ($\epsilon\iota$) makes the condition one of assumed reality. It is certain that if they should receive it John would be the fulfillment of Malachi 4. There is scarcely a passage in Scripture which shows more clearly that the kingdom was being offered to Israel at this time. Its coming was contingent upon one thing: Israel's receiving it by genuine repentance.[17] Because of this John is not here said to be Elijah. He fulfilled Isaiah 40:3 and Malachi 3:1, but not Malachi 4:5-6 because the latter passage is dependent upon the response of the people. Malachi 4:6 says that he shall turn the heart of the fathers to the children and the heart of the children to their fathers; John did not do this. John is the forerunner of the King. He could be Elijah if Israel would but respond correctly.[18] If John were Elijah the kingdom would be Israel's.

d. The Censoriousness of the Generation of the King, **11:16-11:19.** *"But to what shall I compare this generation? It is like children sitting in the market places, who call out to the other children, and say, 'We played the flute for you, and you did not dance; we sang a dirge, and you did not mourn.' For John came neither eating nor drinking, and they say, 'He has a demon!' The Son of Man came eating and drinking, and they say, 'Behold, a gluttonous man and a drunkard, a friend of tax-gatherers and sinners!' Yet wisdom is vindicated by her deeds."* Matthew has set forth proofs of the King's person by referring, in answer to John's question, to the works and words of Jesus. He goes on to make reference to Christ's commendation of John and the Lord's identification of him. Elijah would have come in the person of John and the kingdom would be Israel's if it would receive it. The kingdom has drawn near and its coming is contingent on Israel's repentance. But Israel responds wrongly to the ministry of John and Jesus. Not only do the people fail to repent, but they are brazen enough to censure the herald and the King. Because of this the King likens

17. McClain, *The Greatness of the Kingdom,* pp. 306-307.
18. Darby, *Synopsis,* 3:101.

Israel to children sitting in the marketplace and criticizing other children for not responding to their demands. They cry to John to dance, but he lives like an ascetic. They call to Jesus to fast, but He eats with sinners and ministers to them.[19]

Jesus pointed to the foolishness of Israel by comparing them to children. Now He emphasizes this charge by using a proverb, "But wisdom is justified from her works." The aorist is no doubt gnomic here[20] and the preposition "from" ($\dot{\alpha}\pi\acute{o}$) is used in the sense of the preposition "by" ($\dot{\upsilon}\pi\acute{o}$).[21] Actually the saying forms a bridge to what follows. Israel censured John and Jesus, but the folly of their criticism is sure to be displayed by its result, which is judgment. On the other hand the methods of John and Jesus are certain to be justified.[22]

2. The Indifference to the Message of the King, 11:20-11:24.

11:20-11:24. *Then He began to reproach the cities in which most of His miracles were done, because they did not repent. "Woe to you, Chorazin! Woe to you, Bethsaida! For if the miracles had occurred in Tyre and Sidon which occurred in you, they would have repented long ago in sackcloth and ashes. Nevertheless I say to you, it shall be more tolerable for Tyre and Sidon in the day of judgment, than for you. And you, Capernaum, will not be exalted to heaven, will you? You shall descend to Hades; for if the miracles had occurred in Sodom which occurred in you, it would have remained to this day. Nevertheless I say to you that it shall be more tolerable for the land of Sodom in the day of judgment, than for you."* The first evidence of the King's rejection is the antagonism shown to the methods of John and the Messiah. The second indication is the indifference shown to the message of the King. The King and His disciples had ministered for some time in Galilee, but there was no repentance on the part of the nation. As a result of this indifference Jesus pronounces judgment on those cities in which the great number of His mighty works had been performed.

There are several factors which give significance to this section. First it indicates the new character of the Lord's ministry which commences at this point.

19. Richard Chenevix Trench, *Studies in the Gospels,* p. 160.
20. Bruce, "The Synoptic Gospels," *The Expositor's Greek Testament,* 1:176.
21. M'Neile, *St. Matthew,* p. 159.
22. Plummer, *Exegetical Commentary,* p. 163.

> Those who really wish to know their Bibles should see that we are
> in new country from this verse forward. Draw a thick black line
> between the nineteenth and the twentieth verses. There is a great
> divide here. Truth flows down to opposite oceans from this point.
> We are face to face with a new aspect of the work of Christ. The
> Lord Jesus was henceforth a different Man in His action and in His
> speech. The One Who was the meek and lowly Jesus was about to
> exhibit His strong wrath in no uncertain way.[23]

This change in the tone of the ministry of the King is indicated by the
immediate context. In Matthew the verb "to begin" ($\mathring{\eta}\rho\xi\alpha\tau o$) is never
superfluous; it usually indicates a new movement or a change. This verb
with the adverb "then" ($\tau\acute{o}\tau\epsilon$) in verse twenty confirms the statement of
Barnhouse. In addition a new word is used by the Lord: *woe*. Further-
more, the King upbraids the cities in which He had worked, a thing
hitherto not recorded of the King. The fact that Matthew uses the verb
"to be done" ($\dot{\epsilon}\gamma\acute{\epsilon}\nu o\nu\tau o$) in verse twenty indicates that the work performed in Galilee was looked on as being completed. It ". . . looks back
like a plu-perf. at the Galilean ministry as wholly, or to a large extent,
completed."[24] This is the sense in which it is also used in verse twenty-
one.

A second significant factor is the evidence of completed rejection. If
the cities in which He had performed many mighty works failed to heed
His message, who would? The fact that Matthew uses the word meaning
"power, might, or strength" ($\delta\acute{\nu}\nu\alpha\mu\iota\varsigma$) for Christ's miracles indicates
the power displayed by them, power which authenticated His message
of repentance. The rejection was indicated by simple indifference on the
part of the people. Verse twenty says they did not repent, while verse
twenty-three shows that Capernaum was too proud to repent. Concerning the indifference of the cities Plummer comments, "They perhaps
took a languid interest in His miracles and teaching; but His beneficence
never touched their hearts, and His doctrine produced no change in their
lives."[25] Though crowds followed Him and came to be healed, they
failed to respond to the message.

A third significant contribution of this section to the argument is seen
in the results of rejection, which are twofold. One relates to future
eternal condemnation. That this is in view is seen from verse twenty-
four where the judgment of Sodom is still looked upon as being future.

23. Donald Grey Barnhouse, *His Own Received Him Not, But . . .*, p. 77.
24. M'Neile, *St. Matthew*, p. 159.
25. Plummer, *Exegetical Commentary*, p. 165.

Since Sodom no longer existed, the reference is to the coming judgment of the dead at the Great White Throne. A second result is the removal of the earthly kingdom from that generation of Israel. The nation was not rejected because they had a wrong concept of the kingdom, but because they failed to repent. Jesus was not attempting to change their ideas of an earthly kingdom; rather He was attempting to bring them to the place where they might obtain it.

A fourth factor to note is that which has been seen throughout Christ's ministry, the claims which He makes. Both eternal condemnation and the coming of the kingdom are contingent upon the response one makes to Him. The cities in which He had been working failed; consequently they lost both eternal life and the kingdom for that generation.

3. The Invitation of the King, 11:25-11:30.

This is the third evidence of the rejection of the King, the others being the antagonism displayed toward John and Jesus and the indifference to the King's message. The invitation is an indication of rejection since it is a call to those who had humbly repented to separate themselves from proud Israel and to come to Him. Israel had failed to repent; now the King calls to the repentant to come to Him. Thus a whole new emphasis is given in the invitation of the King.

11:25-11:26. *At that time Jesus answered and said, "I praise Thee, O Father, Lord of heaven and earth, that Thou didst hide these things from the wise and intelligent and didst reveal them to babes. Yes, Father, for thus it was well-pleasing in Thy sight."* The pronoun "that" (ἐκεῖνος) with a word indicating time points to a change of subject. So here the King tenders an invitation to come to Him in sharp contrast to the condemnation just preceding. The fact that the things of the kingdom were hidden from the wise and understanding but revealed to babes shows why Israel failed to repent. That nation was not in the place of humility but in pride; consequently spiritual things could not be revealed to Israel.

11:27. *"All things have been handed over to Me by My Father; and no one knows the Son, except the Father; nor does anyone know the Father, except the Son, and anyone to whom the Son wills to reveal Him."* After the King recognizes the sovereignty of His Father, He openly acknowledges His own authority in verse twenty-seven. The aorist tense of the verb "to be handed over" (παρεδόθη) points back to eternity, the King pre-existing as one who is sovereign with the Father.[26] Thus He lays claim to deity. It is significant that the King further asserts His divine sovereignty by stating that one can only come to know the Father by means of the Son, Jesus being the Son. Furthermore, this is only accomplished by the sovereign grace of the Son who would reveal the Father to whomsoever the Son willed to do so.

11:28-11:30. *"Come to Me, all who are weary and heavy laden, and I will give you rest. Take My yoke upon you, and learn from Me, for I am gentle and humble in heart; and you shall find rest for your souls. For My yoke is easy, and My load is light."* The invitation given here implies two things—the condition of Israel and the rejection of Israel on the part of the Son. The two participles in verse twenty-eight; "weary" ($\kappa o\pi\iota\tilde{\omega}\nu\tau\epsilon\varsigma$) and "heavy-laden" ($\pi\epsilon\phi o\rho\tau\iota\sigma-\mu\acute{\epsilon}\nu o\iota$), describe the condition of Israel.

> The one implies toil, the other endurance. The one refers to the weary search for truth and for relief for a troubled conscience; the other refers to the heavy load of observances that give no relief, and perhaps also the sorrow of life, which, apart from the consolations of a true faith, are so crushing.[27]

The spiritual leaders of Israel had brought them to this place of toiling and bearing burdens. The turbulent history of Israel's past together with their restlessness while their Messiah was with them bore testimony to their need for rest. And this rest was bound up in a person, even Immanuel, the One they were in the process of rejecting.

The invitation also shows that the nation as a group had decided already to reject Christ. Because of this decision Jesus now extends an invitation, not to Israel as a nation, but to individual Jews to come to Him. Despite Israel's rejection He would give these individuals rest.[28] Since the nation rejects Him, He has no alternative but to reject it and to postpone the coming of the kingdom.

B. The Illustrations of the Opposition to the King
12:1-12:50

The antagonism of Israel's religious hierarchy and the indifference of the people are ominous indications that the decision to reject Jesus as the

26. Ibid., p. 168.
27. Ibid., p. 170.
28. Charles L. Feinberg, *Premillennialism or Amillennialism?*, p. 66.

Messiah has been reached. As yet the choice is an inner one, but as a result of this decision the opposition to the King develops and becomes more open. Matthew uses five illustrations involving four basic principles to show how the opposition is manifested and increases. In each there is a negative approach to Jesus and a positive answer by the King.

1. The Contention Concerning the Sabbath, 12:1-12:21.

The first two illustrations of open opposition involve two incidents which concern the Sabbath question. The Sabbath was peculiarly important to the Jew. Just as circumcision marked him as a son of Abraham, so the sign of the Sabbath bore testimony to his relationship to the Mosaic law. Matthew's Gospel is addressed to Jews; this may explain why he included two illustrations involving the Sabbath.

a. The Relationship of the Sabbath to Man, 12:1-12:8.

The first example of opposition is recorded in Matthew 12:1-8.

12:1-12:2. *At that time Jesus went on the Sabbath through the grain-fields, and His disciples became hungry and began to pick the heads of grain and eat. But when the Pharisees saw it, they said to Him, "Behold, Your disciples do what is not lawful to do on a Sabbath."* The illustration is introduced by the demonstrative pronoun "that" (ἐκεῖνος) with a designation of time. In this illustration the Pharisees accuse the Lord's disciples of breaking the Sabbath by plucking grain and eating it. The verb "to begin" (ἤρξατο) of verse one bespeaks the critical attitude of the Pharisees. As soon as the disciples began to pluck and eat, the Pharisees leveled their accusation of them at the Lord.

12:3-12:4. *But He said to them, "Have you not read what David did, when he became hungry, he and his companions; how he entered the house of God, and they ate the consecrated bread, which was not lawful for him to eat, nor for those with him, but for the priests alone?"* In answer to this criticism the King presents a most logical argument. He first refers the Pharisees to the Old Testament Scriptures involving David when he was in rejection. When David was hungry, he and his men ate the shewbread which it was not lawful for them to eat. By recounting this incident Jesus showed the Pharisees that man's needs supersede the law of the Sabbath. But there is also a very strong implication. This is seen in the parallel situation in which Jesus found Himself. David, God's anointed king, in rejection was forced to eat that which it was not lawful to eat. However, he was held guiltless because as long as "...David was rejected and a fugitive, the holy things connected with the ceremonials given to Israel by God ceased to be holy."[29]

David himself points this out in 1 Samuel 21:5, "... the bread is in a manner common, yea, though it were sanctified this day in the vessel (KJV)." "David was the Lord's anointed King. He was rejected, and while he was rejected there was nothing in all Israel that was holy. So he took the bread because, in that moment, *he* was greater than the *bread*."[30] Now the Son of David is in the same position. To pluck and to eat on the Sabbath is not wrong since the rejection of the King voided the restrictions of the Sabbath. As long as Israel refused to receive the King, it was hollow mockery for it to observe the Sabbath.

12:5-12:6. *"Or have you not read in the Law, that on the Sabbath the priests in the temple break the Sabbath, and are innocent? But I say to you, that something greater than the temple is here."* Jesus continues His refutation by alluding to the law's provision for the priest to profane the Sabbath in order for him to carry out his duties in the temple. The work of the temple overrides the sanctity of the Sabbath. Following these words Jesus makes an application. "Something greater ($\mu\epsilon\tilde{\iota}\zeta o\nu$) than the temple is here." The neuter gender of "greater" must not refer to Christ as a person but to His ministry. If the ministry of the temple superseded Sabbath rules, how much more does the work of the Messiah overrule the Sabbath!

12:7-12:8. *"But if you had known what this means, 'I desire compassion, and not a sacrifice,' you would not have condemned the innocent. For the Son of Man is Lord of the Sabbath."* In verses seven and eight the Lord advances another argument which reflects on their spiritual discernment. Their spiritual condition caused them to accuse guiltless ones; they did not know Hosea 6:6 in their experience. Interested only in performing sacrifices for outward show and pride, the truths relative to the person of Jesus had been hidden from them (Matthew 11:25). If they had known mercy they would have been humble as infants and would have had God's revelation concerning the person of His Son on earth. But they did not even know the mockery of their own hypocrisy. The contrary-to-fact condition of verse seven indicates this.[31] Jesus uses this Old Testament passage very effectively to

29. A. C. Gaebelein, *The Gospel of Matthew*, 1:240.
30. Barnhouse, *His Own*, p. 108.
31. Bruce, "The Synoptic Gospels," *The Expositor's Greek Testament*, 1:182.

show their spiritual dullness. In Matthew 9:13 the King shows them that if they had known the meaning of this verse they would have recognized their own needs; here they would have recognized the King.

The conjunction "for" (γάρ) of verse eight shows why they should not have condemned His disciples. Jesus, the Messiah, is Lord also of the Sabbath. Therefore the disciples were "... justified by the presence of the Messiah."[32] Because the Pharisees were blind due to their hardened hypocrisy, they failed to recognize the King and as a result condemned innocent ones.

   b. The Relationship of the Sabbath to Good Deeds, 12:9-12:21. The second illustration of opposition also concerns the Sabbath.

   12:9-12:13. *And departing from there, He went into their synagogue. And behold, there was a man with a withered hand. And they questioned Him, saying, "Is it lawful to heal on the Sabbath?" –in order that they might accuse Him. And He said to them, "What man shall there be among you, who shall have one sheep, and if it falls into a pit on the Sabbath, will he not take hold of it, and lift it out? Of how much more value then is a man than a sheep! So then, it is lawful to do good on the Sabbath."* Then He *said to the man, "Stretch out your hand!" And he stretched it out, and it was restored to normal, like the other.* The King sets forth the principle that, rather than leave the good undone on the Sabbath, it is lawful to do the good.

   12:14. *But the Pharisees went out, and counseled together against Him, as to how they might destroy Him.* As a result of this sound refutation the Pharisees take counsel to destroy Him. The words "to take counsel" (συμβούλιον ἔλαβον) show the Pharisees have reached a definite decision. "The phrase means to come to a conclusion, rather than to deliberate whether or not."[33] The only question now was how to accomplish His destruction.

   12:15-12:16. *But Jesus, aware of this, withdrew from there. And many followed Him, and He healed them all, and warned them not to make Him known.* This action of the Pharisees brings the King to a crucial point in His ministry. M'Neile writes, "The incident marks a crisis in the Lord's life, being the culminating point of the opposition of

---

32. C. G. Montefiore, *The Synoptic Gospels,* 2:189.
33. Plummer, *Exegetical Commentary,* p. 175.

the Jewish religious authorities."[34] As a result of the decision of the Pharisees, Jesus "withdraws" (ἀναχωρέω) from there. But even as He withdraws many follow Him and He heals them. This is the pattern of His ministry until His final and open rejection in chapters twenty-one to twenty-seven—opposition, withdrawal, and continued ministry. Now He charges all not to make Him known. The reason the Lord thus secludes Himself is to prevent open conflict with the Pharisees.[35] Besides, the work of revelation was the Father's (Matthew 11:25).

12:17-12:21. *in order that what was spoken through Isaiah the prophet, might be fulfilled, saying,*

> *"Behold, My Servant whom I have chosen; My Beloved in whom My soul is well pleased; I will put My Spirit upon Him, and He shall proclaim justice to the Gentiles. He will not quarrel, nor cry out; nor will any one hear His voice in the streets. A battered reed He will not break off, and a smoldering wick He will not put out, until He leads justice to victory. And in His name the Gentiles will hope."*

The withdrawal of the King and His command to keep His presence unknown is done in order to fulfill prophecy. The quotation is from Isaiah 42:1-4, a Messianic prophecy. It suits Matthew's argument well. First, it shows how the withdrawal of the King fits the work of the Messiah. He shall not wrangle or cry out in the streets. It is also a fitting picture of His compassion, for he will not break a battered reed or put out a smoldering wick. Thus Bennetch writes, "The very passivity evidenced by the Nazarene here was nothing against, but rather a good argument for, His Messiahship, judging from the ancient prediction of Isaiah it fulfilled."[36]

A second argument presented by the prophecy is the divine approval of the Messiah. Although He does not cry out or engage in open conflicts, He is still God's Servant who shall carry out God's program.

The indication of a future ministry to Gentiles is also very important. In the face of rejection by the nation of Israel Matthew, by Messianic prophecies, prepares his Jewish reader for the proclamation of a universal Savior. The Gentiles shall hope in His name.

34. M'Neile, *St. Matthew,* p. 171.
35. Samuel J. Andrews, *The Life of Our Lord Upon the Earth,* p. 265.
36. John Henry Bennetch, "Matthew: An Apologetic," *Bibliotheca Sacra* 103 (October 1946):480.

Finally, the emphasis on judgment is very fitting. Even Matthew's translation of the Hebrew amplifies this aspect of Messiah's ministry. Concerning Matthew 12:18 M'Neile writes, "$\kappa\rho\iota\sigma\iota\varsigma$ [justice] in Mt. has not the wide meaning of מִשְׁפָּט [judgment], almost 'religion'; he understands it of the fast approaching judgment."[37] The same commentator makes a similar remark concerning verse twenty.

> In Heb. נֶצַח means "permanence," "perpetuity," in Aram. "victory"; the latter was adopted in the Gk. translation which Mt. used . . . For the evangelist the rendering was important: the Lord's earthly activities were those which the prophets predicted of the Messiah, and His final victorious judgement was certain.[38]

Thus Matthew concludes the discussion of the King's conflict with the Pharisees over the principle of the Sabbath with a prophecy in connection with His withdrawal. This is very appropriate since it sets the stage for the coming scenes which are the result of the King's rejection.

2. The Contention Concerning the Power of the King, 12:22-12:37.

The second principle involves the power of the King and revolves about the incident recorded here.

12:22-12:23. *Then there was brought to Him a demon-possessed man who was blind and dumb, and He healed him, so that the dumb man spoke and saw. And all the multitudes were amazed, and began to say, "This man cannot be the Son of David, can he?"* Matthew introduces this incident and the crucial discourse which follows with his characteristic adverb "then" ($\tau\acute{o}\tau\epsilon$). The religious leaders are forced to explain the power of the Messiah after He has healed one who was demon possessed. The sheer amazement of the people is shown by the question introduced with the interrogative particle $\mu\acute{\eta}\tau\iota$. It expects the negative answer. They were saying, "This can't be the Messiah, can it?" Thus their inquiry, while indicating a faint possibility of belief, indicated that their amazement was primarily in unbelief.

12:24. *But when the Pharisees heard it, they said, "This man casts out demons only by Beelzebul the ruler of the demons."* The stubborn Pharisees attempt to establish the unbelief of the people by

---

37. M'Neile, *St. Matthew,* p. 172.
38. Ibid., p. 173.

hurling a vicious accusation at Jesus. The Pharisees see the issue. Either His power is of God or it is of Satan. It is impossible to deny the work which Jesus has performed. Not willing to accept Him as the Messiah, the Pharisees say His work is performed by diabolical power. Their contempt for Him is shown by the pronoun "this" (οὗτος). Matthew has referred to the same accusation before (9:34), but now he uses it to show how it causes an open break between Christ and the Pharisees.

12:25-12:28. *And knowing their thoughts He said to them, "Any kingdom divided against itself is laid waste; and any city or house divided against itself shall not stand. And if Satan casts out Satan, he is divided against himself; how then shall his kingdom stand? And if I by Beelzebul cast out demons, by whom do your sons cast them out? Consequently they shall be your judges. But if I cast out demons by the Spirit of God, then the kingdom of God has come upon you."* The Lord answers the charge which the Pharisees place against Him with three logical affirmations. First, He says that the accusation of the Pharisees is untenable because it is impossible for a kingdom, a city, or even a family to exist when it is divided against itself (Matthew 12:25). Second, the King states in 12:27 that if other exorcists cast out demons, the Pharisees affirm that it is done by divine power.[39] A third reply is seen in the inference the King makes concerning the kingdom of God (12:28). The deduction is clear and simple. The powers which the Pharisees were beholding were clear evidences of the nearness of the kingdom. This sign was a demonstration of Messianic authority.

The verb in verse twenty-eight "to come" (φθάνω), has caused some difficulty. Those who refuse to accept the teaching of Scripture concerning the offer of the kingdom to Israel usually refer to Luke 17:21 in an attempt to interpret Matthew 12:28. There is, however, an ambiguity in the Luke passage which has caused them much difficulty. It involves the adverb ἐντός. While some say it means *within*, others say it is to be translated *among*. Of the two, *among* is by far the better. Major, Manson, and Wright give three reasons why this is so.[40] First, the kingdom of God could not in any way be said to be within His foes, the Pharisees, whom He was then addressing. Second, the kingdom under discussion was not a spiritual one, but the earthly, Jewish, eschatological one.

39. Plummer, *Exegetical Commentary,* p. 177.
40. H. D. A. Major, T. W. Manson, and C. J. Wright, *The Mission and Message of Jesus,* p. 596.

Finally, Jesus always speaks of men entering the kingdom and never of the kingdom entering into men.

But there is even a better meaning for ἐντός than *among*. Colin H. Roberts proves that the word has a broader connotation. He contends that in its occurrences in the papyri it can either be translated as "in your control" or "in your possession."[41] J. Gwyn Griffiths concurs with this and substantiates it with occurrences in classical Greek.[42] Thus Luke 17:21 substantiates the premillennial interpretation of Matthew 12:28. The kingdom of the heavens had drawn near; its nearness was proven by the evidence of signs; and whether it should come or not was in the control of Israel.

Actually φθάνω simply means *to come* or *to arrive*. The fact that the Lord uses it in a first class conditional sentence shows that He assumes the kingdom had come. Whereas the perfect tense had before been used to refer to the condition of the kingdom, the aorist tense is now used. In view of the evident rejection of the King, the kingdom could not now be said to be in the condition of *remaining* at hand. In fact the kingdom is never again preached as having drawn near.

12:29. *"Or how can anyone enter the strong man's house and carry off his property, unless he first binds the strong man? And then he will plunder his house."* The King makes a most interesting statement concerning Satan in verse twenty-nine. Christ by a parable states that in order for kingdom conditions to exist on earth, Satan must first be bound. By this statement He previews John the Apostle's discussion in Revelation 20. Jesus does not say He has bound Satan or is even in the process of doing so. He simply sets the principle before the Pharisees. His works testify to His ability to bind Satan, and therefore they attest His power to establish the kingdom.

12:30-12:33. *"He who is not with Me is against Me; and he who does not gather with Me scatters. Therefore I say to you, any sin and blasphemy shall be forgiven men; but blasphemy against the Spirit shall not be forgiven. And whoever shall speak a word against the Son of Man, it shall be forgiven him; but whoever shall speak against the Holy Spirit, it shall not be forgiven him, either in this age, or in the age to come. Either make the tree good, and its fruit good; or make the tree rotten, and its fruit rotten; for the tree is*

41. Colin H. Roberts, "The Kingdom of Heaven, Lk. XVII.21," *Harvard Theological Review* 41 (January 1948):1-8.
42. J. Gwyn Griffiths, "ἐντός ὑμῶν (Luke xvii.21)," *The Expository Times* 63 (October 1951): 30-31.

known by its fruit. " Instead of joining with Jesus the Pharisees were opposed to Him and were even scattering those that He was gathering. On account of the blasphemous accusation of the Pharisees, the King judges them for having committed the unpardonable sin. Having refused the witness of the Holy Spirit to their hearts, they attributed the work of the Spirit in Christ to Satan. That the Pharisees were working against the Spirit is proven by their words.

In Matthew 7 the King uses the same illustration as He does in Matthew 12:33. In chapter seven He employs it to show that words and works indicate character; here it is utilized to prove that words are the manifestation of the heart. The blasphemy of the Spirit pouring forth from the lips of the Pharisees was that which would condemn them.

12:34-12:37. *"You brood of vipers, how can you, being evil, speak what is good? For the mouth speaks out of that which fills the heart. The good man out of his good treasure brings forth what is good; and the evil man out of his evil treasure brings forth what is evil. And I say to you, that every careless word that men shall speak, they shall render account for it in the day of judgment. For by your words you shall be justified, and by your words you shall be condemned.* " The cleavage between the religious authorities and Jesus is now final and irreparable. Kiddle writes, "It is worth noting that in Mt. the breach between Jesus and the authorities is not definite until the Beelzebub charge."[43]

3. The Contention Concerning the Signs of the King, 12:38-12:45.

The third principle involves the signs of the King and revolves about the incident recorded here.

12:38. *Then some of the scribes and Pharisees answered Him, saying, "Teacher, we want to see a sign from You."* The incident is bound to the preceding by the adverb "then" (τότε). Although their rejection of Him is certain, the scribes and Pharisees approach the King and in antagonistic unbelief seek a sign from Him.

12:39-12:40. *But He answered and said to them, "An evil and adulterous generation craves for a sign; and yet no sign shall be given to it but the sign of Jonah the prophet; for just as Jonah was three days and three nights in the belly of the sea-monster; so shall*

---

43. M. Kiddle, "The Conflict Between the Disciples, the Jews, and the Gentiles in St. Matthew's Gospel, " *The Journal of Theological Studies* 36 (January 1935):37.

the Son of Man be three days and three nights in the heart of the earth." Immediately the King points out their spiritual condition, and because of their intent refuses to comply with their request. He calls them an evil and adulterous generation. From a prophetic standpoint the adjective "adulterous" (μοιχαλίς) is an important word. Israel is called the adulterous wife of Jehovah throughout the Old Testament prophecies (Jeremiah 3:10; Hosea 7:13-16; Isaiah 57:3-8). Israel, by its formalism and hypocrisy, was living in spiritual adultery. The leaders were manifesting this condition by seeking a sign. Unbelievers seek a sign for the sign's sake; a believer sees in it authentication.

Because the scribes and Pharisees were unbelievers, no sign would be given to them, except one. This sign was the death and resurrection of Jesus. The King in using Jonah for an illustration intimates that which is to follow. The only prophet to preach to the Gentiles sent from Israel was Jonah. Gentiles would yet hear the message concerning the Messiah of Israel.

12:41-12:42. *"The men of Nineveh shall stand up with this generation at the judgment, and shall condemn it because they repented at the preaching of Jonah; and behold, something greater than Jonah is here. The Queen of the South shall rise up with this generation at the judgment and shall condemn it; because she came from the ends of the earth to hear the wisdom of Solomon; and behold, something greater than Solomon is here."* The mention of Jonah brings the King to His next point, the judgment of Israel. Nineveh repented at the proclamation of a prophet. Israel failed to respond to the preaching of its Messiah; therefore Nineveh would be a witness against Israel. Likewise, the Queen of Sheba, who marveled at the wisdom of Solomon, would bear testimony against Israel. The reason is patent. Something "greater" (πλεῖον) than Jonah with his proclamation or Solomon with his wisdom here, the King with His kingdom.

It is interesting to note the transition from the sign of Jonah to judgment. The Pharisees believed that a resurrection preceded the judgment.[44] It was natural therefore for the King to proceed from the subject of the resurrection to judgment. The transition is all the more closely knit by the inclusion of Jonah in both.

12:43-12:45. *"Now when the unclean spirit goes out of a man, it passes through waterless places, seeking rest, and does not find it. Then it says, 'I will return to my house from which I came;' and*

---

44. F. W. Green, ed., *The Gospel According to Saint Matthew,* p. 183.

when it comes, it finds it unoccupied, swept, and put in order. Then it goes, and takes along with it seven other spirits more wicked than itself, and they go in and live there; and the last state of that man becomes worse than the first. That is the way it will also be with this evil generation. " Verses forty-three to forty-five, which contain a parable, are joined to the subject of judgment. The Lord uses the illustration of a demon who left his home and returned to find it empty, swept, and adorned. He then finds seven other demons to dwell there. This parable portrays the reason why Israel was not properly responding to the ministry of their Messiah. Under the preaching of John the Baptist and the Lord Jesus, a moral reformation of sorts had taken place. But here is the peril of the unhaunted heart. More and worse evil spirits move in. [45] Israel's house was already filled with demons; therefore it rejected its King.

4. The Question Concerning the Kin of the King, 12:46-12:50.

12:46-12:50. *While He was still speaking to the multitudes, behold, His mother and His brothers were standing outside, seeking to speak to Him. And someone said to Him, "Behold, Your mother and Your brothers are standing outside seeking to speak to You." But He answered the one who was telling Him and said, "Who is My mother and who are My brothers?" And stretching out His hand toward His disciples, He said, "Behold, My mother and My brothers! For whoever shall do the will of My Father who is in heaven, he is My brother and sister and mother."* Perhaps the most subtle of all opposition comes from the family of the King. It is closely linked with the preceding by the words, "While He was still speaking ... " (Ἔτι αὐτοῦ λαλοῦντος). Mark 3:21 gives the occasion for this incident. The family, prompted by friends, is about to seize Jesus because they think He is beside Himself. The King takes this opportunity to instruct His listeners concerning the nature of one's relationship to the Messiah. Participation in the Messianic kingdom is not merely based upon a claim to Abraham's family, but it is contingent upon a spiritual relationship to Christ (Matthew 3:9).

---

45. Cf. Hendriksen, *Gospel of Matthew*, pp. 540-541.

C. The Adaptation of the King to his Opposition
13:1-13:53

The die is cast. The religious leaders have openly declared their opposition to their Messiah. The people of Israel are amazed at the power of Jesus and His speech, but they fail to recognize Him as their King. Not seeing the Messiahship of Jesus in His words and works, they have separated the fruit from the tree. Because of this opposition and spiritual apathy, the King adapts His teaching method and the doctrine concerning the coming of the kingdom to the situation.

An Introduction to Parabolic Instruction

Before this time the King had used parables to *illustrate* the truth; now, however, He *presents* His doctrine in a long discourse composed entirely of parables (Matthew 13:3, 34). This discourse is recorded in Matthew 13. Previously He had proclaimed the nearness of the kingdom, but never again does He do this. Rather, the King in parables instructs His disciples concerning the mysteries of the kingdom.

The Characteristics of the Parabolic Instruction

The Meaning of "Parable." According to the etymology of the word, "parable" ($\pi\alpha\rho\alpha\beta o\lambda\acute{\eta}$) is the act of placing one thing beside another so that a comparison may be made between them.[46] As a result the word came to mean a comparison, illustration, or figure. In the Greek of the Old Testament the word was used to cover many kinds of literary composition.

> $\Pi\alpha\rho\alpha\beta o\lambda\acute{\eta}$ is the LXX. rendering of מָשָׁל some forty-five times; $\Pi\alpha\rho o\iota\mu\acute{\iota}\alpha$ occurs in Prov. 4 and Sir. 5 only. The word denotes utterances of very various kinds: gnomic and poetical utterances ... taunts ... riddles ... [47]

A good comparison of the parable with other modes of composition is made by Kerr.

> ... it differs from a fable in that the latter involves the animal creation, and has it acting contrary to nature, and is always a possible occurrence. It is drawn from nature or from human af-

46. Henry Barclay Swete, *The Parables of the Kingdom*, p. 1.
47. M'Neile, *St. Matthew*, p. 185.

fairs. Furthermore, the teaching of a parable belongs to a higher realm than that of the fable. The myth is different from the parable, because the former is a growth in unhistoric times, and has not like the parable a didactic design. The allegory is more closely akin to the parable, inasmuch as they both are comparisons of one thing with another, but differs from it in that while the former transfers the properties and qualities and relations of one to the other, the latter preserves them apart.[48]

One may conclude then that in the Synoptics a parable denotes an extended comparison between nature or life and the things involving the spiritual life and God's dealings with men.

The Purpose of the Parabolic Instruction. The key to the purpose of these parables is found in the Lord's own explanation (Matthew 13:11-18). He says that He uses parables at this juncture for two purposes—to reveal truth and to conceal it. To the ones who accept the Messiah the truth and interpretation of the parables is revealed (Matthew 11:25-26; 13:11-16). On the other hand, to those who have hardened their hearts the truth is veiled by the parables (Matthew 11:25-26; 13:11-15).

By so concealing the truth the King is following His own injunction not to give that which is holy to dogs nor to cast pearls before swine (Matthew 7:6). In veiling the truth from those with hardened hearts the Lord was actually exercising grace. For, as Plummer says, "They were saved from the guilt of rejecting the truth, for they were not allowed to recognize it."[49]

The Context of the Parabolic Instruction. The context of any parabolic instruction is of primary importance for at least two reasons. First, it indicates the reasons for that type of instruction, and second, it is the basis for the interpretation of the parables. In verse one, the demonstrative pronoun "that" (ἐκεῖνος) is used with a time designation indicating a change of subject or of emphasis. The new thing being introduced here is of course the content and method of the parabolic instruction.

The first reason for the parables at this juncture is found in the attitude of rejection being manifested on the part of Israel. Matthew notes it by writing "on that day" (ἐν τῇ ἡμέρᾳ ἐκείνῃ), that is, the day of the open hostilities with the Pharisees and the misunderstanding of His

48. John H. Kerr, "The Veiled Gospel or the Parabolic Teachings of Jesus," *The Bible Student* 1 (May 1900): 276.

49. Plummer, *Exegetical Commentary,* p. 188.

family. The passive attitude of Israel in it all underscores the imminence of the ultimate rejection. Matthew 13:14-15 indicates that the hardening of Israel's heart had already taken place. Even the manner in which Jesus uses Isaiah's statement confirms this.

> The way the Lord changed the form of the statement is impressive. To Isaiah it was said, "Make the heart of this people fat . . . and shut their eyes; lest they see with their eyes." This Christ adapted to the then present fact: "this people's heart is [already] waxed gross, and their ears are [already] dull of hearing, and their eyes they have [themselves] closed; Lest haply they should perceive, etc.," and "*Therefore* speak I unto them in parables" (Matt. 13:10-15).[50]

It is evident that the kingdom could not come because of the opposition to the King; therefore, the King by means of parables instructs His disciples about the postponement of the kingdom. To instruct the "great multitudes" (ὄχλοι πολλοί, 13:2) of Israel openly about this matter would have engendered greater and premature hatred on the part of Israel for its King. If the ordinary Jew was unable to comprehend the person of the King, he certainly would not understand the postponement of the kingdom. Because of this Jesus instructs His disciples concerning this subject by means of parables. That the parables are closely associated with rejection is attested by the significant fact that in each of the Synoptics the parables follow the clear indication of the rejection of Christ.

Matthew sees a second reason for the Lord's speaking in parables. In verse thirty-five he notes that Jesus fulfilled that which was written in Psalm 78:2. The skillful use Matthew makes of the Old Testament for apologetic purposes is indicated by his application of this Psalm.

Psalm 78 is a review of God's workings in connection with Israel's past history. In introducing his subject, Asaph, the writer of the Psalm, writes the verse which Matthew quotes. Christ "establishes" (πληρωθῇ)[51] the meaning of this verse by His use of parables, for He is indicating God's workings in connection with the kingdom in the light of Israel's rejection of its King.

Not only does the context give the reasons for parabolic instruction, it also provides one of the bases for the interpretation of parables. Illustrations of this fact are found in Luke 14:28-32, where verse thirty-three

---

50. George Henry Lang, *Pictures and Parables*, p. 59.
51. See above, p. 55, for this interpretation of πληρωθῇ.

determines the meaning, and in Luke 15, where verses one and two explain the significance of the parable.[52]

Never can the context conflict with the interpretation of a parable. To look at a parable apart from the setting in which it is presented is to set one's boat adrift in the shifting tides of speculation. The parables of Matthew 13 must be considered in the context of the rejection of the Messiah.

The Content of the Parabolic Instruction

The Significance of "Mystery", (13:11). The content of the parables deals with the mysteries of the kingdom of the heavens. Since the Lord refers to the truths of the kingdom as mysteries, it is important to understand the significance of the word "mystery" ($\mu\nu\sigma\tau\eta\rho\iota\omicron\nu$). Abbott-Smith says that it is used in the New Testament " ... of the counsels of God ... once hidden but now revealed in the gospel or some fact thereof .... "[53] A more comprehensive and exact definition has been formulated.

> ... a $\mu\nu\sigma\tau\eta\rho\iota\omicron\nu$ in the New Testament is some phase of the eternal purposes of God which, although beyond the natural ability of man's intellect to discover or understand, can be and has been made known by divine revelation in God's own appointed time and to those who are illumined by the Spirit of God.[54]

Since the Lord refers to these parables as containing truths which are mysteries, one may infer that they contain facts which were not revealed before the time He spoke them. That this is the significance of $\mu\nu\sigma\tau\eta\rho\iota\omicron\nu$ in Matthew 13 is verified by verses seventeen and thirty-five.

The Mysteries of the Kingdom of the Heavens. It is extremely important that one notes that the new revelation concerns the kingdom of the heavens. The same kingdom is in view in Matthew 13 as the one which was proclaimed as being at hand in Matthew 3:2; 4:17, and 10:7. In chapter thirteen the King is giving additional information concerning the kingdom of heaven, information which has never before been revealed. He is instructing His disciples regarding a hitherto unrevealed period of time prior to the establishment of the kingdom. This new age would not be the promised kingdom, nor would it be, strictly speaking, a kingdom

52. Bernard Ramm, *Protestant Biblical Interpretation*, p. 284.
53. G. Abbott-Smith, *A Manual Greek Lexicon of the New Testament*, p. 298.
54. Thaddeus L. Bradley, "Μνστήριον in the Pauline Literature," (Doctor's dissertation, Dallas Theological Seminary, 1949), p. 49.

in the so-called "mystery form." Thus the mysteries of the kingdom of the heavens relate to the span in which the millennial kingdom is being postponed.

> ... the very outskirts of the subject already force the conclusion that those mysteries refer not *to the nature* of the kingdom, but *to the manner* of its establishment, *the means* employed, *the preparation* for it, *the time* for its manifestation, and such related subjects.[55]

However, there is one sense in which the kingdom can be said to exist during this period in that a portion of the people who shall inherit the kingdom live during this age. That is the explanation of the reference to the kingdom in verse forty-one and like passages elsewhere such as Colossians 1:13. The believers of this age become members of the church which shall form "... the spiritual nucleus for the future Kingdom ..."[56]

Because of this the Lord claims the believers of the church age as the true sons of the kingdom (verse thirty-eight). This term is also used in Matthew 8:11 to refer to the Jews who were supposed to inherit the kingdom but did not because of unbelief. The kingdom exists in this intercalation only in the sense that the sons of the kingdom are present. But strictly speaking the kingdom of the heavens in Matthew 13 refers to the prophesied and coming kingdom on the earth.

The Interpretation of the Parabolic Instruction

Needless to say, Matthew 13 containes a host of interpretive problems which have given birth to many different approaches to the chapter. Generally speaking these approaches may be placed in four categories, each of which will be considered in this discussion.

For Jews Only. The view commonly held by ultradispensationalists states that the parabolic instruction is for Jews only. They argue that the doctrine of the church as composed of Jew and Gentile was not known until it was revealed to Paul; therefore, there is no hint in the gospels of any truth applying to the church.[57] Bullinger claims that since all of the parables in Matthew 13 relate to the kingdom of the heavens, the only

---

55. George N. H. Peters, *The Theocratic Kingdom of Our Lord Jesus, the Christ, as Covenanted in the Old Testament, and Presented in the New Testament,* 1:142.
56. McClain, *The Greatness of the Kingdom,* p. 441.
57. J. C. O'Hair, *God's Grace Manifesto,* pp. 39-40.

people in view are Jews.[58] The kingdom of the heavens, he states, is limited nationally to Israel.[59]

This view is erroneous inasmuch as both of these presuppositions are incorrect. The church, while it was revealed to Paul, was not revealed to him only. Christ clearly gave a prophecy of the church which is recorded in Matthew 16. The ultradispensationalist's idea that the coming earthly kingdom is for Jews only is also incorrect. The King said, as a result of a Gentile's faith, "Many shall come from the east and west, and recline at table with Abraham, and Isaac, and Jacob, in the kingdom of heaven" (Matthew 8:11). Therefore, it is not correct to argue on the basis of these suppositions that Matthew 13 is for the Jews only.

To Correct the Kingdom Concept. Some contend that Christ graciously used these parables in an attempt to correct the mistaken notions which the Jews held of the kingdom.[60] They say He is teaching His audience that He did not come to establish any sort of earthly kingdom at all but rather to found a spiritual one.[61] Thus they practically equate the kingdom of the heavens with the church.[62]

This interpretation has appealed to many as being the correct one. However, it, too, meets with serious difficulties. The first is found in the fact that the church has not yet been mentioned in Matthew. Such a concept was completely foreign to the Jews. If it was difficult for believing and spiritual Jews to grasp the significance of the church at a later time when it was revealed openly, how much less would even the disciples of Jesus understand it when veiled in parables?

In addition, the kingdom of the heavens announced by John, Christ, and the disciples was clearly the literal and earthly one prophesied in the Old Testament.[63] If the kingdom of the heavens was so defined in the preceding portions of Matthew, what is the basis for changing its meaning here? It will also be noted that the Lord never rebukes His disciples for holding to the doctrine of an earthly kingdom. In fact, He encourages them along these lines (Matthew 19:28; 20:20-23; Acts 1:6-7).

The disciples had the same idea of an earthly Messianic kingdom at the end of Christ's life as before (Luke 24:21), and this after all of the

---

58. E. W. Bullinger, ed., *The Companion Bible,* p. 1336.
59. Ibid., pp. 155-57 of Appendix.
60. George A. Denzer, *The Parables of the Kingdom,* pp. 45-61.
61. Siegfried Goebel, *The Parables of Jesus,* p. 41.
62. Oswald T. Allis, *Prophecy and the Church,* p. 80.
63. See above, pp. 61-68.

instruction which the Lord had presented concerning the kingdom. In Matthew 13:16 the Lord pronounces the eyes of the disciples blessed because they see. If they had a completely erroneous concept of the kingdom, Jesus could hardly have made this statement.

Finally, this view completely disregards the Old Testament kingdom prophecies. Invariably those who hold this position refuse to accept the literal interpretation of those prophecies which relate to the earthly kingdom.

To Introduce the Concept of Christendom. The proponents of this view state that, in the light of His rejection, Jesus prepares His disciples for the "going forth" of mercy to Gentiles. They believe the King offered Himself to Israel, and Israel refused Him. Therefore, the King by means of parables is instructing His followers as to a new form of the kingdom which will be in existence while He is absent.

> In one word "the kingdom of the heavens" in Matthew is equivalent with "Christendom." It includes the whole sphere of Christian profession saved and unsaved, so-called Romanists and Protestants, all who are naming the name of Christ. Therefore, the church is not the kingdom of the heavens, though the church is in the kingdom of the heavens.
>
> The Lord teaches in the seven parables how matters will go in the earth while He is not here, and what men will do with that which He brought from heaven and left in the hands of men. [64]

They conclude, therefore, that there is no connection between these parables taught by the Lord Jesus Christ and the teachings of the Old Testament.[65] Many outstanding premillennialists such as Kelly,[66] English,[67] and Habershon[68] hold the same view. However, this view also has its difficulties. The first is the change in meaning which must be given to the term *the kingdom of the heavens.*

> The kingdom of heaven is, according to Schofield, a Jewish, Messianic kingdom, which is both of the past and of the future; it is *not* present. How then can these parables of the kingdom apply to the present age?[69]

---

64. Gaebelein, *The Gospel of Matthew,* 1:263-264.
65. Barnhouse, *His Own,* pp. 169-170.
66. William Kelly, *Lectures on the Gospel of Matthew,* pp. 265-66.
67. E. Schuyler English, *Studies in the Gospel According to Matthew,* pp. 91-92.
68. Ada R. Habershon, *The Study of the Parables,* pp. 112, 118-19.
69. Allis, *Prophecy and the Church,* p. 85.

If one grants that Christ here presents a new concept of the kingdom, then the amillennialist has perfect right to assert that Christ is attempting to correct the prevalent Jewish notions.

A second problem is found in the terminology which those who hold this view use in referring to Christendom. On the basis of Matthew 13:11, Christendom is called the kingdom in its mystery form.[70] However, Christ does not use the phrase *kingdom in mystery form*. Rather, He says the parables concern mysteries of the kingdom of the heavens, that is, hitherto unrevealed truth about the kingdom. It is also stated by the proponents of this view that the kingdom in mystery form contains professors as well as true believers.[71] However, it has been proven before that the kingdom of the heavens is composed only of believers (Matthew 5:3, 10, 20; 6:33; 7:21; 11:11; 18:3).[72]

Finally, the concept of the kingdom in Matthew is always millennial.[73]

To Reveal New Truths Concerning the Kingdom. This view states that the King is giving new revelation concerning the kingdom promised to the Jews. The truths relate to the time of the establishing of the kingdom, the preparation for it, and other such material which had never before been revealed. This approach is the best for several reasons.

First, it is consistent with the uniform New Testament concept of the kingdom.

A second advantage of this view is its agreement with the Old Testament prophecies of the kingdom. The Old Testament expected a judgment to precede the establishment of the kingdom (Daniel 7:21-27); the parables concur (Matthew 13:30, 41-42, 49-50). The Old Testament prophet foresaw the giving of rewards to the righteous which would be manifested in the kingdom (Daniel 12:2-3); the parables present the same truth (Matthew 13:30, 41-42). Daniel's prophecy of the stone "cut out without hands" indicates that the coming of the kingdom was to be supernatural (Daniel 2:34); the parables state the same fact (Matthew 13:30, 40-41). The kingdom was to come suddenly (Isaiah 46:13; Daniel 2:34, 44-45; Malachi 3:1); again the parables agree (Matthew 13:30, 40-41, 48-49). The authority of the prophesied Messianic kingdom was to be universal (Psalm 2:8); the kingdom presented in Matthew 13

---

70. Feinberg, *Premillennialism*, p. 70.
71. William L. Pettingill, *Simple Studies in Matthew*, pp. 155-56.
72. See above, pp. 66-67.
73. See above p. 68.

likewise extends throughout the world (Matthew 13:38-41). The conclusion is patent: the *nature* of the kingdom portrayed in the parables is the same as that pictured by the Old Testament prophets.

This view has the further advantage of being consistent with the New Testament concept of a mystery. Because of the Jewish rejection of the Messiah, the promised kingdom is now held in abeyance. The parables of Matthew 13 reveal new truths involving the preparation for the establishment of the kingdom during this time of postponement which was not predicted in Daniel's seventy weeks or other Old Testament prophecies.

1. The Parables Spoken to the Multitudes, 13:1-13:35.

a. The Setting, **13:1-13:2.** ***On that day Jesus went out of the house, and was sitting by the sea. And great multitudes gathered about Him, so that He got into a boat and sat down, and the whole multitude was standing on the beach.***

A Public Setting. Having left the house in which He was ministering, the Messiah stood by the sea where great crowds gathered about Him. So great was the throng that He sat in a boat, pushed off from the shore, and with His audience standing on the beach He spoke many things to them in parables (Matthew 13:1-3). This crowd heard four parables—the parables of the sower, the parable of the wheat and darnel, the parable of the mustard seed, and the parable of the leaven. They heard no interpretation, just the parables.

A Private Setting. Verse ten states that the disciples came to Jesus, and He gave them the interpretation of the parable of the sower. After the Lord had given these parables to the crowd, He left them and went back into the house (Matthew 13:36). In the house the King explains the parable of the darnel of the field and gives them other parables—the parable of the hidden treasure, the parable of the precious pearl, and the parable of the dragnet.

Thus two simple statements (Matthew 13:1, 36) divide the parables into two groups, those spoken to the crowds and those given only to the disciples. These statements also indicate that the parables were all spoken on one occasion and are not an example of Matthew's tendency to group material. A further proof of their continuity is found in the time designation of verse one, "On that day."

b. The Introduction, 13:3-13:23.

(1) The Parable of the Sower, **13:3-13:9.** *And He spoke many things to them in parables, saying, "Behold, the sower went out to sow; and as he sowed, some seeds fell beside the road, and the birds came and devoured them. And others fell upon the rocky places, where they did not have much soil; and immediately they sprang up, because they had no depth of soil. But when the sun had risen, they were scorched; and because they had no root, they withered away. And others fell among the thorns, and the thorns came up and choked them out. And others fell on the good soil, and yielded a crop, some a hundredfold, some sixty, and some thirty. He who has ears, let him hear."* This parable was given to the multitudes (Matthew 13:3-9) but interpreted to the disciples only (Matthew 13:18-23). Actually this parable serves as an introduction to the remainder of the parables and does not really give any new revelation of the kingdom of heaven. This fact is evident for several reasons.

First, in contrast to the other parables in this chapter, the kingdom is not "likened" to any truth in this parable. None of the gospels uses either the adjective "like" (ὅμοιος) or the verb "to be like" (ὁμοιόω) in connection with the parable of the sower. From this it may be inferred that this parable has no direct connection with new kingdom truths. Second, there is no new revelation found in this parable. The response to the message of God as characterized by the soils was always true. It could not, therefore, be a mystery of the kingdom. Furthermore, just as Christ uses the parable of the householder for application (Matthew 13:52), so He employs this parable as an introduction.

Finally, Mark 4:13 indicates clearly that this parable is introductory to the rest. There the Lord goes on to infer that the understanding of it is basic to comprehending the remainder of the parables. It seems from Mark 4:10 that the explanation of this parable was given after the Lord had left the crowd and returned to the house with His disciples. Matthew, however, introduces the interpretation before he records Christ's presentation of the rest of the parables. In Matthew's account, the plural "parables" in 13:10 indicates the disciples did not ask this question immediately. After a number of parables they became perplexed and addressed their query to the Lord. Matthew moves the question up ahead in the narrative to present the explanation for all these parables to the reader. The fact that He gave the interpretation to the disciples privately is made evident by Matthew nevertheless. Thus

Matthew uses this parable with its interpretation as an introduction to
the series of parables which follows.

(2) The Purpose of the Parables, **13:10-13:17.** *And the disciples
came and said to Him, "Why do You speak to them in parables?"
And He answered and said to them, "To you it has been granted to
know the mysteries of the kingdom of heaven, but to them it has not
been granted. For whoever has, to him shall more be given, and he
shall have an abundance; but whoever does not have, even what he
has shall be taken away from him. Therefore I speak to them in
parables; because while seeing they do not see, and while hearing
they do not hear, nor do they understand. And in their case the
prophecy of Isaiah is being fulfilled, which says,*

> *'You will keep on hearing, but will not understand; and
> you will keep on seeing, but will not perceive; for the
> heart of this people has become dull, and with their ears
> they scarcely hear, and they have closed their eyes; lest
> they should see with their eyes, and hear with their ears,
> and understand with their heart and turn again, and I
> should heal them.'*

*But blessed are your eyes, because they see; and your ears, because
they hear. For truly I say to you, that many prophets and righteous
men desired to see what you see, and did not see it; and to hear what
you hear, and did not hear it."* See above, p. 169.

(3) The Parable of the Sower Explained, **13:18-13:23.** *"Hear then
the parable of the sower. When any one hears the word of the
kingdom, and does not understand it, the evil one comes and
snatches away what has been sown in his heart. This is the one on
whom seed was sown beside the road. And the one on whom seed
was sown on the rocky places, this is the man who hears the word,
and immediately receives it with joy; yet he has no firm root in
himself, but is only temporary, and when affliction or persecution
arises because of the word, immediately he falls away. And the one
on whom seed was sown among the thorns, this is the man who
hears the word, and the worry of the world, and the deceitfulness of
riches choke the word, and it becomes unfruitful. And the one on
whom seed was sown on the good ground, this is the man who hears
the word and understands it; who indeed bears fruit, and brings
forth, some a hundredfold, some sixty, and some thirty."* The four
soils represent four kinds of receptions given to the seed. The seed is the
word of the kingdom (verse nineteen). The fruit spoken of in verse

than what? All must be saved, then.

twenty-three is more revelation and understanding concerning the kingdom. This understanding of the word "fruit" is evident for several reasons.

This interpretation fits the context of the parabolic instruction. The word of the kingdom had been proclaimed to Israel by John, by Jesus, and by the disciples. This parable notes the blindness and dullness of Israel's response to this proclamation. However, some did understand and were growing in understanding (Matthew 11:25).

Second, this view of the fruit fits the Lord's explanation as to why He spoke in parables (Matthew 13:10-17). From those who failed to lay hold of the word of the kingdom or who abused it the word was taken away (Matthew 13:12-15). On the other hand, it was given to the disciples to know because their hearts were conditioned to receive the word of the kingdom (Matthew 13:11-12). It is in connection with this answer to the disciples' question that the interpretation of the parable is given. The Lord desires to conceal the truth from those who are not receptive and to reveal it to receptive hearts. The parable illustrates this principle perfectly. If they could understand this parable, then they were spiritually qualified to understand the remaining ones.

In addition, this interpretation of the fruit fits the explanation of the parable which the King gives to His disciples (Matthew 13:18-23). The introduction to the interpretation of the parable emphasizes understanding. The eyes and ears of the disciples were called blessed because they were seeing and hearing that which the prophets and holy men of old desired to see and hear. "Therefore" ($o\mathring{v}\nu$), they were to listen with all the knowledge hearing is intended to convey.[74] That the fruit represents a fuller comprehension of the kingdom is seen also in the emphasis on understanding in the interpretation (verses nineteen and twenty-three).

Finally, this interpretation is very logical. Seed produces more seed. The word of the kingdom received into the heart would yield more revelation and understanding of it. This new revelation is that which the King is about to give in the remainder of Matthew 13. Only the humble would understand the truth in the parables and manifest a hundredfold, sixtyfold, or thirtyfold increase of their comprehension.

The principle taught by the parable is this: reception of the word of the kingdom in one's heart produces more understanding and revelation of the kingdom. In this way the parable acts as an introduction to the remainder of the parables.

---

74. R. C. H. Lenski, *The Interpretation of St. Matthew's Gospel*, p. 517.

The use of the masculine, demonstrative pronoun "this" (οὗτος) in verses nineteen, twenty, twenty-two, and twenty-three, as well as the masculine participle σπαρείς ("the one on whom was sown," NASB; "what was sown," NIV, RSV), has caused some difficulty. The pronoun and the participle cannot refer to the seed since the word "seed" (σπέρμα) is neuter in gender. Goebel presents the most logical explanation.

> Hence the man, who as hearer of the word is in the first instance the soil which receives the seed, on the other hand, inasmuch as he does not put forth the effect of what he has heard as something different from and alien to himself ... may also be identified with the grain which is the product of the sowing. And the seed, which is in the first instance the word, may also, where it no longer appears as the means, but as the result of the sowing ... be just as well identified with the persons in whom the word heard is effective as the principle of a new personal life.[75]

c. Three Parables of the Kingdom, 13:24-13:33.

(1) The Parable of the Wheat and the Darnel, **13:24-13:30.** *He presented another parable to them, saying, "The kingdom of heaven may be compared to a man who sowed good seed in his field. But while men were sleeping, his enemy came and sowed tares also among the wheat, and went away. But when the wheat sprang up and bore grain, then the tares became evident also. And the slaves of the landowner came and said to him, 'Sir, did you not sow good seed in your field? How then does it have tares?' And he said to them, 'An enemy has done this!' And the slaves said to him, 'Do you want us, then, to go and gather them up?' But he said, 'No; lest while you are gathering up the tares, you may root up the wheat with them. Allow both to grow together until the harvest; and in the time of the harvest I will say to the reapers, "First gather up the tares; and bind them in bundles to burn them up; but gather the wheat into my barn." ' "* The parable of the wheat and darnel given to the crowds is explained to the disciples privately by the Messiah (Matthew 13:36-43). In this parable the Lord uses the verb "to compare" (ὁμοιόω) to make the comparison with the kingdom of heaven, while in the remainder the adjective "like" (ὅμοιος) is used. Actually there is no great difference between these two formulas. The verb like the adjective is simply used to indicate a comparison (cf. Matthew 7:24,

---

75. Siegfried Goebel, *The Parables of Jesus,* p. 47.

26; 11:16; 25:1). It must also be noted that these formulas do not mean that the kingdom of heaven is symbolized by the man, or the mustard seed, or leaven, or any other single object in the parables. It is simply used to introduce a narrative which represents truth relative to the kingdom.

At least three new facts are revealed in the parable of the wheat and darnel. The first is the doctrine of a new age in which the sons of the kingdom were to be sown in the *world* (Matthew 13:38; 28:19-20). That this is completely new is verified by the most casual comparison with Matthew 10:5-6 and 15:22-28. A second fact is also taught; in this new age good and evil would coexist (Matthew 13:30). Finally, the Lord uses this parable to instruct His disciples that this evil would coexist until the kingdom is established (Matthew 13:39-43).[76] The whole age is in view from the ascension until the coming of the Lord to establish the kingdom. Because of this fact the rapture of the church is included in the time span of the parable but is not spoken of as a separate detail.

(2) The Parable of the Mustard Seed, **13:31-13:32.** *He presented another parable to them, saying, "The Kingdom of heaven is like a mustard seed, which a man took and sowed in his field; and this is smaller than all other seeds; but when it is full grown, it is larger than the garden plants, and becomes a tree, so that the birds of the air come and nest in its branches."* The parable of the grain of mustard teaches two things concerning the growth of the kingdom message and its reception in the age preceding the establishment of the kingdom. The first thing seen in the parable is the phenomenal growth of this tiny seed into a tree. This of course is a reference to the extraordinary spread and growth of the kingdom message in the age before the kingdom is established. The King does not picture the coming of the kingdom here since it is impossible to do so in connection with the tree.

A second thing is also taught by this parable, and it is the seemingly prosperous growth in number of those who should be heirs of the kingdom. This is what is meant by the tree becoming so large that the birds of heaven came and dwelled in its branches. This is not necessarily a reference to evil characters among the heirs of the kingdom. The expression occurs frequently in the Old Testament (Daniel 4:12, 21; Ezekiel 17:23; 31:6; Psalm 104:12) and in each case it pictures the prosperity of a person or nation, primarily as seen by men. So here in

---

76. Peters, *Theocratic Kingdom*, 2:421.

Matthew the parable of the grain of mustard describes the prosperous growth in number of the heirs of the kingdom in the sight of men.

The preceding parable had taught the disciples that the field was the world; this parable instructs the followers of the Lord as to how the message of the kingdom would outwardly be received in the world.

(3) The Parable of the Leaven and the Meal, **13:33.** *He spoke another parable to them; "The kingdom of heaven is like leaven, which a woman took, and hid in three pecks of meal, until it was all leavened."* This parable is related in nineteen simple words in the Greek text, but many thousands of words have been written in an attempt to explain it. The discussion revolves about the significance of the word "leaven" (ζύμη). Many contend that the leaven is used here in a good sense and pictures the spread of the gospel throughout the earth. Others state that the word represents evil and is used to illustrate the growth of evil within the group which professes to inherit the kingdom. This latter interpretation has the strongest support. It is consistent with the doctrine of Scripture concerning the evil character of the end of the church age and the tribulation (1 Timothy 4; 2 Timothy 3; Jude; 2 Peter 3; Revelation 6-19).

One of the greatest supports for the interpretation that leaven speaks of evil is the use of the word in Scripture. Invariably leaven pictures sin (Exodus 12; Leviticus 2:11; 6:17; 10:12; Matthew 16:12; Mark 8:15; Luke 12:1; 1 Corinthians 5:6-8; Galatians 5:9). Finally, the verb used here, "to hide" (ἐνέκρυψεν), is very unusual if leaven represents good. It is a much more fitting word if the leaven is to have a sinister effect. This is similar to the idea in the parable of the wheat and darnel. The way the woman hides the leaven in the meal parallels very closely the manner in which the enemy sowed darnel by night.

This parable reveals the fact that evil will run its course and dominate the new age. But it also indicates that when the program of evil has been fulfilled, the kingdom will come. This is indicated by the use of the preposition "until" (ἕως). The definite limit and program of this age is also indicated by the fact that *three measures* of meal are used. The parable stops when this amount is leavened. So the kingdom will come when the evil of this age has run its course.

The parable of the mustard seed indicated what the program of the kingdom would appear to be in the eyes of men; the parable of the leaven gives God's view of it.

d. The Fulfillment of Prophecy, **13:34-13:35.** *All these things Jesus spoke to the multitudes in parables, and He was not talking to them without a parable, so that what was spoken through the prophet might be fulfilled, saying,*

> *"I will open my mouth in parables; I will utter things hidden since the foundation of the world."*

See above, pp. 170-71.

2. The Parables Spoken to the Disciples, 13:36-13:53.

a. The Explanation of the Parable of the Wheat and the Darnel, **13:36-13:43.** *Then He left the multitudes, and went into the house. And His disciples came to Him, saying, "Explain to us the parable of the tares of the field." And He answered and said, "The one who sows the good seed is the Son of Man, and the field is the world; and as for the good seed, these are the sons of the kingdom; and the tares are the sons of the evil one; and the enemy who sowed them is the devil, and the harvest is the end of the age; and the reapers are angels. Therefore just as the tares are gathered up and burned with fire, so shall it be at the end of the age. The Son of Man will send forth His angels, and they will gather out of His kingdom all stumbling blocks, and those who commit lawlessness, and will cast them into the furnace of fire; in that place there shall be weeping and gnashing of teeth. Then the righteous will shine forth as the sun in the kingdom of their Father. He who has ears, let him hear."* See above, pp. 180-81.

b. Three Parables of the Kingdom, 13:44-13:50.

(1) The Parable of the Hidden Treasure, **13:44.** *"The kingdom of heaven is like a treasure hidden in the field; which a man found and hid; and from joy over it he goes and sells all that he has, and buys that field."* This is the fifth of the parables spoken by the Lord in Matthew 13. The great problem of interpretation in this parable is the identification of the treasure. It is evident that the treasure is an allusion to the kingdom viewed from the standpoint of Israel. That is, it looks at Israel's kingdom program.

The parable's hidden state views the dark hours of Israel from the time of Rehoboam, the son of Solomon, to the period of Christ's ministry. The uncovering of the treasure is the coming near of the kingdom in the person of the King. The removal of the kingdom from Israel

(Matthew 21:43) is represented by the hiding of the treasure. The man who sells all he has to buy the field is a clear picture of the condescension and death of Jesus (Philippians 2:5-8).

One point remains unstated. When the man comes again he will unveil the treasure and be very rich. This, of course, pictures the glory of Christ when He comes again in His kingdom.

The mystery revealed in this parable is the putting aside of Israel's kingdom program for a time. The redemption of the treasure has been accomplished, but the unveiling of it has not. This will occur at Christ's second coming to the earth.

(2) The Parable of the Pearl of Great Price, **13:45-13:46.** *"Again, the kingdom of heaven is like a merchant seeking fine pearls, and upon finding one pearl of great value, he went and sold all that he had, and bought it."* The interpretation of this parable is contingent upon the identification of the precious pearl. It seems that the pearl pictures the true church of Jesus Christ. The mention of one pearl is very fitting inasmuch as the New Testament often describes the oneness of the church (1 Corinthians 10:17; 12:12-27; Ephesians 4:4-6). The buying of the pearl is a reference to the redemption of the church by the blood of Christ.

As with the hidden treasure, the revelation of the pearl occurs at the second coming of Christ to establish His kingdom on earth. The mystery revealed is the formation of a new body which also would inherit the kingdom (Ephesians 3:3-6). The pearl being a product of the sea may infer that this group would be taken from the nations of the earth (Matthew 28:19-20).

(3) The Parable of the Dragnet, **13:47-13:50.** *"Again, the kingdom of heaven is like a dragnet cast into the sea, and gathering fish of every kind; and when it was filled, they drew it up on the beach; and they sat down, and gathered the good fish into containers, but the bad they threw away. So it will be at the end of the age; the angels shall come forth, and take out the wicked from among the righteous, and will cast them into the furnace of fire; there shall be weeping and gnashing of teeth."* The parable of the dragnet is the last in Matthew 13 which compares the kingdom of heaven to some truth with the formula "is like" (ὁμοία ἐστὶν). This parable pictures the end of the tribulation period when the judgment of Israel and the nations will take place preceding the actual establishment of the kingdom.

While the Jews expected a judgment to take place before the kingdom would be seen, this parable gives new revelation in connection with the other parables. The other parables taught the disciples of Christ that a new age was to intervene before the coming of the kingdom. This parable revealed the fact that the expected judgment would be postponed until after this new age had been completed.

c. Conclusion: The Parable of the Householder, 13:51-13:53. "Have you understood all these things?" They said to Him, "Yes." And He said to them, "Therefore every scribe who has become a disciple of the kingdom of heaven is like a head of a household, who brings forth out of his treasure things new and old."

And it came about that when Jesus had finished these parables, He departed from there. This parable, strictly speaking, is not a parable of the kingdom. Neither the words "is like" (ὁμοία ἐστὶν) nor the verb "to be like" (ὁμοιόω) are used to introduce it. As the parable of the sower is used to introduce the parables, so this parable applies the responsibility of knowing them to the disciples. The disciples, instructed in the new truths of the kingdom as well as the old, were now responsible to minister these truths. The use of the neuter adjectives "old" or "worn out things" (παλαιά) and "new" or "fresh things" (καινά) is very fitting in this connection.

It is also interesting to note that in this verse the Lord refers to His disciples as scribes. By so doing the Messiah rejected the ministry of the common scribes and appointed His own. His disciples were now responsible for dispensing the whole truth, for only they possessed it.

Matthew with his characteristic transition "And it came about that when Jesus had finished" (καὶ ἐγένετο ὅτε ἐτέλεσεν ὁ Ἰησοῦς), concludes this discourse of Christ and this section of the book. The course of the opposition has been carefully traced. It is now so evident that Christ declares His knowledge of their rejection and adapts His ministry accordingly. He speaks to the multitudes and the disciples in parables in which truths concerning a new kingdom program are revealed. When these are concluded, the King charges His disciples with their responsibility in dispensing the truths of the kingdom.

V. The Reaction of the King (13:54-19:2)

  A. The Withdrawal of the King (13:54-16:12)

    1. The unbelief of the people of Nazareth (13:54-13:58)

    2. The opposition of Herod (14:1-14:36)

      a. The beheading of John (14:1-14:12)

      b. The withdrawal to a desert place (14:13-14:36)

        1) The feeding of the five thousand (14:13-14:21)

        2) The walking on the water (14:22-14:33)

        3) The ministry at Gennesaret (14:34-14:36)

    3. The opposition of the Pharisees and scribes (15:1-15:39)

      a. The dispute over tradition (15:1-15:20)

      b. The withdrawal to Tyre and Sidon (15:21-15:39)

        1) The healing of the daughter of the Canaanitish woman (15:21-15:28)

        2) The ministry by the Sea of Galilee (15:29-15:31)

        3) The feeding of the four thousand (15:32-15:39)

    4. The opposition of the Pharisees and the Sadducees (16:1-16:12)

      a. The request for a sign (16:1-16:4a)

      b. The abandonment by the King (16:4b-16:12)

  B. The Instruction of the Disciples of the King (16:13-19:2)

    1. The revelation concerning the person of the King (16:13-16:17)

    2. The revelation concerning the program of the King (16:18-17:13)

      a. The church (16:18)

      b. Peter and the kingdom (16:19-16:20)

      c. The death and resurrection of the King (16:21-16:27)

      d. The coming kingdom (16:28-17:13)

    3. The instruction concerning the principles of the King (17:14-18:35)

      a. The principle of faith (17:14-17:21)

      b. The death and resurrection of the King (17:22-17:23)

      c. The principle of tribute (17:24-17:27)

      d. The principle of humility (18:1-18:4)

      e. The principle of not causing stumbling (18:5-18:14)

      f. The principle of discipline (18:15-18:20)

      g. The principle of forgiveness (18:21-18:35)

    4. The journey to Jerusalem continued (19:1-19:2)

V. The Reaction of the King

The Messiah has presented Himself to Israel with all of His credentials. However, the nation is not prepared to receive its King and kingdom, and it begins to manifest opposition to His presence. In the face of this hostility the King commences His withdrawal from the religious and political leaders. Then, in preparation for His passion, He instructs His disciples in light of the crucifixion.

A. The Withdrawal of the King
13:54-16:12

The withdrawal of Jesus as presented by Matthew in this section follows a definite pattern. After a manifestation of antagonism on the part of the leaders toward Jesus, He withdraws. Following this withdrawal there is a performance of a mighty work. This series of events occurs twice. The third time opposition arises the King not only withdraws but finally "abandons" ($\kappa\alpha\tau\alpha\lambda\epsilon\acute{\iota}\pi\omega$; "leaves," NASB) the Pharisees and Sadducees (Matthew 16:4).

1. The Unbelief of the People of Nazareth, 13:54-13:58.

13:54-13:58. *And coming to His home town He began teaching them in their synagogue, so that they became astonished, and said, "Where did this man get this wisdom, and these miraculous powers? Is not this the carpenter's son? Is not His mother called Mary, and His brothers, James and Joseph and Simon and Judas? And His sisters, are they not all with us? Where then did this man get all these things?" And they took offense at Him. But Jesus said to*

*them, "A prophet is not without honor except in his home town,
and in his own household." And He did not do many miracles there
because of their unbelief.* This brief paragraph is the key to the section.
The Messiah ministers in His home town of Nazareth in wisdom and in
power. The people are amazed at His words and power but scorn His
person. They refer to Him with the pronoun "this" (οὗτος, 13:55) which
is often a term of contempt (Matthew 12:24). The smallness of the town
of Nazareth is shown by the words "the carpenter's son"; there was only
one carpenter in the village. Yet this tiny town refuses the King of Israel.
What contempt!

It is interesting to note that Matthew calls Jesus the son of Joseph. By
referring to Joseph as His father, Matthew continues to show that Jesus
is *legally* the descendant of David the king. However, Matthew's main
point in including this brief narrative is to show the unbelief of Israel
and its blindness to the person of Christ. Kelly writes, "The manifestation of glory is not denied; but Him in whom it was manifested, is not
received according to God, but judged according to the sight of ap-
prehensions of nature . . . ."[1]

2. The Opposition of Herod, 14:1-14:36.

a. The Beheading of John, **14:1-14:12.** *At that time Herod the tet-
rarch heard the news about Jesus, and said to his servants, "This is
John the Baptist; he has risen from the dead; and that is why
miraculous powers are at work in him." For Herod had seized
John, and bound him, and put him in prison on account of
Herodias, the wife of his brother Philip. For John had been saying
to him, "It is not lawful for you to have her." And although he
wanted to put him to death, he feared the multitude, because they
regarded him as a prophet. But when Herod's birthday came, the
daughter of Herodias danced before them and pleased Herod.
Thereupon he promised with an oath to give her whatever she
asked. And having been prompted by her mother, she said, "Give
me here on a platter the head of John the Baptist." And although he
was grieved, the king commanded it to be given because of his
oaths, and because of his dinner-guests. And he sent and had John
beheaded in the prison. And his head was brought on a platter and
given to the girl; and she brought it to her mother. And his disciples*

---

1. William Kelly, *Lectures on the Gospel of Matthew*, p. 296.

*came and took away the body and buried it; and they went and
reported to Jesus.*

Matthew records in the fourteenth chapter of his Gospel the opposition of Herod. Again this narrative is linked to the preceding by the
pronoun "that" (ἐκεῖνος) with a time designation which at the same
time indicates a slight change in the narrative. When Herod hears of the
mighty works of the Messiah, he concludes that the Messiah is John the
Baptist, whom he had beheaded, raised from the dead.

Herod's reasonings concerning Christ's miracles prove that His works
were supernatural. To Herod they were the kind which would be done by
one who was raised from the dead. It is an important fact that John was
beheaded for righteousness' sake. In so doing he precedes the King who
died because of His righteous character. Plummer notes, "John preceded the Messiah in birth and in mission; and he now precedes Him in
a violent death."[2] The shadow of the King's ultimate rejection and death
begins to loom large and dark over the scene of the King's movements.

b. The Withdrawal to a Desert Place, 14:13-14:36.

(1) The Feeding of the Five Thousand, **14:13-14:21.** *Now when Jesus
heard it, He withdrew from there in a boat, to a lonely place by
Himself; and when the multitudes heard of this, they followed Him
on foot from the cities. And when He came out, He saw a great
multitude, and felt compassion for them, and healed their sick. And
when it was evening, the disciples came to Him, saying, "The place
is desolate, and the time is already past; so send the multitudes
away, that they may go into the villages and buy food for themselves." But Jesus said to them, "They do not need to go away; you
give them something to eat!" And they said to Him, "We have here
only five loaves, and two fish." And He said, "Bring them here to
Me." And ordering the multitudes to recline on the grass, He took
the five loaves and the two fish, and looking up toward heaven, He
blessed the food, and breaking the loaves He gave them to the
disciples, and the disciples gave to the multitudes, and they all ate,
and were satisfied. And they picked up what was left over of the
broken pieces, twelve full baskets. And there were about five
thousand men who ate, aside from women and children.* When
Christ hears of the beheading of His forerunner, He "withdraws"

---

2. Alfred Plummer, *An Exegetical Commentary on the Gospel According to S. Matthew,*
p. 201.

(ἀναχωρέω) into a desert place by Himself. As the imprisonment of John was a signal for the beginning of the King's official ministry (Matthew 4:12), so the death of John signaled the withdrawal and restriction of the Messiah's ministry.

In this desert place the multitudes flock to Him, and the King, moved with compassion, ministers to them. When the day is spent and the crowd is in need of food, the King miraculously feeds them.

This sign was very important to three groups—the disciples, the believing remnant, and the wonder-watching unbelievers. From now on the miracles are primarily for the benefit of the disciples in that they are designed to instruct them. But in addition they confirm the faith of those who believe and the unbelief of the unbelieving masses. That they are for the disciples' training is seen in the fact that the rejection of the Lord is evident. The cities in which He had performed most of His mighty works had already indicated their apathy and opposition. He had left the masses so that He could be apart with the disciples.

Since He is training His disciples, when the crowd's need for food is brought before Him He tells the disciples, "You give them something to eat." Finally, He gave the food to the disciples who gave it to the multitudes. The Lord ministering through them in this way prepares them for their future work in His absence.

This display of power also confirmed the faith of the remnant. The Jews had a tradition that the Messiah would miraculously feed the people with bread from heaven as Moses had done.[3] Certainly the feeding of five thousand men, not counting the women and children, proved the sufficiency of Jesus to provide for Israel as its King. In addition, this great scene must have caused many to look forward to a coming Messianic banquet (Matthew 22:1-13; 26:29; Luke 14:16-24). They would see that this is the One who could fulfill the promise given in Psalm 132:15 and also the request for "daily bread" in the simple prayer recorded in Matthew 6.

This miracle also had its effect on the masses. The fact that they had wrong motives in following Christ is shown clearly in John 6:15-66. Matthew also implies that a blind, fanatical movement on the part of the masses to establish Christ as King was under way. The disciples would delight in such a movement, so he *immediately compelled* them to leave.[4] Then He dismissed the misunderstanding crowd.

---

3. Ibid., p. 206. cf. Deuteronomy 18:15.
4. R. C. H. Lenski, *The Interpretation of St. Matthew's Gospel,* p. 568.

The feeding of the multitudes instructs the disciples, confirms the faith of the believing remnant, and establishes the spiritual blindness of the masses.

(2) The Walking on the Water, **14:22-14:33.** *And immediately He made the disciples get into the boat, and go ahead of Him to the other side, while He sent the multitudes away. And after He had sent the multitudes away, He went up to the mountain by Himself to pray; and when it was evening, He was there alone. But the boat was already many stadia away from the land, battered by the waves; for the wind was contrary. And in the fourth watch of the night He came to them, walking upon the sea. And when the disciples saw Him walking on the sea, they were frightened, saying, "It is a ghost!" And they cried out for fear. But immediately Jesus spoke to them, saying, "Take courage, it is I; do not be afraid." And Peter answered Him and said, "Lord, if it is You, command me to come to You on the water." And He said, "Come!" And Peter got out of the boat, and walked on the water and came toward Jesus. But seeing the wind, he became afraid, and beginning to sink, he cried out, saying, "Lord, save me!" And immediately Jesus stretched out His hand and took hold of him, and said to him, "O you of little faith, why did you doubt?" And when they got into the boat, the wind stopped. And those who were in the boat worshiped Him, saying, "You are certainly God's Son!"* During this time of withdrawal the King also performs a second sign of power, walking on the water. This miracle was again for the purpose of instruction. It instructed the disciples concerning the power of faith; by faith Peter walked on the water with the Lord, and because of lack of faith he began to sink. Perhaps the greatest and most profound lesson concerns the manifestation of His person. The disciples "worshipped" ($\pi\rho o\sigma\kappa\upsilon\nu\acute{e}\omega$) Him and called Him God's Son. Though they adore Him as God's Son, they do not yet recognize him as the Son of God. Plummer succinctly writes, "They are sure that He is more than human; but perhaps even yet they are not sure that He is the Messiah."[5]

This is the first time that Peter comes to the fore in Matthew's Gospel. The Evangelist here presents Peter in all of his impetuosity mixed with his great devotion. In keeping with Matthew's style of writing, these traits, which are first mentioned here, characterize Peter throughout the remainder of the Gospel. More significant is the fact that the place of

5. Plummer, *Exegetical Commentary,* p. 210.

preeminence among the apostles which Peter here assumes is never lost in the rest of Matthew's Gospel.

(3) The Ministry at Gennesaret, **14:34-14:36.** *And when they had crossed over, they came to land at Gennesaret. And when the men of that place recognized Him, they sent into all that surrounding district and brought to Him all who were ill; and they began to entreat Him that they might just touch the fringe of His cloak; and as many as touched it were cured.* When they arrive in the land of Gennesaret, the men of that place recognize Jesus. There He ministers to their sick by healing them. One fact is evident in His work here: they recognize Him for His healing ministry, yet they are blind to His person. In this they differ greatly from the disciples and the believing remnant.

3. The Opposition of the Pharisees and Scribes, 15:1-15:39.

a. The Dispute over Tradition, 15:1-15:20. Matthew 14 records the opposition of the civil authority to the King; Matthew 15 contains an account of the religious opposition. The development of the narrative is the same—opposition, withdrawal, and miracles.

15:1-15:3. *Then some Pharisees and scribes came to Jesus from Jerusalem, saying, "Why do Your disciples transgress the tradition of the elders? For they do not wash their hands when they eat bread." And He answered and said to them, "And why do you yourselves transgress the commandment of God for the sake of your tradition?"* The Pharisees and scribes criticize the disciples of Jesus for transgressing the tradition of the elders. The Lord rebukes them for their concern for ritualism and traditions and their indifference to the righteousness of the law.

There are several significant factors involved in this conflict. It will be noticed that the religious leaders are from Jerusalem and not merely a local synagogue. This indicates the impact of Christ's ministry and also the extent to which the opposition of the Pharisees had been aroused. Evidently the report of the events of Matthew 12:1-45 had already reached Jerusalem and had its repercussions there. It is strange that the capital city of Israel is the source of the greatest antagonism. Yet this is the manifestation of that about which Matthew had hinted in chapter two.

15:4-15:9. *"For God said, 'Honor your father and mother,' and, 'He who speaks evil of father or mother, let him be put to death.'*

But you say, 'Whoever shall say to his father or mother, "Anything of mine you might have been helped by has been given to God," he is not to honor his father or his mother.' And thus you invalidated the word of God for the sake of your tradition. You hypocrites, rightly did Isaiah prophesy of you, saying,
> *'This people honors Me with their lips, but their heart is far away from Me. But in vain do they worship Me, teaching as their doctrines the precepts of men.'"*

A second factor worthy of note is the nature of the conflict. The controversy concerned true righteousness over against hypocrisy. The religious leaders would rather observe the traditions of men than the commandments of God. M'Neile says, "When the ἐντολή [commandment] and the παράδοσις [tradition] clashed, the former was sacrificed to the latter."[6] Because of this Jesus calls them "hypocrites" (verse seven). By their tradition concerning the vow of Corban (15:5-15:6) they had annulled the fifth commandment (the first commandment with promise, the very promise which was associated with the land) and the law of stoning the child who dishonored his parents. To prove that the issue involved hypocrisy the Lord applies Isaiah 29:13 to the religious leaders.

15:10-15:12. *And He called to Himself the multitude, and said to them, "Hear, and understand. Not what enters into the mouth defiles the man, but what proceeds out of the mouth, this defiles the man." Then the disciples came and said to Him, "Do You know that the Pharisees were offended when they heard this statement?"* The break between the religious leaders and Jesus is so evident that the disciples notice it (verse twelve). The Pharisees and scribes, instead of manifesting repentant hearts, display their offense at the words of Christ. The seriousness of this breach and its implications is indicated by the concern which the disciples manifest. No doubt it was dangerous to incur the wrath of these religious leaders from Jerusalem!

15:13-15:14. *But He answered and said, "Every plant which My heavenly Father did not plant shall be rooted up. Let them alone; they are blind guides of the blind. And if a blind man guides a blind man, both will fall into a pit."* A final item is the result of the hypocrisy. It will culminate in judgment. Any candid observer will note the parallels between the language the Lord uses here and the parable of the wheat and darnel. In verse thirteen He refers to the Pharisees and scribes

---

6. Alan Hugh M'Neile, *The Gospel According to St. Matthew,* p. 222.

with their doctrines as "plants." In discussing this word Carr writes, "Not a wild flower, but a cultivated plant or tree . . . ."[7] In other words, the plants to which the Lord makes reference were those deliberately planted by Satan. They look like wheat in their hypocrisy but are really darnel at heart. Just as the householder told his servants to leave the darnel alone, so Christ tells His disciples to leave the religious leaders alone (verse fourteen). In the end the Heavenly Father will judge them.

15:15-15:20. *And Peter answered and said to Him, "Explain the parable to us." And He said, "Are you also still without understanding? Do you not understand that everything that goes into the mouth passes into the stomach, and is eliminated? But the things that proceed out of the mouth come from the heart, and those defile the man. For out of the heart come evil thoughts, murders, adulteries, fornications, thefts, false witness, slanders. These are the things which defile the man; but to eat with unwashed hands does not defile the man."* The Pharisees had defined defilement as an outward thing, when defilement really begins from the heart. An interesting aside in this section is Matthew's continuing emphasis of Peter. Peter is now the spokesman for the group as he approaches Christ and asks Him to make the parable clear to them (verse fifteen).

b. The Withdrawal to Tyre and Sidon, 15:21-15:39. As a result of the opposition of Herod, the King withdrew to a desert place. But now because of the antagonism of the religious leaders of Jerusalem He leaves the land of Israel to go into Gentile country. Again His withdrawal ($\dot{\alpha}\nu\alpha\chi\omega\rho\dot{\epsilon}\omega$) is marked by signs and further ministry.

(1) The Healing of the Daughter of the Canaanitish Woman, **15:21-15:28.** *And Jesus went away from there, and withdrew into the district of Tyre and Sidon. And behold, a Canaanite woman came out from that region, and began to cry out, saying, "Have mercy on me, O Lord, Son of David; my daughter is cruelly demon-possessed." But He did not answer her a word. And His disciples came to Him and kept asking Him, saying, "Send her away, for she is shouting out after us." But He answered and said, "I was sent only to the lost sheep of the house of Israel." But she came and began to bow down before Him, saying, "Lord, help me!" And He answered and said, "It is not good to take the children's bread and*

7. A. Carr, *The Gospel According to St. Matthew,* p. 204.

throw it to the dogs." But she said, "Yes, Lord; but even the dogs feed on the crumbs which fall from their master's table." Then Jesus answered and said to her, "O woman, your faith is great; be it done for you as you wish." And her daughter was healed at once.
The first miracle, the healing of the daughter of the Canaanitish woman, is full of significance. First, it emphasizes the place of the Jew in God's program. The Lord claims that His ministry is for the lost sheep of Israel only and puts off the request of the Gentile woman. David Smith says, "There is no incident in our Lord's earthly ministry more puzzling than this."[8] No doubt Smith's statement is true of those who will not hold the dispensational viewpoint. It is clear that Christ came to offer Himself to His people, and in grace He is prolonging the exclusiveness of His ministry in the hope that Israel will repent. The great love of the Shepherd for Israel is shown by the fact that He calls them "sheep" (verse twenty-four). He still claims the place of the King who shall shepherd Israel (Matthew 2:6; 2 Samuel 5:2). "Children" (verse twenty-six) again emphasizes the kingdom program of the Messiah. Israel will have the leading place among the nations of the world. It is very clear that even though Christ finally does heal the Gentile woman, the preeminent place of Israel is never lost.

The second item significant to Matthew's argument is the place given to the Gentiles. The Gentile mother addresses Jesus, "Lord, Son of David," and Christ does not respond at all. This woman was a descendant of the Canaanites who were to be destroyed when Israel possessed the land (Deuteronomy 20:17). She was of a cursed family who had no right to Messianic blessings, yet she approaches the Lord on the basis of His Messiahship. Lenski writes, "She plainly reveals that she has knowledge of the Messianic hopes of Israel and had heard that they were being connected with Jesus as the promised great descendant of King David."[9] It was because she was of a family which was to have no part in the Messianic blessings of Israel (Zechariah 14:21; Joel 3:17) that the Lord does not respond when she addresses Him in this manner. Since Jesus was sent to Israel to be its Messiah, He could not heal a Gentile who took the position of a Jew.

Then the woman with great insight sees herself in the place of a house dog (not a street hound) in the house of Israel.

8. David Smith, *The Days of His Flesh*, p. 248.
9. Lenski, *Interpretation of Matthew*, p. 594.

She does not claim to be one of the children, and has no thought of depriving them of their bread. She accepts the position of one of the family dogs. But such animals *are* members of the household, and they get what the children do not want. Without confusing the difference between Jews and heathen, and without depriving the Jews of anything that is theirs, He may grant her request. The metaphor which Christ had used as a reason for rejecting her petition she turns into a reason for granting it.[10]

When she comes to Him as a Gentile outside the pale of Jewish blessings, she is helped. She sees that she has no right to their blessings, but turns to Him in faith alone. On the basis of her great faith, not because of her relationship to the covenant people, her request is granted.

In this miracle of mercy there is a clear foreview of Gentile blessing which fits the pattern established in Matthew 1:1 and Romans 15:8-9. The actions of Christ show that He was a minister of the circumcision for the truth of God, for confirmation of the promises made unto the fathers and that the Gentiles might glorify God for His mercy.

(2) The Ministry by the Sea of Galilee, **15:29-15:31.** *And departing from there, Jesus went along by the sea of Galilee, and having gone up to the mountain, He was sitting there. And great multitudes came to Him, bringing with them those who were lame, crippled, blind, dumb, and many others, and they laid them down at His feet; and He healed them, so that the multitude marveled as they saw the dumb speaking, the crippled restored, and the lame walking, and the blind seeing, and they glorified the God of Israel.* Matthew goes on to record a whole series of healing miracles which the Lord performs by the Sea of Galilee. This again is a forecast of Gentile blessings, and the Gentiles here glorify the God of Israel.

(3) The Feeding of the Four Thousand, **15:32-15:39.** *And Jesus summoned to Himself His disciples, and said, "I feel compassion for the multitude, because they have remained with Me now for three days and have nothing to eat; and I do not wish to send them away hungry, lest they faint on the way." And the disciples said to Him, "Where would we get so many loaves in a desert place to satisfy such a great multitude?" And Jesus said to them, "How many loaves do you have?" And they said, "Seven, and a few small fish."*

10. Plummer, *Exegetical Commentary,* p. 217.

And He directed the multitude to sit down on the ground; and He took the seven loaves and the fish; and giving thanks, He broke them and started giving them to the disciples, and the disciples in turn, to the multitudes. And they all ate, and were satisfied, and they picked up what was left over of the broken pieces, seven full baskets. And those who ate were four thousand men, besides women and children. And dismissing the multitudes, He got into the boat, and came to the region of Magadan. Finally the Messiah feeds four thousand men plus the women and the children. The miracle closely parallels that which was recorded in chapter fourteen, the great difference being the fact that Gentiles are fed instead of Jews. A Gentile crowd is evidenced by the facts that they glorified the God of Israel (verse thirty-one) and He was at this time ministering in the midst of the territories of Decapolis (Mark 7:31).[11] A further indication of this fact is seen in the word for "basket" (verse thirty-seven). Σπυρίς has reference to a basket which the Gentiles used; κόφινος is a smaller basket utilized by the Jews.[12] The word for the basket employed by Gentiles is used here and whenever reference is made to this incident (Matthew 16:10; Mark 8:8, 20).

This incident no doubt made a profound impression on the disciples. By it the King taught that He was not only sufficient to minister to Israel but to the world as well. In addition the disciples were instructed that they would be empowered to minister not only to the Jews but also to Gentiles.

4. The Opposition of the Pharisees and the Sadducees, 16:1-16:12.

a. The Request for a Sign, 16:1-16:4a.

16:1. *And the Pharisees and Sadducees came up, and testing Him asked Him to show them a sign from heaven.* Traditionally the Pharisees and Sadducees were bitter opponents (Acts 23:6-10).[13] But their common enmity against Jesus has become so great that it now overshadows their hatred of one another. In a common alliance they come tempting the Lord (the present participle "tempting" [πειράζον- τες] indicates their malicious purpose in coming).

---

11. Brooke Foss Westcott, *Characteristics of the Gospel Miracles,* pp. 12-13.
12. G. Campbell Morgan, *The Gospel According to Matthew,* p. 200.
13. Plummer, *Exegetical Commentary,* p. 221.

The sign for which they ask is one out of heaven. Matthew uses the preposition "from" (ἐκ) to emphasize the heavenly origin of the sign which these religious leaders desired. The Jews were notorious for seeking signs (1 Corinthians 1:22), and because this incident is almost a reduplication of that recorded in chapter twelve, the same characteristic of the Jewish people is emphasized. A superstitious belief existed among the Hebrews that demons could perform works on earth, but only God could execute a sign from heaven.[14] It is true that God had in the past given such signs to Israel by means of Moses, Joshua, Samuel, and Elijah. However, the request was not made in order to reenforce faith but to tempt the Lord. The unbelief of these religious leaders would lead them to refuse the truth of the sign even if the Lord had performed it.[15]

16:2-16:4a. *But He answered and said to them, "When it is evening, you say, 'It will be fair weather, for the sky is red.' And in the morning, 'There will be a storm today, for the sky is red and threatening.' Do you know how to discern the appearance of the sky, but cannot discern the signs of the times? An evil and adulterous generation seeks after a sign; and a sign will not be given it, except the sign of Jonah."* Because of their unbelief the Messiah refuses their request and rebukes them for their spiritual perverseness and blindness. They are so blind in the realm of spiritual things that they fail to discern the signs of the times. The Lord very significantly uses the word "time" (καιρός) here (verse three). He is not thinking of a mere space of time, but of a divine program. This is evident since καιρός denotes a fixed period of time.[16]

But what were the signs of the times which they should have recognized? There are several. One of the clearest was the coming of John. To these very same religious leaders John had claimed to be the fulfillment of Isaiah 40. The Lord had identified John as the promised Elijah of Malachi 4 if Israel would only have accepted Him (Matthew 11:14). A second token of the times was the works of the Messiah. Christ claimed that they were a clear token of the times in Matthew 12:28. Finally, it should have been evident to any discerning student of the Old Testament that Daniel's sixty-ninth week was about to finish its course and usher in the seventieth week of tribulation. However, the stubborn hearts of these ecclesiastical leaders blinded their minds.

---

14. Henry Alford, *The Greek Testament*, 1:169.
15. Lenski, *Interpretation of Matthew*, p. 610.
16. W. E. Vine, *Expository Dictionary of New Testament Words*, 4:138.

b. The Abandonment by the King, **16:4b-16:12.** *And He left them, and went away.*

And the disciples came to the other side and had forgotten to take bread. And Jesus said to them, "Watch out and beware of the leaven of the Pharisees and Sadducees." And they began to discuss among themselves, saying, "It is because we took no bread." But Jesus, aware of this, said, "You men of little faith, why do you discuss among yourselves because you have no bread? Do you not yet understand or remember the five loaves of the five thousand, and how many large baskets you took up? Or the seven loaves of the four thousand, and how many baskets you took up? How is it that you do not understand that I did not speak to you concerning bread? But beware of the leaven of the Pharisees and Sadducees." Then they understood that He did not say to beware of the leaven of bread, but of the teaching of the Pharisees and Sadducees. Because of the opposition of the Pharisees and Sadducees the King abandons them. Heretofore Matthew has used the verb "to withdraw" (ἀναχωρέω); now he employs καταλείπω which means "to forsake, to abandon, or to leave." The Lord turns His back on these religious leaders for the simple reason that they were hopeless and incorrigible.[17]

When the King is alone with His disciples He warns them of the leaven, that is, the doctrine of the Pharisees. Although the doctrines of the Pharisees and Sadducees were extremely different, Matthew joins them together with one article here. Evidently the Evangelist gives reference to the fact that both sects had false doctrine and were in opposition to Christ. The Pharisees by their formalism taught the doctrine of hypocrisy, and the Sadducees set forth the doctrine of rationalism. They are alike in that both are erroneous and opposed to the Messiah.

In this section (Matthew 13:54-16:12), Matthew has traced the continued course of opposition to the King. In the face of this opposition the Lord withdraws twice. In the first withdrawal He ministers to Jews and in the second to Gentiles. This again emphasizes the pattern of the King's ministry as set forth in Matthew 1:1. In the first case the opposition arises from the political realm; the religious leaders are responsible for the antagonism in the second. Finally, the hatred of Israel's leaders becomes so great the King simply abandons them and begins to instruct

17. Plummer, *Exegetical Commentary,* p. 221.

His disciples. From now on the emphasis on signs and miracles begins to wane and the King instead prepares His disciples for His death and resurrection and for the momentous days following that event.

B. The Instruction of the Disciples of the King
16:13-19:2

The King moves about from place to place as a fugitive from the hatred of the Jewish hierarchy. Now He takes His disciples away from the thronging crowds to Caesarea Philippi at the northern extremity of Jewish territory to be with His small group of learners. It is in this place that He makes several great revelations to them concerning His person, His program, and the principles of His kingdom.

1. The Revelation Concerning the Person of the King, 16:13-16:17.

16:13-16:14. *Now when Jesus came into the district of Caesarea Philippi, He began asking His disciples, saying, "Who do people say that the Son of Man is?" And they said, "Some say John the Baptist; some, Elijah; and others, Jeremiah, or one of the prophets."* After the King has come into the area where the Gentile population is predominant, He asks His disciples about the opinions of men concerning His person. The conclusions which Israel had reached proved their rejection. Their thinking bore testimony to the supernatural character of Jesus, but they failed to identify Him as the Messiah.

16:15-16:16. *He said to them, "But who do you say that I am?" And Simon Peter answered and said, "Thou art the Christ, the Son of the living God."* However, the Spirit in grace reveals to Peter and the disciples the fact that Jesus is the Messiah, the Son of the living God. These words are deeply significant. By *Messiah* Peter identified Jesus as the One in whom all of the Old Testament hopes had been placed. He was the fulfillment of their Scriptures. More specifically, Jesus was the Son of the living God. Before (Matthew 14:33) they had acknowledged that He was *a* Son of God, now Peter identifies Him as *the* Son of the only genuine God. The fact that Christ was the Son of God was proof that He was the Messiah of Israel and the King of the future kingdom.

16:17. *And Jesus answered and said to him, "Blessed are you, Simon Barjona, because flesh and blood did not reveal this to you, but My Father who is in heaven."* Because of this great confession on the part of Peter, Christ pronounces him blessed. The Lord is not here giving a reward to Peter but rather is describing his blessed spiritual condition.[18] In calling Peter "Barjona" the Lord emphasizes the human nature of Peter. He in effect says, "You are flesh, and flesh and blood has not revealed this to you, but my Father in heaven." In Jewish literature "flesh and blood" is often used for humanity in contrast to God (Galatians 1:16; Ephesians 6:12; Hebrews 2:14).[19] This revelation to Peter and the disciples reveals their heart condition. They were fertile soil, the babes to whom the Father made revelation concerning the Son and His Kingdom (Matthew 11:25).

In this section Christ already lays claim to both Messiahship and deity. He affirms the truthfulness of Peter's confession by calling Peter blessed and by stating that this revelation is of God.

2. The Revelation Concerning the Program of the King, 16:18-17:13.

a. The Church, **16:18.** *"And I also say to you that you are Peter, and upon this rock I will build My church; and the gates of Hades shall not overpower it."* Following the Father's revelation to Peter and the rest of the disciples concerning the person of Jesus, the Lord Jesus goes on to reveal some matters pertinent to His program and work. The first revelation He makes involves the building of His church on "this rock" (ταύτῃ τῇ πέτρᾳ). One of the great exegetical problems of Bible students for centuries has been the identification of "rock" (τῇ πέτρᾳ) in verse eighteen.

Generally speaking there are three positions which are held—the rock is Peter;[20] the rock is Christ;[21] and the rock is the truth of Peter's

18. Morgan, *Gospel According to Matthew,* p. 210.
19. M'Neile, *St. Matthew,* p. 240.
20. Plummer, *Exegetical Commentary,* pp. 228-229.
21. Morgan, *Gospel According To Matthew,* p. 211.

confession.[22] There are several facts which tend to do away with the first view. In the first place, the Lord could easily have said "on you" (ἐπί σου) to remove the ambiguity. Why should the Lord use the pronoun "this" (ταύτη) if He were speaking directly to Peter as He is in the immediately preceding and following contexts? A second objection is found in the distinctive meanings of πέτρα and πέτρος. Invariably πέτρα is used of a shelf or ledge of rock or of a mass of rock, while πέτρος is used of a stone. Liddell and Scott do not see πέτρος and πέτρα being used in the same sense.[23] They go on to cite πέτρα being used to describe masses of rock rather than separate, loose stones.[24] Some attempt to do away with this distinction by saying Christ spoke in Aramaic, a language in which it is claimed there were no distinctions such as are shown by the Greek. This argument has little support.

> We know too little about the Aramaic to assert that when Jesus spoke these words he used the same Aramaic term in both statements. We should like to know more about the Aramaic as it was spoken at the time of Jesus. Therefore this appeal to the Aramaic substitutes something unknown and hypothetical for what is fully known and insured as true on the basis of the inspired Greek of the holy writers themselves.[25]

A second view holds that the rock is Christ. This view has the advantage of being consistent with the Old Testament use of the word *rock;* it is used symbolically oftentimes of the person of God.[26] However, the third person pronoun "this" (ταύτη) makes this view rather untenable.

A better view is the one which holds that the rock is the truth of Peter's confession. It is the truth of Christ's person and work upon which the church shall be built. This fits the use the Lord makes of ταύτη and also the sense of πέτρα. It is large enough to include the second viewpoint, the position which states Christ is the rock. Thus it concurs with the statements of Paul and Peter (Romans 9:33; Ephesians 2:20; 1 Peter 2:5-8).

The only occurrences of the word "church" (ἐκκλησία) in the gospels are found in Matthew 16:18 and 18:17. This term was not unfamiliar to the Jews of the Lord's day for it was used frequently in the Septuagint

22. M'Neile, *St. Matthew*, p. 241.
23. Henry George Liddell and Robert Scott, *A Greek-English Lexicon*, pp. 1397-1398.
24. Ibid.
25. Lenski, *Interpretation of Matthew*, p. 627.
26. Morgan, *Gospel According to Matthew*, p. 211.

to refer to Israel either as a body or as a congregation.[27] In the New Testament it is also employed with regard to an assembly of citizens with no religious significance whatsoever.[28] However, it is used here with a very distinct meaning.

> ... ἐκκλησία was the only possible word to express the Christian body as distinct from Jews ... He had just ended His public ministry in Galilee, had taken the disciples on a long journey alone, and was about to go to Jerusalem with the avowed intention of being killed; no moment was more suitable for preparing His followers to become a new body, isolated both from the masses and from the civil and religious authorities.[29]

What the Lord designated by this term was something entirely new, an organism which had never before had existence nor was even conceived. The fact that Christ calls it *my* church distinguishes it from all else. The Lord certainly could not say of Israel "My church." A further proof that ἐκκλησία does not allude to anything then in existence is the future tense of the verb "to build" (οἰκοδομέω). He was yet to build the church. The term is an explanation of that which will transpire on the earth from Pentecost until the seventieth week of Daniel preceding the establishment of the kingdom.

A problem also exists as to the meaning of the gates of Hades not overpowering the church. It is generally conceded that the phrase "gates of Hades" (πύλαι ᾅδου) to the Jew designated death.[30] Therefore, the Lord is simply stating the fact that the church as founded on the truth of Christ's person and work would not be held captive by death. A building is only as strong as its foundation (Matthew 7:24-27). Since the confession of Peter was based on the fact that Jesus was the Messiah, the Son of the living God, and because the church was built on that rock, the church had a foundation which could not be shaken by the greatest evidence of Satan's work, death. Thus the Lord was anticipating His own resurrection as well as the resurrection and translation of the church.

b. Peter and the Kingdom, 16:19-16:20.

16:19. *"I will give you the keys of the kingdom of heaven; and whatever you shall bind on earth shall have been bound in heaven, and whatever you shall loose on earth shall have been loosed in*

---

27. M'Neile, *St. Matthew*, p. 241.
28. Marvin R. Vincent, *Word Studies in the New Testament*, 1:93.
29. M'Neile, *St. Matthew*, pp. 241-242.
30. C. Clare Oke, "My Testimony," *The Expository Times* 37 (July 1926): 476.

heaven." Verse nineteen contains further revelation of Christ's program, the place of Peter in the kingdom. While many commentators do not identify the "kingdom" of verse nineteen with the "church" of verse eighteen, most attempt to associate them in some way. Plummer admits that they are not the same.[31] M'Neile believes the kingdom is here the church, although he concedes that this conception is different from that expressed elsewhere in the Lord's teaching.[32] Lenski contends that the church is the earthly side of the kingdom, while the kingdom of the heavens includes both the earthly and the heavenly sides.[33] For several reasons it is best to take the phrase "the kingdom of heaven(s)" ($\dot{\eta}$ $\beta\alpha\sigma\iota\lambda\epsilon\acute{\iota}\alpha$ $\tau\tilde{\omega}\nu$ $o\dot{\upsilon}\rho\alpha\nu\tilde{\omega}\nu$) as a designation of the millennial age.

First, this is consistent with its regular meaning throughout the Gospel of Matthew. Second, the promise of position in the kingdom was foremost in the mind of Peter and the rest of the disciples (Matthew 19:27-28; 20:20-23; Mark 10:35-37). Therefore it is completely natural for Christ to go from the subject of building His church to the matter of promising Peter a position of preeminence in the kingdom. It is the fitting reward for such an outstanding Messianic confession. Indeed, such a procedure is not unusual. In Matthew 19 Peter asks the Lord what should be the disciples' reward for leaving all to follow Him. The Messiah does not promise positions in the church but rather He assures them thrones in the millennial kingdom. The two situations are somewhat parallel in that a promise concerning the future is given as a reward for some good work in relationship to the Messiah's earthly ministry.

In addition, while the announcement concerning the church would have had a profound effect on Peter and the rest of the disciples, it is unlikely that the disciples would have clear insight into the significance of the church. In fact, it seems that it was necessary for the Lord to bring in the subject of the kingdom at this point so that His disciples would not later conclude that the church had taken the place of the kingdom. It is interesting that Matthew, the Gospel which presents the kingdom program most clearly, includes these sayings, while the rest of the gospels omit them. It must be concluded that verse nineteen is a reference to Peter's position in the millennial kingdom because (1) the term always refers to the millennial kingdom in Matthew, (2) the disciples were concerned primarily with their position in the kingdom, (3) the confes-

31. Plummer, *Exegetical Commentary,* p. 230.
32. M'Neile, *St. Matthew,* p. 243.
33. Lenski, *Interpretation of Matthew,* p. 629.

sion is Messianic and so is the reward, and (4) it is necessary for the King to distinguish the church from the kingdom.

> We must ... be careful not to identify the ἐκκλησία [church] with the kingdom. There is nothing here to suggest such identification. The Church was to be built on the rock of the revealed truth that Jesus was the Messiah, the Divine Son. To S. Peter were to be given the keys of the kingdom. The kingdom is here, as elsewhere in this Gospel, the kingdom to be inaugurated when the Son of Man came upon the clouds of heaven ... The ἐκκλησία, on the other hand, was the society of Christ's disciples, who were to wait for it, and who would enter into it when it came. The Church was built upon the truth of the divine Sonship. It was to proclaim the coming kingdom. In that kingdom Peter should hold the keys which conferred authority. [34]

In this verse, the word "keys" (κλείς) could have two meanings. It could mean that Peter would be the one who would open the gates of access to the kingdom to both Jews and Gentiles by being the first to proclaim the gospel to both groups.[35] This view has the support of the Acts account where Peter is recorded as the first to preach the gospel of Jesus' Messiahship to the Jews (Acts 2) and to the Gentiles (Acts 10).

However, the term has a second meaning. It is used of one who is in authority, the keys being a symbol of that authority.[36] To the Hebrews the key was the insignia of the authority which belonged to a scribe.[37] Morgan writes, "The key was the sign, not of priestly office, but of the office of the scribe."[38] These scribes interpreted and taught the law. It seems that Matthew uses "keys" (κλείς) in this second sense.

The Lord is promising Peter an exalted position of great authority in the coming earthly kingdom. This has the support of the rest of the New Testament. In Matthew 19:28 the Messiah promises each of the disciples a throne from which they shall judge the twelve tribes of Israel. In fact, Paul asserts that the saints of this age shall judge the world (1 Corinthians 6:2). The immediate context also supports this view. To Peter was given the authority of binding and loosing. These terms do not refer to the forgiveness of sins.

---

34. Willoughby C. Allen, *A Critical and Exegetical Commentary on the Gospel According to S. Matthew*, p. 177.

35. Vincent, *Word Studies*, 1:96.

36. M'Neile, *St. Matthew*, p. 243; Joseph Henry Thayer, *A Greek-English Lexicon of the New Testament*, p. 348; C. G. Montefiore, *The Synoptic Gospels*, 2:235.

37. Carr, *St. Matthew*, p. 212.

38. Morgan, *Gospel According to Matthew*, p. 215.

The two words are technical expressions, the meaning of which was well understood. To "bind" is to forbid, to "loose" is to permit. Just as a Rabbi of great knowledge would decide what, according to the provisions of the oral Law, was allowed or prohibited, so Peter would decide what, according to the teaching of Christ, was permitted or not.[39]

In other words, "to bind" (δέω) and "to loose" (λύω) are references to the execution of Peter's judicial authority.[40] This authority will be manifested in the coming earthly kingdom according to Christ's promise.

A problem exists as to the meaning of the future perfect periphrastics in Matthew 16:19 ("shall have been bound" and "shall have been loosed"). The Roman Catholic Church bases its sacerdotal authority on this verse, together with Matthew 18:18 and John 20:23.[41] However, this false doctrine is largely the result of an improper translation. Because of Jerome's Latin Vulgate Version, which was made about 400 A.D., many of the translators since then have translated the verbs in Matthew 16:19 as simple futures. Needless to say, the future perfect periphrastics have been ignored in these translations. It is the unanimous testimony of Greek grammarians that the perfect tense denotes a past action, the results of which endure to the present.[42] The periphrastic form of the perfect usually emphasizes the existing state.[43] This changes the complexion of Matthew 16:19 completely.

This is wrongly translated "shall be bound" and "shall be loosed," seeming to make Jesus teach that the apostles' acts will determine the policies of heaven. They should be translated "shall have been bound" and "shall have been loosed." This makes the apostles' acts a matter of inspiration or heavenly guidance.[44]

A good translation is given by Williams, who exercises great care in the translation of the Greek tenses, "And whatever you forbid on earth must be what is already forbidden in heaven, and whatever you permit on earth must be what is already permitted in heaven."[45] Bacon translates it, "Whatever thou dost prohibit on earth will have been prohibited

39. Plummer, *Exegetical Commentary*, p. 231.
40. Vincent, *Word Studies*, 1:96.
41. Joseph Pohle, *Dogmatic Theology*, 10:5-20.
42. Julius R. Mantey, *Was Peter a Pope?*, p. 38.
43. Ernest DeWitt Burton, *Syntax of the Moods and Tenses in New Testament Greek*, p. 40.
44. William Douglas Chamberlain, *An Exegetical Grammar of the Greek New Testament*, p. 80.
45. Charles B. Williams, *The New Testament, A Private Translation in the Language of the People*, p. 47.

in heaven, and whatever thou dost permit on earth will have been permitted in heaven."[46] Cadbury objects to this translation on the basis of the fact that the perfect loses its usual significance in sentences with such general conditions.[47] But while it is true that the point of time in future conditional clauses is very indefinite, the sequence of events usually remains the same.[48] Therefore, the verse is a promise to Peter of a place of authority in the future earthly kingdom. With this promise the Lord gives Peter the basis of the decisions which he shall make. Peter is to discern what is the mind of God and then judge accordingly.

16:20. *Then He warned the disciples that they should tell no one that He was the Christ.* The Lord concludes this revelation of His person and His program with a "warning" (ἐπιτιμάω) to His disciples. They are to tell no one that Jesus is the Christ. The revelation of this fact was to be given by the Father to those whose hearts were spiritually conditioned to the truth (11:27). Since the disciples did not know the hearts of men, they could cast this pearl before swine.

c. The Death and Resurrection of the King, 16:21-16:27. The Lord goes on to reveal to His disciples another aspect of His work—His death and resurrection.

16:21. *From that time Jesus Christ began to show His disciples that He must go to Jerusalem, and suffer many things from the elders and chief priests and scribes, and be killed, and be raised up on the third day.* This revelation is introduced by the words "From that time (Jesus Christ) began" (ἀπὸ τότε ἤρξατο), a phrase which occurs but twice in the book. It is used in Matthew 4:17 to introduce the reader to the ministry of the King in His presentation to Israel. Here it is employed by Matthew to introduce the revelation of the King's ultimate rejection and resurrection. From now on a new emphasis on this fact characterizes the King's instructions. The fact that the Lord now begins to instruct His disciples in preparation for His death and resurrection bears strong testimony to the reaction of Israel to the presence of its King.

The words "He must" (δεῖ) shows the necessity for Jesus to suffer and be raised again. While δεῖ can indicate various kinds of necessity, in this case it is used of divine necessity.[49] It was an imperative because the

---

46. Benjamin W. Bacon, *Studies in Matthew*, p. 302.

47. Henry J. Cadbury, "The Meaning of John 20:23, Matthew 16:19, and Matthew 18:18," *Journal of Biblical Literature* 58 (July 1939): 251.

48. Mantey, *Was Peter a Pope?*, pp. 54-55.

49. Lenski, *Interpretation of Matthew*, p. 634.

Messiah must suffer to fulfill prophecy; He must be raised again for the same reason (Isaiah 53; Acts 2:22-36).

The words which the Lord uses to foretell His death and resurrection emphasize the *official* rejection on the part of Israel. Matthew only of the Synoptics records Christ saying He must go to *Jerusalem,* the capital of Israel. The Messiah was to suffer many things and be killed at the hands of the elders, the chief priests, and scribes. This includes the whole Sanhedrin and indicates a formal trial will be held.[50] The highest judicial body of the land was going to condemn Him. The King is going to be rejected *formally* and *officially* by Israel.

16:22-16:23. *And Peter took Him aside and began to rebuke Him, saying, "God forbid it, Lord! This shall never happen to You." But He turned and said to Peter, "Get behind Me, Satan! You are a stumbling-block to Me; for you are not setting your mind on God's interests, but man's."* Christ's rebuke of Peter for his misguided attempt to turn the Lord from His way indicates that the death of Christ was of God. No doubt this is the significance of Christ's words "you are not setting your mind on God's interests" (οὐ φρονεῖς τὰ τοῦ θεοῦ).

16:24-16:27. *Then Jesus said to His disciples, "If any one wishes to come after Me, let him deny himself, and take up his cross, and follow Me. For whoever wishes to save his life shall lose it; but whoever loses his life for My sake shall find it. For what will a man be profited, if he gains the whole world, and forfeits his soul? Or what will a man give in exchange for his soul? For the Son of Man is going to come in the glory of His Father with His angels; and will then recompense every man according to his deeds."* In verses twenty-four to twenty-six the King discusses the cost of discipleship. The purpose is to show the disciples that glory follows suffering. By including this discussion here Matthew once more emphasizes the program of the Messiah as it is based on Daniel's prophecy. The Messiah must first be cut off (Daniel 9:26), a period of intense trouble begins at a later time (Daniel 9:27), and finally the Son of Man comes in glory to judge the world (Daniel 7:13-14). Thus the disciples must endure suffering, and when the Son of Man comes in His glory, they will be rewarded.

d. The Coming Kingdom, 16:28-17:13. The King has revealed His program regarding the building of a church, Peter's place in the king-

50. M'Neile, *St. Matthew,* p. 244.

dom, and the suffering and resurrection of the Messiah. Now the coming kingdom is discussed more fully.

16:28. *"Truly I say to you, there are some of those who are standing here who shall not taste death until they see the Son of Man coming in His kingdom."* Jesus promises in Matthew 16:28 that some of the disciples who were standing there should not die until they had seen the Son of Man coming in His kingdom. This verse has caused much difficulty. It can hardly refer to the coming of the Son of Man to establish His kingdom as prophesied in the Old Testament simply because the Old Testament kingdom prophecies were not fulfilled in the lifetime of the disciples.

Matthew 16:28 cannot be a prediction of the resurrection and ascension. How is the verb "to come" (ἔρχομαι) to be associated with His resurrection and ascension? Elsewhere the Lord refers to this as His going away (John 16:7). Furthermore, this explanation, because of the Old Testament kingdom prophecies, does not do justice to the statement.

It cannot be a reference to Pentecost as some hold.[51] The Son of Man did not come then. He *sent* the Holy Spirit (John 16:7; Acts 1:5-8). Nor can Matthew 16:28 be a prediction of the destruction of Jerusalem as Trench contends.[52] The only parallel between this event and the coming of the Son of Man is the fact of judgment. But what does this catastrophic event have to do with the coming of the kingdom?

It seems fairly evident that Matthew 16:28 is an anticipation of the transfiguration, which immediately follows this prediction. It must be noted that verse twenty-seven is to be separated from verse twenty-eight in this connection. Verse twenty-seven looks at the establishment of the kingdom in the future, while a promise of seeing the Messiah in His glory is the thought of verse twenty-eight. They are two separate predictions separated by the words "truly I say to you" (ἀμὴν λέγω ὑμῖν).

Matthew 16:28 is attested as a prediction of the transfiguration by several facts. Peter, one of the three who witnessed the transfiguration, interprets it in this manner.

> *For we did not follow cleverly devised tales when we made known to you the power and coming of our Lord Jesus Christ, but we were eyewitnesses of His majesty. For when He received honor and glory from God the Father, such an utterance as this was made to Him by the Majestic Glory, "This is My beloved Son with whom I am well pleased,"–and we ourselves heard this utterance made*

51. Morgan, *Gospel According to Matthew*, p. 221.
52. Richard Chenevix Trench, *Studies in the Gospels*, p. 198.

from heaven when we were with Him on the holy mountain.
(2 Peter 1:16-18.)

A second testimony of the fact that the Lord was anticipating His transfiguration is found in the arrangement of the events in the gospels. All three Synoptics (John omits the account of the transfiguration) place the transfiguration immediately after this prediction of the King. Matthew and Mark link the transfiguration to the promise with the conjunction "and" (*καί*), while Luke uses the words "and it came about" (*ἐγένετο δέ*, Luke 9:28). A third evidence is seen in that only some of the apostles saw the transfiguration. Finally, this explanation fits the meaning. The three disciples saw a foreview of the coming of the kingdom.

17:1-17:13. *And six days later Jesus took with him Peter and James and John his brother, and brought them up to a high mountain by themselves. And He was transfigured before them; and His face shone like the sun, and His garments became as white as light. And behold, Moses and Elijah appeared to them, talking with Him. And Peter answered and said to Jesus, "Lord, it is good for us to be here; if You wish, I will make three tabernacles here, one for You, and one for Moses, and one for Elijah." While he was still speaking, behold, a bright cloud overshadowed them; and behold, a voice out of the cloud, saying, "This is My beloved Son, with whom I am well pleased; hear Him!" And when the disciples heard this, they fell on their faces and were much afraid. And Jesus came to them and touched them and said, "Arise, and do not be afraid." And lifting up their eyes, they saw no one, except Jesus Himself alone. And as they were coming down from the mountain, Jesus commanded them, saying, "Tell the vision to no one until the Son of Man has risen from the dead." And His disciples asked Him, saying, "Why then do the scribes say that Elijah must come first?" And He answered and said, "Elijah is coming and will restore all things; but I say to you, that Elijah already came, and they did not recognize him, but did to him whatever they wished. So also the Son of Man is going to suffer at their hands." Then the disciples understood that He had spoken to them about John the Baptist.* The purpose of the transfiguration was primarily confirmation. It confirmed several vital facts. One of these was the reality of a future kingdom. The very fact that the transfiguration took place attests this. The presence of Old Testament saints on earth with Christ in a glorified state is the greatest possible verification of the kingdom promises in the Old Testament. The reality of this kingdom is also evident from the connection of the transfiguration with the promise of Matthew 16:27-28. The Son of Man was going to come one day to judge the world and establish His kingdom (Matthew 16:27). As an earnest of the coming of the kingdom three disciples were permitted to see the Son of Man in His kingdom (Matthew 16:28). This is exactly the manner in which Peter uses the transfiguration (2 Peter 1:16-21).

A third evidence that the kingdom is still future is seen in the Lord's statement recorded in Matthew 17:9. The King commands the privileged three to tell no one about what they had seen. Israel had rejected its King and now the King is indicating His rejection of Israel. However, the temporal conjunction "until" (ἕως) shows that the proclamation of the King and the kingdom is again to be announced to Israel at some time subsequent to the Lord's resurrection.

A final evidence that the transfiguration is a confirmation of God's kingdom program is seen in the King's comments about Elijah and John the Baptist (Matthew 17:10-12). The disciples were puzzled as to why they should tell no one. The scribes had taught that Elijah was to precede the Messiah in his coming. If this was Elijah, why should not they proclaim his coming? They therefore asked the Lord why the scribes teach this.

The Lord first of all confirms the theological proposition which the scribes had taught. Elijah shall come first, and he shall restore the spiritual state of Israel. But John was Elijah in his coming. However, because of Israel's spiritual blindness and lack of response, John could not restore all things. Rather, John was killed. It is interesting to note that Matthew records this fact as though Israel had a part in John's imprisonment and subsequent death, which preceded the imprisonment and death of the Messiah. "A suffering Forerunner is to be followed by a suffering Messiah."[53]

There is one clear inference from the Lord's statement concerning Elijah and John the Baptist. It is clearly prophesied of Elijah that he shall come and restore the spiritual state of Israel (Malachi 4:5-6). Since John did not accomplish this, the coming of Elijah is still future. One can logically conclude, therefore, that the coming of the kingdom is also postponed and future.

---

53. Plummer, *Exegetical Commentary*, p. 240.

Not only does the transfiguration verify the concept of a future kingdom, it also confirms the person of Jesus as the Messiah. His transformation attests it. He was not merely changed in His outward appearance, but His very form was transformed (μετεμορφώθη, verse two).[54] The very fact that His garments became white is significant.

> ... that wherever λευκός [white] is used here or elsewhere in the New Testament in connection with clothing it always has reference either to that of angels (beings surrounded with glory), or else to the garments of the saints who enter into a glorified state in heaven.[55]

The person of Jesus as the Messiah is also verified by His speaking with Moses and Elijah. M'Neile writes, "The abiding validity of the Law and the Prophets as 'fulfilled' by Christ (Mt. v. 17) is symbolized by the harmonious converse which He holds with their representatives, Moses and Elijah."[56]

The greatest attestation of the person of Jesus is the voice of the Father. The first phrase of the Father's sentence, "This is my beloved Son," is taken from Psalm 2:7, clearly a Messianic Psalm. So also is the second phrase Messianic, being taken from Isaiah 42:1. Even the imperative, "Hear Him," is Messianic. M'Neile says that it "... is added only here ... the point of which is seen by reference to Deut. xviii.15, 'a prophet from your brethren like unto me shall the Lord thy God raise up unto thee, him ye shall hear.'"[57]

The transfiguration confirms a third fact, the necessity of the Messiah's sufferings. Bernardin observes, "It is intended to be a divinely miraculous testimonial not only to the fact of Jesus' Messiahship but also to the truth of His startling statement that the Messiah must suffer and die."[58] This is seen in Luke's account where Moses, Elijah, and the King speak of the Lord's *exodus*. Matthew also infers that the transfiguration is related to Christ's death. The disciples were to tell no one of the transfiguration until the Lord was risen from the dead.

The transfiguration, being a fulfillment of the promise contained in Matthew 16:28, is a confirmation of the kingdom program, the person of the Messiah, and the necessity of Christ's sufferings.

54. Lenski, *Interpretation of Matthew*, pp. 651-652.
55. Joseph B. Bernardin, "The Transfiguration," *Journal of Biblical Theology* 52 (October 1933): 185.
56. M'Neile, *St. Matthew*, p. 251.
57. Ibid, p. 250.
58. Bernardin, "The Transfiguration," p. 181.

3. The Instruction Concerning the Principles of the King, 17:14-18:35.

Because the cross is drawing ever nearer the King prepares His disciples for that event with further instruction. Having given them a revelation of His person and His program, He goes on to instruct His disciples concerning His principles. These principles are given for the purpose of guiding the apostles while the King is absent.

  a. The Principle of Faith, **17:14-17:21.** *And when they came to the multitude, a man came up to Him, falling on his knees before Him, and saying, "Lord, have mercy on my son; for he is an epileptic, and is very ill; for he often falls into the fire, and often into the water. And I brought him to Your disciples, and they could not cure him." And Jesus answered and said, "O unbelieving and perverted generation, how long shall I be with you? How long shall I put up with you? Bring him here to Me." And Jesus rebuked him, and the demon came out of him, and the boy was cured at once.*

  Then the disciples came to Jesus privately and said, "Why could we not cast it out?" And He said to them, "Because of the littleness of your faith; for truly I say to you, if you have faith as a mustard seed, you shall say to this mountain, 'Move from here to there,' and it shall move; and nothing shall be impossible to you. But this kind does not go out except by prayer and fasting. When the Lord returns from the mount where the transfiguration took place, He finds the remainder of His disciples in a strange predicament. They are unable to exorcise a demon from a child. The Lord rebukes that "generation" γενεά is used here in the sense of "a race of people alike in character and pursuits")[59] for their lack of faith and perverseness. He then casts the demon out of the child with a command. When the disciples inquire as to why they could not cast out the demon, the King replies, "Because of the littleness of your faith."

Two items stand out in this incident. The Lord places His finger on the guilt of Israel— they lack faith and are perverted spiritually. In addition, one of these maladies, lack of faith, had infected the disciples. Before this time the King had endowed them with power to perform these works in His absence, and it is evident that they had been successful in this (Matthew 10:8). It may be that they were now cognizant of the King's waning popularity and were beginning to lose faith. The power for them to perform the miracle was there, but they failed to appropriate

59. Thayer, *Greek-English Lexicon,* p. 112.

it. Therefore, the Messiah instructs them as to the power of faith. No
doubt this is to show them the principle of faith in preparation for His
absence.

   b. The Death and Resurrection of the King, **17:22-17:23.** *And while
they were gathering together in Galilee, Jesus said to them, "The
Son of Man is going to be delivered into the hands of men; and they
will kill Him, and He will be raised again on the third day." And
they were deeply grieved.* As the King comes back into Galilee on His
way to Jerusalem, He again tells them of His coming death and resurrection. When the disciples hear this they are very sorry. This is another
indication of their lack of understanding, for they perceive that He is
going to die but fail to see the truth of the resurrection. It is evident that
they did not understand because they did not want to believe it. Lenski
comments, "To the last their minds struggled against the plain meaning
of what was dinned into their ears, and thus what they did not want to
know they actually did not understand."[60]

   c. The Principle of Tribute, 17:24-17:27.

   17:24-17:25a. *And when they had come to Capernaum, those who
collected the two-drachma tax came to Peter, and said, "Does your
teacher not pay the two-drachma tax?" He said, "Yes."* When the
King and the disciples come into Capernaum, Peter is accosted by the
collector of the temple tax. This was a voluntary payment of money
given annually by every Jew over twenty years of age for the maintenance of the temple (Exodus 30:13). The collector inquires of Peter
whether his teacher made a practice of paying this tax. Peter quickly
answers in the affirmative. When the disciples come into the house,
Jesus, knowing what had been said, instructs Peter concerning the principle of tribute.

   17:25b-17:27. *And when he came into the house, Jesus spoke to
him first, saying, "What do you think, Simon? From whom do the
kings of the earth collect customs or poll-tax, from their sons or
from strangers?" And upon his saying, "From strangers," Jesus
said to him, "Consequently the sons are exempt. But, lest we give
them offense, go to the sea, and throw in a hook, and take the first
fish that comes up; and when you open its mouth, you will find a
stater; take that and give it to them for you and Me."* Several facts
stand out in this section. First, the King points out to Peter that He, as
God's Son, is free from any taxation for the maintenance of the temple.

60. Lenski, *Interpretation of Matthew,* pp. 671-672.

In fact, the temple actually belongs to Him (Malachi 3:1). Secondly, Jesus is seen in His ministry of fulfilling all righteousness (Matthew 3:15; 8:4; 22:21). Rather than offend others He pays the tax. Thirdly, the Messiah manifests His divine person. This He does by "anticipating" ($\pi\rho o\acute{\epsilon}\phi\theta\alpha\sigma\epsilon\nu$) the subject in the house, ("Jesus preceded him, saying," lit.), by declaring His sonship with relation to the temple tax, and finally by performing the miracle of the stater in the mouth of the fish.

d. The Principle of Humility, 18:1-18:4. Matthew 18 contains the fourth discourse of five which are recorded in this Gospel. The others are contained in Matthew 5:1-7:27; 10:1-42; 13:1-53, and Matthew 24:1-25:46. The theme of the entire discourse is the necessity of humility, and it is addressed to the disciples of the King. Humility is essential for five reasons. It is necessary (1) for entrance into the kingdom (18:2-3), (2) for greatness in the kingdom (18:4), (3) to prevent offenses (18:5-10), (4) to carry on correct discipline in the church (18:12-20), and (5) in forgiving brethren (18:21-35).

It is well for one to understand the true nature of humility. It is not self-depreciation. Rather humility is the objective discernment of one's position before God. This may often lead to self-depreciation, but not necessarily. What the Lord has in mind in Matthew 18 is an awareness of what one is in God's sight and in His program.

Humility is seen in its relationship to both the kingdom and the church. In verses one to nine the kingdom is in view, and the church is considered in the remaining portion. In both the kingdom and the church humility is a necessity; therefore the Lord does not here make a clear-cut distinction between them.

18:1. At that time the disciples came to Jesus, saying, "Who then is greatest in the kingdom of heaven?" The discourse is introduced with the pronoun "that" ($\acute{\epsilon}\kappa\epsilon\hat{\iota}\nu os$) and a time designation inferring that this discourse is to be separated in thought from the preceding portion. However, the particle "then" ($\check{\alpha}\rho\alpha$) of verse one shows some sort of connection. Mark 9:33-34 presents the situation. The disciples had been arguing about who was to be the greatest. Matthew simply looks back at the events which had placed Peter, as well as James and John, in the preeminent places. As a result of these events the disciples ask a question concerning greatness in the kingdom. It may be noted in passing that the verb "is" ($\acute{\epsilon}\sigma\tau\acute{\iota}\nu$) in verse one does not mean the kingdom has started. The present tense here is used loosely.[61]

61. Montefiore, *The Synoptic Gospels,* 2:247.

18:2-18:4. *And He called a child to Himself and stood him in their midst, and said, "Truly I say to you, unless you are converted and become like children, you shall not enter the kingdom of heaven. Whoever then humbles himself as this child, he is the greatest in the kingdom of heaven."* The King introduces His reply with an authoritative statement, "Truly I say to you" (ἀμὴν λέγω ὑμῖν, cf. 5:18). Humility is so important that entrance into the kingdom is contingent upon it. The necessity of humility is emphasized by the emphatic negation (18:3). Greatness in the kingdom as well as entrance into the kingdom is based on humility (18:4).

    e. The Principle of Not Causing Stumbling, 18:5-18:14.

18:5-18:11. *"And whoever receives one such child in My name receives Me; but whoever causes one of these little ones who believe in Me to stumble, it is better for him that a heavy millstone be hung around his neck, and that he be drowned in the depth of the sea. Woe to the world because of its stumbling-blocks! For it is inevitable that stumbling-blocks come; but woe to that man through whom the stumbling-block comes! And if your hand or your foot causes you to stumble, cut it off and throw it from you; it is better for you to enter life crippled or lame, than having two hands or two feet, to be cast into the eternal fire. And if your eye causes you to stumble, pluck it out, and throw it from you. It is better for you to enter life with one eye, than having two eyes, to be cast into the hell of fire. See that you do not despise one of these little ones, for I say to you, that their angels in heaven continually behold the face of My Father who is in heaven. (For the Son of Man has come to save that which was lost.)* The Lord goes on to establish the importance of humility in living the present life by pointing out the peril of offending believers. In order to avoid this believers are to manifest humility toward one another by receiving one another. In so doing one receives Christ (18:5). The verb the Lord uses here, "to receive" (δέχομαι), means to accept into fellowship.[62] "It implies that a decision of the will towards the object presented has taken place, and that the result of this is manifest."[63] It is a very great sin for one believer to offend another (18:6). Likewise the world is indicted for the offenses which it has caused believers (18:7). Lack of humility can even cause a believer to offend himself (18:8-9). Therefore, every occasion for laying a snare in one's own path is to be

62. Thayer, *Greek-English Lexicon,* p. 130.
63. Hermann Cremer, *Biblico-Theological Lexicon of New Testament Greek,* p. 175.

removed. In verse ten the King makes a strong application, warning His disciples not to offend other believers who are here pictured as children.

18:12-18:14. *"What do you think? If any man has a hundred sheep, and one of them has gone astray, does he not leave the ninety-nine on the mountains and go and search for the one that is straying? And if it turns out that he finds it, truly I say to you, he rejoices over it more than over the ninety-nine which have not gone astray. Thus it is not the will of your Father who is in heaven that one of these little ones perish."* Humility is also imperative in dealing with the brethren who cause offenses. This subject is introduced with the parable of the lost sheep.

> The connexion of the parable of the Lost Sheep (12,13) with what precedes is that God cares for children and for childlike believers as a shepherd cares for his sheep. If one of them is lost, He will make every effort to recover it, and will rejoice greatly if He succeeds. If God takes so much trouble to recover a little one that has strayed, how grievous it must be to cause it to stray ... For the remainder of the chapter the connecting thought is the forgiveness of sins, a subject which is suggested by the parable of the Lost Sheep.[64]

The possession of humility is proven not by passively waiting for one to beg forgiveness and then granting it. Rather, it is manifested by actively seeking out the erring brother and attempting to make him penitent.

f. The Principle of Discipline, 18:15-18:20.

18:15-18:17. *"And if your brother sins, go and reprove him in private; if he listens to you, you have won your brother. But if he does not listen to you, take one or two more with you, so that by the mouth of two or three witnesses every fact may be confirmed. And if he refuses to listen to them, tell it to the church; and if he refuses to listen even to the church, let him be to you as a Gentile and a tax-gatherer."* The Lord then applies the illustration of the above parable (18:12-14) to the method of discipline in the church (15-17). This is the second and last occurrence of the word "church" (ἐκκλησία) in the gospels. It is used in a different sense here from that in Matthew 16:18. In the earlier occurrence it has reference to the body of Christ composed of those who are baptized by the Holy Spirit into Christ (1 Corinthians

---

64. Plummer, *Exegetical Commentary*, p. 252.

12:13). Here it speaks of the local assembly, a body of believers gathered together as a fellowship. Both times the Lord uses the term He is anticipating the future when the church age would intervene between His first and second comings.

Another factor indicates that the Lord is looking ahead to a new age. In verse twenty He states, "Where two or three have gathered together in My name, there am I in their midst." This clearly implies a time when He will be absent from them, a time in which the church would exist. By using the term *brother* in verse fifteen Christ also emphasizes the concept of humility since one would deal with another as a brother and not as his subject.

18:18-18:20. *"Truly I say to you, whatever you shall bind on earth shall have been bound in heaven; and whatever you loose on earth shall have been loosed in heaven. Again I say to you, that if two of you agree on earth about anything that they may ask, it shall be done for them by My Father who is in heaven. For where two or three have gathered together in My name, there I am in their midst."* Verses eighteen to twenty speak of the principle which is to be followed in the discipline. The injunction of verse eighteen concerns the same principle as that of Matthew 16:19 except it is here addressed to all of the disciples. In Matthew 16:19 it was spoken only to Peter. The Lord is indicating to His disciples that, in the church, divine guidance is to be the rule to follow. To Peter the King promised authority in the kingdom, assuring him of guidance in the use of that authority. Now the Lord instructs His disciples concerning the subject of discipline in the church and also promises divine direction in their decisions.

g. The Principle of Forgiveness, 18:21-18:35.

18:21-18:22. *Then Peter came and said to Him, "Lord, how often shall my brother sin against me and I forgive him? Up to seven times?" Jesus said to him, "I do not say to you, up to seven times, but up to seventy times seven."* Finally, Jesus indicates the necessity of humility in forgiving brethren. In nobly suggesting a limit of seven times to extend forgiveness to a brother, Peter far surpasses the traditional rabbinic concept of three times. But Christ says "up to seventy times seven" ($\xi\omega\varsigma\ \dot{\epsilon}\beta\delta o\mu\eta\kappa o\nu\tau\dot{\alpha}\kappa\iota\varsigma\ \dot{\epsilon}\pi\tau\dot{\alpha}$). M'Neile notices the similarity of these numbers to the Septuagint Version of Genesis 4:24.

> The saying in Mt., and the apostle's question leading to it, have
> possibly been framed under the influence of this passage in Gen.:

the unlimited revenge of primitive man has given place to the
unlimited forgiveness of Christians.[65]

18:23-18:35. *"For this reason the kingdom of heaven may be
compared to a certain king who wished to settle accounts with his
slaves. And when he had begun to settle them, there was brought to
him one who owed him ten thousand talents. But since he did not
have the means to repay, his lord commanded him to be sold, along
with his wife and children and all that he had, and repayment to be
made. The slave therefore falling down, prostrated himself before
him, saying, 'Have patience with me, and I will repay you everything.' And the lord of that slave felt compassion and released him
and forgave him the debt. But that slave went out and found one of
his fellow-slaves who owed him a hundred denarii; and he seized
him and began to choke him, saying, 'Pay back what you owe.' So
his fellow-slave fell down and began to entreat him, saying, 'Have
patience with me and I will repay you.' He was unwilling however,
but went and threw him in prison until he should pay back what
was owed. So when his fellow-slaves saw what had happened, they
were deeply grieved and came and reported to their lord all that
had happened. Then summoning him, his lord said to him, 'You
wicked slave, I forgave you all that debt because you entreated me.
Should you not also have had mercy on your fellow-slave, even as I
had mercy on you?' And his lord, moved with anger, handed him
over to the torturers until he should repay all that was owed him. So
shall My heavenly Father also do to you, if each of you does not
forgive his brother from your heart."* The Lord illustrates the principle of humility in forgiveness with the parable of the unmerciful servant. "The 'Therefore,' διὰ τοῦτο [or "For this reason"], marks a close
connexion with the saying."[66] The King links up the duty of forgiving
brethren in this age with the coming kingdom.

> The parable begins with the formula "the kingdom of heaven is
> like." This means nothing more than that a lesson may be drawn
> from what follows, which all who hope to enter the kingdom
> should lay to heart.[67]

In order for one to be able to enter the kingdom he must be forgiven
an infinite amount by God; therefore all who are anticipating entrance

65. M'Neile, *St. Matthew,* p. 268.
66. Plummer, *Exegetical Commentary,* p. 256.
67. Allen, *Commentary on Matthew,* p. 201.

are under obligation to show all possible consideration to others in the matter of forgiveness. The huge amount which the servant owed the king in the parable (verse twenty-four) expresses limitless forgiveness.[68] Therefore, it is necessary (cf. verse thirty-three where "should" [δεῖ] is used in this connection) for the forgiven servant to express humility in forgiving others. In both the church age and the kingdom age, humility is an absolute necessity.

One may ask, "Why does the Lord include this discourse here?" First Christ gave it at this point simply because the disciples needed it. He corrects the pride with which they were anticipating their positions in the kingdom. A second purpose was to instruct the disciples further concerning entrance "into" and greatness "in" the kingdom. Finally, this discourse was given to prepare the disciples for the coming church age. They were to accept all who believed. Perhaps the very ones who were responsible for Christ's death were to be accepted into fellowship if they repented (18:5-6). This discourse gave definite instruction relevant to discipline and forgiveness in the church in the coming age.

4. The Journey to Jerusalem Continued, 19:1-19:2.

19:1-19:2. *And it came about that when Jesus had finished these words, He departed from Galilee, and came into the region of Judea beyond the Jordan; and great multitudes followed Him, and He healed them there.* Matthew concludes the discourse and this section of his Gospel with the familiar words, "And it came about that when Jesus had finished" (καὶ ἐγένετο ὅτε ἐτέλεσεν ὁ ᾽Ιησοῦς). The King continues His journey to Jerusalem by departing from Galilee and entering the regions of Judea on the other side of the Jordan River. Still great multitudes follow Him, and in His love and compassion He heals them.

Two great movements have been traced in this section (Matthew 13:54-19:2)—the continued opposition to the King and the instruction of the disciples. In the first the antagonism resulted in subsequent withdrawals. Finally, the King abandons Israel to take His disciples apart to instruct them in preparation for His departure. Even as He journeys to Jerusalem to suffer and die, He manifests His royal benevolence in healing those who come to Him.

---

68. M'Neile, *St. Matthew,* p. 269.

VI. The Formal Presentation and Rejection of the King (19:3-25:46)
   A. The Continued Instruction of the Disciples (19:3-20:34)
      1. Concerning marriage (19:3-19:12)
         a. The problem of divorce (19:3-19:9)
         b. Marriage and the kingdom (19:10-19:12)
      2. Concerning childlikeness (19:13-19:15)
      3. Concerning the snare of wealth (19:16-19:26)
      4. Concerning rewards (19:27-20:16)
         a. Peter's question (19:27-19:30)
         b. The parabolic illustration (20:1-20:16)
      5. Concerning the passion (20:17-20:19)
      6. Concerning position (20:20-20:28)
      7. The healing of the blind men (20:29-20:34)
   B. The Formal Presentation of the King (21:1-21:17)
      1. The preparation (21:1-21:7)
      2. The entrance into Jerusalem (21:8-21:11)
         a. The homage (21:8-21:9)
         b. The response (21:10-21:11)
      3. The entrance into the temple (21:12-21:17)
         a. The cleansing of the temple (21:12-21:13)
         b. The healing ministry in the temple (21:14-21:17)
   C. The Rejection of the King by the Nation (21:18-22:46)
      1. The fig tree (21:18-21:22)
      2. The conflict with the chief priests and the elders (21:23-22:14)
         a. The question of authority (21:23-21:27)
         b. The parable of the two sons (21:28-21:32)
         c. The parable of the wicked husbandmen (21:33-21:46)
         d. The parable of the royal feast (22:1-22:14)
      3. The conflict with the Pharisees and the Herodians (22:15-22:22)
      4. The conflict with the Sadducees (22:23-22:33)
      5. The conflict with the Pharisees (22:34-22:46)
   D. The Rejection of the Nation by the King (23:1-23:39)
      1. The admonition of the multitudes and the disciples (23:1-23:12)
      2. The indictment of the scribes and Pharisees (23:13-23:36)
      3. The lamentation over Jerusalem (23:37-23:39)
   E. The Predictions of the Rejected King (24:1-25:46)
      Introduction to Various Interpretations of the Olivet Discourse
      1. The setting (24:1-24:2)
      2. The questions of the disciples (24:3)
      3. The warning concerning deception (24:4-24:6)
      4. The general description of the end time (24:7-24:14)
      5. The abomination of desolation (24:15-24:22)
      6. The coming of the Son of Man (24:23-24:31)
      7. The parabolic admonition (24:32-25:30)
         a. The parable of the fig tree (24:32-24:42)
         b. The parable of the watchful householder (24:43-24:44)
         c. The parable of the two servants (24:45-24:51)
         d. The parable of the ten virgins (25:1-25:13)
         e. The parable of the talents (25:14-25:30)
      8. The judgment of the nations (25:31-25:46)

VI. The Formal
Presentation and Rejection
of the King

With great care Matthew has recorded the presentation of the King's credentials to Israel. But that nation, blind and stiffnecked, refuses to accept Jesus as the Messiah. As a result of this response, the King begins to instruct His disciples in the light of His coming death and resurrection. That instruction is continued in this section (Matthew 19:3-25:46). This portion of Matthew also contains the Lord's greatest prophetic discussion, the Olivet discourse. The outstanding event is the Lord's so-called triumphal entry into Jerusalem and the nation's formal rejection of His person.

A. The Continued Instruction of the Disciples
19:3-20:34

1. Concerning Marriage, 19:3-19:12.

a. The Problem of Divorce, 19:3-19:9.

19:3. *And some Pharisees came to Him, testing Him, and saying, "Is it lawful for a man to divorce his wife for any cause at all?"* In the regions of Judea beyond Jordan, the King makes His way to Jerusalem and the Pharisees approach Him with the malicious purpose of "tempting" (πειράζω) Him. The Pharisees, Christ's avowed enemies, are now determined to destroy Him, so they come to Him with a test question concerning divorce.[1] John had been placed in prison and then killed because of his stand on the divorce question (Matthew 14:3-5). No doubt

---

1. For a discussion of the two views of divorce current in the Lord's day see Alfred Edersheim, *The Life and Times of Jesus the Messiah,* 2:333-334.

the Pharisees already knew the Lord's position from previous statements which He had made (Luke 16:17-18; Matthew 5:31-32). It may be that these Pharisees in asking this question purposed to entangle Jesus in the same political snare as the one that had removed John from the scene.

19:4-19:6. *And He answered and said, "Have you not read, that He who created them from the beginning made them male and female, and said, 'For this cause a man shall leave his father and mother, and shall cleave to his wife; and the two shall become one flesh'? Consequently they are no more two, but one flesh. What therefore God has joined together, let no man separate."* The King fearlessly responds in asserting that the marriage bond is indissoluble for four reasons. In the beginning God created one man for one woman (verse four).[2] He did not make provision for either polygamy, polyandry, or divorce by making more men than women or more women than men. Secondly, the marriage bond is the strongest of all family relationships (verse five). A third reason is seen in the fact that a man and wife are looked upon as being one flesh (verses five and six). Finally, since God ordained marriage, the consummation of marriage is looked upon as being a work of God not to be put asunder by man (verse six).

19:7-19:8. *They said to Him, "Why then did Moses command to give her a certificate and divorce her?" He said to them, "Because of your hardness of heart, Moses permitted you to divorce your wives; but from the beginning it has not been this way."* The Pharisees, ever alert to their opportunities of disparaging the Lord's ministry, ask, "Why, then, did Moses command to give her a bill of divorcement and to put her away?" Again the King refutes their insinuation that He was ignorant of the law of Moses or that He was disregarding it. The Pharisees said that Moses commanded it; Christ corrects them and says he *permitted* divorce, a provision for their primitive spiritual condition. In the beginning a higher ideal existed.

> Moses regulated, but thereby conceded, the practice of divorce; both were with a view to (πρός) the nation's (ὑμῶν) hardness of heart: since they persist in falling short of the ideal of Eden, let it at least be within limits.[3]

19:9. *"And I say to you, whoever divorces his wife, except for immorality, and marries another commits adultery."* Thus the Lord

2. Alfred Plummer, *An Exegetical Commentary on the Gospel According to S. Matthew,* p. 260.
3. Alan Hugh M'Neile, *The Gospel According to St. Matthew,* p. 273.

224

lays an indictment at the feet of the Pharisees. If they had really had a *No! they did desire the ideal.* heart for the things of God, they would have desired the highest ideal and not the lowest. In verse nine the Lord uses the words "And I say to you" (λέγω δὲ ὑμῖν) in the same manner as He did in chapter five. He speaks authoritatively of the true meaning of the Old Testament in asserting that there is to be no divorce except for adultery.

b. Marriage and the Kingdom, **19:10-19:12.** *The disciples said to Him, "If the relationship of the man with his wife is like this, it is better not to marry." But He said to them, "Not all men can accept this statement, but only those to whom it has been given. For there are eunuchs who were born that way from their mother's womb; and there are eunuchs who were made eunuchs by men; and there are also eunuchs who made themselves eunuchs for the sake of the kingdom of heaven. He who is able to accept this let him accept it."* At this the disciples say that, if this is the case, it is better not to marry at all. However, the Lord did not intend for the disciples to reach the conclusion of marital abstinence based solely upon the reason of convenience.[4] But for the sake of the work of the kingdom it is best, for those who are able, not to marry.

Verses one to twelve indicate the continuing progress of the argument. The Pharisees persist in their opposition to the Messiah of Israel. In the face of this antagonism the King continues to manifest His authority. Above all, the disciples are taught the primacy of the work of the kingdom. There can be no doubt but that the Lord is here preparing them for the time when He shall be absent and the work will be left in their hands.

2. Concerning Childlikeness, 19:13-19:15.

19:13-19:15. *Then some children were brought to Him so that He might lay His hands on them and pray; and the disciples rebuked them. But Jesus said, "Let the children alone, and do not hinder them from coming to Me; for the kingdom of heaven belongs to such as these." And after laying His hands on them, He departed from there.* As the King continues to instruct His disciples the subject of children intrudes itself. The great contribution of this passage is the stress placed upon the character of those who enter the kingdom. Christ is not saying that children are the only ones who inherit the kingdom,

4. C. G. Montefiore, *The Synoptic Gospels,* 2:262-66.

but He is saying that childlike trust and humility are essential for entrance. It will be noted in this connection that the pronoun is "such as
these" (τοιούτων) and not "these" (τούτων).[5]

The emphasis on children in Matthew is interesting. In connection
with the kingdom and with praise, Matthew refers to them in 11:25;
18:2-4; 19:13-14; and 21:15-16. The Evangelist uses the character of
children to sharply contrast the distinction between their faith and
humility and Israel's unbelief and blindness.

3. Concerning the Snare of Wealth, 19:16-19:26.

A rich young ruler, whose quest for eternal life brings him to the
Lord, causes the subject of riches and entrance into the kingdom to be
discussed.

19:16. *And behold, one came to Him and said, "Teacher, what
good thing shall I do that I may obtain eternal life?"* This incident
emphasizes three facts. It indicates primarily the misconception concerning the requirements for entrance into the kingdom. The young man
asks, "What good thing shall I do that I may obtain eternal life?" He
believes (1) that entrance is contingent upon some outstanding act, and
(2) that he is able to do it. He does not ask "How?" but "What?"

19:17-19:19. *And He said to him, "Why are you asking Me about
what is good? There is only One who is good; but if you wish to
enter into life, keep the commandments." He said to Him, "Which
ones?" And Jesus said, "You shall not commit murder; You shall
not commit adultery; You shall not steal; You shall not bear false
witness; Honor your father and mother; and You shall love your
neighbor as yourself."* The second question of the young man also
reveals the condition of Israel. When the Lord tells him to be keeping
the commandments, he asks, "Which ones (ποίας)?" The scribes and
Pharisees had catalogued the commandments, misinterpreted them, and
added so many of their own that the man took the Lord's command as
being a bit ambiguous. He questions, "What sort of commandments?"

19:20-19:22. *The young man said to Him, "All these things I have
kept; what am I still lacking?" Jesus said to him, "If you wish to be
complete, go and sell your possessions and give to the poor, and you
shall have treasure in heaven; and come, follow Me." But when the
young man heard this statement, he went away grieved; for he was*

---

5. Plummer, *Exegetical Commentary,* p. 262.

one who owned much property. The third statement of the young ruler further confirms the blindness of his generation. He blandly asserts that he has always kept the commandments which the Lord enumerates. He had followed the doctrines of the scribes and Pharisees (Matthew 5:20), but not the interpretation of the Lord (Matthew 5:21-7:6). His final response put the lie to these words.

19:23-19:25. *And Jesus said to His disciples, "Truly I say to you, it is hard for a rich man to enter the kingdom of heaven. And again I say to you, it is easier for a camel to go through the eye of a needle, than for a rich man to enter the kingdom of God." And when the disciples heard this, they were very astonished and said, "Then who can be saved?"* Finally, the amazement and question of the disciples at the Lord's statement (Matthew 19:25) attest the dullness of all of Israel.

> Possibly the Twelve still had the belief that earthly prosperity is a sign of piety, for God has promised to bless the substance of the religious man. If, therefore, to be wealthy is to be excluded from the Kingdom, who can be saved?[6]

19:26. *And looking upon them Jesus said to them, "With men this is impossible, but with God all things are possible."* In response to the disciples' question the Lord looks at them and points them to God's work instead of man's. This reply well illustrates the work of Christ on earth. As Jesus was dealing with the young ruler, He was constantly attempting to turn the man away from himself to God. In the same manner the Lord also attempted in His ministry to turn Israel to God. The Forerunner preached repentance to turn their minds to God; Christ and His disciples proclaimed the same message for the same purpose. Now the disciples themselves were looking at men; therefore the King points to God who is able to accomplish anything.

In recording this incident Matthew uses the words "eternal life" for the first time. It is interesting to note that the Lord here associates eternal life with entrance into the kingdom (Matthew 19:16, 23, 24). This interchange of terms is also illustrated well in Mark 9:43-47. The King, though no longer proclaiming the nearness of the kingdom, still preaches the possibility of entrance into the kingdom by faith. The fact that the disciples of the Lord would enter the kingdom by means of a resurrection may also be intimated by these words. The only occurrence of "eternal life" ($\zeta\omega\grave{\eta}\nu$ $\alpha\iota\acute{\omega}\nu\iota\sigma\nu$) in the Septuagint is found in Daniel 12:2 where it is the result of the resurrection of the godly. Matthew,

6. Ibid., p. 269.

therefore, may be giving a foreview of a postponement of the kingdom which could be longer than the apostles would live.

4. Concerning Rewards, 19:27-20:16.

a. Peter's Question, 19:27-19:30. A question asked by Peter makes an easy bridge from the subject of wealth as a snare to the topic of rewards in the kingdom.

19:27. *Then Peter answered and said to Him, "Behold, we have left everything and followed You; what then will there be for us?"* Simon remembers the Lord's statement to the rich young man, "If you wish to be complete, go and sell your possessions and give to the poor, and you shall have treasure in heaven; and come, follow Me." He asks the King what those who had made this sacrifice could expect to receive. The introductory adverb "then" (τότε) of verse twenty-seven marks the change of subject, while the word "then" (ἄρα) found in Peter's question indicates the connection with the preceding. The Lord goes on to answer Peter's question with the promise of reward and a warning (Matthew 19:27-30). Then a parable, recorded in Matthew 20:1-16, is used by Christ to illustrate the warning of Matthew 19:30.

19:28. *And Jesus said to them, "Truly I say to you, that you who have followed Me, in the regeneration when the Son of Man will sit on His glorious throne, you also shall sit upon twelve thrones, judging the twelve tribes of Israel."* The promise to Peter contains some very significant facts relative to Matthew's argument. The first is found in the word "regeneration" (παλιγγενεσία). This concept would not be a bit ambiguous to the average Israelite. It was the belief of the Jews that the Messiah, after His advent, would create a new heaven and a new earth.[7] The Old Testament prophecy of Isaiah (65:17; 66:22) was the solid foundation for this doctrine. The expectation of a "new birth" was also commonplace in apocalyptic literature.[8] The Lord does not disprove this doctrine but rather strongly endorses it. He even promises the apostles a place of authority in this future kingdom which He terms *a regeneration.*

> The twelve apostles are here given a special place and prerogative. παλιγγενεσία is a word only found here and in one other passage

7. Willoughby C. Allen, *A Critical and Exegetical Commentary on the Gospel According to S. Matthew,* p. 212.

8. F. W. Green, *The Gospel According to Saint Matthew,* p. 222.

(Titus iii.5) in the New Testament. It is used by Josephus for the
new birth of the Jewish nation after the return from the Babylonian
exile, and by Philo of the new birth of the earth after the flood and
after its destruction by fire. The new birth here denotes the world
or Israel at the time of the second advent—at the Parousia. The
Son of man is Jesus, who sits upon his Messianic throne.[9]

A second important factor in the Lord's answer to Peter is also found
in verse twenty-eight. There the King refers to the Son of Man sitting
upon the throne of His glory. This is an allusion to Daniel 7:13-14 where
the Ancient of Days gives the kingdom to the Son of Man. Again the
Messiah endorses the view of a coming kingdom when He shall rule.

The reference to the twelve judging the twelve tribes is also significant. This is a reference to Daniel 7:22 as well as Isaiah 1:26. It must be
noted that judgment here refers to government. "In the O.T. κρίνειν [to
judge] often means 'govern' (e.g. Ps. ix.4, 8)."[10] The Lord thus confirms the promise He had already given to Peter (Matthew 16:19) and
enlarges it to include all of the apostles. They are to be rulers over Israel
in the kingdom.

19:29-19:30. *"And everyone who has left houses or brothers or
sisters or father or mother or children or farms for My name's sake,
shall receive many times as much, and shall inherit eternal life. But
many who are first will be last; and the last, first."* A fourth factor is
the general promise given to all who forsake earthly relationships and
worldly possessions for the sake of Christ. They shall receive manifold
in return and in addition inherit life eternal.

> ... the καί joining the two clauses is the usual "and," not a καί
> *epexegeticum,* which, moreover, would be exceedingly harsh here.
> The promise is to the effect that in the future kingdom of God,
> every one shall receive manifold recompense for his special sac-
> rifices, and in addition shall inherit the supreme blessing of eternal
> life.[11]

Finally, the Lord by His statements makes some very daring claims.
He affirms that because the disciples have followed Him they will have
great places of authority in the regeneration. So also those who forsake
all for the sake of the Messiah will be abundantly rewarded. But the
greatest claim is His assertion of being the Son of Man of Daniel 7:13.

9. Montefiore, *The Synoptic Gospels,* 2:270.
10. M'Neile, *St. Matthew,* p. 282.
11. Siegfried Goebel, *The Parables of Jesus,* p. 300.

This is a clear reference to the Messiah who shall rule the world in judgment and put down every authority. That these are genuine assertions is evident from the almost casual manner in which the words were spoken.

    b. The Parabolic Illustration, **20:1-20:16.** *"For the kingdom of heaven is like a landowner who went out early in the morning to hire laborers for his vineyard. And when he had agreed with the laborers for a denarius for the day, he sent them into his vineyard. And he went out about the third hour and saw others standing idle in the market place; and to those he said, 'You too go into the vineyard, and whatever is right I will give you.' And so they went. Again he went out about the sixth and the ninth hour, and did the same thing. And about the eleventh hour he went out, and found others standing; and he said to them, 'Why have you been standing here idle all day long?' They said to him, 'Because no one hired us.' He said to them, 'You too go into the vineyard.' And when evening had come, the owner of the vineyard said to his foreman, 'Call the laborers and pay them their wages, beginning with the last group to the first.' And when those hired about the eleventh hour came, each one received a denarius. And when those hired first came, they thought that they would receive more; and they also received each one a denarius. And when they received it, they grumbled at the landowner, saying, 'These last men have worked only one hour, and you have made them equal to us who have borne the burden and the scorching heat of the day.' But he answered and said to one of them, 'Friend, I am doing you no wrong; did you not agree with me for a denarius? Take what is yours and go your way, but I wish to give to this last man the same as to you. Is it not lawful for me to do what I wish with what is my own? Or is your eye envious because I am generous?' Thus the last shall be first, and the first last."* Verse thirty contains a warning in connection with rewards, and this warning is illustrated by the parable recorded here. The conjunction "for" (γάρ) of Matthew 20:1 with the repetition of the thought of Matthew 19:30 in Matthew 20:16 indicate this connection. Several principles are given in this parable in relationship to the subject of rewards. Plummer states, "As to the householder's fairness, there can be no question. He kept faith with those who made an agreement with him, and he was the sole judge of what the work of the others was worth to him."[12] In verse

---

12. Plummer, *Exegetical Commentary,* p. 273.

four, the householder promises to pay those who were hired at the third hour a wage which was just or "right" (δίκαιος). This emphasis on the fairness of the householder is a good answer to Peter's question. The apostles were assured that their future reward would be a just one.

In addition, the parable prepares the disciples for the entrance of a new group of people, Gentiles, into the kingdom. The Jews like the first group of workers had the promises; the Gentiles like the later group had none. Yet both would have equal opportunities for reward. In fact, the church is promised that it would judge the world (1 Corinthians 6:2; Revelation 2:26), a promise very much like that given to Peter and the disciples (Matthew 16:19; 19:28).

A second principle taught by this parable is the fact that God is also gracious in giving His rewards. The householder by his actions is said to be "generous" (ἀγαθός). Therefore, when he acts according to his will (verse fifteen), he performs that which is in sovereign grace.[13] Again this is a reply to Peter's question. The rewards are of grace and not of works.

Finally, this parable was a lesson to the disciples that outward circumstances do not determine the reward. This was the great lesson of the parable. One group of workers had contracts, others merely had the promise of a just wage, and still others were only told to work. The five groups involved all worked for a different length of time. The men accomplished varying amounts of work. Yet all were rewarded with the same amount of money. "In the distribution of rewards no distinction will be made between first and last."[14] Thus the first will be last and the last first.

5. Concerning the Passion, 20:17-20:19.

20:17-20:19. *And as Jesus was about to go up to Jerusalem, He took the twelve disciples aside by themselves, and on the way He said to them, "Behold, we are going up to Jerusalem; and the Son of Man will be delivered up to the chief priests and scribes, and they will condemn Him to death, and will deliver Him up to the Gentiles to mock and scourge and crucify Him, and on the third day He will be raised up."* The King with His little band of disciples is now going directly toward Jerusalem. In preparation for the events which shall

13. Edersheim, *Life and Times,* 2:419.
14. Plummer, *Exegetical Commentary,* p. 274.

transpire with such rapidity there, the Lord makes a fourth announcement of His death and resurrection (Matthew 20:17-19). This is by far the most detailed that He has given. In Matthew 16:21 the Lord said His sufferings were a necessity ($\delta\epsilon\hat{\iota}$); in 20:22 He tells His disciples they are about to be ($\mu\acute{\epsilon}\lambda\lambda\epsilon\iota$); and now He is in the process of going to Jerusalem where those things will transpire. The program of Christ's death is outlined more fully here than previously. He is to be delivered to the Sanhedrin where He will be condemned. Since they have no authority to put a man to death, the King will be delivered to the Gentiles to be mocked, scourged, and crucified. This is the first time that death by crucifixion has been predicted.

The King is on His way to Jerusalem to die. But even in these circumstances the majestic person of the King is displayed by His prophetic statements and His confident dignity. The response of the disciples to this affirmation of the Lord's death and resurrection is not given here. The Evangelist is concerned primarily with showing the person of Christ. This he does by recording these very specific statements of Jesus.

6. Concerning Position, 20:20-20:28.

20:20-20:28. *Then the mother of the sons of Zebedee came to Him with her sons, bowing down, and making a request of Him. And he said to her, "What do you wish?" She said to Him, "Command that in Your kingdom these two sons of mine may sit, one on Your right and one on Your left." But Jesus answered and said, "You do not know what you are asking for. Are you able to drink the cup that I am about to drink?" They said to Him, "We are able." He said to them, "My cup you shall drink; but to sit on My right and on My left, this is not Mine to give, but it is for those for whom it has been prepared by My Father." And hearing this, the ten became indignant at the two brothers. But Jesus called them to Himself, and said, "You know that the rulers of the Gentiles lord it over them, and their great men exercise authority over them. It is not so among you, but whoever wishes to become great among you shall be your servant, and whoever wishes to be first among you shall be your slave; just as the Son of Man did not come to be served, but to serve, and to give His life a ransom for many."*

With the adverb "then" ($\tau\acute{o}\tau\epsilon$) Matthew moves to the next subject. The mother of James and John beseeches the King to give the two seats of authority next to Him to her sons when He comes into His kingdom. The Lord assures James and John that they shall suffer for Him, but the places of authority which they seek are reserved only for those for whom they are prepared. Because of the agressiveness of the sons of Zebedee, the ten become indignant with them. From this situation the Lord Jesus gives a brief discourse on the subject of positions in the kingdom. From this discussion there is much to be gleaned, not only with reference to positions in the kingdom, but also in connection with Matthew's argument.

It is important to notice that the Lord does not dispute the disciples' concept of the kingdom. This argument for the doctrine of a Messianic kingdom could possibly be discounted if this incident occurred at the very beginning of the Lord's ministry. However, this event transpires within days of the crucifixion. Certainly Christ would have corrected this important idea by now if the disciples' thinking was faulty. However, the Lord does nothing of the sort; rather He corrects the apostles' concept of *greatness in the kingdom*.

A second important factor is seen in how the King prepares His disciples for His absence and their subsequent sufferings. The "cup" ($\pi o \tau \acute{\eta} \rho \iota o \nu$) of verses twenty-two and twenty-three refers to the destiny of suffering.[15] It was used in the Old Testament of the sufferings of God's wrath against sin.[16] Here it specifically indicates the passion of Christ and the trials the apostles would endure for His sake. While the disciples did not comprehend the import of these words at this time, it did fortify them for the future when they would suffer and understand their meaning.

A third item to note is the fact that the disciples were prepared for the coming of the kingdom, but not for positions in it. They had repented and trusted in Jesus as their Messiah, but they failed to learn the lesson of humility which the King had been teaching in chapter eighteen. This lack of humility is seen in the request of James and John for places of prominence in the kingdom. The indignation of the rest of the disciples at the two showed that all of them lacked this element in their spiritual character. They were perturbed, not because of the Lord's response to the request of the two, but because of the request. "All alike wanted the premier position, and they felt that these brothers had taken an unfair advantage of them."[17]

15. R. C. H. Lenski, *The Interpretation of St. Matthew's Gospel*, p. 787.
16. A. Carr, *The Gospel According to St. Matthew*, p. 237.
17. Theodore H. Robinson, *The Gospel of Matthew*, p. 167.

Finally, their lack of humility is indicated by the fact that the King had to instruct them further along this line (Matthew 20:25-28). In chapter eighteen the King set the example of children before them; in chapter twenty a contrast with earthly rulers is made. In the kingdom the secular principle of greatness is reversed. The teaching of greatness in this section is even more direct and forcible than that which the King had just completed in Matthew 19:27-20:16. They were heirs of the kingdom, but were not yet prepared for authority in the kingdom. This they would learn in the future.

A great lesson is taught by this incident: greatness comes by humility. It is most interesting to note the progression in the Lord's instruction. Greatness is dependent upon being a "servant" (διάκονος) of others but primacy comes from being a "slave" (δοῦλος) of others.

> Δοῦλος, perhaps from δέω, *to bind,* is the *bondman,* representing the permanent *relation* of servitude. Διάκονος, probably from the same root as διώκω, *to pursue,* represents a servant, not in his relation, but in his *activity.*[18]

The Lord will have the preeminent place since He came not to be ministered unto, but to minister and to give His life a ransom for many (verse twenty-eight). This fact is the supreme illustration of how greatness in the kingdom is attained. It was because of this that Christ could not give the places of prominence to James and John. The offices are given according to fitness. As Morgan comments, "When God prepares an office for a man, He prepares the man for the office; and there is perfect fitness."[19]

A fifth important fact which is underscored in this section is the person of Christ. If humility is the prerequisite to greatness, Christ is the greatest since He is infinitely more humble than any human. Plummer writes, "To be great is to be the servant (διάκονος) of many; to be first is to be the bond-servant (δοῦλος) of many; to be supreme is to give one's life for many."[20] Another indication of His deity is the fact that His life is to be a ransom for many. Only God could make this claim. The very fact that the Lord said "the Son of man has come" indicates His existence in eternity past. "'The Son of Man came' implies the preexistence of the Son; it is not a mere synonym for being born

18. Marvin R. Vincent, *Word Studies in the New Testament,* 1:112.
19. G. Campbell Morgan, *The Gospel According to Matthew,* p. 247.
20. Plummer, *Exegetical Commentary,* p. 280.

(xviii.11; Lk. xix.10)."[21] Jesus did not rebuke the mother of James and John for attributing Messiahship to Him. He only pointed out the suffering that was involved. The conjunction "but" ($\dot{\alpha}\lambda\lambda\dot{\alpha}$) of verse twenty-three, which follows the clause "this is not Mine to give," in no way detracts from Christ's person. It is here equivalent to $\epsilon\dot{\iota}\ \mu\dot{\eta}$ [the word "except"].[22] The position and the man are both fitted by the Father. Therefore, Christ could not arbitrarily give these places to two disciples.

A final factor is the revelation of Christ's work. Before this time Christ asserted that He would be crucified, but He had never said what this would accomplish. Now He reveals that His life will be a ransom for many (verse twenty-eight). Concerning the word "ransom" ($\lambda\dot{\upsilon}$-$\tau\rho o\nu$), Robertson writes, "The word translated 'ransom' is the one commonly employed in the papyri as the price paid for a slave who is then set free by the one who bought him, the purchase money for manumitting slaves."[23] The word "for" ($\dot{\alpha}\nu\tau\dot{\iota}$) indicates the substitutional aspect of the work of the Lord Jesus.[24] This is seen not only from the meaning of the preposition, but also from the context. Robertson says, "... the context renders any other resultant idea out of the question."[25] Thus the King makes a great revelation of the work which He shall accomplish on the cross. His death will provide the means whereby the many shall gain entrance into the kingdom.

7. The Healing of the Blind Men, 20:29-20:34.

20:29-20:34. *And as they were going out from Jericho, a great multitude followed Him. And behold, two blind men sitting by the road, hearing that Jesus was passing by, cried out, saying, "Lord, have mercy on us, Son of David!" And the multitude sternly told them to be quiet; but they cried out all the more, saying, "Lord, have mercy on us, Son of David!" And Jesus stopped and called them, and said, "What do you wish Me to do for you?" They said to Him, "Lord, we want our eyes to be opened." And moved with compassion, Jesus touched their eyes; and immediately they received their sight, and followed Him.*

21. Ibid.

22. Blomfield Jackson, "Note on Matt. xx 23 and Mark x 40," *The Journal of Theological Studies* 6 (January 1905): 237-240.

23. Archibald Thomas Robertson, *Word Pictures in the New Testament*, 1:163.

24. A. T. Robertson, *A Grammar of the Greek New Testament in the Light of Historical Research*, p. 573.

25. Ibid.

With the conjunction "and" (καί) and a genitive absolute grammatical construction, Matthew continues to carefully trace the final journey of the King to the capital city. As the Messiah leaves Jericho, a city situated about fifteen miles from Jerusalem, a huge crowd follows Him. Two blind men call to Him. Though rebuked by the multitude, the men continue their cry. In compassion the King stops, touches their eyes, and heals them. Invariably commentators note that Matthew speaks of *two* blind men, and *two* lepers, and they puzzle about the number. It is evident that Matthew, writing for a Jewish reader, would emphasize two since this number was the minimum required to establish the truth of a testimony (Deuteronomy 17:6).

It is most interesting to note the title by which the multitude identifies their King. "The ὅτι ["that," verse thirty] is equivalent to quotation marks. They heard the crowd cry, *"Jesus is passing!"* [26] Thus the attitude of rejection on the part of Israel is indicated in that they fail to recognize Him as the Messiah, the Son of David. Later they take up the cry in hysterical frenzy, but not in true belief. To them He could only be the Messiah in Jerusalem.

On the other hand, the blind ones call upon Jesus by His Messianic title, Son of David. It is well recognized that this was a Messianic name. Morison writes, "It was a current appellation of the Messiah." [27] The blind men, in contrast to the masses of Israel, have spiritual sight and genuine faith in Jesus as the Messiah and King.

It is interesting to note that this is the last public miracle which the Lord performs. Though rejected, He still manifests Himself as the Son of David, the Messiah. This is important. The kingdom was no longer near, but entrance was still possible in the future if they would trust in Jesus as their King. These would enter the kingdom by means of the resurrection. This is one reason why the King, completely cognizant of His rejection, continues to present Himself as the Messiah by His entrance into Jerusalem. Thus this miracle forms a fitting prelude to that great event which Matthew is about to recount. [28]

---

26. Vincent, *Word Studies,* 1:112.
27. James Morison, *A Practical Commentary on the Gospel According to St. Matthew,* p. 365.
28. Lenski, *Interpretation of Matthew,* p. 797.

B. The Formal Presentation of the King
21:1-21:17

The formal presentation of the King involves the so-called triumphal entry of Jesus into Jerusalem. In this section, Matthew also includes the cleansing of the temple and the Lord's conflict with the Jewish hierarchy in the temple.

1. The Preparation, 21:1-21:7.

21:1-21:3. *And when they had approached Jerusalem and had come to Bethphage, to the Mount of Olives, then Jesus sent two disciples, saying to them, "Go into the village opposite you, and immediately you will find a donkey tied there and a colt with her; untie them, and bring them to Me. And if anyone says something to you, you shall say, 'The Lord has need of them;' and immediately he will send them."* The simple phrase "and when" (καὶ ὅτε) marks the transition in the narrative. The careful preparation which the Lord makes indicates His sovereignty. That which is about to transpire is no accident. Detailed and deliberate instructions are given to the disciples. In this situation the King was not placed in the midst of a popular clamor, but He intentionally was causing it. What is significant is the fact that this action was so contrary to His preceding ministry. After His rejection was evident, the King had carefully withdrawn from the cities and avoided the religious leaders, but now He intentionally and openly parades into Jerusalem in the midst of the hierarchy.[29] Even as He sends His disciples for the animals He manifests great authority. The King tells them to explain to the one who would question them, "The *Lord* has need of them." Except for the doubtful passage in Matthew 28:6, this is the only place in Matthew's Gospel where the expression "the Lord" (ὁ κύριος) is used of Christ, and here He applies it to Himself.[30] The term denotes power and authority.

21:4-21:7. *Now this took place that what was spoken through the prophet might be fulfilled, saying,*
> *"Say to the Daughter of Zion,*
> *'Behold your King is coming to you,*
> *Gentle, and mounted upon a donkey,*
> *Even upon a colt, the foal of a beast of burden.'"*

---

29. Morgan, *Gospel According to Matthew*, p. 249.
30. Robertson, *Word Pictures*, 1:165-166.

And the disciples went and did just as Jesus had directed them, and brought the donkey and the colt, and laid on them their garments; on which He sat. Verse four is a comment by Matthew in which he makes one of his typical apologetic introductions of an Old Testament prophecy. The quotation is composed of two Old Testament passages— Isaiah 62:11 and Zechariah 9:9. The Evangelist shows that the Lord purposely did these things in order that the prophecy of Zechariah might be fulfilled. When the two disciples find the ass and her foal, the events transpire exactly as they were predicted by the Messiah. All these things occur at or near Bethphage, which means "house of unripe figs."[31] The Lord was coming to Jerusalem which, like an unripe fig tree, was unprepared for the coming of its King.

The significant thing in these first seven verses is the use Matthew makes of the prophecies of Isaiah and Zechariah. Each phrase is significant. Rather than use the first clauses of Zechariah 9:9, Matthew introduces the Zechariah passage with a phrase from Isaiah 62:11, "Say to the daughter of Zion." The Zechariah passage actually has, "Rejoice greatly, O daughter of Zion; shout in triumph, O daughter of Jerusalem." But this would not fit into Matthew's argument since Jerusalem failed to recognize its King. Jerusalem had to have its King pointed out; therefore the Evangelist substitutes the words of Isaiah to give the passage more meaning. "The substitution is interpretative."[32] Since Zion is another term for Jerusalem or a particular portion of that city, the phrase *daughter of Zion* must refer to the inhabitants of Jerusalem.[33] Jerusalem is to awake out of its lethargy and note the coming of its King.

The use of Zechariah 9:9 is very appropriate since the Jews generally acknowledge that it is a Messianic prophecy.[34] The words "Behold your King" ($\iota\delta o\grave{v}$ $\acute{o}$ $\beta\alpha\sigma\iota\lambda\epsilon\acute{v}\varsigma$ $\sigma o\upsilon$) are extremely important. Matthew could hardly make the presentation of the royalty of Jesus more explicit. To Israel Matthew writes, "Behold, your King!" These words are the theme of this Jewish Gospel. The first time Jerusalem was told of the King's presence in Israel was at the coming of the Magi (2:2). In the Sermon on the Mount the Lord reminds His listeners that Jerusalem belongs to the great King (5:35). Now Jerusalem is to see its King, but

31. Ibid., 1:165.
32. Lenski, *Interpretation of Matthew*, p. 802.
33. E. W. G. Masterman, "Zion," *The International Standard Bible Encyclopaedia*, 5:3150.
34. A. C. Gaebelein, *The Gospel of Matthew*, 2:125.

the city perplexed as to His identity fails to own Him as its Messiah.

It is very significant that Matthew does not quote Zechariah 9:9 in its entirety. He carefully and prudently omits, "He is just and endowed with salvation," a sentence equivalent to "He is righteous and endued with salvation."[35] Although the Lord is ever righteous, He did not come at this time to bring Israel's national salvation. Israel rejected its King; therefore Matthew omits this part of the prophecy.

The great emphasis of the prophecy is on the meekness and lowliness of the King in His coming. This is more readily noted in the Hebrew text of Zechariah.

> The Hebrew word expresses the condition of one, who is bowed down, brought low through oppression, affliction, desolation, poverty, persecution, bereavement; but only if, at the same time, he had in him the fruit of all these, in lowliness of mind, submission to God, piety.[36]

The idea of lowliness is further emphasized by His riding on an ass. "Since the times of Solomon no king bestrode an ass."[37] This coming in meekness and lowliness is in sharp contrast with the coming prophesied in Daniel 7:13. The Jews had much difficulty in attempting to reconcile these two passages.[38] How could the Messiah come in the clouds of heaven and also upon an ass? The answer is found in two comings. He will yet come in the clouds to be the King of Israel's kingdom; here He comes meek and lowly to present Himself to Israel as its King.

2. The Entrance Into Jerusalem, 21:8-21:11.

a. The Homage, 21:8-21:9. The actual presentation of the King to Israel can be discussed under three headings as far as Matthew's argument is concerned—the homage, the response, and the significance of the presentation.

21:8. *And most of the multitude spread their garments in the road, and others were cutting branches from the trees, and spreading them in the road.* As the King rides the ass the majority of the crowd throw their garments in His pathway while others keep strewing

---

35. Charles L. Feinberg, *God Remembers,* pp. 127-128.
36. E. B. Pusey, *The Minor Prophets,* 2:403.
37. Lenski, *Interpretation of Matthew,* p. 805.
38. Gaebelein, *The Gospel of Matthew,* 2:126.

branches before Him. To make a carpet out of garments for the way of a
King is said to be a common form of homage to this day.[39] The waving
of palm branches was done to welcome kings.[40] Every outward indication pointed to the entrance of a king into Jerusalem.

21:9. *And the multitudes going before Him, and those who followed after were crying out, saying,*
> *"Hosanna to the Son of David;*
> *Blessed is He who comes in the name of the Lord;*
> *Hosanna in the highest!"*

The cry of the crowds also attested the royal character of Christ's
entry. The word *Hosanna* is significant. M'Neile comments,
"'Hosanna' is from Ps. cxviii.25, the last of the Hallel psalms which
would soon be sung at the Passover. It is the Heb. נָא יָשַׁע הוֹ (for
הוֹשִׁיעָה) 'save we pray Thee,' not the Aram. אוֹשַׁעְנָא 'save us.' "[41]
It seems, however, that the term came to signify *praise* or *glory* rather
than its literal Hebrew meaning.[42] This may be its sense in "Hosanna in
the highest" and also in Revelation 7:9 where the great multitude cries,
"Salvation to our God." It is not legitimate, however, to rob this cry of
its Messianic significance on this basis. The praise given to the "Son of
David" is clearly a Messianic title.[43] It is taken from Psalm 118 " . . .
which celebrates the millennial sabbath brought in by the Messiah, then
to be acknowledged by the people."[44]

Another peculiarly Messianic characteristic of this passage is the
participle translated "He who comes" (ὁ ἐρχόμενος). "'He that cometh' (*Habba*) was a recognized Messianic title."[45] The verb also speaks
of all that the Messiah would bring with Him. Thus when the crowds
pronounce Him blessed (a perfect participle), they are welcoming Him
with all of His blessings.

> The enthusiastic multitudes thus acclaim Jesus as being blessed by
> Jehovah, not merely with a verbal benediction, but, as Jehovah
> always blesses, with the gifts and the treasures implied in the

---

39. Plummer, *Exegetical Commentary,* p. 286.
40. Edersheim, *Life and Times,* 2:372.
41. M'Neile, *St. Matthew,* p. 296.
42. Gustaf Dalman, *The Words of Jesus,* p. 221.
43. Robinson, *The Gospel of Matthew,* p. 171.
44. J. N. Darby, *Synopsis of the Books of the Bible,* 3:112.
45. Carr, *St. Matthew,* p. 242.

benedictory words; and they acclaim him as coming and bringing
all these blessings to them and to their capital and their nation.[46]

b. The Response, **21:10-21:11.** **And when He had entered**
Jerusalem, all the city was stirred, saying, "Who is this?" And the
multitudes were saying, "This is the prophet Jesus, from Nazareth
in Galilee." It is interesting to note the response to this great display of
homage. The city was shaken as by an earthquake. The Authorized
Version's rendering, "was moved," hardly does justice to the verb "to
be stirred" (σείω). The response of the city indicates that there were
two groups involved. The cry of praise arose largely from the people
who were visiting Jerusalem for the feast; the question originated from
the inhabitants of the city. Only once before had the city been similarly
affected and that also was because of the King (Matthew 2:3). The
movement was of such a size as to shake the city, but the people are only
aroused enough to inquire, "Who is this?" They go no further.

The shouting multitude answers, "This is the prophet Jesus, from
Nazareth of Galilee." This answer is a vivid portrayal of the blindness
of Israel. It is not said that He is the Messiah; He is recognized only as a
prophet, and that from miserable Nazareth. The very people among
whom He had performed His many marvelous miracles own Him only
as a prophet (Matthew 16:13-14; 21:46).

The Significance of the Presentation. The significance of the triumphal entry is tremendous in this Gospel. To Matthew it is the final and
official presentation of Jesus to Israel as its Messiah. This is evident for
several reasons. The first is the manner in which Christ acts throughout
this whole course of events. He deliberately makes very careful preparation to fulfill every detail of the prophecy of Zechariah 9:9. In addition
He planned His movements with understanding of their significance.
Morgan says, "It is evident also that He acted with knowledge. This is
manifested in the detailed instructions."[47] The acknowledgment which
He gives to the praise indicates that the Lord presented Himself to Israel
(Matthew 21:16). When the religious leaders ask the Lord, "Do you hear
what these are saying?" the King responds, "Yes."

A second indication of the fact that Jesus presented Himself to Israel
is seen in that the people recognized it as such. All of Jerusalem and the
teeming multitudes in that city for the celebration of the feast noticed
His Messianic entrance. Johnson writes, ". . . the people understood the

46. Lenski, *Interpretation of Matthew,* p. 809.
47. Morgan, *Gospel According to Matthew,* p. 249.

significance of the event, although their ideas of Him were no doubt deficient (*Cf.* 21:8-11, 46)."[48]

A third proof that the Lord presented Himself as the King of Israel is seen in the parables which the Messiah gives following this event.[49] The parable of the husbandmen (Matthew 21:33-43) clearly teaches that the Messiah has come to Israel but has been rejected. The close connection of the parable with the entrance into Jerusalem indicates that the interpretation of the parable is bound up with that event.

A fourth indication of the presentation of the King to Israel is the time in which it occurred. Sir Robert Anderson has shown that the entry of Christ into Jerusalem occurred on the very day that the sixty-ninth week of Daniel's prophecy had run out.[50] This is the exact time in which the Messiah was to come (Daniel 9:25).

Because Israel refused to accept the King when He was presented in exact fulfillment of their Scripture, their unbelief was confirmed beyond the shadow of a doubt. The reception which was given the King was without genuine faith and understanding. However, it did give a brief glimpse of that which will characterize the King's reception when He appears to Israel for a second time.

3. The Entrance Into the Temple, 21:12-21:17.

a. *The Cleansing of the Temple,* **21:12-21:13.** *And Jesus entered the temple and cast out all those who were buying and selling in the temple, and overturned the tables of the money-changers and the seats of those who were selling doves. And He said to them, "It is written, 'My house shall be called a house of prayer;' but you are making it a robbers' den."* The King is next seen in the temple. There He casts out all the ones who were carrying on commerce, overturns the tables of the money changers and the ones selling doves. Matthew uses one article with the participle "selling" ($\pi\omega\lambda o\tilde{v}\nu\tau\alpha\varsigma$) and the participle "buying" ($\dot{\alpha}\gamma o\rho\dot{\alpha}\zeta o\nu\tau\alpha\varsigma$) indicating that the ones who were carrying on this commerce in the temple were looked upon as being in one class. The Lord's action is justified by His words, "You are making it a robbers' den." That is, the temple had become a garrison for a group of

48. S. Lewis Johnson, Jr., "The Argument of Matthew," *Bibliotheca Sacra,* 112 (April 1955): 151.
49. Ibid.
50. Robert Anderson, *The Coming Prince,* pp. 127-28.

bandits.[51] This fits the use the Messiah makes of Jeremiah 7:11. Jeremiah 7:10 says that the Jews, after committing all sorts of sins, would plead deliverance from the consequences of those sins simply because they came to the temple.

> *"Will you steal, murder, and commit adultery ... then come and stand before Me in this house, which is called by My name, and say 'We are delivered!' –that you may do all these abominations? Has this house, which is called by My name, become a den of robbers in your sight?"*

The Jews of the Lord's day were doing just exactly this. "No matter what they do even by violating the sanctity of their Temple, they imagine that their adherence to this Temple will protect and shield them from any penalty."[52]

Several factors stand out in this section. It is significant that He comes suddenly to the temple to cleanse it. While this event is not a fulfillment of Malachi 3:1, it certainly is a preview of its ultimate fulfillment. For this reason Matthew emphasizes the temple throughout this passage (21:12, 13, 14, 15). As a result of this cleansing and the one recorded in John 2, it was possible for the first time in centuries for the temple to be used as it was intended. This is indeed a preview of the future. It is also important to note that here the King comes in judgment. This again is in accordance with Malachi 3:3-5. The King is to purify the sons of Levi and come in judgment in the day He establishes His kingdom.

A third significant factor is the emphasis on the King's person. M'Neile comments, "The narrative does not suggest that the buyers and sellers submitted to expulsion because Jesus was supported by a crowd of followers. It was the power of character that did the deed."[53] A fourth point worth noting is the omission which the Lord makes in His quotation of Isaiah 56:7. He omits "for all the peoples." This is due to the fact that the King is viewing His ministry as yet limited to Israel. Finally, the deplorable condition of Israel is evident from this passage. The temple had degenerated to the place where it was a hideout for professional bandits; still Israel honored it as a holy sanctuary.

b. The Healing Ministry in the Temple, **21:14-21:17.** *And the blind and the lame came to Him in the temple, and He healed them. But*

---

51. Carr, *St. Matthew*, p. 244.
52. Lenski, *Interpretation of Matthew*, p. 816.
53. M'Neile, *St. Matthew*, p. 299.

*when the chief priests and the scribes saw the wonderful things that
He had done, and the children who were crying out in the temple
and saying, "Hosanna to the Son of David," they became indignant,
and said to Him, "Do You hear what these are saying?" And Jesus
said to them, "Yes; have you never read, 'out of the mouth of
infants and nursing babes Thou has prepared praise for Thyself'?"
And He left them and went out of the city to Bethany, and lodged
there.* After this incident the Messiah heals the blind and the lame in the
temple. As He does the children cry out, "Hosanna to the Son of
David!" At this the high priests and the scribes are moved with indignation. It was not just the cries of the children that provoked them, but the
works which Christ did as well. The miracles are called "wonderful
things" (θαυμάσια) here because that is the way they appeared to the
Sanhedrists.[54] The Lord turns then to rebuke these religious leaders for
their ignorance of spiritual things.

Again several factors contribute to Matthew's argument in this section. One of the main ones is the claim which Christ makes. When
asked if He hears the shouts of the children acclaiming that He is the
Son of David, He answers, "Yes." All of the shouts of the triumphal
entry and the cries of the children are accepted by Him. Thereby the
Lord lays claim to being the Messiah. The use that Jesus makes of
Psalm 8 (verse sixteen) is also significant. This Psalm is a prophecy of
praise which men will offer to God for the conditions that exist during
the millennium. Therefore the praise of the children at this point is a
foreview of the adoration which will be Christ's in the future.

These few verses also indicate the blind and savage hostility that
existed toward Jesus on the part of many. Healing in the temple and
being praised by children infuriated the hierarchy. Finally, this passage
shows that Christ is about to reject Israel. Verse seventeen says that He
forsook them and went outside of the city. Emphasis is placed on His
leaving by the use Matthew makes of the verbs "to leave and to go
forth," and the preposition "out" (καταλείπω, ἐξέρχομαι, and ἔξω).

---

54. Lenski, *Interpretation of Matthew*, p. 817.

C. The Rejection of the King by the Nation
21:18-22:46

1. The Fig Tree, 21:18-21:22.

21:18-21:19. *Now in the morning, when He returned to the city, He became hungry. And seeing a lone fig tree by the road, He came to it, and found nothing on it except leaves only; and He said to it, "No longer shall there ever be any fruit from you." And at once the fig tree withered.* Matthew skillfully introduces the record of Israel's rejection of Jesus with the account of the withering of the fig tree. As Christ returns to Jerusalem the next day He becomes hungry. Expecting to find figs on a fig tree, He finds none and curses the tree. Presently the tree withers.

It is generally accepted that the tree represents Israel.

> The cursing of the fig tree has always been regarded as of symbolic import, the tree being in Christ's mind an emblem of the Jewish people, with a great show of religion and no fruit of real godliness. This hypothesis is very credible.[55]

For Israel to be represented by a vine or a vineyard is common enough (cf. Luke 13:6-9; Hosea 9:10, 16; Micah 7:1). "Just as the 'cleansing' of the Temple was a symbolic denunciation by the Messiah ... so the withering of the fig tree was a symbolic denunciation by Him of the Jewish nation ..."[56] If the tree is taken to represent Israel, then the cursing of the tree represents the judgment of that nation for its false profession. "As a symbol of moral and religious character, the tree was a deceiver and a hypocrite; and for this the Lord pronounces a symbolical judgment upon it."[57] It is significant that of all the miracles which Christ is recorded to have performed, this is the only miracle of judgment.[58] The reason it occurs here is to mark the future of that generation of Jews who failed to accept their Messiah. Christ is not condemning Israel forever, but he is judging that generation forever. It would never see the kingdom.

21:20-21:22. *And seeing this, the disciples marveled, saying, "How did the fig tree wither at once?" And Jesus answered and said*

---

55. Alexander Balmain Bruce, "The Synoptic Gospels," *The Expositor's Greek Testament,* 1:264.

56. R.V.G. Tasker, *The Gospel According to St. Matthew,* p. 201.

57. Plummer, *Exegetical Commentary,* p. 291.

58. Morgan, *Gospel According to Matthew,* p. 253.

*to them, "Truly I say to you, if you have faith, and do not doubt,
you shall not only do what was done to the fig tree, but even if you
say to this mountain, 'Be taken up and cast into the sea,' it shall
happen. And everything you ask in prayer, believing, you shall
receive."* When the disciples ask Him how He accomplished this, the
Lord uses the opportunity to instruct them concerning faith. They were
taught this lesson before (Matthew 17:20), but they failed to comprehend it. The fact that Matthew lays such stress on faith at this point
indicates why Israel failed to recognize Jesus as the Messiah. If they
would have had faith in God, they would have trusted in Jesus as the
Messiah (John 8:42). Since they lacked faith, they did not perceive
Him; therefore the power of God to establish the kingdom was not
theirs.

2. The Conflict with the Chief Priests and the Elders, 21:23-22:14.

a. The Question of Authority, 21:23-21:27. With the connective (καί)
and a genitive absolute grammatical construction, Matthew goes on to
describe the conflict which arises between the King and the leaders of
Israel. In one day there are conflicts with the chief priests and elders
(21:23-22:14), the Pharisees and the Herodians (22:15-22), the Sadducees (22:23-33), and the Pharisees and Sadducees (22:34-46).

21:23-21:27. *And when He had come into the temple, the chief
priests and the elders of the people came to Him as He was teaching,
and said, "By what authority are You doing these things, and who
gave You this authority?" But Jesus answered and said to them, "I
will ask you one thing too, which if you tell Me, I will also tell you by
what authority I do these things. The baptism of John was from
what source, from heaven or from men?" And they began reasoning among themselves, saying, "If we say, 'From heaven,' He will
say to us, 'Then why did you not believe him?' But if we say, 'From
men,' we fear the multitude; for they all hold John to be a prophet." And they answered Jesus and said, "We do not know." He
also said to them, "Neither will I tell you by what authority I do
these things."* When the King comes into the temple to resume His
ministry, the chief priests and elders question Him concerning His authority. "The ἐξουσία [authority] is both the right and the power that
goes with this right."[59] They phrase two questions but they really ask
the same thing. Bruce writes, ". . . the second question is but an echo of
the first: the quality of the authority (ποίᾳ) depends on its source."[60]

59. Lenski, *Interpretation of Matthew,* p. 826.
60. Bruce, "The Synoptic Gospels," *The Expositor's Greek Testament,* 1:265.

Christ answers their question with one of His own. He was not dodging the issue; to answer one question with another was very common.[61] Unable to face the consequences of a definite answer the religious leaders say, "We don't know," and leave.

It is significant to note that in this brief encounter the religious leaders come to Jesus for the purpose of judging Him. This is nowhere stated but it is a clear inference. If they did not assume the position of judges, why should they ask the Lord a question concerning the source of His authority?

This little episode also explains why the religious hierarchy failed to recognize Jesus as the Messiah. God had revealed Himself through the "preaching" (κήρυγμα) and work of John, but they *refused* to believe (verse twenty-five). Because of this God could not reveal Christ to them (Matthew 11:25).

A third important factor indicated in this brief event is the judgment of these leaders. They were judged by Christ. In His refusal to answer much the same question the disciples had just asked Him, the Lord indicates His rejection of them. This fact is borne out by the following parables. Not only does the King judge them, but they judge themselves. They admitted that they refused to believe John (verse twenty-five). By showing their fear of the people they indicated they would not stand for their convictions. And finally by saying, "We don't know," they attested their inability to be the spiritual leaders of the people.[62] They lacked spiritual discernment.

The Messianic significance of John is also shown in this passage. Verse twenty-five clearly intimates that John pointed to Jesus as the Messiah. John did the work of Elijah, but he could not be Elijah since Israel refused Jesus as its Messiah.

It is interesting to note how Matthew uses this event as an introduction to the three following parables. This of course is in line with Matthew's style of using events to introduce doctrine. The understanding of these parables is impossible unless they are read in the light of the context of Matthew 21:23-27. The first parable, the parable of the two sons, portrays the conduct of the religious leaders (21:28-21:32); the second illustrates the results of their actions (21:33-21:46); and the third reveals their judgment (22:1-22:14).

---

61. Plummer, *Exegetical Commentary*, p. 293.
62. Carr, *St. Matthew*, p. 246.

b. The Parable of the Two Sons, **21:28-21:32.** *"But what do you think? A man had two sons, and he came to the first and said, 'Son, go work today in the vineyard.' And he answered and said, 'I will, sir;' and he did not go. And he came to the second and said the same thing. But he answered and said, 'I will not;' yet he afterward regretted it and went. Which of the two did the will of his father?" They said, "The latter." Jesus said to them, "Truly I say to you that the tax-gatherers and harlots will get into the kingdom of God before you. For John came to you in the way of righteousness and you did not believe him; but the tax-gatherers and harlots did believe him; and you, seeing this, did not even feel remorse afterward so as to believe him."* In the parable of the two sons, the King judges the elders and chief priests. But even as He does this the Lord manifests His great love by calling the two sons "children" (τέκνα). The great object of the parable is to point out the hypocrisy of Israel's religious leaders. This is accomplished in several ways. The disobedient son, when asked to work in the vineyard, answers with an emphatic "I (will)" (ἐγώ), a vivid portrayal of the self-confidence of these religious leaders. In verse thirty-one the emphasis is on *doing* and not on *saying*. The elders and chief priests were guilty of saying without doing. Their sanctimony is further affirmed by their unbelief in John's message. Although the Baptist came in the way of righteousness, they refused him. Therefore they are shown to be hypocrites. Furthermore, they were not moved to faith by the sight of those who produced righteous lives as a result of faith in John's message. The Baptist's proclamation together with the testimony of those who believed should have caused them to exercise faith also.

The verb which is used in verse thirty-one, "to get in before" (προάγουσιν), is significant. Those who were the most despised in the land were entering the kingdom, while the elders and chief priests were not. Thus Christ judged the religious hierarchy. However, the present tense and the prefix "before" (πρό) indicate that it was still possible for the leaders to enter the kingdom. Therefore, by pointing out their sin, the King was acting in grace. If they would acknowledge their need and believe in Christ, they would enter.

It is well to note also that, while the kingdom is no longer proclaimed as having drawn near, entrance is still being accomplished. The inference is that participation in the kingdom will come about at a much later time, possibly after those who were then entering had died; therefore, the kingdom must be postponed.

c. The Parable of the Wicked Husbandmen, 21:33-21:46. The King then asks them to hear another parable, that of the wicked husbandmen.

21:33. *"Listen to another parable. There was a landowner who planted a vineyard and put a wall around it and dug a wine press in it, and built a tower, and rented it out to vine-growers, and went on a journey."* In describing the vineyard and the householder's provision for it, the Lord uses the language of Isaiah 5:2. However, Christ employs the figure of the vineyard in a different sense than Isaiah. In Isaiah 5 it is a representation of Israel; in Matthew 21 it is a picture of the kingdom (cf. Isaiah 5:7; Matthew 21:43). The detailed description of the vineyard is given to indicate the owner of this vineyard has provided for its well-being with the utmost care.[63]

21:34-21:46. *"And when the harvest time approached, he sent his slaves to the vine-growers to receive his produce. And the vine-growers took his slaves and beat one, and killed another, and stoned a third. Again he sent another group of slaves larger than the first; and they did the same thing to them. But afterward he sent his son to them, saying, 'They will respect my son.' But when the vine-growers saw the son, they said among themselves, 'This is the heir; come, let us kill him, and seize his inheritance.' And they took him, and cast him out of the vineyard, and killed him. Therefore when the owner of the vineyard comes, what will he do to those vine-growers?"* They said to Him, *"He will bring those wretches to a wretched end, and will rent out the vineyard to other vine-growers, who will pay him the proceeds at the proper seasons."* Jesus said to them, *"Did you never read in the Scriptures,*
'The stone which the builders rejected,
This became the chief corner stone;
This came about from the Lord,
And it is marvelous in our eyes'?

Therefore I say to you, the kingdom of God will be taken away from you, and be given to a nation producing the fruit of it. And he who falls on this stone will be broken to pieces; but on whomever it falls, it will scatter him like dust." And when the chief priests and the Pharisees heard His parables, they understood that He was speaking about them. And when they sought to seize Him, they became afraid of the multitudes, because they held Him to be a prophet.* In verse forty-two the figure is changed from a vineyard to a stone, but the

---

63. M'Neile, *St. Matthew,* p. 308.

same thought is carried on. The wicked husbandmen kill the heir, and
the parable stops there. In the parable of the stone the heir who is killed
is represented by the rejected stone. In this manner the parable of the
stone takes the rejected One, who is Christ, from death to glory (verse
forty-two) and judgment (verse forty-four). This latter parable is contained in Psalm 118:22, a portion of Scripture so familiar that the Lord
says, "Did you never (οὐδέποτε) read in the Scriptures ...?" In Psalm
118 as well as in Matthew 21:42 the stone is a figure of Christ.[64] He was
rejected and now is at the right hand of the Father waiting to take His
pre-eminent place on earth. The verb "to reject" (ἀποδοκιμάζω) in
verse forty-two is very appropriate since it means "... to reject *after
trial* ..."[65]

Because Israel rejected its Messiah the King says, "The kingdom of
God shall be taken from you and shall be given to a nation bringing forth
its fruits" (verse forty- three). This verse looks back to the parable of the
wicked husbandmen and especially verse forty-one. Thus the parable
becomes fairly evident. The owner of the vineyard is God. The husbandmen represent Israel. The servants are God's messengers sent to
Israel and so shamefully treated by that nation (1 Kings 18:4; 19:10;
22:24; 2 Chronicles 24:20-21; Nehemiah 9:26; Jeremiah 2:30; 20:1-2;
26:20-23; 37:15; 38:6). A problem exists as to the identity of the vineyard. Some say it is Israel on the basis of Isaiah 5:7 and other Old
Testament passages such as Jeremiah 2:21 and Psalm 80:8.[66] However,
there are some rather serious difficulties with this view. It would be very
difficult to explain how Israel could be taken from its leaders and given
to another nation in the light of Matthew 21:43. The Lord identifies the
vineyard with the kingdom of God. As was stated before, the term
kingdom of God in Matthew always refers to the future millennial kingdom on earth.[67] Therefore Christ is saying that the privilege for entrance
into the kingdom would be taken from Israel and given to another
nation. But this raises another problem: who is the "nation" (ἔθνει)?

Gaebelein believes the nation refers to the Jewish remnant. He writes,
"The nation is Israel still, but that believing remnant of the nation,
living when the Lord comes."[68] But the difficulty with this explanation

64. Siegfried Goebel, *The Parables of Jesus*, pp. 335-36.
65. M'Neile, *St. Matthew*, p. 311.
66. Lenski, *Interpretation of Matthew*, pp. 835-837; Gaebelein, *The Gospel of Matthew*, 2:136.
67. See above., pp. 67-68.
68. Gaebelein, *The Gospel of Matthew*, 2:138.

250

is seen in that "nation" (ἔθνος) is used and not "generation" (γενεά) or "offspring" (γέννημα). Gaebelein also states, "The Church is called the Body of Christ, the Bride of Christ, the Habitation of God by the Spirit, the Lamb's Wife, but never a nation."[69] This statement can be very seriously disputed. 1 Peter 2:9 and Romans 10:19 definitely refer to the church as a nation.

Kiddle holds that the disciples are the ones to whom the kingdom is given. He writes, "... He meant that it should be given to the disciples, not to the Gentiles, though the Gentiles were to have a share in it."[70] But how could the disciples be called a nation? This interpretation has no support whatsoever from the rest of the New Testament.

Bruce states that ἔθνος is a clear reference to the heathen world.[71] But the noun is singular here, which is not the equivalent of τὰ ἔθνη, the Gentiles.[72] In addition, it cannot be said that the Gentiles as a group are bringing forth the fruit of the kingdom.

A fourth view states that the nation is the church. This position is the most tenable for several reasons. The church is said to enter into the blessings of the kingdom (Galatians 3:7-9, 29; Romans 11:20-24). McClain sees a genuine relationship between the kingdom and the church today, a relationship which qualifies the church for these kingdom blessings.

> In another sense, however, it might be said that the Mediatorial Kingdom does have a present *de jure* existence, even prior to its establishment. This is true, first, in the sense that God is today saving and preparing in the *ekklesia* [church] the members of the royal family who are destined to rule with Christ in the future established kingdom; and, second, in the sense that, as those born into the royal family, we enter *judicially* into the kingdom before its establishment, a divine action so remarkable that Paul speaks of it as a translation (Col. 1:13).[73]

Not only does the church inherit the kingdom with Israel, but the church is also called a nation (1 Peter 2:9-10; Romans 10:19). The logical conclusion is, therefore, that the church is the nation to whom the kingdom is given in Matthew 21:43.

---

69. Ibid.
70. M. Kiddle, "The Conflict Between the Disciples, the Jews, and the Gentiles in St. Matthew's Gospel," *The Journal of Theological Studies* 36 (January 1935): 34.
71. Bruce, "The Synoptic Gospels," *The Expositor's Greek Testament,* 1:268.
72. Lenski, *Interpretation of Matthew,* p. 844.
73. Alva J. McClain, *The Greatness of the Kingdom,* p. 439.

It must not be concluded from this that the kingdom is removed forever from Israel. This is impossible due to the promises given to Abraham and David. The promises are addressed to Israel as a nation. That Israel is yet to be restored to the place of blessing is asserted by Paul in Romans 11:26-27.

Again there are several notable factors relative to the argument in this passage which need to be observed. First, the leaders are as intent as ever to take Christ (Matthew 21:46). In addition the people are still blind to the person of Jesus; they hold Him to be a mere prophet (Matthew 21:46). A third significant observation pertains to the claims of Jesus. He maintains that He is the Messiah in the parables. As the Son and Heir of the vineyard He is different from the servants who represent the prophets. The stone which the builders rejected becomes the Head of the corner. The One who made these claims must be the Christ. In addition, the Lord foretold His death. In the parables the heir is killed and the stone is rejected, implying clearly that Christ would be put to death by the leaders of the land. A fifth fact is one which relates to this church age. For the first time the King speaks openly and clearly to someone outside of the circle of the disciples about a new age. This is full proof that the kingdom was no longer near at hand.

This passage also makes a sixth revelation. The stone would become the head of the corner, and if it should fall on anyone, it would winnow him. Thus the implication is clearly made that Christ's death would not end His work with Israel. He would be resurrected to a prominent place. Finally, this passage teaches that Christ will yet come in judgment. Verse forty-four teaches that the one trusting in Christ would be despised by Israel and the world. But the one who would be condemned by Christ at His second coming will be ground to powder (cf. Daniel 2:35, 44-45).

d. The Parable of the Royal Feast, 22:1-22:14. The third of a trilogy of parables spoken with the religious leaders in view is now recorded. All these are a result of the encounter of Matthew 21:23-27. Unlike the other two, this parable is introduced by a verb which likens the kingdom of heaven to certain facts related in the parable of the royal banquet. To make this comparison Matthew uses the aorist passive of the verb "to be compared" (ὡμοιώθη).

22:1-22:14. *And Jesus answered and spoke to them again in parables, saying, "The kingdom of heaven may be compared to a king, who gave a wedding feast for his son. And he sent out his slaves to*

*call those who had been invited to the wedding feast, and they were
unwilling to come. Again he sent out other slaves saying, 'Tell those
who have been invited, "Behold, I have prepared my dinner; my
oxen and my fattened livestock are all butchered and everything is
ready; come to the wedding feast."' But they paid no attention and
went their way, one to his own farm, another to his business, and
the rest seized his slaves and mistreated them and killed them. But
the king was enraged and sent his armies, and destroyed those
murderers, and set their city on fire. Then he said to his slaves,
'The wedding is ready, but those who were invited were not worthy.
Go therefore to the main highways, and as many as you find there,
invite to the wedding feast.' And those slaves went out into the
streets, and gathered together all they found, both evil and good;
and the wedding hall was filled with dinner guests. But when the
king came in to look over the dinner guests, he saw there a man not
dressed in wedding clothes, and he said to him, 'Friend, how did
you come in here without wedding clothes?' And he was speechless.
Then the king said to the servants, 'Bind him hand and foot, and
cast him into the outer darkness; in that place there shall be weeping and gnashing of teeth.' For many are called, but few are cho-
sen."* Before the interpretation of the parable is presented several features will be discussed. It will be noted that invitations had been sent out
at a considerable time before the feast. Very near to the actual time of
the feast servants are sent out to call those who had previously been
invited (verse three). This is in accord with an Eastern custom.[74] When
the third invitation is tendered (verse four), the nearness of the banquet
is emphasized by the statement, "I have prepared my dinner" (τὸ ἄρισ-
τόν μου ἡτοίμακα). This meal was not the banquet supper, but the
early meal.[75] The early meal had already been prepared; therefore the
banquet was very near. In fact, the oxen and fatlings had already been
killed and everything was in readiness. When the king's servants were
shamefully mistreated, he sent them out to gather in everyone who
would come both good and bad (verse ten). The evil men were killed
and their city burned. At the feast the son of the king reviews the guests
and finds one improperly attired. Confronted by the king's son, the
guest is dumbfounded because of his deliberate offense (verses eleven
and twelve). The use Matthew makes of the words for "not" and "with-

---

74. Goebel, *The Parables of Jesus*, p. 351.
75. Edersheim, *Life and Times*, 2:427.

out" (οὐ and μή) in verses eleven and twelve emphasizes the willful sin of this fellow.

> This distinction between the two negative particles rests on the law of the Greek language, according to which οὐ and its compounds stand where something is to be denied as a *matter of fact,* and μή and its compounds when something is to be denied as a matter of *thought.*[76]

The interpretation of this parable is very important to Matthew's argument. In the parable the king is a representation of God the Father, and the son is God's Son, Jesus Christ. "Those who had been invited" (κεκλημένοι) are the Jews. The four invitations represent the various invitations of God to enter the kingdom. The first invitation, which is not recorded, evidently refers to all of the Old Testament preparation for the coming of the kingdom. The second invitation is an allusion to the work of the Baptist and Jesus. The ministry of the apostles to Israel before and after the death of Christ is pictured in the third invitation. The last is a call to Gentiles to participate and looks at the present age. The destruction of Jerusalem is anticipated in the burning of the city.

A problem exists as to the translation of γάμος. Most commentators take it to refer to a wedding feast. On the basis of this it would be possible for it to refer to the marriage supper of the church and Christ. However, there is a difficulty with this view. According to this position, the wedding was ready and the invitations were sent out before the church existed. But γάμος can also refer to any large banquet.[77] It is used in Esther 9:22 to designate the feast by which the Jews celebrated their deliverance from Haman's plot. Cremer notes that it is not used with this meaning in profane Greek, but he does acknowledge that it is used in this sense in the Scriptures.[78]

It seems best to take γάμος to mean simply a festive banquet here. There is no mention of a marriage or a bride. Rather, the great emphasis is placed on the royalty of the persons giving the banquet. Since Jesus (Matthew 8:11) as well as the Jews pictured the kingdom in terms of a banquet, it seems best to conclude that the King is here referring to participation in the kingdom. The man who attempts to participate in the kingdom but is evicted is used to demonstrate the judgment preceding the kingdom. The Messiah refers to *one* man to point out to the Jew the

---

76. Vincent, *Word Studies,* 1:121.

77. Alexander Balmain Bruce, *The Parabolic Teaching of Christ,* p. 465.

78. Hermann Cremer, *Biblico-Theological Lexicon of New Testament Greek,* p. 666.

fact that the judgment was to be on the basis of individual standing and not mere nationality. The judgment is executed by the King's servants. The agents of the King are designated in three ways. His messengers are called "slaves" (δοῦλοι), his soldiers are designated as armies" (στρατεύματα), and his servants as "servants" (διάκονοι). This latter group is evidently a reference to the angels (Matthew 13:41-42).

This parable very dramatically emphasizes the fact that the kingdom had drawn near. The feast was already made by the king for his son (Matthew 22:2). The guests had only to come to enjoy it. The obstinacy of the Jews is also portrayed in this parable. The verb "to will" (θέλω) emphasizes the deliberate choice of those who refused to come (verse three). The Jews were more interested in their own things than the things of God. Others were so belligerent that they mistreated the servants of the King. In addition, this parable intimates that another offer of the kingdom was to be given to Israel after the death and resurrection of Jesus Christ. If John and Jesus are represented as being sent out first to remind the called of their invitation, then the subsequent invitation must take place after the cross. Such an offer is recorded in Acts 3:12-26.

Another great truth pictured in this parable is the grace of God. This is shown by the repeated callings extended by the servants to the feast. There may also be a picture of the Son of God becoming a servant (Philippians 2:7), although this is not stated. A very important fact revealed in the parable is the fact that the offer of the kingdom was a genuine one. The kingdom in all of its reality was as prepared and near as was the feast of the parable.

The parable also teaches the reader of this Gospel that the kingdom was postponed.

> The calling of other guests now (still going on) takes the place of the first invitation—a new exigency and preparation being evolved—and the supper, until these guests are obtained ... *is postponed* to the Second Advent. ...[79]

This is substantiated by the events of the parable as recorded in verses seven, eight, and nine. The parable further affirms that which Christ stated in Matthew 8:11 and 21:43. The privilege of entrance into the kingdom was to be extended to others than the Jews. Another doctrine taught by this parable is the truth that a judgment shall precede the

---

79. George N. H. Peters, *The Theocratic Kingdom of Our Lord Jesus, the Christ, as Covenanted in the Old Testament, and Presented in the New Testament*, 1:379.

establishment of the kingdom. This of course is taught by the expulsion of the improperly attired intruder. The alternative to entrance into the kingdom is weeping and gnashing of teeth, a term used to refer to the punishment of those who fail to enter the kingdom (Matthew 8:12; 13:42, 50; 24:51; 25:30; Luke 13:28).

Another very significant fact is seen in this parable: God provides the means of entrance into the kingdom for those who desire it. The participle "dressed" (ἐνδεδυμένον) in verse eleven is passive. It may be inferred, therefore, that the king provided the guests with the proper garments. Although it is disputed whether this was an Oriental custom or not, it seems evident from certain Old Testament passages that it was common enough (Genesis 45:22; Judges 14:12, 19; 2 Kings 5:22; 10:22; Esther 6:8; 8:15).[80] It pictures perfectly the fact that God attires everyone who turns to Him with the proper garments for His presence and His kingdom.

Finally, the parable teaches that a general call does not constitute or guarantee election (verse fourteen). The Israelites took great pride in the fact that they as a nation possessed the kingdom promises. But this of itself did not mean each Jew was elected to it. Entrance was an individual responsibility, and that is what Christ is emphasizing in the last portion of the parable.

3. The Conflict With the Pharisees and the Herodians, 22:15-22:22.

22:15-22:22. *Then the Pharisees went and counseled together how they might trap Him in what He said. And they sent their disciples to Him, along with the Herodians, saying, "Teacher, we know that You are truthful and teach the way of God in truth, and defer to no one; for You are not partial to any. Tell us therefore, what do You think? Is it lawful to give a poll-tax to Caesar, or not?" But Jesus perceived their malice, and said, "Why are you testing Me, you hypocrites? Show Me the coin used for the poll-tax." And they brought Him a denarius. And he said to them, "Whose likeness and inscription is this?" They said to Him, "Caesar's." Then He said to them, "Then render to Caesar the things that are Caesar's; and to God the things that are God's." And hearing this, they marveled, and leaving Him, they went away.* The Pharisees in league with the Herodians attempt to snare Jesus in His words with a question concerning the capitation tax. The King answers that, if they were enjoying the benefits of a certain government, they should render that government its due as well as giving God that which belongs to Him. There is a great difference between the verbs "to give" (δοῦναι, 22:117) and "to render" (ἀπόδοτε, 22:21). "The questioners had said δοῦναι (v. 17), as though of a gift which might be withheld; the Lord replies with ἀπό δοτε, the payment of a rightful due."[81]

This incident reveals the terrible enmity of the leaders of Israel for Jesus. Traditionally the Pharisees and Herodians were bitterly opposed to one another. But their hatred for Christ is greater than their dislike of one another. This episode also provided a means for the King to instruct His disciples in preparation for His absence. Although they were heirs of the kingdom, they were to maintain allegiance to their earthly rulers.

4. The Conflict With the Sadducees, 22:23-22:33.

22:23-22:33. *On that day some Sadducees (who say there is no resurrection) came to Him and questioned Him, saying, "Teacher, Moses said, 'If a man dies, having no children, his brother as next of kin shall marry his wife, and raise up an offspring to his brother.' Now there were seven brothers with us; and the first married and died, and having no offspring left his wife to his brother; so also the second, and the third, down to the seventh. And last of all, the woman died. In the resurrection therefore whose wife of the seven shall she be? For they all had her." But Jesus answered and said to them, "You are mistaken, not understanding the Scriptures, or the power of God. For in the resurrection they neither marry, nor are given in marriage, but are like angels in heaven. But regarding the resurrection of the dead, have you not read that which was spoken to you by God, saying, 'I am the God of Abraham, and the God of Isaac, and the God of Jacob'? God is not the God of the dead but of the living." And when the multitudes heard this, they were astonished at His teaching.*

The Evangelist now narrates a conflict which the King has with the Sadducees. Matthew uses the pronoun "that" (ἐκεῖνος) with a time designation to note a change of groups. The Sadducees, who believed in neither the resurrection nor spirits and angels (Acts 23:8), approach Christ with a theological riddle. "It was probably an old conundrum

81. M'Neile, *St. Matthew*, pp. 319-320.

that they had used to the discomfiture of the Pharisees."[82]

This incident reveals several facts relative to Matthew's argument. It shows the intensity of the opposition to Christ's ministry. This is the third group to accost the King with malicious intent on the same day. The guilt of this group of Israel's leaders is also revealed. They were ignorant of the Scriptures and God's power. For Christ to prove the existence of spirits after death pulverized one of the main doctrines of the Sadducees (Acts 23:8). The implication of this fact is this: if God is able to makes one's spirit exist after death, then He is certainly capable of a resurrection. But the fact that God could translate bodies into another existence was unknown to them. The resurrection is the means by which many would enter the kingdom; therefore Christ defends it. In addition Christ's use of Exodus 3:6 (verse thirty-two) indicates that the patriarchs would also participate in the kingdom. "The promises made to the fathers remained sure, and the fathers were living to enjoy these promises hereafter."[83] This is a positive proof of a future resurrection. For the patriarchs to participate in the promises, they had to be resurrected.

5. The Conflict With the Pharisees, 22:34-22:46.

22:34. *But when the Pharisees heard that He had put the Sadducees to silence, they gathered themselves together.* The remainder of Matthew 22 is concerned with the antagonism of the Pharisees to the words and works of the King. Gleefully they gather about Christ after He so effectively muzzled the Sadducees. But even though the Lord has silenced their foes, the Pharisees still oppose Him. The very words translated "together" (ἐπὶ τὸ αὐτό) in verse thirty-four manifest this opposition.

> The expression was possibly suggested by Ps. ii.2 ...; cf. Ac. iv. 26f., where the words from the Ps. are followed by συνήχθησαν ["they were gathered together"] ... ἐπὶ τὸν ἅγιον παῖδά σου Ἰησοῦν ["against Thy holy servant Jesus"].[84]

22:35-22:36. *And one of them, a lawyer, asked Him a question, testing Him, "Teacher, which is the great commandment in the*

82. Robertson, *Word Pictures*, 1:176.
83. J. N. Darby, *Synopsis*, 3:116.
84. M'Neile, *St. Matthew*, p. 324.

Law?" Although the Pharisees were generally very antagonistic to Christ, one lawyer evidently impressed by the way Jesus answered His previous questioners, tested the Lord with a question. It does not seem that this question was asked with a malicious intent, but for the purpose of finding more about Jesus Christ. The question concerned the commandments of the law, a pertinent problem.

> The scribes declared that there were 248 affirmative precepts, as many as the members of the human body; and 365 negative precepts, as many as the days in the year; the total being 613, the number of letters in the Decalogue. Of these they called some *light* and some *heavy.* [85]

Therefore the lawyer desired to know what kind of a commandment is great in the law. "The man is not asking which is the one supreme commandment, but what *class* of commandments is in the first rank." [86]

22:37-22:40. *And He said to him, "'You shall love the Lord your God with all your heart, and with all your soul, and with all your mind.' This is the great and foremost commandment. And a second is like it, 'You shall love your neighbor as yourself.' On these two commandments depend the whole Law and the Prophets."* The King precisely and accurately answers. Mark includes the clause ". . . is much more than all burnt offerings and sacrifices" (Mark 12:33). Matthew omits this since it might offend his Jewish reader, and the point is well made without it. This incident is valuable for pointing out the spiritual blindness of the Pharisees. They had missed the essence of Old Testament doctrine in their concern over phylacteries, the fringes of their garments, and ceremonial cleanness. It also was an excellent means for the King to teach His disciples what should be their hallmark. This doctrine of love even comprehends that which the Lord had taught in verse twenty-one.

22:41-22:46. *Now while the Pharisees were gathered together, Jesus asked them a question, saying, "What do you think about the Christ, whose son is He?" They said to Him, "The son of David." He said to them, "Then how does David in the Spirit call Him 'Lord,' saying,*

> *'The Lord said to my Lord,*
> *"Sit at My right hand,*
> *Until I put Thine enemies beneath Thy feet."'*

85. Vincent, *Word Studies,* 1:122.
86. Plummer, *Exegetical Commentary,* p. 308.

If David then calls Him 'Lord,' how is He his son?" And no one was able to answer Him a word, nor did anyone dare from that day on to ask Him another question. The Messiah then asks a question of the Pharisees. He asks them to reconcile the fact that, although the Messiah is David's Son, David under the inspiration of the Holy Spirit calls Him "Lord" (Psalm 110:1). The Pharisees were unable to answer the problem because of their obstinancy; the answer stood before them.

Jesus makes some startling revelations concerning Himself in these few statements. The humanity of the Christ is affirmed by the common knowledge among the Jews of the fact that He was called the Son of David. The deity of the Messiah is set forth here, too. In Psalm 110:1 "... one divine person speaks to the other."[87] It further expresses the pre-existence of the Messiah. He lived in David's time, *before* the Christ came to earth. This Psalm, used so often in the New Testament, also indicates that David by inspiration of the Holy Spirit spoke of a kingdom. God was to make the enemies of the Messiah the footstool of the Christ. The context of this Psalm is Messianic and looks forward to the establishment of the kingdom. The temporal conjunction "until" ($\xi\omega\varsigma$) anticipates the time when this will be accomplished. No wonder the Pharisees were put to silence. For Christ to assert His deity was only the outworking of His person, and they could not deny the theological premise of His assertions.

D. The Rejection of the Nation by the King
23:1-23:39.

1. The Admonition of the Multitudes and the Disciples, 23:1-23:12.

Now that the rejection of the King on the part of Israel and its leaders is clearly evident, the King declares His rejection of that nation.

23:1. *Then Jesus spoke to the multitudes and to His disciples,* Matthew uses his characteristic introductory adverb "then" ($\tau\acute{o}\tau\epsilon$) to present this aspect of his argument (Matthew 23:1-39). Before the King denounces the scribes and Pharisees, He instructs those about Him with regard to the position and practice of these religious leaders. Evidently there were three groups of people massed about Christ as He was in the temple at this time—the disciples, the multitudes, and the scribes and Pharisees. The first twelve verses are addressed to the multitudes and

87. Lenski, *Interpretation of Matthew,* p. 888.

the disciples while the scribes and Pharisees also listened. In this instruction several factors stand out.

23:2. *saying, "The scribes and the Pharisees have seated themselves in the chair of Moses;* . . . The law is still looked upon as being authoritative and in force (Matthew 23:2, 23).[88] Only a few aspects of the new church age have yet been made known by Jesus Christ, and the freedom from the law revealed in the age of grace was not among them. Therefore, the Lord speaks from His position of being under the law and indicates that He is still acting as a minister of the circumcision (Romans 15:8).

23:3-23:7. *"therefore all that they tell you, do and observe, but do not do according to their deeds; for they say things, and do not do them. And they tie up heavy loads, and lay them on men's shoulders; but they themselves are unwilling to move them with so much as a finger. But they do all their deeds to be noticed by men; for they broaden their phylacteries, and lengthen the tassels of their garments. And they love the place of honor at banquets, and the chief seats in the synagogues, and respectful greetings in the market places, and being called by men, Rabbi."* A second factor which is underscored in these twelve verses is the sin which gripped the scribes and Pharisees, hypocrisy (Matthew 23:3, 5-7). This is enlarged upon in Christ's indictment of them (Matthew 23:13-33). The error of the doctrine of these religious leaders is also seen. They drove men under the law and failed to lead them by the law to faith in God. In attempting to keep the minutiae of the law they did not realize that they were missing its moral principles (Matthew 23:23; 9:13; 12:7; 15:4-6).

23:8-23:12. *"But do not be called Rabbi; for One is your Teacher, and you are all brothers. And do not call anyone on earth your father; for One is your Father, He who is in heaven. And do not be called leaders; for One is your Leader, that is, Christ. But the greatest among you shall be your servant. And whoever exalts himself shall be humbled; and whoever humbles himself shall be exalted."* A fourth important fact is revealed here. Since the religious leaders of Israel were rejected by the Messiah, the disciples of Jesus were taking their place in the program of God. The emphatic pronoun "you" (ὑμεῖς) in verse eight, the understood subject of the first clause, stresses the fact that the disciples were yet to have the position of leadership. Matthew 13:52 had hinted at much the same fact.

88. Ibid., p. 909.

2. The Indictment of the Scribes and Pharisees, 23:13-23:36.

23:13-23:36. *"But woe to you, scribes and Pharisees, hypocrites, because you shut off the kingdom of heaven from men, for you do not enter in yourselves; nor do you allow those who are entering to go in. (Woe to you, scribes and Pharisees, hypocrites, because you devour widows' houses, even while for a pretense you make long prayers; therefore you shall receive greater condemnation.)*

Woe to you, scribes and Pharisees, hypocrites, because you travel about on sea and land to make one proselyte; and when he becomes one, you make him twice as much a son of hell as yourselves.

Woe to you, blind guides, who say, 'Whoever swears by the temple, that is nothing; but whoever swears by the gold of the temple, he is obligated.' You fools and blind men; which is more important, the gold, or the temple that sanctified the gold? And, 'Whoever swears by the altar, that is nothing, but whoever swears by the offering upon it, he is obligated.' You blind men, which is more important, the offering or the altar that sanctifies the offering? Therefore he who swears, swears both by the altar and by everything on it. And he who swears by the temple, swears both by the temple and by Him who dwells within it. And he who swears by heaven, swears both by the throne of God and by Him who sits upon it.

Woe to you, scribes and Pharisees, hypocrites! For you tithe mint and dill and cummin, and have neglected the weightier provisions of the law: justice and mercy and faithfulness; but these are the things you should have done without neglecting the others. You blind guides, who strain out a gnat and swallow a camel!

Woe to you, scribes and Pharisees, hypocrites! For you clean the outside of the cup and of the dish, but inside they are full of robbery and self-indulgence. You blind Pharisee, first clean the inside of the cup and of the dish, so that the outside of it may become clean also.

Woe to you, scribes and Pharisees, hypocrites! For you are like whitewashed tombs which on the outside appear beautiful, but inside they are full of dead men's bones and all uncleanness. Even so you too outwardly appear righteous to men, but inwardly you are full of hypocrisy and lawlessness.

Woe to you, scribes and Pharisees, hypocrites! For you build the tombs of the prophets and adorn the monuments of the righteous, and say, 'If we had been living in the days of our fathers, we would not have been partners with them in shedding the blood of the prophets.' Consequently you bear witness against yourselves, that you are sons of those who murdered the prophets. Fill up then the measure of the guilt of your fathers. You serpents, you brood of vipers, how shall you escape the sentence of hell? Therefore, behold, I am sending you prophets and wise men and scribes; some of them you will kill and crucify, and some of them you will scourge in your synagogues, and persecute from city to city; that upon you may fall the guilt of all the righteous blood shed on earth, from the blood of righteous Abel to the blood of Zechariah, the son of Berechiah, whom you murdered between the temple and the altar. Truly I say to you, all these things shall come upon this generation."

In this indictment, the word *woe* occurs seven times in connection with the scribes and Pharisees (Matthew 23:13, 15, 16, 23, 25, 27, 29).

> Every one of the seven "woes" is an exclamation like the "blessed" in the Beatitudes. It does not state a wish but a fact. It is not a curse that calls down calamity but a calm, true judgment and verdict rendered by the supreme Judge himself. Hence six of these judgments have the evidence attached by means of a causal ὅτι ["because"] clause which furnishes the full reason for the verdict "woe;" and in the remaining judgment (v. 16) the varied form of expression does the same by means of an apposition.[89]

The first three announcements of woe are given because of the doctrine of the scribes and Pharisees, the last three because of their character. The middle one is transitional dealing with both.[90]

These religious leaders are found to be guilty of the sin of hypocrisy. In this the Lord's doctrine can be compared to what He taught in the Sermon on the Mount. There the King indicated the character of true righteousness; here He emphasizes the nature of hypocrisy. In associating this sin with the scribes and Pharisees, Christ emphasizes their guilt (23:32, 33). He asks, "How shall you escape the sentence of hell?" Plummer writes, "The quotation has no answer; it is implied that they cannot escape this judgment."[91]

It is important, however, to note a second item. The perversity of the religious leaders of Israel does not excuse the people of Israel. They were guilty of willfully following blind guides. In verse thirty-five the Lord is not blaming the scribes and Pharisees of His day for the murder

89. Ibid., p. 903.
90. Plummer, *Exegetical Commentary,* p. 317.
91. Ibid., p. 321.

of God's representatives on earth, but He is stating that the nation as a whole is guilty of what was done in preceding generations.[92] It is clear, therefore, that the nation as well as the leaders were held as being guilty in God's sight.

Perhaps the most outstanding element of these verses is the severity of the words and the emphasis on judgment. The Lord uses such words as hypocrites (seven times), son of hell, blind guides, fools, whitewashed tombs, serpents, and brood of vipers in connection with the scribes and Pharisees. It is evident that Christ is casting them aside as hopeless and giving them up to their own desires. These leaders even bore witness to themselves that they were the descendants of those who had killed the prophets (verses thirty to thirty-one). Christ said, "By so saying, you bear witness to the murder-taint in your blood."[93] This is further proven by the fact that the Messiah was sending (present tense) to Israel prophets, wise men, and scribes. Of these, they would kill and crucify some, others they would scourge in their synagogues, and still others they would persecute from city to city. The King had Himself in mind as well as those who would bear witness to Israel subsequent to His death. From this point the King goes on to pronounce judgment on that generation.

> In the case of the Jews, the limit of misbehavior had been almost reached, and with the murder of the Messiah and His Apostles would be transgressed. The destruction of Jerusalem and the dispersion of the nation was at once the inevitable consequence.[94]

The principle by which this judgment is meted out is explained very well by Lenski.

> Divine justice is not as superficial as ours; it demands more than a reckoning for individual and separate crimes. Each crime, when it is re-enacted, involves a guilt that reaches back to the beginning. The last acts "allow" or sanction all the former that were of the same type, and so the last acts involve guiltiness for all.[95]

The fact that the judgment for all this violence should come upon "this generation" ($\tau\grave{\eta}\nu$ $\gamma\epsilon\nu\epsilon\grave{\alpha}\nu$ $\tau\alpha\acute{\upsilon}\tau\eta\nu$) indicates its imminence.

All hope for a turning of Israel to God in repentance has gone. The King therefore has no alternative but to reject that nation for the time

92. Ibid., p. 323.
93. Allen, *Commentary on Matthew*, p. 249.
94. Plummer, *Exegetical Commentary*, pp. 320-321.
95. Lenski, *Interpretation of Matthew*, pp. 918-919.

being with regard to its kingdom program. The clear announcement of this decision is seen in these verses of Matthew's Gospel.

3. The Lamentation over Jerusalem, 23:37-23:39.

23:37-23:39. *"O Jerusalem, Jerusalem, who kills the prophets and stones those who are sent to her! How often I wanted to gather your children together, the way a hen gathers her chicks under her wings, and you were unwilling. Behold, your house is being left to you desolate. For I say to you, from now on you shall not see Me until you say, 'Blessed is He who comes in the name of the Lord.'"* Having declared His rejection of Israel, the King sadly laments over the capital city of the Jewish nation. In these verses Jerusalem is looked upon as a representative of the nation of Israel in its attitude and actions toward God. The repetition of Jerusalem in this expression of sorrow indicates the Lord's great love for Israel and reminds one of David's cry at the death of Absalom (2 Samuel 18:33; 19:4). Even the word *woe* has the implication of sorrow.[96]

This lamentation also reveals the willfulness of Israel's rejection. By using the verb "to want or will" ($\theta\acute{\epsilon}\lambda\omega$) twice in verse thirty-seven, the Lord shows that Israel was a rebellious nation, constantly pitting its will against God's. This attitude of withstanding God was manifested constantly as the "city of peace" murdered those sent to it by God.

But even in this expression of sorrow there are indications of certain judgment. The solemnity of this final pronunciation is marked by Christ's words, "For I say to you ..." ($\lambda\acute{\epsilon}\gamma\omega$ $\gamma\grave{\alpha}\rho$ $\dot{\upsilon}\mu\widetilde{\iota}\nu$...), in verse thirty-nine. The rabbis spoke of the Messiah as the Shekinah who would give Israel rest and blessing.[97] Thus by His departure, the Messiah was leaving Israel's house (evidently an allusion to the temple) to them. Another indication of His rejection of Israel are the words *your house*. The King no longer lays claim to the temple as being His (cf. Matthew 5:35; 17:25-26; 21:12-16). That the departure of the Messiah was inescapable is indicated by the double negative $o\dot{\upsilon}$ $\mu\acute{\eta}$ (translated "not") of Matthew 23:39.

It is extremely important for one to note that Christ's rejection of Israel is not an eternal one. The word "until" ($\acute{\epsilon}\omega\varsigma$) of verse thirty-nine together with the following statement affirms the fact that Christ will

96. Ibid., p. 903.
97. Gaebelein, *The Gospel of Matthew,* 2:162-163.

come again to a repentant nation to establish the promised millennial kingdom.

Finally, Christ makes some striking claims in these few statements. He clearly associates Himself with God who had in former generations sent prophets to Israel. He further implies that His departure will leave Israel's house empty. And finally, when He comes again the nation will cry out, "Blessed is He who comes in the name of the Lord."

E. The Predictions of the Rejected King
24:1-25:46

The nation has rejected its King and the King has rejected Israel. All is now in readiness for the cutting off of the Messiah. But before this occurs, the Lord presents His famous and much discussed Olivet Discourse, contained in Matthew 24 and 25, with parallel accounts in Mark 13 and Luke 21. This discourse, delivered privately to the disciples, is the longest prophetic message of Christ.

Introduction to Various
Interpretations of the Olivet Discourse

The difficulty of this portion of God's Word is well-known. Widely divergent interpretations and approaches have been set forth in an attempt to interpret the Olivet Discourse.

Past Fulfillment. There are none who actually believe the entire discourse has already been fulfilled. This nomenclature is simply used to identify those who take much of it as having been fulfilled in the destruction of Jerusalem. Kik, an amillennialist who holds this view, divides the discourse at Matthew 24:34.

> If the literal and well-defined meaning of this verse is accepted, it will be seen that this verse divides the chapter into two sections. Section One speaks of events which were to occur to the generation living at the time that Christ spoke these words. Section Two speaks of events to occur at the Second Coming of the Lord. Verse 34 is the division point of the two sections.[98]

However, in order to substantiate this view, Kik is forced to wildly spiritualize Matthew 24:29-31. One illustration from verse twenty-nine will suffice.

98. J. Marcellus Kik, *Matthew Twenty-Four, An Exposition*, p. 9.

If the sun, moon, and stars refer to the Jewish nation and its
prerogatives, then we have seen the fulfillment of this prophecy.
The Jewish nation has been darkened and no longer shines for
God. This has been true ever since the tribulation of those days . . .
The Sun of Judaism has been darkened; as the moon it no longer
reflects the Light of God; bright stars, as were the prophets, no
longer shine in the Israel of the flesh.[99]

The difficulty of this approach is very evident when such a method of
interpretation must be used to substantiate it. All of the events predicted
in this section simply have not come to pass. Much of Matthew 24:1-34
has not been fulfilled in any sense of the word.

Fulfillment in the Church Age. Some hold that Matthew 24 and 25
describe the general conditions between Christ's two advents. These
usually state that the Lord is emphasizing the great events preceding His
coming or *parousia.* No rapture of the church takes place, so therefore
these words are addressed directly to the church. Berkhof, another
amillennialist, contends that this view is the correct one.[100]

This view, too, is inconsistent with the doctrine of the church revealed in other Scripture. The church will not continue on through the
period of the tribulation but will be raptured before that time (Revelation
3:10; 1 Thessalonians 1:9-10; 5:9). Yet it is clear that at least a portion of
the discourse deals with the tribulation (Matthew 24:8, 13-15, 21, 22,
29). Therefore, to assert that this passage refers to the church age is
inaccurate.

Fulfillment in the Tribulation. Many premillenarians assert that the
Olivet Discourse as recorded in Matthew is entirely future. The answer
to the question which the disciples ask concerning the destruction of the
temple is passed over by Matthew but is recorded by Luke. Matthew
records only the reply to the second question according to this position.

Here the answer as to the impending ruin, already given in the
parable of the marriage feast (Matt. xxii. 7) is passed by; and the
Lord passes on to the second question, which rightly brings together the sign of His coming and of the completion of the age.[101]

This answer, of course, is then made to refer to the end time or the
tribulation.

99. Ibid., p. 65.
100. L. Berkhof, *Systematic Theology,* pp. 696-707.
101. W. Kelly, *The Lord's Prophecy on Olivet in Matthew XXIV. XXV.,* pp. 6-7.

Although this view has much to commend it, there is a difficulty which is inherent in it also. Why would Matthew include the first question of the disciples and then leave the answer unrecorded? If the second question is answered, how can one with consistent logic contend that in Matthew the first is not? A fourth view which is consistent with the context and with the argument of Matthew will be presented in the discussion of the argument of the Olivet Discourse.

1. The Setting, 24:1-24:2.

24:1-24:2. *And Jesus came out from the temple and was going away when His disciples came up to point out the temple buildings to Him. And He answered and said to them, "Do you not see all these things? Truly I say to you, not one stone here shall be left upon another, which will not be torn down."* The setting of this discourse is very important. The King has been rejected. Just previous to this instruction, Christ had severely denounced the Pharisees and told them that the blood of the prophets would come upon that generation (Matthew 23:35-36). Then in His lament over Jerusalem He announces the forsaking of the house of Israel (Matthew 23:38). Finally, Christ makes a very startling and disconcerting assertion in Matthew 24. As the King leaves the temple, the disciples point out the buildings of the temple to Him. Although it was built by Herod the Great, the Jews were very proud of this magnificent structure. In reply to the disciples' statements, the Lord states that, " ... not one here shall be left upon another, which will not be torn down." This statement is given with great force because of the aorist passive subjunctive of the verb "to leave" with the double negative οὐ μή (translated "not").

2. The Questions of the Disciples, 24:3.

24:3. *And as He was sitting on the Mount of Olives, the disciples came to Him privately, saying, "Tell us, when will these things be, and what will be the sign of Your coming, and of the end of the age?"* Naturally this assertion together with the ones which Christ had made just previously prompted the curiosity of the disciples. When they are alone with Him on the Mount of Olives, they ask Him, "When will these things be, and what will be the sign of Your coming, and of the end of the age?" While many see three questions here, the disciples are really asking two. The words "coming" (παρουσίας) and "end" (συν-

τελείας) are joined together by one article and the conjunction "and" ~~GRANDVILLE~~
(καί); therefore, these two words actually are two parts of one question. ~~SHARP RULE.~~
The word "coming" (παρουσία) is very interesting. In classical
Greek it had more the meaning of "presence" than "arrival."[102] However, it came to be used in the second and third century A. D. for the
visit of a king or other official.[103] It may be that the disciples are already
using the terms in this latter sense. They were convinced that Jesus was
the Messiah who would yet manifest Himself as the King of Israel in His
coming. Furthermore, the word ". . . intimates that the return of the
Messiah in glory will not result, like the First Coming, in a transitory
stay, but will inaugurate an *abiding presence.*"[104]

But the problem remains, what is the meaning of the disciples' questions? Edersheim contends that the two questions involve two separate
thoughts—the destruction of Jerusalem and Christ's second coming.

> . . . in the very saying which gave rise to their question, Christ had
> placed an indefinite period between the two. Between the desola-
> tion of the House and their new welcome to Him, would intervene
> a period of indefinite length, during which they would not see Him
> again.[105]

The basis of Edersheim's interpretation is correct, that is, Christ did
place an indefinite period of time between His forsaking of Israel and
His coming again. However, it appears that the disciples did not associate the destruction of the temple with the departure of the Lord, but
rather with His coming again. Therefore, the two questions involve a
single thought rather than two separate ones.

The King's statements had a very special meaning to the disciples. In
their minds they had developed a chronology of events in the following
sequence: (1) the departure of the King, (2) after a period of time the
destruction of Jerusalem, and (3) immediately after Jerusalem's devasta-
tion the presence of the Messiah. They had good scriptural ground for
this since Zechariah 14:1-2 describes the razing of Jerusalem. The same
passage goes on to describe the coming of the Lord to destroy the
nations which warred against Jerusalem (Zechariah 14:3-8). Following
this the millennial kingdom is established (Zechariah 14:9-11). This
sequence is so clearly in view that Luke records the question concerning
the destruction of Jerusalem only (Luke 21:7). That is, the disciples took

102. Abbott-Smith, *A Manual Greek Lexicon of the New Testament*, p. 347.
103. M'Neile, *St. Matthew*, p. 345.
104. Plummer, *Exegetical Commentary*, p. 329.
105. Edersheim, *Life and Times*, 2:432-433.

the destruction of Jerusalem to be completely eschatological. Therefore, Luke records this question only, as though Jerusalem's destruction would mark the coming of the King to reign. Bruce is correct when he asserts, "The questioners took for granted that all three things went together: destruction of temple, advent of Son of Man, end of the current age."[106]

3. The Warning Concerning Deception, 24:4-24:6.

24:4-24:6. *And Jesus answered and said to them, "See to it that no one misleads you. For many will come in My name, saying, 'I am the Christ,' and will mislead many. And you will be hearing of wars and rumors of wars; see that you are not frightened, for those things must take place, but that is not yet the end."* Christ now warns the disciples against being deceived. It is significant that each of the Synoptic Gospels begins the Lord's answer with the verb translated "see to it" (βλέπετε) and the warning. The key to understanding the discourse is found in this first sentence. The disciples thought that the destruction of Jerusalem with its great temple would usher in the end of the age. The Lord separates the two ideas and warns the disciples against being deceived by the destruction of Jerusalem and other such catastrophes. The razing of the temple and the presence of wars and rumors of wars do not necessarily signify the nearness of the end. Therefore the disciples are warned against the things which could lead them astray such as false messiahs and wars or cold wars.

The use of the words "those things must take place" (δεῖ γενέσθαι) reveals the prophetic nature of the discourse (verse 6). This clause is characteristically apocalyptic (Daniel 2:28, 29, 45; Revelation 1:1; 4:1; 22:6). In the New Testament, the verb "to be necessary" (δεῖ) is not only used of logical necessity but also of ". . . a necessity beyond human comprehension, grounded in the will of God . . ."[107] Evidences of this idea are found in Mark 8:31; 9:11; 13:10; Luke 24:7, 26; John 20:9; Acts 3:21; 1 Corinthians 15:25, 53; and 2 Corinthians 5:10. It is necessary for these things to come to pass in the future, but the disciples are told that these events do not mark out the end time. Cranfield comments, "These things do not constitute a sign that the End is just round the corner; and

---

106. Bruce, "Synoptic Gospels," *The Expositor's Greek Testament,* 1:289.

107. C. E. B. Cranfield, "St. Mark 13," *Scottish Journal of Theology,* 6 (July 1953): 289.

the disciples of Jesus are warned against giving heed to sensational rumors that the Parousia is upon them."[108]

4. The General Description of the End Time, 24:7-24:14.

After warning His disciples lest they should be deceived by the presence of false messiahs and wars, the Lord goes on to give a very general picture of the period just preceding His coming.

24:7. *"For nation will rise against nation, and kingdom against kingdom, and in various places there will be famines and earthquakes."* The conjunction "for" (γάρ) of verse seven introduces the reason why false messiahs, wars, and cold wars do not mark off the end time. Verse six evidently has reference to local situations, but verse seven looks at a worldwide conflict. The beginning of the end is to be indicated by universal war as well as famines and earthquakes in various places. M'Neile writes in commenting on verse seven, "The horrors described are not local disturbances, but are spread over the known world; nations and kingdoms are in hostility with one another.'[109] These are the things which indicate the beginning of the end. It is interesting to note in this connection how Luke uses the phrase "But before all these things" (πρὸ δὲ τούτων πάντων, Luke 21:12). The same universal catastrophes are used by Luke to indicate the nearness of the end. During this time of tribulation, those who will be followers of the Lord will be hated and persecuted.

24:8. *"But all these things are merely the beginning of birthpangs."* The words "all these things" (πάντα ταῦτα) look back to the things spoken of in verse seven. The picture portrayed in the words "the beginning of birth pangs" (ἀρχὴ ὠδίνων) is a vivid one. Just as the first labor pangs of a pregnant woman indicate the nearness of the birth of a child, so these great signs anticipate the end of the age and the beginning of a new one. Mark uses these words in the same sense and with the same connective as does Matthew.

24:9-24:13. *"Then they will deliver you up to tribulation, and will kill you, and you will be hated by all nations on account of My name. And at that time many will fall away and will betray one another and hate one another. And many false prophets will arise, and will mislead many. And because lawlessness is increased, most*

108. Ibid.
109. M'Neile, *St. Matthew,* p. 346.

271

people's love will grow cold. But the one who endures to the end, it is he who shall be saved." The occurrences of the adverb translated "then" or "at that time" (τότε) in verses nine and ten introduce further description of the end time. The persecution of Christ's followers, the offending of many, the betraying and hating of one another, false prophets deceiving many, lawlessness, and the growing cold of love will characterize that period of time. Even so a few will endure to the end (verse thirteen). In this verse the word "end" (τέλος) has the idea of an endurance that is complete. The thought is that the one "sticking it out" shall be saved.

24:14. *"And this gospel of the kingdom shall be preached in the whole world for a witness to all the nations, and then the end shall come.*" The final great sign preceding the end of the age is the universal proclamation of the gospel of the kingdom. "This Gospel of the Kingdom ... means 'the good tidings in this discourse that the Kingdom is near.'"[110] The message will be much the same as that which was proclaimed by John the Baptist, Jesus Christ, and the disciples. This universal testimony will accomplish three things. It will provide opportunity for all the world to hear of the person and work of the King and the essence of the kingdom. Second, it will cause many to turn in faith to God. Finally, a basis of judgment will be provided. For those who accept the message, entrance into the kingdom awaits. But eternal damnation accrues to those who refuse the gospel of the kingdom.

When these catastrophic events transpire together with the universal proclamation of the gospel of the kingdom, then the end shall come. Thus Christ gives a very general description of the events which will transpire preceding the end of the age.

5. The Abomination of Desolation, 24:15-24:22.

24:15. *"Therefore when you see the abomination of desolation which was spoken of through Daniel the prophet, standing in the holy place (let the reader understand).*" The King becomes very specific concerning the end time by referring to the abomination of desolation. The Greek particle translated "therefore" (οὖν) links this section very closely to the preceding. Both passages speak of the end of the age, but Matthew 24:15-22 particularizes one great event in that

110. Ibid., p. 347.

time. That event is the standing of the prophesied abomination of desolation in the holy place.

The nomenclature "the Abomination of Desolation" (τὸ βδέλυγμα τῆς ἐρημώσεως) is very significant. It is clear from Christ's own words that the term arises from Daniel's prophecy. It occurs in Daniel 9:27; 11:31; and 12:11.

> "The abomination of desolation," an allusion to Daniel, as Mt. notes, is the LXX. equivalent for שִׁקּוּץ הַשֹּׁמֵם (Dan. xi. 31) and שִׁקּוּץ שֹׁמֵם (xii. 11), "an abominable thing that layeth waste," referring to ix. 27.[111]

In the Septuagint the plural "desolations" (ἐρημώσεων) is found in Daniel 9:27, while the singular "desolation" (ἐρημώσεως) is used in Daniel 12:11. In Daniel 12:11 exactly the same formula is used as occurs in Matthew 24:15. Since the singular is employed in 1 Maccabees 1:54, it seems that the singular includes the idea of the plural. Morison writes, "The two representations, the singular and the plural, are but two phases of one substantive idea."[112] The word "desolation" is used in connection with the word "abomination."

> The significance of the use of τῆς ἐρημώσεως (equivalent to the Hebrew participle *shomem*) to qualify it is that the abominable thing causes the Temple to be deserted, the pious worshippers avoiding the Temple on its account.[113]

The word "abomination" (βδέλυγμα) is used in the Bible of that which is particularly detestable to God and rejected by Him. It is used with particular reference to heathen gods and to articles connected with them.[114] It may be concluded then that the abomination of desolation spoken of in Daniel's prophecy and referred to by Christ is an idol set up in the temple by the man of sin who is opposed to Jesus Christ.

Since the Lord's statement concerning the abomination of desolation is based on Daniel's prophecy of seventy weeks, it is well to note the chronology of Daniel 9:24-27. Daniel prophesies that from the decree of Artaxerxes—given to Nehemiah to restore and rebuild Jerusalem—until the coming of Israel's King is the period of sixty-nine weeks of years. This period of time was culminated when Christ made His triumphal

111. Ibid.
112. Morison, *A Practical Commentary*, p. 465.
113. Cranfield, "St. Mark 13," pp. 298-299.
114. Ibid., p. 298.

entry into Jerusalem.[115] But because Israel rejected its King, the calendar of the events of the seventieth week had to be postponed. Consequently, the great time of tribulation spoken of in connection with that period of time (Daniel 12:1) has been put off into the future. This future period of time will be inaugurated with the signing of the covenant by the nation Israel with the wicked prince that shall come. In the middle of the week, or after three and a half years, that wicked prince will cause the temple worship at Jerusalem to cease. At that time, the abomination of desolation will be introduced in the temple.

Because many have refused to believe that Daniel's prophecy of the seventieth week is still future, various other explanations have also been advanced. Some say the abomination of desolation is a reference to the conduct of the Zealots in the temple just previous to the Roman siege of Jerusalem.[116] However, this interpretation fails to give full meaning to *abomination* since there was no idolatry in the action of the Zealots. Others contend that Christ is using the expression in speaking of the introduction of Roman standards bearing the image of Caesar.[117] The Roman army brought their ensigns into the temple and there offered sacrifices to them, acclaiming Titus to be the emperor. However, this view also is fraught with difficulties. The images on the Roman standards had been introduced into Jerusalem many times before.[118] In addition, the warning to flee at the sight of the abomination would be useless if this interpretation is taken. The terrible ravages of the siege had already taken their toll by the time the sacrifices were offered to the ensigns of the Roman army. Bruce takes the abomination to be the Roman army at the fall of Jerusalem. However, this view also misses the significance of abomination.

The abomination of desolation must be a future event in God's eschatological program for several reasons. First, the context of Christ's words refers to a yet future time. Neither of the events spoken of in verses fourteen or twenty-one have been fulfilled. In verse twenty-nine, Christ speaks of His coming in close connection with the events described in Matthew 24:15. Second, Daniel's seventieth week has been postponed until the end times. Third, Mark in the parallel passages uses the masculine participle "standing" ($\dot{\epsilon}\sigma\tau\eta\kappa\acute{o}\tau\alpha$) in connection with the

115. See above, p. 242.

116. Henry Alford, *The Greek Testament*, 1:239; Lenski, *Interpretation of Matthew*, p. 938.

117. Kik, *Matthew Twenty-Four*, p. 45; Morison, *A Practical Commentary*, pp. 467-468; J. W. Shepard, *The Christ of the Gospels*, p. 517; Vincent, *Word Studies*, 1:128.

118. Alford, *The Greek Testament*, 1:239.

abomination of desolation. That is, he looked on the abomination as being manifested by a person who sets himself up as God in the temple. This has never been done since Christ spoke these words. Fourth, other Scripture yet anticipates the manifestation of the man of sin as the abomination (2 Thessalonians 2:3-4; Revelation 13:11-18).

24:16-24:22. *"Then let those who are in Judea flee to the mountains; let him who is on the housetop not go down to get the things out that are in his house; and let him who is in the field not turn back to get his cloak. But woe to those who are with child and to those who nurse babes in those days! But pray that your flight may not be in the winter, or on a Sabbath; for then there will be a great tribulation, such as has not occurred since the beginning of the world until now, nor ever shall. And unless those days had been cut short, no life would have been saved; but for the sake of the elect those days shall be cut short."* The Lord then offers admonition. When the abomination of desolation stands in the holy place, then the fastest possible escape from Jerusalem and Judea is to be made. There are two reasons why this is so—it is the last possible moment for escape, and terrible tribulation is about to come. So great will be the tribulation that if God in His mercy would not shorten it, no flesh would be saved (verse twenty-two). But on account of the heirs of the kingdom then dwelling on the earth, God will cut off that time of trouble.

6. The Coming of the Son of Man, 24:23-24:31.

Having warned His disciples about the tribulation of the last times, the King describes His coming.

24:23-24:27. *"Then if any one says to you, 'Behold, here is the Christ,' or 'There He is,' do not believe him. For false Christs and false prophets will arise and will show great signs and wonders, so as to mislead, if possible, even the elect. Behold, I have told you in advance. If therefore they say to you, 'Behold, He is in the wilderness,' do not go forth, or, 'Behold, He is in the inner rooms,' do not believe them. For just as the lightning comes from the east, and flashes even to the west, so shall the coming of the Son of Man be."* He begins this with a warning concerning false prophets who set forth false messiahs. These false prophets are demoniacally inspired to the extent that they are able to perform deceiving signs. Thus it is needful for the King to describe what His coming will not be like. It will not be

so obscure that He must be pointed out. Rather, Christ's coming will be
as manifest and evident as a bolt of lightning stretching from sky to sky.

24:28. *"Wherever the corpse is, there the vultures will gather."*
The gnomic saying of verse twenty-eight has engendered some difficulty.

> Who acts like eagles that pounce on carrion to fatten upon the
> reeking flesh? Why these false Christs and these false prophets?
> They seek to get an advantage from the dead body of their nation.
> So Jesus says to his disciples: "When you hear these cries to come
> here or there in connection with false Christs and false prophets,
> remember that Christ comes in a glory that is instant and visible to
> the whole world, and that you have in those raucous cries only
> another case of eagles going to feast on carrion."[119]

The King vividly portrays the state of Israel by referring to it with the
word "corpse" ($\pi\tau\hat{\omega}\mu\alpha$). It is lifeless and hopeless and going into
putrefication. "It is fit only for vultures."[120] Thus the nation is and will
be in such a spiritual condition that false prophets will be able to feast on
it as vultures consume the flesh of a dead and decaying body.

24:29. *"But immediately after the tribulation of those days the
sun will be darkened, and the moon will not give its light, and the
stars will fall from the sky, and the powers of the heavens will be
shaken,"* After this negative admonition, Christ gives a positive de-
scription of His coming (Matthew 24:29-31). "Immediately" ($\epsilon\dot{v}\theta\dot{\epsilon}\omega\varsigma$)
following the time of great tribulation, there will be signs in the
heavenly bodies. The sun shall be darkened and the moon will not give
its light; stars will fall from their places. The phrase "powers of the
heavens" ($\delta\upsilon\nu\dot{\alpha}\mu\epsilon\iota\varsigma\ \tau\hat{\omega}\nu\ o\dot{v}\rho\alpha\nu\hat{\omega}\nu$) is a reference to the sun, moon,
and stars, spoken of in a summary fashion.[121] Thus the Lord describes
the astronomical bodies being shaken as the earth is in an earthquake.
The tribulation, the signs in the stellar spaces, and the sign of the Son of
Man are all marks of Christ's coming again.

24:30. *"and then the sign of the Son of Man will appear in the
sky, and then all the tribes of the earth will mourn, and they will see
the Son of Man coming on the clouds of the sky with power and
great glory."* A problem exists as to the identification of the sign of the
Son of Man. Of the various suggestions, three have proved to be the
most popular. The patristic fathers held that the sign was the display of

119. Lenski, *Interpretation of Matthew*, p. 946.
120. Ibid.
121. M'Neile, *St. Matthew*, p. 352.

the cross in the heavens. Alford concurs with this.[122] Others take the sign to be a shining light like the Shekinah glory of the Old Testament which will surround the Son of Man.[123] Still others say the sign is the coming of Christ Himself.[124] It seems that Christ is here alluding to Daniel 7:13. He shall come in glory as prophesied by the prophet Daniel. Allen paraphrases it, "Then shall appear the well-known sign of the Son of Man predicted by Daniel."[125] The clouds of heaven refer to the superhuman majesty of the person of the King.[126] At this glorious sight all the tribes of the earth shall mourn (cf. Zechariah 12:12).

24:31. *"And He will send forth His angels with a great trumpet and they will gather together His elect from the four winds, from one end of the sky to the other."* When He comes the King will send forth His angels to regather His people Israel from the extremities of the earth. Many expositors take this to be a reference not to Israel but to the gathering of the church. For several important reasons it is evident that the faithful of Israel are in view. First of all, the word "elect" (ἐκλεκ - τός) is used in the Old Testament of Israel (1 Chronicles 16:13; Psalm 105:6, 43; 106:5; Isaiah 41:8, 43:20; 45:4). It was not only used of Israel as a nation but also of the faithful ones in that nation (Isaiah 65:9, 15, 22). It is in this latter sense that Christ uses it here. When He comes again, the believing remnant of Israel will be regathered from the corners of the earth to be placed in the land. This is prophesied clearly in the Old Testament (Jeremiah 16:14-15; Isaiah 11:11-16; 27:13). Herein is the second evidence that the church is not in view in this passage. A third is found in the Jewish context of the discourse from Matthew 24:3-25:30. Such terms as the gospel of the kingdom (24:14), the holy place (24:15), the sabbath (24:20), and the Messiah (24:23-24) indicate that Israel as a nation is in view. Fourthly, the discourse relates to the end time described in Daniel's prophecy of the seventieth week (Matthew 24:15). Finally, the church cannot be in view since it will not go through the tribulation period (Revelation 3:10; Romans 5:9; 1 Thessalonians 1:9-10; 5:9).

It may be concluded then that Christ will come in glory with His church (Colossians 3:4) and with His angels (Matthew 16:27) at the

122. Alford, *The Greek Testament*, 1:243.

123. E. Schuyler English, *Studies in the Gospel According to Matthew*, p. 177; Gaebelein, *The Gospel of Matthew*, 2:209; M'Neile, *St. Matthew*, p. 352.

124. Allen, *Commentary on Matthew*, pp. 258-259; Darby, *Synopsis*, 3:125; Kelly, *Lectures on Matthew*, p. 27; Lenski, *Interpretation of Matthew*, p. 948.

125. Allen, *Commentary on Matthew*, p. 259.

126. Plummer, *Exegetical Commentary*, p. 336.

close of the tribulation period. At that time He will send forth His angels
to regather faithful Israel to its land (Matthew 24:31) and also to gather
out the wicked of the world for judgment (Matthew 13:39, 41; 24:40, 41;
25:31; 2 Thessalonians 1:7-8).

7. The Parabolic Admonition, 24:32-25:30.

Thus far in the discourse the King has warned the disciples not to be
deceived concerning the end times. There will be wars and rumors of
wars (and the destruction of Jerusalem with its temple), but that is not
the end. The end is indicated by certain definite signs—world wars,
famines, earthquakes, universal social disturbances, the worldwide
proclamation of the gospel of the kingdom, and the appearance of the
abomination of desolation in the holy place. The Son of Man will then
come to establish His universal kingdom. His appearance will be of
such a supernatural character that no one will doubt Who it is that has
come. On the basis of these facts, the King admonishes His disciples by
means of a series of parables (Matthew 24:32-25:30).

a. The Parable of the Fig Tree, 24:32-24:42.

24:32-24:35. *"Now learn the parable from the fig tree: when its
branch has already become tender, and puts forth its leaves, you
know that summer is near; even so you too, when you see all these
things, recognize that He is near, right at the door. Truly I say to
you, this generation will not pass away until all these things take
place. Heaven and earth will pass away, but My words shall not
pass away."* The first parable which Christ employs is the parable of the
fig tree. The lesson of the parable is rather simple: when the signs of the
end appear the coming of the Son of Man is very near. However, there
are several difficulties in the words of the Lord in this section. One
involves the meaning of "this generation" ($\dot{\eta}$ $\gamma\epsilon\nu\epsilon\grave{\alpha}$ $\alpha\mathring{v}\tau\eta$) in verse
thirty-four. Some take it to refer to the generation which was contempo-
rary with Christ and assert that the Lord made an error. M'Neile writes,
"It is impossible to escape the conclusion that Jesus, as Man, expected
the End within the lifetime of His contemporaries . . . ."[127] This is untenable. While it is true that Christ in His *kenosis* (emptying, Philippians
2:7) subjected Himself to the voluntary non-use of His divine attributes,
it can never be said that He was in error in His human nature. From His

127. M'Neile, *St. Matthew,* p. 355.

human nature He may admit ignorance (Matthew 24:36), but never does He propagate error from this ignorance.

Others refer "generation" ($\gamma\epsilon\nu\epsilon\acute{\alpha}$) to the contemporaries of Christ and make the prophecies apply to the destruction of Jerusalem.[128] This view has great difficulty in attempting to find the fulfillment of the prophecies in the first century. The only means whereby they can say that the Son of Man came, the sun was darkened, or the gospel of the kingdom was universally proclaimed, is to "spiritualize" their meaning.

A third interpretation lays great stress on the verb translated "to take place" ($\gamma\acute{\epsilon}\nu\eta\tau\alpha\iota$) which occurs at this point in all three Synoptics. Because the word means *to begin, to have a beginning,* it is asserted that Christ is here telling His disciples that the prophesied events will begin their course in that generation.[129] This approach fails to note the significance of the words "all these things" ($\pi\acute{\alpha}\nu\tau\alpha$ $\tau\alpha\tilde{\upsilon}\tau\alpha$) in the same verse. It could hardly be said that all these things began to be in the lifetime of the disciples. How could Christ begin His coming at the time when it is described as being like lightning? Nor does this explanation fit the meaning of verse thirty-three.

Still another interpretation is set forth which makes "generation" ($\gamma\epsilon\nu\epsilon\acute{\alpha}$) refer to the Jewish people.[130] Thus the words of the King would be a promise that the Jewish people would never be wiped off the face of the earth. This is a legitimate interpretation since $\gamma\epsilon\nu\epsilon\acute{\alpha}$ can mean "race, stock, or lineage."[131]

There is, however, still another meaning attached to the phrase. It is very possible to take it as a reference to the generation which will be living at the end time when the signs of Christ's coming appear.[132] The meaning then becomes that the same generation which sees the beginning will see the end. Of the latter two interpretations, this is the better. Although it is true that the Jewish race will continue until the end, the context does not support this view as well as the other. These words were spoken with the word "near" ($\grave{\epsilon}\gamma\gamma\acute{\upsilon}\varsigma$) in view (verse thirty-two). When the tree is tender and it puts forth leaves, then the summer is known to be near. Thus the first sign of the Son of Man's coming

128. Kik, *Matthew Twenty-Four,* pp. 10-12; Plummer, *Exegetical Commentary,* p. 338.

129. Cranfield, "St. Mark 13," 7 (July 1954): 291; C. E. Stowe, "The Eschatology of Christ, With Special Reference to the Discourse in Matt. XXIV. and XXV.;" *Bibliotheca Sacra* 7 (July 1850): 471.

130. English, *Studies in Matthew,* p. 179; Gaebelein, *The Gospel of Matthew,* 2:215.

131. Cremer, *Biblico-Theological Lexicon,* pp. 148-149.

132. Carl Armerding, *The Olivet Discourse,* p. 44; Charles Lee Feinberg, *Israel in the Last Days: The Olivet Discourse,* p. 22; F. W. Grant, *The Numerical Bible,* 5:230.

indicates its proximity. It is so close that the generation that is alive when the first sign appears will live to see the coming of Christ. This view faces one great objection. It is claimed by its opponents that the demonstrative pronoun "this" ($\alpha\breve{\upsilon}\tau\eta$) prevents one from referring $\gamma\epsilon\nu\epsilon\acute{\alpha}$ to any other generation than the contemporary one.[133] To prove their point they refer to Matthew 11:16; 12:41-45; 23:36; Luke 11:50, 51; 17:25 and other passages. However, in so doing, they rigidly limit the basic meaning of the demonstrative. Winer writes, "The pronoun $o\mathring{\upsilon}\tau os$ sometimes refers, not to the noun locally nearest, but to one more remote, which, as the principal subject, was *mentally* the nearest, the most present to the writer's thoughts ..."[134] The subject in the thought of Christ is the end time. It seems best, therefore, to refer $\gamma\epsilon\nu\epsilon\acute{\alpha}$ to the future generation which shall be living at the time of Christ's second coming.

24:36. *"But of that day and hour no one knows, not even the angels of heaven, nor the Son, but the Father alone."* Verse thirty-six is most interesting in view of what has just been spoken by the Lord Jesus. He has given definite signs which will indicate the general nearness of His coming. However, the definite day or hour is known by no one except the Father. This verse becomes the main proposition which is developed from this point to Matthew 25:30. Since no one knows the day or hour, the believer is to watch and be prepared at any moment for His coming.

24:37-24:39. *"For the coming of the Son of Man will be just like the days of Noah. For as in those days which were before the flood they were eating and drinking, they were marrying and giving in marriage, until the day that Noah entered the ark, and they did not understand until the flood came and took them all away, so shall the coming of the Son of Man be."* The word "as" ($\omega\sigma\pi\epsilon\rho$) of verse thirty-seven introduces a comparison between the days of Noah and Christ's second coming to the earth. The likeness is seen in the suddenness of the coming of the judgment and the unpreparedness of the world for it.

> The special point of the analogy is not that the generation that was swept away by the Flood was exceptionally wicked; none of the occupations mentioned are sinful; but that it was so absorbed in its worldly pursuits that it paid no attention to solemn warnings.[135]

133. Kik, *Matthew Twenty-Four*, pp. 10-12; Plummer, *Exegetical Commentary*, p. 338.

134. George Benedict Winer, *Grammar of the Idiom of the New Testament*, p. 157.

135. Plummer, *Exegetical Commentary*, p. 340.

24:40-24:41. *"Then there shall be two men in the field; one will be taken, and one will be left. Two women will be grinding at the mill; one will be taken, and one will be left."* A problem exists as to the identification of the ones who are taken in verses forty and forty-one. Is this a description of the rapture of the church or of the taking of the wicked to judgment? Those who take the former position argue that "to take" (παραλαμβάνω), the verb used here, is to be differentiated from "to take" (αἴρω), the verb used in verse thirty-nine.[136] It is asserted that παραλαμβάνω signifies the act whereby Christ receives His own to Himself. However, παραλαμβάνω is also used in a bad sense (cf. Matthew 4:5, 8; John 19:16). Since it is parallel in thought with those who were taken in the judgment of the flood, it is best to refer the verb to those who are taken for judgment preceding the establishment of the kingdom. The difference in verbs can be accounted for on the basis of accuracy of description. "The flood came and swept them all away" is a good translation.[137]

> It will be a taking away judicially and in judgment. The ones left will enjoy the blessings of Christ's reign on earth, just as Noah and his family were left to continue life on earth. This is the opposite of the rapture, where those who are left go into the judgment of the Great Tribulation.[138]

24:42. *"Therefore be on the alert, for you do not know which day your Lord is coming."* Verse forty-two is the application of verses thirty-two to forty-one. The people living during the end time are to be on the alert (present imperative). The signs will give a general warning, but they will not be so specific as to designate the day or hour. Therefore, when the signs appear, they are to watch.

b. The Parable of the Watchful Householder, **24:43-24:44.** *"But be sure of this, that if the head of the house had known at what time of the night the thief was coming, he would have been on the alert and would not have allowed his house to be broken into. For this reason you be ready too; for the Son of Man is coming at an hour when you do not think He will."* The conjunction "but" is used to connect the next illustration, the example of the watchful householder, to the pre-

---

136. Benjamin Wills Newton, *The Prophecy of the Lord Jesus as Contained in Matthew XXIV. and XXV.*, p. 87.

137. Morison, *A Practical Commentary*, p. 489; Charles B. Williams, *The New Testament, A Private Translation in the Language of the People*, p. 66.

138. Feinberg, *Israel in Last Days*, p. 27.

ceding. The pronoun translated "at what" (ποία) in verse forty-three and "which" in verse forty-two is almost equivalent to the pronoun "which" (τίνι).[139] If the householder had known which watch the thief should come, he would have watched for him and not permitted his house to be broken into. The lesson is evident. When the householder knows the general time in which the thief should come, he prepares himself accordingly. "For this reason" (διὰ τοῦτο) the believers of the age of the tribulation should be prepared. The signs of the end will equip them to know generally or "in which watch" the Son of Man should come.

   c. *The Parable of the Two Servants,* **24:45-24:51.** *"Who then is the faithful and sensible slave whom his master put in charge of his household to give them their food at the proper time? Blessed is that slave whom his master finds so doing when he comes. Truly I say to you, that he will put him in charge of all his possessions. But if that evil slave says in his heart, 'My master is not coming for a long time,' and shall begin to beat his fellow-slaves and eat and drink with drunkards; the master of that slave will come on a day when he does not expect him and at an hour which he does not know, and shall cut him in pieces and assign him a place with the hypocrites; weeping shall be there and the gnashing of teeth."*

   The next illustration is bound to Matthew 24:32-44 by the word "then" (ἄρα). The account of the two servants illustrates the two attitudes men will have in the end time with relationship to the King's coming to the earth to judge and to reign. One will be characterized by faithfulness and wisdom and the other by wickedness. The sequence which is followed in each case is significant. In the first, faithfulness and wisdom issue in good works which in turn result in reward. This reward is blessing in the coming kingdom. M'Neile notes, "The reward of faithfulness is to be trusted with higher responsibilities; cf. xxv. 21, 23, Lk. xvi. 10a. Since the parable deals with the Parousia, the words apply to higher activities in the age to come."[140] On the other hand, the evil character of a man brings forth sin which results in punishment. This punishment is described as "weeping and gnashing of teeth." Invariably throughout Matthew this phrase refers to the retribution of those who are judged before the millennial kingdom is established (Matthew 8:12; 13:42, 50; 22:13; 25:30).

139. Plummer, *Exegetical Commentary,* p. 340.
140. M'Neile, *St. Matthew,* p. 358.

d. The Parable of the Ten Virgins, 25:1-25:13.

25:1. *"Then the kingdom of heaven will be comparable to ten virgins, who took their lamps, and went out to meet the bridegroom."* Matthew introduces the parable of the ten virgins with his characteristic adverb "then" (τότε). There is some debate as to who is represented by these virgins. Many believe they picture the church at the coming of the Lord.[141] The premillenarians who hold this view contend that τότε refers to Matthew 24:45-51 which is said to deal with the church. They further argue that the period of waiting is too long to take place in the tribulation.[142] It is also said that the title *Son of Man* does not occur in this parable, nor is the phrase *times or seasons* to be found.[143] It is asserted that these phrases are associated with the ministry of the Messiah on earth. Finally, they contend that the tribulation cannot be in view since no Old Testament prophecy is quoted. It can be seen that at best these are arguments from silence.

This parable as well as the next one deals with the Jews in the tribulation period. This is seen from various facts. The context favors this view (Matthew 24:3, 8, 14, 15, 27, 30, 31, 33, 42, 44, 47, 51). The subject being discussed is the end time, the final years before the kingdom is established. At this time the church will be absent from the earth.[144] Therefore this section deals with a Jewish period of time. Secondly, the adverb "then" (τότε) of Matthew 25:1 connects this passage with 24:51. The last phrase of that verse is always employed in connection with the judgment preceding the establishment of the kingdom.[145] Finally, the subject matter of the parables of the ten virgins and of the talents is closely connected with Matthew 24:45-51. M'Neile notes this in writing, "In XXIV. 45 the slave was 'faithful and prudent;' the present parable gives an instance of φρόνιμοι [prudent], the following of πιστοί [faithful]."[146]

The future passive form of the verb "to compare" (ὁμοιωθήσεται) in verse one looks forward to the King's coming to reign. At that time the particular phase of the kingdom of heaven illustrated by the ten

141. Carr, *St. Matthew,* p. 275; Gaebelein, *The Gospel of Matthew,* 2:225-236; Plummer, *Exegetical Commentary,* p. 343.
142. Gaebelein, *The Gospel of Matthew,* 2:228.
143. L. Laurenson, *Messiah, the Prince,* p. 165.
144. See above, pp. 265-66.
145. See above, pp. 255-56.
146. M'Neile, *St. Matthew,* p. 359.

virgins will be true.[147] The particular aspect of the kingdom pictured by the parable is the need for preparation in light of the coming of the King.

In order to understand the parable, one must be familiar with the custom of marriage in the East.[148] At a considerable time previous to the actual marriage the marriage was contracted. At this time the couple was considered to be betrothed. Then, after some time had elapsed, the bridegroom would go to the bride's home where a marriage ceremony took place. Then the bridegroom and the bride would go to the home of the bridegroom in a long procession. There a great marriage festival would be held. The scene of this parable is laid near the bridegroom's house where the virgins are waiting for the bridegroom to return from the house of the bride. They are anticipating joining the procession and entering into the festive banquet at the house of the bridegroom.

25:2-25:12. *"And five of them were foolish, and five were prudent. For when the foolish took their lamps, they took no oil with them, but the prudent took oil in flasks along with their lamps. Now while the bridegroom was delaying, they all got drowsy and began to sleep. But at midnight there was a shout, 'Behold, the bridegroom! Come out to meet him.' Then all those virgins arose, and trimmed their lamps. And the foolish said to the prudent, 'Give us some of your oil, for our lamps are going out.' But the prudent answered, saying, 'No, there will not be enough for us and you too; go instead to the dealers and buy some for yourselves.' And while they were going away to make the purchase, the bridegroom came, and those who were ready went in with him to the wedding feast; and the door was shut. And later the other virgins also came, saying, 'Lord, Lord, open up for us.' But he answered and said, 'Truly I say to you, I do not know you.'"* In the parable, the ten virgins represent Israel in the tribulation period as they wait for the coming of their King. The noun form translated "to meet" ($\dot{v}\pi\dot{\alpha}\nu\tau\eta\sigma\iota\varsigma$) which occurs in verse one is significant. It connotes an official welcome of a newly arrived dignitary.[149] Evidently, the more general signs of the coming of the Son of Man had been displayed already since they are pictured as going forth to meet the bridegroom. They knew His coming was near. The five wise virgins illustrate those Jews who not only anticipate the Messiah's coming but also prepare for it. The foolishness

147. Peters, *Theocratic Kingdom*, 3:306.
148. Peters, *Theocratic Kingdom*, 3:301; Richard Chenevix Trench, *Notes on the Parables of Our Lord*, pp. 200-201.
149. M'Neile, *St. Matthew*, p. 360.

of the other five prefigures the stupidity of the Israelites who wait for Christ's coming but do not properly prepare for it. They know He is coming but are spiritually unprepared nevertheless. Perhaps their spiritual condition will be analagous to the Jews at the Lord's first coming. With eyes only for the physical benefits of the kingdom, the foolish Jews fail to prepare themselves spiritually for its coming. The prepared enter the kingdom as pictured by the banquet, but the unprepared are excluded. The foolishness of the five unprepared virgins is accentuated by the fact that they slept when they should have used the time for preparation. So Israel should use the time of tribulation.

Verse ten describes very well the suddenness of the coming of the King. The genitive absolute indicates that while the foolish virgins were going to obtain oil, the bridegroom came. In addition there seems to be very little interval between the cry, "Behold, the bridegroom!" and the arrival of the procession.[150] Christ had already predicted this (Matthew 24:27, 39, 50).

Verses ten to twelve picture the judgment of the Jewish nation before the establishment of the kingdom. "The closed door, which to those who were ready meant security and untold bliss, to the others meant banishment and untold gloom."[151] The expression "Lord, lord" (Κύριε, κύριε) reminds one of Matthew 7:21-23 where the same scene is being described.

Like Matthew 24:48 and 25:18, verse five indicates that a period of time would elapse between the first signs of the King's coming and His actual appearance. This is no reason to assume that the parable does not deal with the tribulation period. It merely points up the fact that there will be a span of time between the signs of the end and the end.

25:13. *"Be on the alert then, for you do not know the day nor the hour."* The lesson of the parable is presented in verse thirteen and is linked to the parable by the Greek word translated "then" (οὖν). The verb "to be on the alert" (γρηγορεῖτε) has the idea not only of watching but also of being prepared.[152] The Israelites are to be ready for the coming of the King even as they watch for Him in the tribulation period.

e. The Parable of the Talents, 25:14-25:30.

25:14. *"For it is just like a man about to go on a journey, who called his own slaves, and entrusted his possessions to them."* The

150. Plummer, *Exegetical Commentary,* p. 345.
151. Ibid., p. 346.
152. M'Neile, *St. Matthew,* p. 363.

conjunction "for" (γάρ) of verse fourteen links the parable of the talents to the application given in verse thirteen.[153] Therefore, verse thirteen is the key to the meaning of the parable. This illustration of the talents presents the same truth as the first parable, but a different phase of it is seen.

In the first, spiritual preparation for the coming of the King is emphasized; in this parable, service performed in preparation for Christ's coming is set forth. Plummer compares the two parables in writing, "That of the Virgins tells nothing about working for the Bridegroom during the delay. That of the Talents teaches that the time of waiting must be a time of service."[154] The use of the word "slave" (δοῦλος) throughout the parable substantiates this view. The interpretation of this parable, like the preceding, deals with the judgment of Israel at the close of the tribulation period (Matthew 25:21, 23, 30).

25:15-25:18. *"And to one he gave five talents, to another, two, and to another, one, each according to his own ability; and he went on his journey. Immediately the one who had received the five talents went and traded with them, and gained five more talents. In the same manner the one who had received the two talents gained two more. But he who received the one talent went away and dug in the ground, and hid his master's money."* The problem of this parable concerns the servant who received one talent. Is he a believer who receives no rewards or is he a lost man? It is evident from the punishment of this servant that he, like the five foolish virgins, is a lost man.

> He did not know his Master—he did not trust in Him. He could not even do that which was consistent with his own thoughts. He waited for some authorization which would be a security against the character his heart falsely gave his Master.[155]

It must be remembered that the slaves are not Christians of the church age but Jews in the tribulation period. And the large sum of money "... suggests the greatness of the privileges entrusted by God to the Jews."[156] It may be that the responsibility involved is the proclamation of the gospel of the kingdom to the ends of the earth. Those who have a heart for the kingdom faithfully discharge their responsibility, while those who have no real concern for its spiritual realities fail.

153. Ibid., p. 364.
154. Plummer, *Exegetical Commentary,* p. 347.
155. Darby, *Synopsis,* 3:131.
156. M'Neile, *St. Matthew,* p. 364.

25:19-25:30. *"Now after a long time the master of those slaves came and settled accounts with them. And the one who had received the five talents came up and brought five more talents, saying, 'Master, you entrusted five talents to me; see, I have gained five more talents.' His master said to him, 'Well done, good and faithful slave; you were faithful with a few things, I will put you in charge of many things, enter into the joy of your master.' The one also who had received the two talents came up and said, 'Master, you entrusted to me two talents; see, I have gained two more talents.' His master said to him, 'Well done, good and faithful slave; you were faithful with a few things, I will put you in charge of many things; enter into the joy of your master.' And the one also who had received the one talent came up and said, 'Master, I knew you to be a hard man, reaping where you did not sow, and gathering where you scattered no seed. And I was afraid, and went away and hid your talent in the ground; see, you have what is yours.' But his master answered and said to him, 'You wicked, lazy slave, you knew that I reap where I did not sow, and gather where I scattered no seed? Then you ought to have put my money in the bank, and on my arrival I would have received my money back with interest. Therefore take away the talent from him, and give it to the one who has the ten talents.' For to everyone who has shall more be given, and he shall have an abundance; but from the one who does not have, even what he does have shall be taken away. And cast out the worthless slave into the outer darkness; in that place there shall be weeping and gnashing of teeth."* The rewards given to the faithful servants will be further responsibility and privilege in the coming kingdom. "The joy of your master" is a designation of the bliss in the coming kingdom.[157] Verse twenty-nine is most interesting in connection with the judgment. The Lord spoke almost the same words when He judged the contemporary generation of Israel for their spiritual dullness (Matthew 13:12). In the parables of that chapter, the ones who had spiritual perception would receive new truths concerning the kingdom. Those who were spiritually blind would be completely shut off from further light by the parables. So here the heirs of the kingdom will receive greater blessing, while the ones who do not inherit it will be shut off from even an opportunity for entrance. Those who do receive rewards will be rewarded according to their faithfulness and not the measure of their work. Plummer comments, "The lesson of the Talents is,

157. Ibid., p. 365.

that men with different gifts may make an equally good (or bad) use of them, and be proportionately requited."[158]

The last three parables give practical instructions in the light of the King's coming to judge and to reign. The principle which underlies each is the same one which was given in the Sermon on the Mount (Matthew 7:16-21). The fruit of faithfulness and preparedness would indicate the character of those living in the days before His coming. In each parable, character is manifested by works. This thought forms the key to the following passage which deals with the judgment of the nations (Matthew 25:31-46).

8. The Judgment of the Nations, 25:31-25:46.

The Gospel of Matthew has been called "the Gospel of judgment."[159] Throughout this Gospel there are allusions to judgment which justify this statement (Matthew 3:12; 6:2, 5, 16; 7:24-27; 13:30, 48-49; 18:23-34; 20:1-16; 21:33-41; 22:1-14; 24:45-51; 25:1-12, 14-30). This is only natural since one of the main subjects of Matthew is the kingdom, and preceding the kingdom is judgment.[160] The closing words of the Olivet Discourse concern the judgment of the nations, the last event before the kingdom on earth is established.

A problem exists as to the identification of this judgment. Certain theologians and commentators maintain that there is but one general judgment and Matthew 25:31-46 is a description of it.[161] This view is due to a confusion of the Great White Throne judgment spoken of in Revelation 20 with the judgment of the nations.

Several facts indicate that these two judgments are distinct. In Matthew 25, there is no mention of a resurrection; the judgment concerns the living nations. "The word translated 'nations' is *never,* according to the uniform testimony of critics and scholars, used to designate 'the dead,' unless this be a solitary exception."[162] Three classes of people are mentioned in this judgment—the sheep, the goats, and "my brethren." At the Great White Throne judgment, only the wicked are before the Judge (Revelation 20:13-15). At the judgment of the nations, some inherit the kingdom while others are eternally punished. Only the

158. Plummer, *Exegetical Commentary,* p. 348.
159. Ibid.
160. See above, p. 69.
161. Kik, *Matthew Twenty-Four,* pp. 92-97; Lenski, *Interpretation of Matthew,* pp. 986-88; Shepard, *The Christ of the Gospels,* pp. 528-529.
162. Peters, *Theocratic Kingdom,* 2:374.

lake of fire is mentioned as the destiny of those who are judged at the Great White Throne judgment. The judgement of the nations takes place after the tribulation, while the Great White Throne judgment occurs after the millennium. This judgement then must not be confused with the judgment of the wicked dead. It concerns "all the nations" (πάντα τὰ ἔθνη) living at the time of Christ's return to reign.

25:31. *"But when the Son of Man comes in His glory, and all the angels with Him, then He will sit on His glorious throne."* The time of the judgment is indicated by the words "when" (ὅταν) and "then" (τότε) of verse thirty-one. When the Son of Man comes in His glory with all His angels, this judgment will occur. This is in complete agreement with the prophecy of Daniel 7:9-14 and 22-27.

25:32-25:34. *"And all the nations will be gathered before Him; and He will separate them from one another, as the shepherd separates the sheep from the goats; and He will put the sheep on His right, and the goats on the left. Then the King will say to those on His right, 'Come, you who are blessed of My Father, inherit the kingdom prepared for you from the foundation of the world."* The purpose of the judgment is to determine who of the people living on the earth at the time of the King's return will inherit the kingdom and who will be cast into eternal punishment (Matthew 25:34, 41, 46). Verse thirty-four gives a very important description of this kingdom. It is the one which has been prepared from the foundation of the world. This indicates two things. First, it shows that the establishment of God's kingdom on earth has been God's purpose since the creation of the world. Each dispensation has proven man's incapacity for it. At the end time, God, by His marvelous grace and power, will accomplish His desire, a kingdom on earth among men. Second, this statement indicates that this kingdom must be the fulfillment of the promises and covenants to Adam and Eve (Genesis 3:15), to Abraham (Genesis 12, 15, 17, 21), to David (2 Samuel 7:12-16), and to the Jewish nation (Ezekiel 34:20-31; Jeremiah 31:31-40; Zechariah 10:5-12).[163]

Thus, the kingdom will include the resurrected saints of the Old Testament, the church (Colossians 1:13; 3:4; 2 Peter 1:10-11), and the righteous people living at the time of the judgment of the nations. It is important to note that this judgment concerns "entrance into" and "exclusion from" the promised and covenanted earthly kingdom for those who are alive on the earth when the King comes to reign.

163. Ibid., 2:375.

Still another problem exists. It involves the identification of "all the
nations" (πάντα τὰ ἔθνη, verse thirty-two). Generally, "the nations"
(τὰ ἔθνη) refers to the Gentiles as distinct from the Jews.[164] However,
the phrase "all the nations" (πάντα τὰ ἔθνη) can be more inclusive and
designate the whole human race living at one particular time (Matthew
28:19; Mark 13:10; Romans 16:26; Revelation 15:4). The same term is
also used more exclusively to refer to Gentiles only (Luke 21:24; Acts
14:16). In this sense it is equivalent to הַגּוֹיִם in the Old Testament.[165]
Thus, Matthew could possibly be referring to Gentiles as distinguished
from Israel or to the whole human race including Jews.

25:35-25:46. *"'For I was hungry, and you gave Me something to
eat; I was thirsty, and you gave Me drink; I was a stranger, and you
invited Me in; naked, and you clothed Me; I was sick, and you
visited Me; I was in prison, and you came to Me.' Then the righteous will answer Him, saying, 'Lord, when did we see You hungry,
and feed You, or thirsty, and give You drink? And when did we see
You a stranger, and invite You in, or naked, and clothe You? And
when did we see You sick, or in prison, and come to You?' And the
King will answer and say to them, 'Truly I say to you, to the extent
that you did it to one of these brothers of Mine, even the least of
them, you did it to Me.' Then He will also say to those on His left,
'Depart from Me, accursed ones, into the eternal fire which has
been prepared for the devil and his angels; for I was hungry, and
you gave Me nothing to eat; I was thirsty, and you gave Me nothing
to drink; I was a stranger, and you did not invite Me in; naked, and
you did not clothe Me; sick, and in prison, and you did not visit
Me.' Then they themselves also will answer, saying, 'Lord, when
did we see You hungry, or thirsty, or a stranger, or naked, or sick,
or in prison, and did not take care of You?' Then He will answer
them, saying, 'Truly I say to you, to the extent that you did not do it
to one of the least of these, you did not do it to Me.' And these will
go away into eternal punishment, but the righteous into eternal
life."* It is important to note that three groups of people are spoken of in
this passage—the sheep, the goats, and the group designated by Christ
as "brothers of Mine" (verse forty). The key to the identification of all
three is the interpretation of "brothers of Mine." Some say it refers to

164. Abbott-Smith, *A Manual Lexicon*, pp. 129-30; Joseph Henry Thayer, *A Greek-
English Lexicon of the New Testament*, p. 168; Vincent, *Word Studies*, 1:135.
165. Thayer, *Greek-English Lexicon*, p. 168.

Christians.[166] But if this is so, who are the sheep? Others state it is used
as a name for the Jews.[167] But the term seems to have more significance
than this (Matthew 12:50). It seems best to say that "brothers of Mine"
is a designation of the godly remnant of Israel that will proclaim the
gospel of the kingdom unto every nation of the world.[168] Since all of the
ungodly Jews will be removed from the earth at the end of the tribulation (Zechariah 13:8-9), the sheep and goats must include "all the na-
tions" ($\pi\alpha\nu\tau\alpha$ $\tau\alpha\xi\theta\nu\eta$) living on the earth at this time.

If the sheep and goats comprise the living Gentiles at the time of the
judgment, what is the basis of dividing them into two groups? The
criterion is the treatment of the Jewish evangelists in the tribulation
(Matthew 25:40, 45). Those among the Gentiles that respond to the
message indicate the genuineness of the response by their treatment of
the messengers. Passiveness and even belligerence toward the Jewish
proclaimers of the kingdom is the attitude of those who have no heart for
the kingdom. None will have any excuse since the gospel will have been
proclaimed to all (Isaiah 24:13-15; Matthew 24:14).

> The King's messengers, immediately before He appears in glory,
> will go forth preaching the gospel of the kingdom everywhere; and
> when the King takes His throne, those that received the gospel of
> the kingdom among the nations are recognized as "sheep," and the
> despisers perish as "goats."[169]

Those Gentiles who accept the message with its messengers will enter
into the kingdom with Israel's remnant (Isaiah 56:3-8; 57:13; Ezekiel
47:22-23). The unbelieving Gentiles will go into eternal punishment.
Thus the kingdom will be initiated with only the righteous inhabiting it.

The relationship which Christ claims to sustain with His brethren in
this discourse is very similar to that of Jehovah and Israel in the Old
Testament (Isaiah 63:9; Zechariah 2:8; cf. Acts 9:4). Since this would be
very evident to the well-instructed Israelite, the King forcibly declares
the greatness of His person. He further states that He would come as the
King sitting on a throne of glory. As Jehovah He is associated with His
people and as the Judge of the universe He decrees righteous judgments.

This whole discourse again reflects the Lord's emphasis on righteousness. It is a righteousness founded in faith in God which in turn, by

166. Peters, *Theocratic Kingdom*, 2:376.
167. Donald Grey Barnhouse, *Romans. Vol. 1: Man's Ruin. God's Wrath.*, 2:38-39.
168. Allen, *Commentary on Matthew*, p. 265; Darby, *Synopsis*, 3:133; Feinberg, *Israel in
the Last Days*, p. 46; Gaebelein, *The Gospel of Matthew*, 2:246-247.
169. William Kelly, *Lectures on Matthew*, p. 485.

God's grace, empowers the whole man to live a new and righteous life.
Genuine faith results in life, and life manifests itself in righteousness.
Thus, works are the evidence of faith. It is on this basis that some shall
enter the kingdom and others shall be condemned. Righteousness involves the whole man. That is why Christ said, "You will know them by
their fruits" (Matthew 7:20).

26:1a. *And it came about that when Jesus had finished all these
words, ...* Kiddle correctly maintains that the climax of Matthew's
argument is reached at Matthew 25:46.[170] Matthew notes this with the
final occurrence of his indication of a change in emphasis, the words
"And it came about when Jesus had finished" (καὶ ἐγένετο ὅτε ἐτέλεσεν ὁ 'Ιησοῦς, 26:1). He has at this point accomplished his main purposes in presenting the credentials of the King and the kingdom program
of the Jews. The King has shown Himself by His words and His works
to be Israel's Messiah. Because Israel refused to accept Him as their
King, the kingdom is taken from them and given to a nation bringing
forth fruit worthy of repentance. However, this situation will exist only
until the Son of Man comes in His glory. At that time, all unrighteous-
ness will be vindicated and Christ shall reign as Israel's King over the
nations of the earth.

170. Kiddle, "Conflict Between the Disciples," p. 44.

VII. The Crucifixion and the Resurrection of the King (26:1-28:20)
   A. The Crucifixion of the King (26:1-27:66)
      1. The preparation (26:1-26:46)
         a. The setting (26:1-26:5)
         b. The anointing at Bethany (26:6-26:13)
         c. The agreement to the betrayal (26:14-26:16)
         d. The Passover supper (26:17-26:29)
         e. The prediction of the denials (26:30-26:35)
         f. The agonizing in Gethsemane (26:36-26:46)
      2. The arrest (26:47-26:56)
      3. The trials (26:57-27:26)
         a. Before Caiaphas (26:57-26:68)
         b. The denials of Peter (26:69-26:75)
         c. The remorse of Judas (27:3-27:10)
         d. Before Pilate (27:1-27:2, 27:11-27:26)
      4. The cross (27:27-27:56)
         a. The mocking (27:27-27:31)
         b. The passing of the King (27:32-27:50)
         c. The supernatural occurrences (27:51-27:56)
      5. The burial (27:57-27:66)
         a. The burial by Joseph of Arimathea (27:57-27:61)
         b. The sealing of the tomb (27:62-27:66)

   B. The Resurrection of the King (28:1-28:20)

      1. The empty tomb (28:1-28:10)
      2. The false report (28:11-28:15)
      3. The final instructions of the King (28:16-28:20)

VII. The Crucifixion and the Resurrection of the King

Relentlessly the events of the King's life move toward His death on the cross. He has completed His public manifestation to Israel and the nation has rejected Him. In addition, the disciples have been instructed concerning the rejection of Israel and the spiritual basis of entrance into the earthly kingdom. All that remains is the work of the Messiah to provide the means whereby those who exercise faith in Him may enter His kingdom. This work, the death and resurrection of the King, is recounted very succinctly by Matthew. In a large part Matthew's argument is accomplished, and these last events form a fitting conclusion to his book since Jesus here moves through defeat unto victory.

A. The Crucifixion of the King
26:1-27:66.

1. The Preparation, 26:1-26:46.

Several final events occur in preparation for the passion of Christ. The King is anointed, Judas contracts with the Jewish leaders to betray the Lord, the passover supper with its final instructions to the eleven is observed, and Christ agonizes in prayer in Gethsemane in the shadow of the cross.

a. The Setting, **26:1-26:5.** *And it came about that when Jesus had finished all these words, He said to His disciples, "You know that after two days the Passover is coming, and the Son of Man is to be delivered up for crucifixion." Then the chief priests and the elders of the people were gathered together in the court of the high priest,*

*named Caiaphas; and they plotted together to seize Jesus by stealth,
and kill Him. But they were saying, "Not during the festival, lest a
riot occur among the people."* The setting is one of contrasts. In His
majesty and with all calmness, the King announces that He shall
die on a cross in two days. The contrast is introduced with the word
"then" (τότε) in verse three. At the time Christ was predicting His
death, the leaders were plotting to kill Him. The contrast is seen in their
plans and the Lord's predictions. He said He would be crucified in two
days; they said that they should not take Him during the feast since
Jerusalem would be so crowded with people that a riot could result.

This gathering of the religious leaders emphasizes their terrible condition. In the very place where there should have been justice, there was
lawlessness. The religious leaders come to the spiritual head of Israel
and he promotes their evil deed. What an indictment of the Jewish
religious system Matthew places before his Jewish reader! However, the
people are also to blame. By adding the genitive phrase "of the people"
(τοῦ λαοῦ), Matthew intimates "... that the hostile hierarchy consisted
largely of *representatives* of the people; they were popular leaders and
teachers."[1]

These religious leaders knew they could not take Israel's King by
argument (Matthew 22:46), and they dared not take Him by force
(Matthew 21:46); therefore they had no recourse but deceit if they were
going to put Him out of the way.

b. *The Anointing at Bethany,* **26:6-26:13.** *Now when Jesus was in
Bethany, at the home of Simon the leper, a woman came to Him
with an alabaster vial of very costly perfume, and she poured it
upon His head as He reclined at table. But the disciples were indignant when they saw this, and said, "What is the point of this waste?
For this perfume might have been sold for a high price and the
money given to the poor." But Jesus, aware of this, said to them,
"Why do you bother the woman? For she has done a good deed to
Me. For the poor you have with you always; but you do not always
have Me. For when she poured this perfume upon My body, she did
it to prepare Me for burial. Truly I say to you, wherever this gospel
is preached in the whole world, what this woman has done shall also
be spoken of in memory of her."* At Bethany, a woman whom
Matthew leaves unnamed pours a vial of very costly perfume on Christ's

---

1. Alfred Plummer, *An Exegetical Commentary on the Gospel According to S. Matthew,*
p. 353.

head. Again the incident is marked by a contrast, a contrast between the devotion of the woman and the debased attitude of the disciples. Motivated by her devotion and perhaps by her spiritual insight, she prepares the Lord's body for burial.

  c. The Agreement to the Betrayal, **26:14-26:16.** ***Then one of the twelve, named Judas Iscariot, went to the chief priests, and said, "What are you willing to give me to deliver Him up to you?" And they weighed out to him thirty pieces of silver. And from then on he began looking for a good opportunity to betray Him.*** Matthew employs his characteristic adverb "then" (τότε) to introduce the account of Judas' contract with the high priests to betray Christ. Although τότε is sometimes used by Matthew to mark off one event from another, it seems as though it is used here to indicate that the rebuke of the Lord was the occasion for the action of Judas described here.[2]

  In describing the transaction, Matthew uses the words of Zechariah 11:12. He does not here refer to the thirty pieces of silver as being the fulfillment of prophecy, but he is very precise in quoting it nevertheless. This Matthew does with a purpose.

> Mt. (26:15) of course does not *quote* this, using the Hebrew words of the original, nor does he refer to the prophecy; but in here preparing the way for the real quotation, which comes in 27:9f., he is concerned to make the verbal correspondence with scripture as close as possible ... That the money was delivered to Judas then and there is neither said nor necessarily implied, and Mt.'s concern was only with the correspondence.[3]

  What a picture Matthew portrays of Judas! Moses' law declared that thirty pieces of silver were the compensation for a slave gored to death by an ox (Exodus 21:32). The spiritual blindness of Judas Iscariot was such that he sold the Messiah of Israel for the price of a common slave that could be purchased any day.

  d. The Passover Supper, 26:17-26:29. At the Passover supper, two startling revelations are made: one of the twelve disciples was going to betray Christ and the Lord reveals His relationship to the new covenant prophesied in the Old Testament.

---

  2. Alan Hugh M'Neile, *The Gospel According to St. Matthew,* p. 376; Plummer, *Exegetical Commentary,* p. 356.
  3. Charles C. Torrey, "The Foundry of the Second Temple at Jerusalem," *Journal of Biblical Literature* 55 (December 1936): 249.

26:17-26:19. *Now on the first day of the Feast of Unleavened Bread the disciples came to Jesus, saying, "Where do You want us to prepare for You to eat the Passover?" And He said, "Go into the city to a certain man, and say to him, 'The Teacher says, "My time is at hand; I am to keep the Passover at your house with My disciples."' And the disciples did as Jesus had directed them; and they prepared the Passover.* The place where the little band was going to observe the supper was not revealed by the King. This secrecy was a necessity. Had Judas known beforehand where Jesus with His disciples was going to observe the Passover meal, it is very probable that the traitor would have disclosed it to the religious leaders.

26:20-26:25. *Now when evening had come, He was reclining at table with the twelve disciples. And as they were eating, He said, "Truly I say to you that one of you will betray Me." And being deeply grieved, they each one began to say to Him, "Surely not I, Lord?" And He answered and said, "He who dipped his hand with Me in the bowl is the one who will betray Me. The Son of Man is to go, just as it is written of Him; but woe to that man through whom the Son of Man is betrayed! It would have been good for that man if he had not been born." And Judas, who was betraying Him, answered and said, "Surely it is not I, Rabbi?" He said to him, "You have said it yourself."* While they were eating the supper, Christ made an outstanding announcement. One of the twelve was going to betray Him. The disciples had heard previously His predictions concerning His death and resurrection, but this horrible truth of betrayal was completely new. For the fulfillment of prophecy the King sees the necessity for His death, but woe to the man who betrays Him. Finally, Judas asks the Lord, "Surely it is not I, Rabbi?" In calling Jesus "Rabbi" ($\rho\alpha\beta\beta\acute{\iota}$), Judas used a different word from "Lord" ($K\acute{\upsilon}\rho\iota\epsilon$), the title employed by the eleven. The address used by the eleven at this time may mean "divine Lord;" to Judas Christ is but a rabbi.[4] In reply to the question of Judas the Lord states "You have said it yourself" ($\sigma\grave{\upsilon}\ \epsilon\grave{\iota}\pi\alpha\varsigma$). This is clearly a restrained affirmation.[5]

26:26. *And while they were eating, Jesus took some bread, and after a blessing, He broke it and gave it to the disciples, and said, "Take, eat; this is My body."* The second revelation which the Lord Jesus makes at the supper concerns His relationship to the new cove-

---

4. R. C. H. Lenski, *The Interpretation of St. Matthew's Gospel*, p. 1019.

5. A. Carr, *The Gospel According to St. Matthew*, p. 290; Gustaf Dalman, *The Words of Jesus;* M'Neile, *St. Matthew*, p. 381; Plummer, *Exegetical Commentary*, p. 361.

nant. While they were eating, Jesus, having taken bread and blessed it, broke it and gave it to His disciples saying, "Take, eat; this is My body." This act of the Lord had great significance although the disciples could have had only a very cloudy perspective of it at this time. The Israelites partook of the Passover lamb in remembrance of God's preservation of Israel's firstborn. That preservation occurred in Egypt by means of the death of a lamb for each Jewish family. As the lamb's blood applied to the doorposts preserved life, so the death of Christ's body would bring salvation to those who believed on Him. The partaking of the broken bread was to remind the disciples of that fact.

26:27-26:28. *And He took a cup and gave thanks, and gave it to them, saying, "Drink from it, all of you; for this is My blood of the covenant, which is to be shed on behalf of many for forgiveness of sins."* After the King had given thanks for the cup, He gave it to the disciples saying, "Drink from it, all of you; for this is My blood of the covenant, which is to be shed on behalf of many for forgiveness of sins." The significance of the covenant spoken of here has been debated by many. In order for one to properly understand these verses, certain basic facts must be understood. The first of these is the meaning of the word "covenant" (διαθήκη). While it can mean *testament* in the sense of a will, it is better to take it to mean *covenant*. In fact, Lightfoot contends that it is never found in any other sense in the New Testament except in Hebrews 9:15-17 which he calls an exceptional case.[6] It is probable that even the Hebrews 9 passage should be considered as referring to a covenant. Furthermore, διαθήκη is the Greek equivalent of the Hebrew word which usually has the sense of a covenant.[7] The meaning *covenant* here is also indicated by the fact that *testament* does not fit the context as well.

But this raises a question. To what covenant does Christ refer by these famous words? It seems that the King is looking back to the prophesied new covenant also known as the everlasting covenant and the covenant of peace (Jeremiah 31:31-34; 32:37-40; Ezekiel 34:25-31; 37:26-28). This is what would immediately flash into the mind of the average Jew. In fact, it could refer to no other covenant since no other covenant was still unconfirmed. The remission of sins pointed out here is one of the tenets of the new covenant which indicates Jeremiah's prophesied covenant was the covenant under consideration in Matthew 26.

6. J. B. Lightfoot, *The Epistle of St. Paul to the Galatians,* p. 141.
7. Marvin R. Vincent, *Word Studies in the New Testament,* 1:138.

Finally, Luke in the parallel passage uses the words "the new covenant" (ἡ καινὴ διαθήκη). The Lord is therefore inaugurating the new covenant to replace the old worn out Mosaic covenant. The words spoken by the Lord Jesus are very close to those spoken by Moses at Sinai. M'Neile comments, "The reference is to Exod. xxiv. 4-8, ἰδοὺ τὸ αἷμα τῆς διαθήκης, [behold the blood of the covenant], the inauguration of God's covenant with Israel at Sinai."[8] It is evident therefore that the King is speaking of His death as being the means of establishing the prophesied new covenant.

The new covenant prophesied in the Old Testament has some very definite provisions. It is clearly and definitely made with the nation of Israel exclusively.

> It is given to *"the house of Israel and the house of Judah,"* which, as all commentators admit (however they may afterward spiritualize), in its literal aspect denotes the Jewish people. It is *the same* people, too, that were "scattered," "plucked up," "destroyed," and "afflicted," who shall be restored to their "land" and "cities."[9]

The provisions of this covenant are the following: regeneration (Jeremiah 31:33), forgiveness of sins (Jeremiah 31:34), spiritual blessings (Jeremiah 31:34; 32:38-40), the regathering of Israel (Jeremiah 32:37), God's everlasting presence with Israel in His sanctuary (Ezekiel 37:26-28), an everlasting covenant (Jeremiah 32:40; Ezekiel 37:26), and safety and prosperity in the land (Jeremiah 32:37; Ezekiel 34:25-31). It can be seen that these elements of the new covenant pertain to Israel in the kingdom age.

The relationship of Christ's blood to the new covenant is stated very definitely by the Lord. His blood is the basis of it since it is shed on behalf of many for forgiveness of sins. The word "many" (πολλῶν) of verse twenty-eight looks back to the words spoken by the King in Matthew 20:28 and anticipates the command of Christ to His disciples to make disciples of every nation (Matthew 28:19). In addition, the blood of Christ ratifies the new covenant (Exodus 24:8).[10]

When all these facts are analyzed, a very crucial problem takes shape. If the new covenant is with Israel and pertains to the kingdom age, what

---

8. M'Neile, *St. Matthew*, p. 382.

9. George N. H. Peters, *The Theocratic Kingdom of Our Lord Jesus, the Christ, as Covenanted in the Old Testament, and Presented in the New Testament*, 1:322.

10. Plummer, *Exegetical Commentary*, p. 364.

relationship does Christ's ratification of it have to do with the present church age? This problem is answered in four general ways.

The amillennialist generally contends that the New Testament church simply takes the place of the Israel of the Old Testament. The promises given to Israel find their fulfillment in the church. Therefore, the new covenant prophesied in the Old Testament is fulfilled completely in the church. Thus Carr asserts, "The Mediator of the New Covenant is ratifying it with the Princes of the New Israel."[11] The error of this position is very evident. The church simply does not fulfill the promises given to Israel in the new covenant. It does not dwell in peace and safety in the land of Palestine. The covenant was made with Israel and it must find its ultimate fulfillment in that nation.

Some premillennialists contend that the new covenant is with Israel only and has no relationship to the church.

> The new covenant is founded on the blood here drunk in figure. The old was done away. Blood was required to establish the new. At the same time the covenant itself was not established; but everything was done on God's part. The blood was not shed to give force to a covenant of judgment like the first: it was shed for those who received Jesus, while waiting for the time when the covenant itself would be established with Israel in grace.[12]

However, to assert that there is one new covenant with Israel only having no relationship to the church is erroneous for several reasons. First, Paul in 2 Corinthians 3:6 clearly states that he is a minister of a new covenant. It is certain that his ministry was not confined to Israel only. He was the minister of a new covenant then in effect which was applicable in the church to Jew and Gentile alike. Second, in 1 Corinthians 11:25, Paul quotes the Lord in saying, "This cup is the new covenant in My blood." Therefore, the new covenant must be in effect today, and it must sustain some relationship to the church. Third, advocates of the view that there is one covenant only with one application to Israel argue that Jeremiah 31 is addressed to the Jews. This is true. However, this does not hinder the possibility of participation of the church in its blessings. The church will enjoy the blessings of the kingdom, but there is no hint in the Old Testament of such a group participating in it. The very fact that the church was unknown to the Old Testament prophets made it impossible for them to prophesy concerning the relationship of

11. Carr, *St. Matthew*, p. 291.
12. J. N. Darby, *Synopsis of the Books of the Bible*, 3:281; cf. L. Laurenson, *Messiah, the Prince*, pp. 187-88.

the church to the new covenant. Finally, in Hebrews 8:6 and 9:15, Christ is said to be the mediator of a new and better covenant now. If His mediatorship is present, then the covenant upon which His mediatorship is based must be present.

Other premillennialists believe there are two new covenants, one to be made with Israel in the kingdom age and one made with the church.[13] This view also has difficulty in reconciling two new covenants with New Testament revelation. For instance, Hebrews 8:8-12 is a quotation of Jeremiah 31:31-34, a prophecy of Israel's new covenant. This Jewish covenant is made the basis of the appeal which the writer of Hebrews makes to Christian experience in Hebrews 10:15-17. If this covenant spoken of in Jeremiah finds fulfillment only in the millennium, then the writer of Hebrews has erred in applying it to believers in the church.[14] Second, there is no basis in the New Testament for the idea of two separate and distinct new covenants. Paul was clear in his delineation between the church and Israel in God's program (Romans 9-11). Why then would he not have been specific in pointing out the difference between two new covenants? Third, to make two new covenants tends to engender confusion where confusion is unnecessary.

A fourth position is more tenable. It asserts that the new covenant was made with Israel and will ultimately find its fulfillment in that nation, but in the meantime the church enters into certain blessings of the new covenant.[15] This is evident for several reasons. First, a new covenant is in effect now (2 Corinthians 3:6; Galatians 4:21-31; Hebrews 8:6; 9:15). It must therefore sustain some sort of relationship to the church. Second, the church is not the fulfillment of all of the promises of the new covenant. It is not being regathered to Palestine and dwelling there in peace, prosperity, and safety. It must be concluded, therefore, that the church benefits from certain spiritual blessings of the new covenant such as regeneration and the forgiveness of sins, but all the blessings will be Israel's as manifested in the future earthly kingdom. It was impossible for the Old Testament prophets to predict the relationship of the church to the new covenant since the church was unknown to them (Ephesians 3:1-13). Since the King has provided the basis of establishing the new covenant with Israel, it is very possible for some of the spiritual

13. Lewis Sperry Chafer, *Systematic Theology,* 4:325; Charles Caldwell Ryrie, *The Basis of the Premillennial Faith,* pp. 115-25; John F. Walvoord, "The New Covenant With Israel," *Bibliotheca Sacra* 110 (July 1953): 203-204.

14. Bernard Ramm, *Protestant Biblical Interpretation,* p. 264.

15. William Kelly, *Lectures on the Gospel of Matthew,* p. 491; C. I. Scofield, ed., *The Scofield Reference Bible,* pp. 1297-98, note.

benefits to be available in the church age. The church's relationship to the new covenant is parallel in certain respects to its connection with the kingdom promises of Israel. The church is constituted, blessed, and directed by the same Person who shall bring about the literal Jewish kingdom. It also will reign with Christ during the millennial age. In a parallel manner, the church participates in the benefits of the new covenant. Therefore, in instituting the new covenant, Christ makes provision for this covenant to include the present program of the church as well as the future age of Israel.

26:29. *"But I say to you, I will not drink of this fruit of the vine from now on until that day when I drink it new with you in my Father's kingdom."* Verse twenty-nine is important for several reasons. It indicates that the death of the Lord is very near.[16] It also points to a definite eschatological program. Allen writes, "The words are striking and unexpected. They seem to be a solemn farewell. But instead of a promise of a future return, we have this allusion to the joys of the Messianic kingdom."[17]

The new wine pictures the joy of the kingdom very well. "And the wine symbolizes the joy is 'new' ($\kappa\alpha\iota\nu\acute{o}\nu$), because everything in the Kingdom is new (Rev. iii. 12, v. 9, xxi. 1, 5)," writes Plummer.[18] He goes on to say, "It will be joy transformed and glorified; joy so different from the joys experienced here that the heart of man cannot conceive it."[19] By these words, the Lord looks forward to the time when the kingdom will be on earth. Finally, by these words the Lord indicates that the disciples are to live and labor in anticipation of seeing the Messiah with them in God's millennial kingdom.

e. The Prediction of the Denials, **26:30-26:35.** *And after singing a hymn, they went out to the Mount of Olives.*

Then Jesus said to them, "You will all fall away because of Me this night, for it is written, 'I will strike down the shepherd, and the sheep of the flock shall be scattered.' But after I have been raised, I will go before you to Galilee." But Peter answered and said to Him, "Even though all may fall away because of you, I will never fall away." Jesus said to him, "Truly I say to you that this very night, before a cock crows, you shall deny Me three times." Peter said to

---

16. M'Neile, *St. Matthew,* p. 383.
17. Willoughby C. Allen, *A Critical and Exegetical Commentary on the Gospel According to S. Matthew,* p. 277.
18. Plummer, *Exegetical Commentary,* p. 365.
19. Ibid.

*Him, "Even if I must die with You, I will not deny You." All the
disciples said the same thing too.* On the Mount of Olives the Lord
tells His disciples that they all will fall away because of Him that night.
To enforce these words the King quotes Zechariah 13:7. "It sets forth the
general principle, soon to be so sadly illustrated by the conduct of the
Apostles, that the striking down of the shepherd means the scattering of
the sheep."[20] The Messiah goes on to encourage them, however, by
telling them that He would be raised again and would go before them
into Galilee. But Peter, refusing to accept his place as a sheep in the
flock, impetuously declares his total allegiance. The King once again
points out the weakness of the flesh by prophesying a threefold denial
within a few hours. Peter still refuses to accept this and reaffirms his
allegiance. The remainder of the disciples concur with Peter.

   f. The Agonizing in Gethsemane, **26:36-26:46.** *Then Jesus came
with them to a place called Gethsemane, and said to His disciples,
"Sit here while I go over there and pray." And He took with Him
Peter and the two sons of Zebedee, and began to be grieved and
distressed. Then He said to them, "My soul is deeply grieved, to the
point of death; remain here and keep watch with Me." And He went
a little beyond them, and fell on His face and prayed, saying, "My
Father, if it is possible, let this cup pass from Me; yet not as I will,
but as Thou wilt." And He came to the disciples and found them
sleeping, and said to Peter, "So, you men could not keep watch with
Me for one hour? Keep watching and praying, that you may not
enter into temptation; the spirit is willing, but the flesh is weak." He
went away again a second time and prayed, saying, "My Father, if
this cannot pass away unless I drink it, Thy will be done." And He
came back and found them sleeping, for their eyes were heavy. And
He left them again, and went away and prayed a third time, saying
the same thing once more. Then He came to the disciples, and said
to them, "Are you still sleeping and taking your rest? Behold, the
hour is at hand and the Son of Man is being betrayed into the hands
of sinners. Arise, let us be going; behold, the one who betrays Me is
at hand!"* The Evangelist introduces a sharp contrast to the preceding
with the word "then" (τότε). Immediately following the confident
boasting of Peter and the disciples, Christ is seen as being conscious of

20. Ibid., p. 367.

the weakness of His humanity.[21] But even as He agonizes in prayer to His Father for the will of the Father to be accomplished, the disciples fail to stay awake and watch.

In this passage Matthew lays great stress on the anguish of the King. He begins to be sorrowful and is deeply troubled. The verb "to be distressed" (ἀδημονέω) is of doubtful derivation but came to imply "... a restless, distracted, shrinking from some trouble, or thought of trouble, which nevertheless cannot be escaped."[22] In addition His soul is "grieved" (περίλυπος). In His prayer, His sorrow is so great that He addresses His Father with "My Father" (πάτερ μου) instead of His usual "Father" (πάτερ).

In the whole time of prayer, He is progressively more aware of the sufferings which are ahead of Him. In His first petition the condition is positive (verse thirty-nine), but in the second it is negative (verse forty-two). "The second prayer, as given by Mt., shews an advance upon the first, as though the Lord had steeled Himself to realize that the cup could not pass from Him."[23] Finally, He boldly asserts, "Let us be going" (ἄγωμεν, verse forty-six). This has been misunderstood to mean, "Let us flee." However, Plummer is correct in affirming, "The meaning is 'Let us go to meet this peril' (Jn. xviii. 4). His hour is come, and He is anxious to fulfill all that is required of Him."[24]

2. The Arrest, 26:47-26:56.

26:47-26:56. *And while He was still speaking, behold, Judas, one of the twelve, came up, accompanied by a great multitude with swords and clubs, from the chief priests and elders of the people. Now he who was betraying Him gave them a sign, saying, "Whomever I shall kiss, He is the one; seize Him." And immediately he came to Jesus and said, "Hail, Rabbi;" and kissed Him. And Jesus said to him, "Friend, do what you have come for." Then they came and laid hands on Jesus and seized Him. And behold, one of those who were with Jesus reached and drew out his sword, and struck the slave of the high priest, and cut off his ear. Then Jesus said to him, "Put your sword back into its place; for all those who take up the sword shall perish by the sword. Or do you think that I*

21. Ibid., p. 368.
22. M'Neile, *St. Matthew*, p. 389.
23. Ibid., p. 392.
24. Plummer, *Exegetical Commentary*, p. 372.

cannot appeal to My Father, and He will at once put at My disposal more than twelve legions of angels? How then shall the Scriptures be fulfilled, that it must happen this way?" At that time Jesus said to the multitudes, "Have you come out with swords and clubs to arrest Me as though I were a robber? Every day I used to sit in the temple teaching and you did not seize Me. But all this has taken place that the Scriptures of the prophets may be fulfilled." Then all the disciples left Him and fled.

The betrayal and arrest of Jesus is now recorded. When Judas betrays Jesus with a kiss, a zealous disciple severs the ear from the high priest's servant. Christ assumes complete command of the situation and reproves His rash defender. If it were the Father's will for the Messiah not to suffer, He could bid twelve legions of angelic beings to His aid. "It is characteristic of this gospel that the authority and kingly majesty of Jesus should be suggested at a moment when every hope seemed to have perished."[25] The Lord not only reprimands His disciple, but He also reproves the crowd which is taking Him. Even in His arrest Jesus is King.

But "all this" (τοῦτο ὅλον) came to pass that the Old Testament Scriptures might be fulfilled. This factor is so important that attention is drawn to it twice (verses fifty-four and fifty-six). The fulfillment of prophecy is imperative to One who is the Messiah.

3. The Trials, 26:57-27:26.

   a. Before Caiaphas, **26:57-26:68.** *And those who had seized Jesus led Him away to Caiaphas, the high priest, where the scribes and the elders were gathered together. But Peter also followed Him at a distance as far as the courtyard of the high priest, and entered in, and sat down with the officers to see the outcome. Now the chief priests and the whole Council kept trying to obtain false testimony against Jesus, in order that they might put Him to death; and they did not find it, even though many false witnesses came forward. But later on two came forward, and said, "This man stated, 'I am able to destroy the temple of God and to rebuild it in three days.'" And the high priest stood up and said to Him, "Do You make no answer? What is it that these men are testifying against You?" But Jesus kept silent. And the high priest said to Him, "I adjure You by the living*

25. Carr, *St. Matthew*, p. 295.

*God, that You tell us whether You are the Christ, the Son of God."
Jesus said to him, "You have said it yourself; nevertheless I tell you,
hereafter you shall see the Son of Man sitting at the right hand of
Power, and coming on the clouds of heaven." Then the high priest
tore his robes, saying, "He has blasphemed! What further need do
we have of witnesses? Behold, you have now heard the blasphemy;
what do you think?" They answered and said, "He is deserving of
death!" Then they spat in His face and beat Him with their fists,
and others slapped Him, and said, "Prophesy to us, You Christ;
who is the one who hit You?"* The righteousness of Christ is emphasized by the injustice of His trials. One of the outstanding factors of the
Jewish trial before Caiaphas is its illegal character.

> ... even the ordinary legal rules were disregarded in the following
> particulars: (a) The examination by Annas without witnesses. (b)
> The trial by night. (c) The sentence on the first day of trial. (d) The
> trial of a capital charge on the day before the Sabbath. (e) The
> suborning of witnesses. (f) The direct interrogation by the High
> Priest.[26]

This trial was but a farce acknowledging the decision which Israel had
reached long before.

In his record of this trial Matthew emphasizes a second factor, the
greatness of Jesus Christ. This is indicated first by the fact that the
religious leaders could find no fault in Him even when they resorted to
false witnesses. Second, His composure and silence attested the holiness of His person. M'Neile notes, "His silence condemned judge and
witness alike ..."[27] Third, Jesus clearly affirms that He is the Messiah,
the Son of God. By the use of testimony the high priest forced a reply
from the Lord.[28] The affirmative reply which the Lord gives in answer
to the high priest's adjuration means Jesus *swears* that He is no less than
the Son of God.[29] Fourth, the King declares that in the future, He will be
manifested in the glory of Israel's Messiah coming to earth to reign. He
affirms, "Hereafter you shall see the Son of Man sitting at the right hand
of Power, and coming on the clouds of heaven."

---

26. Ibid., p. 297; cf. John James Maclaren, "Jesus Christ, Arrest and Trial Of," *The
International Standard Bible Encyclopaedia*, 3:1671-1672.
27. M'Neile, *St. Matthew*, p. 400.
28. Frank Morison, *Who Moved the Stone?*, pp. 25-26.
29. Lenski, *Interpretation of Matthew*, p. 1064.

The unmistakable reference here was to a pair of the greatest Kingdom prophecies of the Old Testament, Psalm 110:1 and Daniel 7:13, and Christ applied them to Himself ... The high priest, better schooled than some theologians, understood his regal claim, rent his clothing judicially, and called upon his fellow judges to pronounce Him "guilty of death" (Matt. 26:66).[30]

b. The Denials of Peter, **26:69-26:75.** *Now Peter was sitting outside in the courtyard, and a certain servant-girl came to him and said, "You too were with Jesus the Galilean." But he denied it before them all, saying, "I do not know what you are talking about." And when he had gone out to the gateway, another servant-girl saw him and said to those who were there, "This man was with Jesus of Nazareth." And again he denied it with an oath, "I do not know the man." And a little later the bystanders came up and said to Peter, "Surely you too are one of them; for the way you talk gives you away." Then he began to curse and swear, "I do not know the man!" And immediately a cock crowed. And Peter remembered the word which Jesus had said, "Before a cock crows, you will deny Me three times." And he went out and wept bitterly.* The tragedy of the last hours becomes greater with the complete collapse of Peter's boldness in the flesh. Before the cock sounded its clarion call, Peter had denied his Lord three times just as Christ had predicted.

c. The Remorse of Judas, **27:3-27:10.** *Then when Judas, who had betrayed Him, saw that He had been condemned, he felt remorse and returned the thirty pieces of silver to the chief priests and elders, saying, "I have sinned by betraying innocent blood." But they said, "What is that to us? See to that yourself!" And he threw the pieces of silver into the sanctuary and departed; and he went away and hanged himself. And the chief priests took the pieces of silver and said, "It is not lawful to put them into the temple treasury, since it is the price of blood." And they counseled together and with the money bought the Potter's Field as a burial place for strangers. For this reason that field has been called the Field of Blood to this day. Then that which was spoken through Jeremiah the prophet was fulfilled, saying, "And they took the thirty pieces of silver, the price of the one whose price had been set by the sons of Israel; and they gave them for the Potter's Field, as the Lord directed me."* At the birth of Jesus, Joseph wondered (Matthew 1:19); in

30. Alva J. McClain, *The Greatness of the Kingdom,* p. 380.

the midst of Christ's ministry, John the Baptist doubted (Matthew 11:2-3); at the time of His death, Peter denies Him; but these three in contrast to Judas are divinely aided to exercise a deeper faith in Christ. In sharp contrast to Peter's bitter sorrow, Judas, beyond spiritual help, is filled with fatal remorse. Having cast his money into the temple, he departs and hangs himself. It must be remembered that the verb translated "to feel remorse" (μεταμέλομαι) is to be distinguished from the verb translated "to repent" (μετανοέω). The former does not indicate ". . . sorrow for moral obliquity and sin against God, but annoyance at the consequences of an act or course of acts, and chagrin at not having known better."[31] The remorse of Judas at seeing Christ led away to Pilate attests the holy character of Jesus.

The importance of Judas' act of remorse and the subsequent purchase of the potter's field is found in the fulfillment of prophecy. To the last bitter detail, the path of the Messiah's life was foretold by the prophets centuries before.[32]

d. Before Pilate, 27:1-27:2, 27:11-27:26. Now when morning had come, all the chief priests and the elders of the people took counsel against Jesus to put Him to death; and they bound Him, and led Him away, and delivered Him up to Pilate the governor.

Now Jesus stood before the governor, and the governor questioned Him, saying, "Are you the King of the Jews?" And Jesus said to him, "It is as you say." And while He was being accused by the chief priests and elders, He made no answer. Then Pilate said to Him, "Do You not hear how many things they testify against You?" And He did not answer him with regard to even a single charge, so that the governor was quite amazed. Now at the feast the governor was accustomed to release for the multitude any one prisoner whom they wanted. And they were holding at that time a notorious prisoner, called Barabbas. When therefore they were gathered together, Pilate said to them, "Whom do you want me to release for you? Barabbas, or Jesus who is called Christ?" For he knew that because of envy they had delivered Him up. And while he was sitting on the judgment-seat, his wife sent to him, saying, "Have nothing to do with that righteous Man; for last night I suffered greatly in a dream because of Him." But the chief priests and the elders persuaded the

31. Vincent, *Word Studies*, 1:117.
32. For the exegetical difficulty met in verse nine and its allusion to Jeremiah, see Charles L. Feinberg, *God Remembers*, pp. 167-169.

multitudes to ask for Barabbas, and to put Jesus to death. But the
governor answered and said to them, "Which of the two do you
want me to release for you?" And they said, "Barabbas." Pilate
said to them, "What then shall I do with Jesus who is called
Christ?" They all said, "Let Him be crucified!" And he said, "Why,
what evil has He done?" But they kept shouting all the more, say-
ing, "Let Him be crucified!" And when Pilate saw that he was
accomplishing nothing, but rather that a riot was starting, he took
water and washed his hands in front of the multitude, saying, "I am
innocent of this Man's blood; see to that yourselves." And all the
people answered and said, "His blood be on us and on our chil-
dren!" Then he released Barabbas for them; but Jesus he scourged
and delivered over to be crucified. The charge against Jesus before
Caiaphas was religious in nature; in Pilate's court the charge is political.
This was the intention of the Jews. The political aspect is further emphasized by the introduction of the title "the King of the Jews" (ὁ
βασιλεὺς τῶν Ἰουδαίων), a title which has not been used in Matthew
since the account of the King's infancy (Matthew 2:2). The significance
of the King's reply to the question of the procurator is great. It indicates
clearly the nature of Christ's kingdom. The charge that Jesus claimed to
be the King of the Jews probably originated from Israel's leaders. When
Pilate therefore asks Jesus if the charge of regal claims is true, it carries
with it all the implications of the prophesied Jewish kingdom and the
King answers accordingly. Since Jesus answers in the affirmative, He
thereby lays claim to being the promised Jewish Messiah and King.

Not only is the political aspect of the trial emphasized, the guilt of the
people of Israel is also set forward. Matthew first quietly intimates their
sin with the genitive form "of the people" (τοῦ λαοῦ, Matthew 26:3,
47; 27:1). But now he shows how the fickle and blind people actively
turn against their King at the behest of their hypocritical leaders
(Matthew 27:20, 22, 23). Their success in persuading the people is
indicated by the fervor of the mob. Verse twenty-three says "They kept
shouting all the more" (περισσῶς ἔκραζον). The final indication of
the nation's guilt in this passage are the words "all the people" (πᾶς ὁ
λαός) of verse twenty-five. They *all* spoke these dreadful words of
self-condemnation. By replacing the word "multitudes" (ὄχλος) of
verse twenty with the word "people" (λαός), the nation is seen as
invoking this guilt upon itself.[33] The viciousness of their anger could

33. M'Neile, *St. Matthew*, p. 413.

hardly be described more graphically than by this horrible utterance.

As the trial before Caiaphas was distinguished by its illegality, so this examination before Pilate is characterized by its injustice. Pilate knew why Christ had been taken (verse eighteen), but he acted as a weak and vacillating politician and not as a representative of the justice of the Roman government.

4. The Cross, 27:27-27:56.

a. The Mocking, **27:27-27:31.** ***Then the soldiers of the governor took Jesus into the Praetorium and gathered the whole Roman cohort around Him. And they stripped Him, and put a scarlet robe on Him. And after weaving a crown of thorns, they put it on His head, and a reed in His right hand; and they kneeled down before Him and mocked Him, saying, "Hail, King of the Jews!" And they spat on Him, and took the reed and began to beat Him on the head. And after they had mocked Him, they took His robe off and put His garments on Him, and led Him away to crucify Him.*** In the common hall Christ is shamefully mistreated and mocked. Not realizing that the King of the Jews is actually before them, the soldiers of the governor taunt and deride Him. The prophecy recorded in Matthew 20:19 has now been partially fulfilled; the crucifixion fulfills the remainder.

b. The Passing of the King, **27:32-27:50.** ***And as they were coming out, they found a certain Cyrenian named Simon; this man they pressed into service to bear His cross.***

And when they had come to a place called Golgotha, which means Place of a Skull, they gave Him wine to drink mingled with gall; and after tasting it, He was unwilling to drink. And when they had crucified Him, they divided up His garments among themselves, casting lots; and sitting down, they began to keep watch over Him there. And they put up above His head the charge against Him which read, "THIS IS JESUS THE KING OF THE JEWS." At that time two robbers were crucified with Him, one on the right and one on the left. And those who were passing by were hurling abuse at Him, wagging their heads, and saying, "You who destroy the temple and rebuild it in three days, save Yourself! If You are the Son of God, come down from the cross." In the same way the chief priests, along with the scribes and elders, were mocking Him, and saying,

"He saved others; He cannot save Himself. He is the King of Israel; let Him now come down from the cross, and we shall believe in Him. He trusts in God; let Him deliver Him now, if He takes pleasure in Him; for He said, 'I am the Son of God.'" And the robbers also who had been crucified with Him were casting the same insult at Him.

Now from the sixth hour darkness fell upon all the land until the ninth hour. And about the ninth hour Jesus cried out with a loud voice, saying, "Eli, Eli lama sabachthani?" that is, "My God, My God, why hast Thou forsaken Me?" And some of those who were standing there, when they heard it, began saying, "This man is calling for Elijah." And immediately one of them ran, and taking a sponge, he filled it with sour wine, and put it on a reed, and gave Him a drink. But the rest of them said, "Let us see whether Elijah will come to save Him." And Jesus cried out again with a loud voice, and yielded up His spirit. Matthew describes the actual crucifixion very briefly. As far as his argument is concerned, four things stand out. The foremost of these is the fulfillment of prophecy. Matthew does not even once in this passage introduce the prophecy in his usual manner. Rather, he weaves the Old Testament Scripture into his account. To describe the drink offered to Jesus, Matthew uses the words of Psalm 69:21 (verses thirty-four and forty-eight). The division of Christ's garments among the soldiers was forseen in Psalm 22:18 (verse thirty-five). Psalm 22:7 is employed to describe the mockery of the people (verse thirty-nine). Their very words were prophesied in Psalm 22:8 (verse forty-three). Finally, the cry of Christ to His Father was spoken in Psalm 22:1 (verse forty-six). There may also be an allusion to Isaiah 53:12 in the fact that the Lord was crucified between two robbers (verse thirty-eight). Although Matthew does not employ his usual formula, the words would be so familiar to the average Israelite that such a formula would be unnecessary at this point.

The second significant factor which stands out is the extreme mockery. Christ is blasphemed by the mob (Matthew 27:39-40, 49), by the religious leaders (Matthew 27:41-43), and even by the thieves (Matthew 27:44).

The superscription is the third important fact. "This is Jesus the King of the Jews" is actually the theme of the book, though it here is used in sheer derision. The scoffers blindly state in mockery what they shall one day acknowledge in truth, Jesus is the King of Israel.

The final significant factor is the manner in which Matthew emphasizes the fact that the death of Jesus was a voluntary laying down of His

life. Jesus dismissed His spirit. To describe this act Matthew employs
the aorist active of the verb "to give up or yield" (ἀφῆκεν). The King's
authority is manifested even in His dying breath.

    c. The Supernatural Occurrences, 27:51-27:56. **27:51-27:53.** *And*
behold, the veil of the temple was torn in two from top to bottom,
and the earth shook; and the rocks were split, and the tombs were
opened; and many bodies of the saints who had fallen asleep were
raised; and coming out of the tombs after His resurrection they
entered the holy city and appeared to many. The divine implications
of the crucifixion of Christ are attested by the supernatural occurrences
accompanying it. The miraculous darkness attested the awfulness of the
crucifixion (verse forty-five). In the rending of the veil of the temple
God indicated that by Christ's death a new and living way of access had
been given (Matthew 27:51; Hebrews 6:19; 9:1-14; 10:19-22). This miracle also pointed out very forcibly that the efficacy of Christ's blood had
abrogated the old Jewish system. The earthquake and the splitting of
"the rocks" (αἱ πέτραι) attested the greatness of the One who was
being crucified (verse fifty-one). Finally, the opening of the graves and
the appearance in the holy city of the dead saints who had arisen affirmed that the King had authority over life and death.

    27:54. *Now the centurion, and those who were with him keeping*
guard over Jesus, when they saw the earthquake and the things that
were happening, became very frightened and said, "Truly this was
the Son of God!" Because of the earthquake and the other circumstances attending the crucifixion, the Gentiles acknowledge the supernatural character of the Crucified One. This is a further indictment of
stubborn Israel.

    27:55-27:56. *And many women were there looking on from a*
distance, who had followed Jesus from Galilee, ministering to Him;
among whom was Mary Magdalene, along with Mary the mother of
James and Joseph, and the mother of the sons of Zebedee. The only
ones that Matthew records to have in any way identified themselves
with Christ in this dark hour are some women from Galilee who had
ministered to Him. This is a further indictment of the frightened disciples.

5. The Burial, 27:57-27:66.

    a. The Burial by Joseph of Arimathea, **27:57-27:61.** *And when it*
was evening, there came a rich man from Arimathea, named

Joseph, who himself had also become a disciple of Jesus. This man came to Pilate and asked for the body of Jesus. Then Pilate ordered it to be given over to him. And Joseph took the body and wrapped it in a clean linen cloth, and laid it in his own new tomb, which he had hewn out in the rock; and he rolled a large stone against the entrance of the tomb and went away. And Mary Magdalene was there, and the other Mary, sitting opposite the grave. Isaiah 53:9 is fulfilled in the burial of Jesus in the tomb of Joseph of Arimathea. Matthew stresses the fact that Joseph is a rich man by the emphatic position of πλούσιος. Having rolled a huge stone in front of the door of the tomb, Joseph departs leaving two mourning women sitting nearby in quiet reverence.

   b. The Sealing of the Tomb, 27:62-27:66. Now on the next day, which is the one after the preparation, the chief priests and the Pharisees gathered together with Pilate, and said, "Sir, we remember that when he was still alive that deceiver said, 'After three days I am to rise again.' Therefore, give orders for the grave to be made secure until the third day, lest the disciples come and steal Him away and say to the people, 'He has risen from the dead,' and the last deception will be worse than the first." Pilate said to them, "You have a guard; go, make it as secure as you know how." And they went and made the grave secure, and along with the guard they set a seal on the stone. The strange circumstances whereby the tomb was sealed are recorded here. The Evangelist uses this event for two purposes. It underscored in a very special way the corruptness of Israel's leaders and the willfulness of their rejection of Jesus. They went so far as to break the sabbath in order to make provision for sealing the tomb of Him whom they accused of breaking the sacred day. They themselves were deceivers (Matthew 26:4) and hypocrites (Matthew 23), yet they accused the Lord of being a deceiver. Their hatred of the King is revealed by the sneering way in which they refer to Him as "that deceiver" (ἐκεῖνος ὁ πλάνος). Actually, their suspicions of what the disciples would do were indications of what they would do if they were in the same situation as Christ's disciples.

   The second purpose for which this little episode is recorded is to emphasize the security of the tomb. The tomb was hewn out of solid rock (verse sixty). The word used here is not the word used for a "stone" (πέτρος) but the word used for a mass of rock (πέτρα) (cf. Matthew 16:18). The only exit was the opening of the tomb. The very fact that the Jewish leaders were given authority to seal it as they desired points out the hopelessness of anyone stealing the body. Matthew emphasizes this by using the verb "to make secure" (ἀσφαλίζω) three times and the verb translated "set a seal" (σφραγίζω) once in these few verses. Furthermore, the tomb was guarded by soldiers. That these were Romans is indicated by the word "guard" (κουστωδία) which is a Latin word. It was impossible for the disciples to steal the body. Thus Matthew proves that the only possible way for Christ to leave the tomb was by means of the resurrection. This is the primary purpose for the inclusion of this event in Matthew's Gospel.

B. The Resurrection of the King
28:1-28:20.

1. The Empty Tomb, 28:1-28:10.

28:1-28:10. *Now late on the Sabbath, as it began to dawn toward the first day of the week, Mary Magdalene and the other Mary came to look at the grave. And behold, a severe earthquake had occurred, for an angel of the Lord descended from heaven and came and rolled away the stone and sat upon it. And his appearance was like lightning, and his garment as white as snow; and the guards shook for fear of him, and became like dead men. And the angel answered and said to the women, "Do not be afraid; for I know that you are looking for Jesus who has been crucified. He is not here, for He has risen, just as He said. Come, see the place where He was lying. And go quickly and tell His disciples that He has risen from the dead; and behold, He is going before you into Galilee, there you will see Him; behold, I have told you." And they departed quickly from the tomb with fear and great joy and ran to report it to His disciples. And behold, Jesus met them and greeted them. And they came up and took hold of His feet and worshiped Him. Then Jesus said to them, "Do not be afraid; go and take word to My brethren to leave for Galilee, and there they shall see Me."*
Matthew is very brief in his account of the resurrection, but one thing he emphasizes is the empty tomb. This is attested by several witnesses. The first is an angel of the Lord. In the beginning of the Gospel an angel of the Lord announced the incarnation; here an angel of the Lord pro-

claims the resurrection.[34] The very appearance of the latter angel was heralded by an earthquake. The second group of witnesses to the empty tomb were the soldiers who certainly must have given an unwilling testimony. The third group are the women who declared it to the disciples. The fourth group who attest the fact of an empty tomb are the religious leaders. Their very actions indicate this. M'Neile comments that the "... Jews, no less than the Christians, were convinced that the Resurrection involved an empty grave."[35]

2. The False Report, 28:11-28:15.

28:11-28:15. *Now while they were on their way, behold, some of the guard came into the city and reported to the chief priests all that had happened. And when they had assembled with the elders and counseled together, they gave a large sum of money to the soldiers, and said, "You are to say, 'His disciples came by night and stole Him away while we were asleep.' And if this should come to the governor's ears, we will win him over and keep you out of trouble." And they took the money and did as they had been instructed; and this story was widely spread among the Jews, and is to this day.* Matthew's brief account of the resurrection and the King's post resurrection appearances also stress the false report circulated by the soldiers and the religious authorities. This has great apologetic value for Matthew's Gospel. For one thing, it stresses the terrible character of the leaders of Israel. In contrast to the devotion of the two Marys (Matthew 28:1-10), these men resort to lies because they refused to believe (Matthew 28:11-15). Therefore, they are responsible for propagating a lie by bribing the soldiers.

A second apologetic feature is the explanation which this account gives concerning the false report which was commonly circulated among the Jews in Matthew's day. The Evangelist is very careful to defend (1) the virgin birth, and (2) the resurrection. His account of the resurrection, though brief, is tightly woven and provides a good defense of the fact of the Messiah's resurrection.

The reason for Matthew's diligence in approaching the resurrection in such an apologetic manner is evident since so much is dependent upon the resurrection of the Messiah. It authenticated His person. To the

34. Plummer, *Exegetical Commentary*, p. 417.
35. M'Neile, *St. Matthew*, p. 428.

nation of Israel, His resurrection was the sign of the prophet Jonah (Matthew 12:38-39) attesting the fact that Jesus was the Messiah. The reason Matthew says nothing about the ascension is bound up in this point. If Jesus is the Messiah, then an account of the ascension is both unnecessary and self-evident to the Israelite. He would yet come in clouds of glory. What mattered to Matthew was that Jesus was Israel's Messiah and the resurrection proved that fact; therefore he goes no further. Second, the resurrection validated Christ's prophecies concerning His rising from the dead (Matthew 16:21; 17:22-23; 20:17-19). Finally, the message of the King involving the character of the kingdom, the offer of the kingdom, and the offer's withdrawal are all involved in the resurrection, for the resurrection verifies the truthfulness of all that Christ ever spoke.

3. The Final Instructions of the King, 28:16-28:20.

28:16-28:17. *But the eleven disciples proceeded to Galilee, to the mountain which Jesus had designated. And when they saw Him, they worshiped Him; but some were doubtful.* The final instructions of the resurrected King are given to the disciples in Galilee. He has instructed His disciples to meet Him in Galilee for three reasons: (1) Jerusalem rejected its King and is being left to itself. (2) Galilee is the place of the King's ministry in Matthew's Gospel. (3) The King had already prophesied that He would regather them in Galilee (Matthew 26:32).

28:18. *And Jesus came up and spoke to them, saying, "All authority has been given to Me in heaven and on earth."* Matthew concludes this Gospel the way he does with two purposes in mind. One is to present the claims of Christ and the other is to place before the reader the commission of the King. In these final verses, some of the greatest statements are made concerning Jesus Christ. He lays claim to possessing all authority. The aorist form of the verb "to give" ($\dot{\epsilon}\delta\acute{o}\theta\eta$) notes this as already given to Him. The Authorized Version errs in translating $\dot{\epsilon}\xi o\nu\sigma\acute{\iota}\alpha$ as "power." It should be *authority* which is far more inclusive.

> Not merely power or might ($\delta\acute{\upsilon}\nu\alpha\mu\iota\varsigma$), such as a great conqueror might claim, but "*authority*" ($\dot{\epsilon}\xi o\nu\sigma\acute{\iota}\alpha$), as something which is His by right, conferred upon Him by One who has the right to bestow it (Rev. ii. 27).[36]

36. Plummer, *Exegetical Commentary,* p. 428.

This authority is all-inclusive for it is *all* authority in heaven and upon the earth. The fact that this has been conferred on Christ makes possible the answer to the petition of the model prayer, "(Let) thy will be done on earth as it is in heaven" (Matthew 6:10). The coming of the Son of Man as described in Daniel 7:13-14 was now possible.

28:19-28:20. *"Go therefore and make disciples of all the nations, baptizing them in the name of the Father and the Son and the Holy Spirit, teaching them to observe all that I commanded you; and lo, I am with you always, even to the end of the age."* Not only does the Messiah claim to possess all authority, but He also places Himself on an equal level with the Father and the Holy Spirit. He instructs His disciples to baptize into the name of the Father, of the Son, and of the Holy Spirit. Finally, the King claims to be universally present with His own every day of the age (Matthew 28:20).

The second purpose of Matthew in writing this passage was to present the final commission of the King to His disciples. The commission is based on the greatness of the Messiah's person whether the word "therefore" (οὖν) of verse nineteen is accepted as genuine or not.[37] This command is in sharp contrast to what the Lord had previously ordered and practiced (Matthew 10:5-6; 15:24). This can only be explained on the basis of a kingdom offer to Israel. Because of their spiritual condition, the people of Israel had rejected their King and the kingdom was taken from them. Now it was given to another nation, the church.[38]

There has been no little difference of opinion as to the interpretation of Matthew 28:19-20. Some believe that the great commission of Matthew applies to the Jews only.[39] It is associated with the prophecy of Matthew 24:14, and the disciples are made to represent the Jewish remnant of the tribulation period. While it is true that Matthew 24:14 does refer to the tribulation period, there is no need to limit the commission of Matthew 28:19-20 to that future time. This is evident for several reasons.

For one thing, the words "end of the age" (συντελείας αἰῶνος), an expression peculiar to this Gospel, is used by the Lord of the period of time extending from the beginning of the church age to the end of the tribulation period (Matthew 13:39, 40, 49). The commission, therefore, applies to the church as well as to the saints of the tribulation. In

37. M'Neile, *St. Matthew*, p. 435.
38. See above, pp. 251-52.
39. Gaebelein, *The Gospel of Matthew*, 2:323; George Williams, *The Student's Commentary on the Holy Scriptures*, pp. 730-31.

addition, the church is composed of people from all nations. If the disciples are to give the kingdom to a nation (the church) bringing forth its fruits, then they must go to all the nations, including Israel.

Finally, Matthew uses this command to weave the final thread of his argument. The purpose of his Gospel was to prove to Israel that Jesus is the Messiah. The inquiring Jew would ask, "If Jesus is our King, where is our kingdom?" Matthew has indicated that the kingdom was offered to Israel, rejected by them, and postponed by God. At the present time and until the end of the tribulation the kingdom is being offered to the Gentiles (Romans 11). Therefore, the disciples are to disciple all nations. At the end of the age the kingdom of Israel will be inaugurated by the return of Israel's King.

The method which the apostles were to use to disciple the nations is indicated by the two participles of verses nineteen and twenty. The participle "baptizing" ($\beta\alpha\pi\tau\iota\zeta o\nu\tau\epsilon\varsigma$) is a reference to water baptism which is to be a testimony to initial faith in the Messiah. This baptism differs from John's baptism in several particulars.[40] John's baptism was restricted to one nation; this baptism is universal. John's baptism was a preparation for the coming of the Messiah; this baptism is based on the work which the Messiah who came has already accomplished. John's baptism marked an incomplete experience with reference to the Messiah; this baptism indicates a complete position in Christ (Acts 19:1-6; Colossians 2:9-10).

The participle "teaching" ($\delta\iota\delta\acute{\alpha}\sigma\kappa o\nu\tau\epsilon\varsigma$) indicates the second phase of making disciples. The apostles were to teach their converts to observe all things whatsoever Christ had commanded them. The verb "to command" ($\dot{\epsilon}\nu\epsilon\tau\epsilon\iota\lambda\acute{\alpha}\mu\eta\nu$) can refer to two things. It may mean the apostles are to teach everything which Christ had preached and taught during His whole earthly ministry. The word may also be interpreted here in a more restricted sense. Christ could be saying that the disciples were to instruct their converts in a definite course of instruction. The disciples had been commanded previously as to what they were to teach, and the Lord here refers to that. This seems best since the King did not instruct by means of commandments. In addition, the word "whatsoever" ($\acute{o}\sigma\alpha$, 28:20 KJV) restricts the teaching ministry of the disciples to what Christ had commanded them to teach.

Matthew includes the mixed response to the resurrection appearance of Christ so that those who were evangelizing would be encouraged. If

40. Lenski, *Interpretation of Matthew*, p. 1178.

some doubted when the resurrected Christ appeared, there certainly would be many who would not believe the message of the King and His kingdom. So Matthew closes his Gospel with the comforting words, "And lo, I am with you always, even to the end of the age."

Conclusion

Conclusion

I. The Argument Reviewed

The genealogy of Jesus attests His royal lineage; His virgin birth proves that He is God incarnate. Before He is manifested to Israel, the forerunner, John the Baptist, appears. In the ministry of the Baptist, Matthew shows that prophetic Scripture is fulfilled. When Jesus is baptized, He receives divine commendation, and this together with the temptation of the King proves that He is morally qualified to rule. Matthew then proceeds to reveal the King's ability to legislate and to judge by recording the Sermon on the Mount. The power of the King to bring about the kingdom conditions is then indicated by His gracious miracles of healing, power, and restoration. The manifestation of the King's presence and the nearness of the kingdom is further announced throughout Israel by the twelve disciples.

It is soon evident, however, that Israel is not interested in a King who reigns righteously. Controversies arise with regard to the sabbath, the origin of the King's power, and the signs of the King. Because of the opposition to His ministry, the King announces a new development in the kingdom program. This is revealed in parables so that the mysteries of the kingdom may be concealed from the unrepentant.

In the face of continued opposition, the King begins a series of withdrawals and instructs His disciples in preparation for His death on the cross. When it is revealed to the disciples that He is the Messiah, the son of God, He announces that He will build His church on this fact. However, the church does not take Israel's place in the kingdom program for He proves by means of the transfiguration that He will yet reign on earth. The spiritual principles which are to guide the disciples are also set forth in this section. At the "triumphal entry," the King is formally presented to Israel and rejected by that nation. At this point, the Messiah publicly reveals that because of Israel's rejection of its King, the kingdom is taken from them and given to another nation which will bring forth its fruits. On the Mount of Olives the King gives an extended eschatological discourse concerning the end times.

The last portion of the Gospel is an account of the King's passion. In His death many great prophecies are fulfilled, and in His resurrection He gives to the nation of Israel the sign of the prophet Jonah. This section proves that it is the King of the Jews who was crucified and rose again. The final commission of Jesus to His disciples is the command which is to guide His own until He comes again to reign.

II. Why Israel Rejected Its King

One may well ask, "Why did Israel reject its King when He offered Himself and the longed-for kingdom?" Several reasons may be given. One of the main reasons is seen in the fact that Israel refused to acknowledge the prophecies concerning a suffering Messiah and looked only for a glorious leader.[1] A second explanation is found in the unrepentant condition of the Jews. Because Israel would not repent, God could not reveal the fact of the Messiahship of Jesus and other spiritual truths (Matthew 7:6; 11:25; 13:11; 16:17). The high spiritual requirements which Christ set before Israel for entrance into the kingdom may be a third factor (Matthew 5:20; 18:3; 19:23-24).[2] A fourth reason is seen in His scathing denunciation of the ruling classes and the current religious practices (Matthew 5:20; 6:5, 16; 9:12-13; 12:7, 34; 15:1-20; 16:4; 19:3-10; 23:1-39). A final explanation is found in the fact that He associated with sinners (Matthew 9:10-13).[3] In summary, it may be said that because Jesus did not do what Israel wanted Him to do, they refused to have Him as their Messiah (Matthew 11:16-19).

Despite the fact that Israel rejected Jesus, Matthew agrees with Paul that Jesus is Israel's Messiah. Yet the church today by God's mercy enters into the place of blessing (Romans 11:1-36; 15:8-13), and shall reign with Christ in Israel's future glory.

> Jesus shall reign where'er the sun
> Does his successive journeys run;
> His kingdom spread from shore to shore
> Till moons shall wax and wane no more.[4]

1. Donald Grey Barnhouse, *Romans. Vol 1: Man's Ruin. God's Wrath.*, 1:39.
2. Alva J. McClain, *The Greatness of the Kingdom*, p. 383.
3. Ibid.
4. Isaac Watts

Appendix:
Comments on Authorship
and Date

Authorship

The Problems of Authorship

It would be ludicrous to convey the impression that a thorough discussion of the problem of authorship could be presented in this brief appendix. Mountains of books have been written concerning the problem of the authorship of the Synoptic Gospels. In such a discussion as this, one can only briefly outline the problems, sketch a few of the proposed solutions, and then tender a conclusion.

The Problem of the Logia. The first problem concerns the matter of Matthew's Logia. The subject first appears in Papias's statement, "Matthew indeed then collected the oracles in the Hebrew language, and each one interpreted them as he was able."[1] This statement cannot be lightly regarded since Papias lived in the first half of the second century. Because the idea of a Hebrew gospel written by Matthew is confirmed by many of the fathers, a statement of Papias cannot be considered inaccurate. Irenaeus, who died about 155 A.D., confirms this concept. He writes, "Matthew also issued a written gospel among the Hebrews in their own dialect, while Peter and Paul were preaching at Rome, and laying the foundations of the church."[2] As a result of these statements, a problem has plagued New Testament scholars for decades. What happened to Matthew's Logia? Are they related to the Greek Gospel bearing his name? If so, what is the relationship between the Gospel now attributed to Matthew and the Logia?

1. Eusebius, *The Ecclesiastical History,* p. 296.
2. Irenaeus, "Against Heresies," *The Ante-Nicene Fathers,* p. 414.

The Problem of Sources. A second problem concerns the relationship of the Gospel of Matthew to proposed sources, particularly Mark. There is much in Mark that is also contained in Matthew. Wherever Matthew uses the word "immediately" (εὐθύς), it is found in the parallel portion of Mark.[3] "Ninety-two per cent of the Gospel of Mark appears in the Gospel of Matthew ...."[4] Another says, "We find, for example, that the substance of 606 out of the 661 verses of Mark appears in Matthew...."[5] Whenever Mark uses the term *Son of Man,* Matthew also uses it, although Matthew uses it more than Mark.[6]

Another evidence of a rather close relationship is seen in the historical order. Plummer[7] points out that Matthew seems to follow Mark's order, and others agree with this conclusion.

> ... the common order of the three Synoptists is the order of Mark, since Mark and Matthew sometimes agree in order against Luke, and Mark and Luke still more frequently against Matthew, while Matthew and Luke never agree in order against Mark.[8]

Since there is so much common material in Matthew and Mark, a problem confronts the New Testament. What is the relationship of Matthew to Mark? Did Matthew use Mark and other sources such as the proposed Q when he wrote his Greek Gospel?

The Problem of the Writer's Identity. A third problem concerns the writer of the book. Nowhere in the Gospel does the writer identify himself. It is common knowledge that the superscription was not written by the author but was affixed by others for identification. Therefore this cannot be considered a proof of Matthew's authorship. Who then wrote the Gospel? Did the Apostle Matthew write it?

Proposed Solutions to the Problems of Authorship

Since so many questions have been raised concerning the origin of Matthew's Gospel, there has come into being a multiplicity of solutions. A few of the better known and more popular are presented here.

3. Archibald Thomas Robertson, *A Grammar of the Greek New Testament in the Light of Historical Research,* p. 549.

4. Ernest Cadman Colwell, *What is the Best New Testament?,* p. 56.

5. F. F. Bruce, *Are the New Testament Documents Reliable?,* p. 31.

6. Alfred Plummer, *An Exegetical Commentary on the Gospel According to S. Matthew,* p. xxvi.

7. Ibid., p. xviii.

8. Bruce, *New Testament Documents,* p. 34.

Matthew Is the Work of a Later Compiler. A common theory asserts that Matthew wrote the Hebrew Logia and later a compiler translated them into Greek and used them with Mark to write the Gospel now bearing Matthew's name.[9] This view is well defended by Plummer.[10]

On first appearance this theory is very attractive. However, it meets with a serious difficulty: the *Greek* Matthew was quoted very early. Ignatius, the *Didache,* and the *Shepherd of Hermas* all quote from it.[11] They do not say they are quoting Matthew's Gospel, but their quotes coincide more exactly with Matthew than either Mark or Luke.[12] In referring to the early date of the Greek Gospel of Matthew, another writer states, "This work, used by the earliest churchmen whose writing have come down to us, is our Greek Gospel."[13] Since this Greek Gospel was in common circulation at such an early date, it seems very unlikely that a compiler other than Matthew or one of his contemporaries could have performed this work. In addition, the internal evidence favors the idea of Matthean authorship.[14]

Still another factor which militates against the theory of a later compiler is the general agreement among New Testament scholars regarding the unlikelihood of a Greek translation from an Aramaic *(Hebrew)* source.

> The non-Marcan materials of Matthew and Luke came to them from Greek sources; there can be no possible doubt of that, as an hour's examination of the non-Marcan parallels in Matthew and Luke will show.[15]

This is borne out by the fact that Aramaic words are retained in the Greek text in Matthew, which would not be true if that Gospel was translated from Aramaic to Greek. Cases in point are Matthew 1:23; 27:33, and 27:46.

Matthew Used the Logia and Mark. Another solution is much like the former. It propounds the theory that Matthew the Apostle translated his Hebrew Logia into Greek and compiled them with the Gospel of Mark

9. Willoughby C. Allen, *A Critical and Exegetical Commentary on the Gospel According to S. Matthew,* pp. lxxix-lxxxiii.

10. Plummer, *Exegetical Commentary,* pp. vii-xi.

11. Merrill C. Tenney, *The Genius of the Gospels,* pp. 35-36.

12. Ibid.

13. Wendell S. Reilly, "The Origin of St. Matthew's Gospel," *The Catholic Biblical Quarterly* 2 (October 1940): 323.

14. Henry Clarence Thiessen, *Introduction to the New Testament,* pp. 132-33.

15. Edgar J. Goodspeed, *An Introduction to the New Testament,* p. 174.

to produce his Gospel. This is a strong possibility, but as was stated in the preceding paragraph, there is no evidence that the non-Marcan parallels were translated from Aramaic *(Hebrew)*.

Another difficulty with this view is that Matthew was an apostle. Why would an eyewitness depend on another? It seems strange that Matthew would use Mark as a source to describe a banquet held in his own house (Matthew 9:9-13; Mark 2:13-17).

Matthew Is a Translation of the Logia. A third view is propounded by Zahn.[16] He says Matthew wrote a Hebrew Gospel, and it was later translated by someone else into Greek. This translation is our Gospel of Matthew. However, the Greek Gospel of Matthew bears no evidence of being a translation.[17]

Matthew Used Mark, a Translation of the Logia of Matthew. A fourth solution is set forth by those who say Matthew wrote the Hebrew Logia. These were translated by Mark into Greek and became the Gospel of Mark, then Matthew used Mark as a source for his Gospel. Bruce suggests this as a possibility.[18]

This view also has its difficulties. If Matthew could write both Greek and Aramaic *(Hebrew)*, why would he depend upon someone else to translate his own Logia? Second, it seems very improbable that Mark used Matthew's Logia as a source. In the New Testament, the term *logia* is used to refer to an oracle, and as such it may indicate any revelation which God gives (Romans 3:2; Hebrews 5:12; 1 Peter 4:11; Acts 7:38).[19] The word was used by the ecclesiastical writers to refer to the precepts and sayings of Jesus.[20] Therefore, the Logia of Matthew must be a reference to a written collection of the sayings of the Lord which Matthew made in Aramaic *(Hebrew)*.

If Mark translated Matthew's Logia and used it as a foundation for his Gospel, it would certainly seem that Mark would contain much discourse material. However, the very opposite is true; it is commonly recognized that Mark contains narrative portions of Christ's activity and very little of His discourses. Besides being very involved, this theory lacks much in the way of support.

---

16. Theodore Zahn, *Introduction to the New Testament*, 2:515-522.
17. Alfred M. Perry, "The Growth of the Gospels," *The Interpreter's Bible*, 7:67-68.
18. Bruce, *New Testament Documents*, pp. 40-41.
19. G. Abbott-Smith, *A Manual Greek Lexicon of the New Testament*, p. 270.
20. Joseph Henry Thayer, *A Greek-English Lexicon of the New Testament*, p. 379.

Appendix

Matthew Wrote Two Accounts. A fifth solution posits the idea that Matthew wrote two independent accounts, one the Hebrew Logia and the other the Greek Gospel extant today. This view appears to be very plausible. However, if this position is taken, it will undoubtedly be met with much opposition.

> In spite of the widespread and undisputed tradition of the second century, which from Papias downward declares our first Gospel the direct handiwork of the Apostle Matthew, modern criticism is unanimous in declaring it irreconcilable with the contents.[21]

In the light of this opposition, this solution must be carefully defended.

That Matthew is the author of the Greek Gospel is shown by the external evidence of tradition which today is generally recognized. But the Matthean authorship can also be shown on the basis of internal evidence. The writer of Matthew is a Palestinian Jew.[22] He is well acquainted with the geography of Palestine (Matthew 2:1, 23; 3:1, 5, 13; 4:12, 13, 23-25; 8:5, 23, 28; 14:34; 15:32, 39; 16:13; 17:1; 19:1; 20:29; 21:1, 17; 26:6). Jewish history, customs, ideas, and classes of people are familiar to him (Matthew 1:18-19; 2:1, 4, 22; 14:1; 26:3, 57, 59; 27:2, 11, 13). The writer is familiar with the Old Testament Scriptures (Matthew 1:2-16, 22-23; 2:6, 15, 17-18, 23; 4:14-16; 8:17; 12:17-21; 13:35; 21:4-5; 27:9). The terminology which the writer uses betrays his nationality (Matthew 2:20, 21; 4:5; 27:53; 5:35; 10:6; 15:24; 17:24-27; 5:47; 6:7, 32; 18:17). A final indication that the writer was a Palestinian Jew is found in the use of the word "then" ($\tau\acute{o}\tau\epsilon$). While a non-Palestinian Jew may have been familiar with Aramaic, it is rather unlikely. "It is probable that the frequency of its occurrence in this Gospel is due to Matthew's thinking in Aramaic."[23] Therefore, the use of $\tau\acute{o}\tau\epsilon$ reflects the Palestinian background of the writer.

It may be inferred that this Palestinian Jew was Matthew, the publican. As a publican he must have been literate and accustomed to keeping written records. It is perfectly logical to conclude that he wrote the Gospel from records he kept during the Lord's ministry. Even clearer evidence is seen in the terminology used in Matthew's Gospel with reference to money. "There is more frequent mention of money in this

21. B. W. Bacon, "Why 'According to Matthew'?," *The Expositor* 46 (October 1920): 294.
22. Ernest DeWitt Burton, "The Purpose and Plan of the Gospel of Matthew," *The Biblical World* 11 (January 1898): 37-38.
23. Thiessen, *Introduction,* p. 139.

Gospel than in any of the others, and more and rarer coins are introduced."[24] Matthew uses three terms for money which occur nowhere else (Matthew 17:24, 27; 18:24). "He also uses GOLD *(chrusos);* SILVER *(arguros);* and BRASS *(chalkos,* x. 9), which do not occur in Mark, Luke, or John . . ."[25] Matthew alone speaks of the talent which was a sum so large that only Matthew of the gospel writers would have handled it.

> Such references are natural in the writing of one who had been a tax collector. There are also references to debt *(opheile),* to account-taking, or reckoning *(sunairo,* with *logos),* and to money-changers *(trapezites),* which do not occur elsewhere (except "debt"), but which a "publican" would naturally make (xviii. 23, 24, 27; xxv. 19, 27).[26]

Still another evidence for the Matthean authorship of the Gospel is the emphasis placed on Capernaum, Matthew's home. It is mentioned in a matter of fact manner only in 8:5 and 17:24; otherwise some special aspect or description is attached to it. In 4:13 an extended description of the city is given with the additional note of fulfilled prophecy; in 9:1 it is called the Lord's own city; and in 11:23 Capernaum is spoken of in the Lord's denunciation and deprecation of the cities in which He had ministered with no positive response.

The fact that Matthew does not ascribe the work to himself is an indication the work was not a forgery. A compiler probably would have attached the name of an apostle to the document so that it would win acceptance. Matthew does not affix his name to the Gospel because he was a very humble man. He call himself Matthew, *the tax-gatherer* (10:3). Matthew does not record the parable of the Pharisee and the publican or the story of Zacchaeus, the publican who restored fourfold all that he had defrauded, lest it exalt his position. Rather, Matthew associates the publicans with sinners and tax collectors (9:11; 21:31-32). Because of his humility, it is to be expected that Matthew would not assert himself to be the author of so great a work.

Conclusion. While there are indications that Matthew may have used Mark to a certain extent, such a premise does not yet stand as proven. It is safe to say that Matthew wrote a Hebrew document which was uninspired and lost. He also wrote a Greek Gospel which is inspired. This

24. W. Graham Scroggie, *A Guide to the Gospels,* p. 247.
25. Ibid., p. 275.
26. Ibid.

Greek Gospel is the Gospel According to Matthew. To go beyond this, one must enter the realm of conjecture.

Date

The Problem of Date

Another great problem involves the date of writing of the Gospel of Matthew. Was it written before or after the destruction of Jerusalem in 70 A.D.? How long before or after that date was it written?

The Solution to the Problem of Date

It was written no doubt before 70 A.D. The city of Jerusalem was still standing at the time of writing. This is shown by the fact that Matthew refers to it as the "holy city" as though it was still in existence (4:5; 27:53). He does not mention its destruction as having been accomplished at any point. In addition, he refers to the customs of the Jews as continuing "to this day" as though they were uninterrupted and unchanged (27:8; 28:15). Since the first church was Jewish and Matthew's Gospel is characteristically Jewish, the Gospel of Matthew must have been written fairly early. A plausible date would be between 50 and 70 A.D.[27]

Conclusion

One may conclude then that Matthew, the publican, wrote the Gospel ascribed to him. The use he made of sources is unknown; what he wrote is the inspired Word of God. The date of his Gospel may be placed somewhere between 50 and 70 A.D.

27. Merrill C. Tenney, *New Testament Survey,* p. 143.

Bibliography

A. Texts

Bullinger, E. W., ed. *The Companion Bible.* Reprint ed., Grand Rapids: Zondervan Bible Publishers, 1964.

Grant, F. W., ed. *The Numerical Bible.* 7 vols. Neptune, N. J.: Loizeaux Brothers, 1899.

Rahlfs, Alfred, ed. *Septuaginta.* 2 vols. New York: American Bible Society, 1935.

Scofield, C. I., ed. *The Scofield Reference Bible.* New York: Oxford University Press, 1917.

Williams, Charles B. *The New Testament, A Private Translation in the Language of the People.* Chicago: Moody Press, 1937.

B. Greek Materials

Abbott-Smith, G. *A Manual Greek Lexicon of the New Testament.* Edinburgh: T. & T. Clark, 1937.

Bauer, Walter. *A Greek-English Lexicon of the New Testament and Other Early Christian Literature.* Translated by William F. Arndt and F. Wilbur Gingrich; 2d English ed. revised by F. Wilbur Gingrich and Frederick W. Danker from Walter Bauer's 5th ed.

Burton, Ernest DeWitt. *Syntax of the Moods and Tenses in New Testament Greek.* 3d ed. Chicago: University of Chicago Press, 1900; reprint ed., Grand Rapids: Kregel Publications, 1976.

Chamberlain, William Douglas. *An Exegetical Grammer of the Greek New Testament.* New York: The Macmillan Co., n. d.

Cremer, Hermann. *Biblico-Theological Lexicon of New Testament Greek.* Translated by William Urwick. 4th English ed. Edinburgh: T. & T. Clark, 1895.

Delling, Gerhard. "παρθένος." In *Theological Dictionary of the New Testament.* Vol. 5, pp. 826-837. Edited by Gerhard Kittel. Translated and edited by Geoffrey W. Bromiley. Grand Rapids: Wm. B. Eerdmans Publishing Co., 1967.

Hatch, Edwin, and Henry A. Redpath. *A Concordance to the Septuagint and the Other Greek Versions of the Old Testament.* 2 vols. Graz, Austria: Akademische Druck-U. Verlagsanstalt, 1954.

Liddell, Henry George, and Robert Scott. *A Greek-English Lexicon with a Supplement.* Revised by Henry Stuart Jones. Oxford: The Clarendon Press, 1968.

337

Moulton, James Hope, and George Milligan. *The Vocabulary of the Greek Testament*. Grand Rapids: Wm. B. Eerdmans Publishing Co., 1930.

Moulton, W. F., and A. S. Geden, eds. *A Concordance to the Greek Testament*. 5th ed. revised by H. K. Moulton. Edinburgh: T. & T. Clark, 1978.

Robertson, A. T. *A Grammar of the Greek New Testament in the Light of Historical Research*. Nashville: Broadman Press, 1934.

Schrenk, Gottlob. "Βιάζομαι, Βιαστής." In *Theological Dictionary of the New Testament*. Vol. 1, pp. 609-614. Edited by Gerhard Kittel. Translated and edited by Geoffrey W. Bromiley. Grand Rapids: Wm. B. Eerdmans Publishing Co., 1967.

Strathmann. "Μάρτυς, μαρτυρέω, μαρτυρία, μαρτύριον." In *Theological Dictionary of the New Testament*. Vol. 4, pp. 474-508.

Thayer, Joseph Henry. *A Greek-English Lexicon of the New Testament*. 4th ed. Grand Rapids: Zondervan Publishing House, 1978.

Vincent, Marvin R. *Word Studies in the New Testament*. 4 vols. New York: Charles Scribner's Sons, 1887: reprint ed., Grand Rapids: Wm. B. Eerdmans Publishing Co., 1946.

Vine, W. E. *An Expository Dictionary of New Testament Words*. Old Tappan, N. J.: Fleming H. Revell Co., 1940.

Wigram, George V., ed. *The Englishman's Greek Concordance of the New Testament*. 9th ed. London: Samuel Bagster and Sons, 1844; reprint ed., Grand Rapids: Zondervan Publishing House, 1970.

Winer, George Benedict. *Grammar of the Idiom of the New Testament*. Translated from the 7th German ed. by J. Henry Thayer. Philadelphia: Smith, English, & Co., 1874.

C. Commentaries

Alford, Henry. *The Greek Testament*. 4 vols. Reprint ed., Grand Rapids: Baker Book House, [n. d.].

Allen, Willoughby C. *A Critical and Exegetical Commentary on the Gospel According to S. Matthew*. 3d ed. The International Critical Commentary on the Holy Scriptures of the Old and New Testaments. Edinburgh: T. & T. Clark, 1912.

Argyle, A. W. *The Gospel According to Matthew*. The Cambridge Bible Commentary on the New English Bible. London: Cambridge University Press, 1963.

Bacon, Benjamin W. *Studies in Matthew*. New York: Henry Holt and Co., 1930.

Barclay, William. *The Gospel of Matthew.* 2 Vols. Edinburgh: The Saint Andrew Press, 1956.

Barnhouse, Donald Grey. *Romans. Vol. 1: Man's Ruin. God's Wrath.* Grand Rapids: Wm. B. Eerdmans Publishing Co., 1952.

Bruce, Alexander Balmain. "The Synoptic Gospels," *The Expositor's Greek Testament.* W. Robertson Nicoll, ed. Grand Rapids: Wm. B. Eerdmans Publishing Co., 1910.

Carr, A. *The Gospel According to St. Matthew.* Cambridge: University Press, 1913.

Darby, J. N. *Synopsis of the Books of the Bible.* 5 vols. Kingston on Thames: Stow Hill Bible and Tract Depot, n. d.

Davies, W. D. *The Sermon on the Mount.* London: Cambridge University Press, 1966.

English, E. Schuyler. *Studies in the Gospel According to Matthew.* New York: Fleming H. Revell Co., 1935.

Feinberg, Charles L. *God Remembers, A Study of Zechariah.* 4th ed. Portland, Oreg.: Multnomah Press, 1979.

Fenton, J. C. *Saint Matthew.* Westminster Pelican Commentaries. Philadelphia: The Westminster Press, 1978.

Gaebelein, A. C. *The Gospel of Matthew, An Exposition.* 2 vols. in one. Neptune, N. J.: Loizeaux Brothers, 1910.

Godet, F. *A Commentary on the Gospel of St. Luke.* 2 vols. Edinburgh: T. & T. Clark, n. d.

Grant, Frederick C., ed. *Nelson's Bible Commentary.* 7 vols. New York: Thomas Nelson & Sons, 1962.

Green, F. W., ed. *The Gospel According to Saint Matthew in the Revised Version.* The Clarendon Bible. Oxford: The Clarendon Press, 1936.

Hendriksen, William. *New Testament Commentary, Exposition of the Gospel According to Matthew.* Grand Rapids: Baker Book House, 1973.

Hill, David. *New Century Bible, The Gospel of Matthew.* Greenwood, S. C.: The Attic Press, Inc., 1972.

Johnson, Sherman E., and George A. Buttrick. "The Gospel According to St. Matthew," in *The Interpreter's Bible.* Vol. 7, pp. 231-625. Edited by George Arthur Buttrick. Nashville: Abingdon Press, 1952.

Kelly, William. *Lectures on the Gospel of Matthew.* New York: Loizeaux Brothers, n. d.

Knox, Ronald. *A Commentary on the Gospels.* New York: Sheed & Ward, 1954.

Lange, John Peter. *Commentary on the Holy Scriptures, Critical, Doctrinal and Homiletical*. Translated from the German by Philip Schaff. 12 vols. Grand Rapids: Zondervan Publishing House, [n. d.].

Laurenson, L. *Messiah, the Prince*. New York: Loizeaux Brothers, 1924.

Lenski, R. C. H. *The Interpretation of St. Matthew's Gospel*. Minneapolis: Augsburg Publishing House, 1943.

Levertoff, P. P., and H. L. Goudge. "The Gospel According to St. Matthew." In *A New Commentary on Holy Scripture Including the Apocrypha*. New York: The Macmillan Co., 1928.

Lightfoot, J. B. *The Epistle of St. Paul to the Galatians*. Grand Rapids: Zondervan Publishing House, [n. d.].

Makrakis, Apostolos. *Interpretation of the Entire New Testament*. Translated by Albert George Alexander. 2 vols. Chicago: Orthodox Christian Educational Society, 1949.

M'Neile, Alan Hugh. *The Gospel According to St. Matthew*. London: Macmillan & Co., 1915.

Montefiore, C. G. *The Synoptic Gospels*. 2 vols. Rev. ed. New York: KTAV, 1968.

Morgan, G. Campbell. *The Gospel According to Matthew*. Old Tappan, N. J.: Fleming H. Revell Co., 1929.

Morison, James. *A Practical Commentary on the Gospel According to St. Matthew*. Boston: N. J. Bartlett & Co., 1884.

Perry, Alfred M. "The Growth of the Gospels." In *The Interpreter's Bible*. Vol. 7, pp. 60-74. Edited by George Arthur Buttrick. Nashville: Abingdon Press, 1952.

Pettingill, William L. *Simple Studies in Matthew*. Findlay, Ohio: Dunham Publishing Co., n.d.

Plummer, Alfred. *An Exegetical Commentary on the Gospel According to S. Matthew*. Grand Rapids: Wm. B. Eerdmans Publishing Co., 1953.

Pusey, E. B. *The Minor Prophets*. 2 vols. Grand Rapids: Baker Book House, 1950.

Robertson, Archibald Thomas. *Word Pictures in the New Testament*. 6 vols. Nashville: Broadman Press, 1930.

Robinson, Theodore H. *The Gospel of Matthew*. The Moffatt New Testament Commentary. London: Hodder and Stoughton, 1928.

Ryle, J. C. *Expository Thoughts on the Gospels*. Reprint ed., Grand Rapids: Baker Book House, 1977.

Schweizer, Eduard. *Good News According to Matthew*. Translated by David E. Green. Atlanta: John Knox Press, 1975.

Smith, George Adam. *The Book of Isaiah*. 2 vols. New York: A. C. Armstrong and Son, 1902.

Tasker, R.V.G. *The Gospel According to St. Matthew*. Grand Rapids: Wm. B. Eerdmans Publishing Company, 1961

Vos, Howard F. *Matthew, A Study Guide Commentary*. Grand Rapids: Zondervan Publishing House, 1979.

Williams, George. *The Student's Commentary on the Holy Scriptures*. 4th ed. Grand Rapids: Kregel Publications, 1949.

D. Books

Allis, Oswald T. *Prophecy and the Church*. Philadelphia: The Presbyterian and Reformed Publishing Co., 1945.

Anderson, Robert. *The Coming Prince*. Grand Rapids: Kregel Publications, 1975.

Andrews, Samuel J. *The Life of Our Lord Upon the Earth*. New York: Charles Scribner's Sons, 1891.

Armerding, Carl. *The Olivet Discourse*. Findlay, Ohio: Dunham Publishing Co., n. d.

Barnett, Albert E. *Understanding the Parables of our Lord*. Chicago: Alec R. Allenson, Inc., 1954.

Barnhouse, Donald Grey. *His Own Received Him Not, But ...* New York: Fleming H. Revell Co., 1933.

Beecher, Willis J. *The Prophets and the Promise*. New York: Thomas Y. Crowell, 1905; reprint ed., Grand Rapids: Baker Book House, 1975.

Broughton, Len G. *Kingdom Parables and Their Teaching*. London: Hodder and Stoughton, 1910.

Bruce, Alexander Balmain. *The Galilean Gospel*. New York: Eaton & Mains, n. d.

_____. *The Parabolic Teaching of Christ*. London: Hodder and Stoughton, 1895.

Bruce, F. F. *Are the New Testament Documents Reliable?* 5th Rev. ed., Downers Grove, Illinois: InterVarsity Press, 1960.

Bullinger, E. W. *Leaven: Its Biblical Usage and Interpretation*. London: Eyre & Spottiswoode, 1907.

Burton, Ernest DeWitt. *A Short Introduction to the Gospels*. Chicago: The University of Chicago Press, 1904.

Colwell, Ernest Cadman. *What Is the Best New Testament?* Chicago: The University of Chicago Press, 1952.

Cooper, David L. *Future Events Revealed.* Los Angeles: David L. Cooper, 1935.

Dalman, Gustaf. *The Words of Jesus.* Edinburgh: T. & T. Clark, 1909.

Denzer, George A. *The Parables of the Kingdom.* Washington, D.C.: The Catholic University of America Press, 1945.

Dibelius, Martin. *The Sermon on the Mount.* New York: Charles Scribner's Sons, 1940.

Dodd, C. H. *The Parables of the Kingdom.* Rev. ed., Great Britain: William Collins Sons & Co. Ltd., Glasgow, 1961.

Dods, Marcus. *The Parables of Our Lord.* New York: Fleming H. Revell Co., n. d.

Dykes, J. Oswald. *The Manifesto of the King. 2d ed.,* London: James Nisbet & Co., 1883.

Edersheim, Alfred. *The Life and Times of Jesus the Messiah.* Grand Rapids: Wm. B. Eerdmans Publishing Co., 1971.

_____. *Prophecy and History.* New York: Anson D. F. Randolph & Co., 1885.

Eusebius. *The Ecclesiastical History.* Translated by Kirsopp Lake and J. E. L. Oulton. 2 vols. New York: G. P. Putnam's Sons, 1932.

Feinberg, Charles Lee. *Israel in the Last Days: The Olivet Discourse.* Altadena, California: Emeth Publications, 1953.

_____. *Premillennialism or Amillennialism?* Wheaton: Van Kampen Press, 1954.

Fraser, Alexander. *The First Four Parables of the Kingdom of Heaven.* Pittsburgh: The Evangelical Fellowship, Inc., 1945.

Gaebelein, Arno Clemens. *His Last Words.* New York: Our Hope, n. d.

Goebel, Siegfried. *The Parables of Jesus.* Translated by Professor Banks. Edinburgh: T. & T. Clark, 1913.

Goodspeed, Edgar J. *An Introduction to the New Testament.* Chicago: University of Chicago Press, 1937.

Gore, Charles. *The Sermon on the Mount.* London: John Murray, 1896.

Habershon, Ada R. *The Study of the Parables.* Grand Rapids: Kregel Publications, 1904.

Hamilton, Frank. *The Bible and the Millennium.* Ventor, New Jersey: Rev. Frank Hamilton, n. d.

Hicks, George E. *John the Baptist.* London: Pickering & Inglis Ltd., n. d.

Hogg, C. F., and J. B. Watson. *On the Sermon on the Mount.* 2d ed., London: Pickering and Inglis, 1934.

Humberd, R. I. *The Virgin Birth.* Flora, Indiana: R. I. Humberd Christian Book Depot, n. d.

Hunter, Archibald M. *The Message of the New Testament.* Philadelphia: The Westminster Press, 1944.

_____. *A Pattern for Life: An Exposition of the Sermon on the Mount.* Rev. ed., Philadelphia: The Westminster Press, 1966.

Irenaeus, "Against Heresies." In *The Ante-Nicene Fathers. Translations of the Writings of the Fathers down to A.D. 325.* Vol. 1, pp. 309-567. Edited by Alexander Roberts and James Donaldson. Revised by A. Cleveland Coxe. Grand Rapids: Wm. B. Eerdmans Publishing Co., 1975.

Jukes, Andrew. *The Characteristic Differences of the Four Gospels.* London: James Nisbet & Co., 1878.

Kelly, W. *The Lord's Prophecy on Olivet in Matthew XXIV. XXV.* London: T. Weston, 1903.

Kepler, Thomas S. *Jesus' Design for Living.* New York: Abingdon Press, 1955.

Kik, J. Marcellus. *Matthew Twenty-Four, An Exposition.* Swengel, Pennsylvania: Bible Truth Depot, n. d.

King, Guy H. *New Order.* London: Marshall, Morgan & Scott, Ltd., 1943.

Kittel, D. Gerhard. *Lexicographia Sacra.* London: Society for Promoting Christian Knowledge, 1938.

Kraeling, Carl H. *John the Baptist.* New York: Charles Scribner's Sons, 1951.

Lang, George Henry. *Pictures and Parables.* London: Paternoster Press, 1955.

Lindsell, Harold. *A Christian Philosophy of Missions.* Wheaton: Van Kampen Press, 1949.

Major, H. D. A. *Basic Christianity.* Oxford: Basil Blackwell, 1944.

_____, T. W. Manson, and C. J. Wright. *The Mission and Message of Jesus.* New York: E. P. Dutton and Co., Inc., 1938.

Mantey, Julius R. *Was Peter A Pope?* Chicago: Moody Press, 1949.

Martin, Hugh. *The Beatitudes.* New York: Harper & Brothers, 1953.

McClain, Alva J. *The Greatness of the Kingdom, An Inductive Study of the Kingdom of God.* Winona Lake, Indiana: BMH Books, 1959.

McNeile, Alan Hugh. *An Introduction to the Study of the New Testament*. 2d ed. edited by C. S. Williams. Oxford: The Clarendon Press, 1953.

Meyer, F. B. *The Directory of the Devout Life*. New York: Fleming H. Revell Co., 1904.

_____. *John the Baptist*. Fort Washington, Pa.: Christian Literature Crusade, 1975.

Miller, Earl. *The Kingdom of God and the Kingdom of Heaven*. Meadville, Pennsylvania: By the Author, 1950.

Montizambert, Eric. *The Flame of Life*. Greenwich, Connecticut: The Seabury Press, 1955.

Morgan, G. Campbell, *The Crises of the Christ*. Old Tappan, N. J.: Fleming H. Revell Co., 1936.

_____. *The Parables of the Kingdom*. London: Hodder and Stoughton, 1907.

_____. *The Parables and Metaphors of Our Lord*. Old Tappan, N.J.: Fleming H. Revell Co., 1956.

Morison, Frank. *Who Moved the Stone?* Grand Rapids: Zondervan Publishing House, 1958.

Newton, Benjamin Wills. *The Prophecy of the Lord Jesus as Contained in Matthew XXIV. and XXV.* London: Houlston & Sons, 1902.

O'Brien, John A. *The Faith of Millions, The Credentials of the Catholic Religion*. Rev. ed., Huntington, Indiana: Our Sunday Visitor, 1974.

O'Hair, J. C. *God's Grace Manifesto*. Chicago: J. C. O'Hair, n. d.

Peak, Luther C. *Studies in the Gospel of the King and the Kingdom*. Dallas: Baptist Beacon Publishing House, 1942.

Pentecost, J. Dwight. *Things to Come*. Grand Rapids: Zondervan Publishing House, 1958.

Peters, George N. H. *The Theocratic Kingdom of our Lord Jesus, the Christ, as Covenanted in the Old Testament, and Presented in the New Testament*. 3 vols. New York: Funk and Wagnalls, 1884; reprint ed., Grand Rapids: Kregel Publications, 1972.

Pink, Arthur W. *An Exposition of the Sermon on the Mount*. Swengel, Pennsylvania: Bible Truth Depot, 1950.

Ramm, Bernard. *Protestant Biblical Interpretation*. 3rd ed., Grand Rapids: Baker Book House, 1970.

Reynolds, Henry Robert. *John the Baptist*. London: Hodder and Stoughton, 1874.

Robertson, A. T. *A Harmony of the Gospels for Students of the Life of Christ*. New York: Harper and Row Publishers, 1922.

_____. *The Christ of the Logia*. London: Hodder & Stoughton Limited, 1924.

Ross, J. J. *The Kingdom in Mystery*. New York: Fleming H. Revell Co., 1920.

Ryrie, Charles Caldwell. *The Basis of the Premillennial Faith*. Neptune, N.J.: Loizeaux Brothers, 1954.

Sauer, Erich. *From Eternity to Eternity*. Translated by G. H. Lang. Grand Rapids: Wm. B. Eerdmans Publishing Co., 1954.

_____. *The Triumph of the Crucified*. Translated by G. H. Lang. Grand Rapids: Wm. B. Eerdmans Publishing Co., 1951.

Schweitzer, Albert. *The Quest of the Historical Jesus*. Translated by W. Montgomery. New York: The Macmillan Co., 1961.

Scott, Ernest F. *The Purpose of the Gospels*. New York: Charles Scribner's Sons, 1949.

Scroggie, W. Graham. *A Guide to the Gospels*. Old Tappan, N. J.: Fleming H. Revell Co., 1975.

Shepard, J. W. *The Christ of the Gospels*. Grand Rapids: Wm. B. Eerdmans Publishing Company, 1939.

Smith, David. *The Days of His Flesh, the Earthly Life of Our Lord and Savior Jesus Christ*. Grand Rapids: Baker Book House, 1976.

Stamm, Frederick Keller. *Seeing the Multitudes*. New York: Harper & Brothers, 1943.

Strombeck, J. F. *First the Rapture*. Moline, Illinois: Strombeck Agency, Inc., 1950.

Strong, Augustus H. *Popular Lectures on the Books of the New Testament*. Philadelphia: The Griffith & Rowland Press, 1914.

Swete, Henry Barclay. *The Parables of the Kingdom*. London: Macmillan and Co., Limited, 1920.

Talbot, Louis T. *Why Four Gospels?* Los Angeles: By the Author, 1944.

Taylor, William M. *The Parables of Our Saviour*. 13th ed., New York: A. C. Armstrong & Son, 1906; reprint ed., Grand Rapids: Kregel Publications, 1975.

Tenney, Merrill C. *The Genius of the Gospels*. Grand Rapids: Wm. B. Eerdmans Publishing Company, 1951.

Thiessen, Henry Clarence. *Introduction to the New Testament*. Grand Rapids: Wm. B. Eerdmans Publishing Company, 1943.

Tholuck, A. *Exposition, Doctrinal and Philological, of Christ's Sermon on the Mount According to the Gospel of Matthew*. 2d ed., Translated by Robert Menzies. 2 vols. Edinburgh: Thomas Clark, 1843.

Thompson, Ernest Trice. *The Sermon on the Mount*. Richmond: John Knox Press, 1946.

Thurneysen, Eduard. *The Sermon on the Mount*. Richmond: John Knox Press, 1964.

Trench, Richard Chenevix. *Notes on the Miracles of Our Lord*. Grand Rapids: Baker Book House, 1949.

_____. *Notes on the Parables of Our Lord*. Grand Rapids: Baker Book House, 1948.

_____. *Studies in the Gospels*. 3rd ed., Grand Rapids: Baker Book House, 1979.

Von Dobschutz, Ernst. *The Eschatology of the Gospels*. London: Hodder and Stoughton, 1910.

Westcott, Brooke Foss. *Characteristics of the Gospel Miracles*. London: Macmillan and Co., 1859.

Williams, Isaac. *Thoughts on the Study of the Holy Gospels*. London: Rivingtons, 1876.

Wilson, Edmund. *The Scrolls from the Dead Sea*. New York: Oxford University Press, 1955.

Windisch, Hans. *The Meaning of the Sermon on the Mount*. Translated by S. MacLean Gilmour. Philadelphia: The Westminster Press, 1937.

Zahn, Theodore. *Introduction to the New Testament*. Translated from the 3d German ed. by John Moore Trout, William Arnot Mather, Louis Hodous, Edward Strong Worcester, William Hoyt Worrell, Rowland Backus Dodge. 3 vols. Grand Rapids: Kregel Publications, 1953.

E. Theologies

Berkhof, L. *Systematic Theology*. 4th ed., Grand Rapids: Wm. B. Eerdmans Publishing Company, 1941.

Chafer, Lewis Sperry. *Systematic Theology*. 8 vols. Dallas: Dallas Seminary Press, 1947.

Hodge, Charles. *Systematic Theology*. 3 vols. Grand Rapids: William B. Eerdmans Publishing Company, [n. d.].

Pohle, Joseph. *Dogmatic Theology*. Edited by Arthur Pruess. 12 vols. St. Louis: B. Herder Book Co., 1911.

Stauffer, Ethelbert. *New Testament Theology*. Translated by John Marsh. London: SCM Press Ltd., 1955.

F. Encyclopedia Articles

A Dictionary of the Bible. S. v. "Salvation, Saviour," by W. Adams Brown.

A Dictionary of the Bible. Extra vol. S. v. "Sermon on the Mount," by C. W. Votaw.

The International Standard Bible Encyclopedia, 1939 ed. S. v. "Jesus Christ, Arrest and Trial of," by John James Maclaren. "The Sermon on the Mount," by Russell Benjamin Miller. "Zion," by E. W. G. Masterman.

G. Periodical Articles

Aiken, Warwick, "A Continental Divide in Scripture Interpretation, The Parable of the Leaven," *Bibliotheca Sacra* 95 (April 1938): 219-230.

Arendzen, J. P., "Re-writing St. Matthew," *The Expositor* 16 (November 1918): 316-73.

Bacon, B. W., "Why 'According to Matthew'?" *The Expositor* 46 (October 1920): 289-310.

Barnes, A. S., "Suggestions on the Origin of the Gospel According to St. Matthew," *The Journal of Theological Studies* 6 (January 1905): 187-203.

Bennetch, John Henry, "Matthew: An Apologetic," *Bibliotheca Sacra* 103 (April 1946): 238-46; (October 1946): 477-84.

Bernardin, Joseph B., "The Transfiguration," *Journal of Biblical Theology* 52 (October 1933): 181-89.

Bevan, T. W., "The Four Anointings," *The Expository Times* 39 (December 1927): 137-39.

Bindley, T. Herbert, "Eschatology in the Lord's Prayer," *The Expositor* 17 (October 1919): 315-20.

Black, Matthew, "The Aramaic of τον αρτον ημων τον επιουσιον," *The Journal of Theological Studies* 42 (July 1941): 186-89.

————, "Let the Dead Bury Their Dead," *The Expository Times* 61 (April 1950): 219-20.

Burch, Vacher, "The Meaning and Function of the 'Church' in Matthew 18:15 ff.," *The Expositor* 18 (September 1919): 233-40.

————, "Some Suggestions on the Text and Interpretation of Matthew 16:18-19," *The Expositor 17* (March 1919): 219-28.

Burrows, Millar, "Thy Kingdom Come," *Journal of Biblical Literature* 74 (January 1955): 1-8.

Burton, Ernest DeWitt, "The Purpose and Plan of the Gospel of Matthew," *The Biblical World* 11 (January 1898): 37-44; (February 1898): 91-101.

Cadbury, Henry J., "The Meaning of John 20:23; Matthew 16:19; and Matthew 18:18," *Journal of Biblical Literature* 58 (July 1939): 251-54.

Carpus, S., "The Sermon on the Mount," *The Expositor* 1 (January 1875): 70-88; (February 1875): 128-42; (March 1875): 196-211.

Chafer, Lewis Sperry, "The Teachings of Christ Incarnate," *Bibliotheca Sacra* 108 (October 1951): 410; 109 (January 1952): 4-36.

Charles, R. H., "Two Parables: A Study," *The Expository Times* 35 (March 1924): 265-69.

Colson, F. H. "The Divorce Exception in St. Matthew," *The Expositor* 11 (June 1916): 438-46.

Cotter, A. C. "The Eschatological Discourse," *The Catholic Biblical Quarterly* 1 (April 1939): 125-32; (July 1939): 204-13.

Cranfield, C. E. B., "St. Mark 13," *Scottish Journal of Theology* 6 (April 1953): 165-96; (July 1953): 287-303; 7 (April 1954): 284-303.

Creed, J. M., "The Kingdom of God Has Come," *The Expository Times* 48 (January 1937): 184-185.

Dods, Marcus, "The Righteousness of Christ's Kingdom," *The Expositor* 9 (January 1894): 70-79.

Donn, T. M., "'Let the Dead Bury Their Dead' (Mt viii. 22, Lk ix. 60)," *The Expository Times* 61 (September 1950): 384.

Dublin, John, "The Gates of Hades," *The Expositor* 11 (June 1916): 401-9.

English, Thomas R., "The Purpose and Plan of Matthew's Gospel," *The Bible Student* 1 (April 1900): 219-22.

Feredey, W. W., "Thoughts on the Lord's Prayer," *Our Hope* 42 (September 1935): 173-78.

Gaebelein, Arno C., "Does the Parable of the Wheat and the Tares Teach that the Church Will Go Through the Great Tribulation?" *Our Hope* 16 (December 1909): 387-90.

————, "The Temptations of the Lord Jesus Christ," *Our Hope* 6 (May 1900): 337-45.

Gale, Herbert M., "A Suggestion Concerning Matthew 16," *Journal of Biblical Literature* 60 (July 1941): 255-60.

Griffiths, J. Gwyn, "ἐντός ὑμῶν (Luke xvii. 21)," *The Expository Times* 63 (October 1951): 30-31.

Hasler, J. Ireland, "The Incident of the Syrophoenician Woman (Matt. xv. 21-28; Mark vii. 24-30)," *The Expository Times* 45 (July 1934): 459-61.

Hatch, William H. P., "A Note on Matthew 6:33," *The Harvard*

Theological Review 38 (October 1945): 270-72.

Hayman, Herbert S., "The Parable of the Pearl Merchant: Matthew xiii. 45, 46," *The Expository Times* 49 (December 1937): 142.

Hogg, C. F., "The Lord's Pleasure in the Centurion's Faith," *The Expository Times* 47 (October 1935): 44-45.

Hoyle, R. Birch, "The Lord's Prayer in History," *The Biblical Review* 17 (April 1932): 210-26.

Jackson, Blomfield, "Note on Matt. XX 23 and Mark X 40," *The Journal of Theological Studies* 6 (January 1905): 237-40.

Johnson, S. Lewis, Jr., "The Argument of Matthew," *Bibliotheca Sacra* 112 (April 1955): 143-53.

—————, "The Message of John the Baptist," *Bibliotheca Sacra* 113 (January 1956): 30-36.

Johnson, Sherman E., "The Biblical Quotations in Matthew," *The Harvard Theological Review* 36 (April 1943): 135-53.

Kerr, John H. "The Veiled Gospel or the Parabolic Teachings of Jesus," *The Bible Student* 1 (May 1900): 275-82.

Kiddle, M. "The Conflict Between the Disciples, the Jews, and the Gentiles in St. Matthew's Gospel," *The Journal of Theological Studies* 36 (January 1935): 33-44.

—————, "The Death of Jesus and the Admission of the Gentiles in St. Mark," *The Journal of Theological Studies* 35 (January 1934): 45-50.

Kleber, Albert, "The Lord's Prayer and the Decalog," *The Catholic Biblical Quarterly* 3 (October 1941): 302-20.

Mantey, J. R., "The Mistranslation of the Perfect Tense in John 20:23; Mt. 16:19, and Mt. 18:18," *Journal of Biblical Literature* 58 (July 1939): 243-49.

Matulich, Silvano G., "The Kingdom of the Heavens in the Gospel of St. Matthew," *Catholic Biblical Quarterly* 3 (January 1949): 43-49.

McClellan, William H., "Homiletical Notes on the Magi: Gospel for the Feast of Epiphany," *The Catholic Biblical Quarterly* 1 (January 1939): 72.

McPheeters, Wm. M., "Christ as an Interpreter of Scripture," *The Bible Student* 1 (April 1900): 223-29.

Minear, Paul S., "The Coming of the Son of Man," *Theology Today* 9 (January 1953): 489-93.

Moffatt, James, "Augustine on the Lord's Prayer," *The Expositor* 17 (October 1919): 259-72.

—————, "Cyprian on the Lord's Prayer," *The Expositor* 18 (September 1919): 176-89.

Montefiore, C. G., "Rabbinic Conceptions of Repentance," *The Jewish Quarterly Review* 16 (January 1904): 209-57.

Oke, C. Clare, "My Testimony," *The Expository Times* 37 (July 1926): 476-78.

Oulton, J. E. L., "An Interpretation of Matthew xvi. 18," *The Expository Times* 48 (August 1937): 525-26.

Perowne, J. J. Stewart, "The Laws of the Kingdom and the Invitation of the King," *The Expositor* 7 (March 1878): 215-23.

Reid, James, "The Parable of the Ten Virgins (Matt. XXV. 1-13)," *The Expository Times* 37 (June 1926): 447-51.

Reilly, Wendell S., "The Origin of St. Matthew's Gospel," *The Catholic Biblical Quarterly* 2 (October 1940): 323.

Riach, John L., "The Day for Action," *The Expository Times* 61 (July 1950): 306-8.

Roberts, Colin H., "The Kingdom of Heaven (Lk. XVII. 21), " *Harvard Theological Review* 41 (January 1948): 1-8.

Smith, Samuel M., "The Decalogue and the Beatitudes," *The Bible Student* 1 (April 1900): 198-202.

Stowe, C. E., "The Eschatology of Christ, with Special Reference to the Discourse in Matt. XXIV. and XXV.," *Bibliotheca Sacra* 7 (July 1850): 452-78.

Torrey, Charles C., "The Foundry of the Second Temple at Jerusalem," *Journal of Biblical Literature* 55 (December 1936): 247-60.

Vos, Geerhardus, "The Kingdom of God," *The Bible Student* 1 (May 1900): 282-89.

————, "The Ministry of John the Baptist," *The Bible Student* 1 (January 1900): 26-32.

Walvoord, John F., "The New Covenant With Israel," *Bibliotheca Sacra* 110 (July 1953): 193-205.

Zenos, A. C., "The Herods," *The Bible Student* 2 (August 1900): 89-94.

H. Unpublished Materials

Andrus, Roger Joel. "The Parable of the Ten Virgins." Master's thesis, Dallas Theological Seminary, 1946.

Bradley, Thaddeus L. "Μυστήριον in the Pauline Literature." Doctor's dissertation, Dallas Theological Seminary, 1949.

Campbell, Donald Keith. "Interpretation and Exposition of the Sermon on the Mount." Doctor's dissertation, Dallas Theological Seminary, 1953.

Eastman, Robert Carter. "A Correlation of the Three Accounts of the Olivet Discourse." Master's thesis, Dallas Theological Seminary, 1954.

Hepp, John, Jr. "The Kingdom: New Testament Meaning and Relation to the Church." Master's thesis, Dallas Theological Seminary, 1955.

Johnson, S. Lewis, Jr. "The Gospel of Matthew." Class lecture notes, Dallas Theological Seminary, 1955-56.

Lopston, Gordon Paul. "A Consideration of Some Problems in Matthew, Chapter Sixteen, Verses Thirteen Through Twenty, From the Standpoint of the Greek Text." Master's thesis, Dallas Theological Seminary, 1954.

Pentecost, J. Dwight. "The Judgment of the Nations." Master's thesis, Dallas Theological Seminary, 1941.

Rand, James F. "The Eschatology of the Olivet Discourse." Doctor's dissertation, Dallas Theological Seminary, 1954.

Rayburn, Robert Gibson. "Matthew Thirteen, Christ's Prophetic Picture of Christendom." Doctor's dissertation, Dallas Theological Seminary, 1944.

Rowe, Harley Edward. "The Kingdom in Matthew." Master's thesis, Dallas Theological Seminary, 1955.

Shiery, Floyd William. "John the Baptist." Doctor's dissertation, Dallas Theological Seminary, 1942.

Wood, Ralph E. "The Olivet Discourse in Matthew 24-25." Master's thesis, Dallas Theological Seminary, 1954.

Subject Index

Apostles, 137, 141, 143, 144, 228,
264, 304, 319. *See also* disciples
Aramaic, 15, 67, 96, 109, 162,
240, 329, 331
Gospel of Matthew, 329-332
the Lord spoke, 67, 202
Archelaus, 56
Assyrians, 82
At hand, 69
Augustus, 51

Babylon, deportation to, 40, 41,
49, 229
Banquet, 124, 253, 261, 284
Messianic, 190, 285
Baptism
Christian, 319
of fire, 70
of Jesus, 71-73, 81, 91
of John, 59, 60, 71, 72, 92, 246,
319
of proselytes, 59, 60
of the Holy Spirit, 70, 71
Pharisees coming for, 68
Barabbas, 309, 310
Bathsheba, 40
Beatitudes, 86, 94-97, 263
Beelzebul, 141, 162, 163, 165
Bethany, 244, 296
Bethlehem, 20, 47, 48, 50-55
Rachel's tomb near, 56
Bethsaida, 154
Betrothal, 42, 43, 284
Binding and loosing, 205, 206
Blind
guides, 262, 263
leaders of, 193
men, 133, 235, 236
spiritually, 51, 52, 287
Blindness
of Judas, 297
of Pharisees, 259
spiritual, of Israel, 188, 190,
191, 198, 211, 226, 241
Blood
field of, 308
of Christ, 300, 301, 310, 313
of the covenant, 300

of the prophets, 263
shed upon the earth, 263
Branch, 57

Caesar, 256, 274
Caiaphas, 296
trial before, 306-308, 310, 311
Canaanitish woman, 19, 194-196
Capernaum, 82, 129, 154, 214, 332
Centurion, 313
servant of, 123, 124
Ceremonial
cleansing, 17
defilement, 16
Children, 216, 225, 226, 234, 244,
248
Chorazin, 154
Christ, 16, 20, 39, 47, 307, 309
sufferings of, 63, 64, 232. *See
also* Messiah
Christendom, 173-175
Christian life, standards of, 94
Church, 217, 283, 301, 303, 327
a body distinct from Jews, 203
age, 64, 88, 129, 132, 218, 252,
267, 283, 286, 300, 318
building of, 201-203, 208, 323
Christ gave prophecy of, 173
Christ returns with, 277, 278
composed of all nations, 318
discipline in, 215, 217, 218
end has evil character, 182
future tense, 203, 218
included in kingdom, 289
in place of blessing, 324
kingdom program to, 19, 172,
204, 251, 289, 301, 318
local assembly, 218
marriage supper, 254
not in tribulation, 267, 277
not mentioned until Matthew
sixteen, 88
not the kingdom, 68, 89, 173,
204, 205, 323
not yet revealed, 62
of Jesus Christ, 20
oneness described in New
Testament, 184

new, 301
not condemned forever, 245
people of, 135
preeminent place never lost by,
195, 252
regathered, 277, 278, 300
rejected by Jesus, 157, 211, 244,
260-266
rejected their King, 37, 51, 83,
208, 211, 236, 265, 266, 274
rejection not permanent, 265
religious leaders, denounced,
51, 244, 263
represented by fig tree, 245
represented by husbandmen, 250
represented by Jerusalem, 265
represented by virgins, 283, 284
sons of, 308
state of, 276
twelve tribes of, 137, 205, 228
unbelief, 188, 226, 242.
See also Jews
Irenaeus, 17, 327
Isaac, 39, 123, 173, 257

Jacob, 56, 123, 173, 257
James, son of Zebedee, 84, 137,
210, 215, 232, 234, 304
Jeconiah, 38
Jericho, 235, 236
Jerusalem, 21, 49, 51, 59, 63, 85,
203, 214, 245, 274, 275, 296,
317, 333
city of peace, 265
city of the King, 89, 103, 238
designations in Matthew, 16
destruction of, 209, 254, 264,
266, 269, 279, 333
did not recognize its king, 238
Holy city, 76, 313, 333
Jesus entrance and ministry in,
240ff
Jesus to go to, 207, 208, 220,
223, 231, 232, 236, 239, 240
lamentation over, 265
rebuilt, 273
religious leaders of 82, 192-194

Jesus, 114, 159, 272. *See also*
Christ; King; Messiah
Character, 155
all powerful, 122, 127, 134,
137
authority, 21, 100, 118, 148,
156, 237, 246-256
claimed deity, 157
compassion, 135, 136, 161
equality with Father and Holy
Spirit, 318
glory of, 184, 209-212, 250
greatness, 97, 98, 137, 234,
252, 307, 313, 318
is God, 201, 260, 323
moral character, 74-78, 81,
121
power over men, 84, 243
power over Satan, 129, 164
power to forgive sins on earth,
129, 134
righteous, 307, 309
sovereign, 37, 237
supernatural, 42, 50, 127
theanthropic person, 46, 58,
76
truthfulness, 317
worshipped by disciples, 191
wrath, 155
Life (chronological). *See also*
Jesus: *Work and Ministry*
kenosis, 278
supernatural conception, 43, 45
virgin birth, 39, 316, 323
birth, 54, 121, 285, 324
infancy, 48, 310
childhood, 48, 54, 56, 58
baptized by John 71-73, 81,
91, 121, 323
anointed with Holy Spirit, 73,
161
acknowledged by Father, 73,
74, 323
temptation, 74-78, 91, 121,
323
questioned by John, 148
hostility toward, 128, 130,
147, 152, 170

Author Index

Goudge, H. L., 24
Grant, Frederick C., 15, 24
Grant, F. W., 279
Green, F. W., 60, 70, 131, 135,
  166, 228
Griffiths, J. Gwyn, 164

Habershon, Ada R., 174
Hendriksen, William, 15, 25, 49,
  143, 167
Hill, David, 15, 20
Hodge, Charles, 43
Hogg, C. F., 88, 103
Hunter, Archibald M., 59, 88, 98,
  103, 104, 108, 125, 237

Irenaeus, 327

Jackson, Blomfield, 235
Johnson, Sherman E., 18, 51, 52
Johnson, S. Lewis, Jr., 37, 41, 61,
  69, 75, 78, 81, 242

Kelly, William, 37, 72, 89, 174,
  188, 267, 302
Kepler, Thomas S., 88
Kerr, John H., 169
Kiddle, M., 165, 251, 292
Kik, J. Marcellus, 266, 267, 274,
  279, 280, 288
Kittel, Gerhard, 87

Lang, George H., 170
Lange, John Peter, 52
Laurenson, L. 283, 301
Lenski, R. C. H., 57, 174, 190,
  195, 198, 202, 204, 207, 212,
  214, 233, 236, 238, 239, 241,
  243, 244, 246, 250, 251, 260,
  263-265, 276, 288, 298, 307,
  319
Levertoff, P. P., 24
Liddell, Henry George, 202
Lightfoot, J. B., 299

McClain, Alva J., 61, 62, 65, 69,
  110, 149, 153, 172, 251, 308,
  324

Maclaren, John James, 307
McClellan, William H., 49
McNeile, Alan Hugh, 63
M'Neile, Alan Hugh, 36, 38, 39,
  42-45, 53, 55, 56, 59, 70, 71,
  78, 82, 84, 85, 95, 96, 100, 102,
  106, 111, 118, 127, 128, 137,
  139, 141, 143, 149, 150, 154,
  155, 161, 162, 168, 193,
  201-205, 208, 212, 219, 220,
  224, 229, 240, 243, 249, 250,
  257, 258, 269, 271-273, 276,
  278, 282-287, 297, 300, 303,
  305, 307, 310, 316, 318
McPheeters, William M., 101
Major, H. D. A., 86, 163
Manson, T. W., 163
Mantey, Julius R., 206, 207
Marsh, John, 108
Masterman, E. W. G., 238
Miller, Earl, 66
Milligan, George, 50, 51, 60, 114,
  127
Montefiore, C. G., 69, 72, 95, 96,
  105, 143, 160, 215, 225, 229
Morgan, G. Campbell, 49, 72, 97,
  201, 202, 205, 209, 234, 237,
  241, 245, 273
Morison, Frank, 307
Morison, James, 52, 57, 60, 70,
  105, 236, 281
Moulton, James H., 50, 51, 60,
  114, 127

Newton, Benjamin Wills, 281

O'Hair, J. C., 172
Oke, C. Clare, 203

Perry, Alfred M., 330
Peters, George N. H., 62, 78, 83,
  126, 172, 181, 255, 283, 284,
  288-290, 300
Pettingill, William L., 89, 175
Plummer, Alfred, 22, 49, 52, 55,
  57, 60, 68, 72, 84, 99, 104, 115,
  124, 126, 127, 133, 136-138,
  148, 154, 155, 157, 160, 163,

374

Scripture Index

Mark

Luke

John

Greek Index

Greek Index

Greek Index